Hanging in Judgment

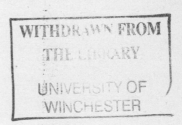

Hanging in Judgment

*Religion and the Death Penalty in England
from the Bloody Code to Abolition*

Harry Potter

When the Father of evil sought to ensnare the Lord and
Master of the world within his toils, he quoted scripture. He
is still at work and fills the minds of good and pious men
with the preposterous paradox, that the blessed book of life
contains a death injunction binding on Christians.

Charles Phillips, *Vacation Thoughts on Capital Punishment*, 1856

SCM PRESS LTD

For Adam

ISBN 0 334 02533 8

First published 1993 by
SCM Press Ltd
26–30 Tottenham Road London N1 4BZ

Phototypeset by Intype, London
Printed in Great Britain by
Mackays of Chatham, Kent

Contents

Acknowledgments

St George's House, Windsor, was the inspiration behind this work. As preparation for a month's course there I had to produce a paper on a chosen field, and so my researches began.

Throughout I have received considerable help from librarians, archivists, former members of the Prison Department, and other participants in the hanging issue. My thanks are due to the curators of the Lincoln, York, and Buckinghamshire Public Records Offices, and to the staff of the Lambeth Palace Library, the Society of Friends Library, the Home Office Library, the Howard League, the Cambridge University Library, and the Radzinowicz Criminology Library, Cambridge. Martin Farell of the Institute for the Study and Treatment of Delinquency was not only helpful but very hospitable. Retired members of the prison service gave me a unique insight into the hanging process from a participant's viewpoint, each remembering events which are still painful to recall. My particular gratitude is due to the Rt Revd Leslie Lloyd Rees, former Chaplain General, the Revd John Williams, former Deputy Chaplain General, the late Revd Fred Sisley, former prison chaplain, and Mr Rodney Llwellyn and Mr Michael Gale, both former Governors. Tom Johns of the Prison Service Chaplaincy aided my researches into material from Lancaster Castle. Lord Soper also provided me with valuable comments from his own experiences. Nevil Hutchinson, Peta Dunstan, Morag McNiven, and Toby Forward read and commented on earlier drafts of this work. Jonathan White was invaluable in reading the proofs.

Introduction

In 1810 the Archbishop of Canterbury, Charles Manners Sutton, and six other bishops voted in the House of Lords against a Bill which would have abolished the death penalty for stealing five shillings from a shop. In 1969 the Archbishop of Canterbury, Michael Ramsey, and eighteen other bishops voted in favour of the total abolition of the death penalty.

In its preservation, as in its abolition, the Church of England played a signal part, the more so in the former than in the latter. The following chapters trace the story of hanging's long heyday, and sudden eclipse, giving special attention to the role of the churches and in particular the Church of England. Their central importance is explained by the fact that hanging was an institution which demanded, and even craved for, religious sanction. The Church by Law Established provided the intellectual and theological justification for hanging, and suggested the means by which those aspects of it which gave rise to most public outcry could be amended and thus hanging be preserved. Judicial killing was sanctioned by bishops, and its execution presided over by chaplains. Had the church denounced it, it would have withered and died, as indeed it did quickly and without hope of resuscitation in the 1960s. Only in the 1950s, long after all other progressive religious and secular opinion had ranged itself against capital punishment, did the Church of England take a firm stand in favour of abolition. Of the other arguments that sustained it – deterrence, and retribution – neither could prevail when the religious imprimatur had gone. For at least a hundred years that imprimatur preserved and sanctified the judicial taking of life. Then suddenly and totally the sanction was withdrawn, and what had been done in God's name became unconscionable.

England is a particularly good country for a study such as this since nowhere in the rest of Europe were the statistics so well kept or the arguments on both sides so well documented. The work of the abolitionist organizations and the evidence taken by a succession of select committees and royal commissions provide a unique and authoritative store of material. Some aspects of the issue, such as the statistical evidence relating to capital punishment as a deterrent, have been given but passing mention. Of necessity, however, the role of religion has had to be placed in the wider framework of the Parliamentary and extra-Parliamentary battles on the hanging issue. Thus this book provides the first general history of capital punishment in England for thirty years, and the only one to cover the period from the Homicide Act of 1957 to final abolition in 1969.

1 The Universal Medicine

The Bloody Code in Execution and Apologetic

> You are to be hanged not for stealing horses, but that horses may not
> be stolen.
>
> *Mr Justice Buller*[1]

> It is an attribute to God himself,
> And earthly power doth then show likest God's
> When mercy seasons justice.
>
> *William Shakespeare*[2]

> The Bloody Code was monstrous and ineffectual. Its vice lay in the
> enormous disproportion it maintained between offences and
> penalties . . . It gave the impression of a world in which 'great thieves
> hang little ones'. It was not justice that was administered; it was a war that
> was waged between two classes of the community.
>
> *The Times*[3]

In 1806 the abolitionist historian Thomas Clarkson, reflecting on the state of
the English criminal law, lamented that a nation which professed itself
Christian had 'reverted to the severity of pagan antiquity'. He had supposed
that 'the advantages of civil and religious liberty, and those of a reformed
religion, would have had their influence in the correction of our judgments,
and in the benevolent disposition of our will', and that lenity and mercy in our
dealings with criminals would have supplanted the full rigours of the law.
Instead 'we seem to hurry them off the stage of life, by means of a code which
annexes death to two hundred different offences, as if we had allowed our
laws to be written by the bloody pen of the pagan Draco'.[4]

This was to misrepresent the general tenor of classical antiquity, as it was
to misjudge the effect of 'reformed religion'. Both Athens at her apogee and
Rome as a republic had mild capital laws. Draco's notoriously savage code
was repealed by his successor, Solon, with the exception that the death penalty
was retained for homicide. In the days of the Roman Republic citizens were
exiled rather than executed, and Cicero could boast that 'the ill-omened tree
had long been buried in the darkness of antiquity, and overwhelmed by the
light of liberty'.[5]

Although the early church fathers had opposed capital punishment,[6] and sometimes Christians were disbarred from high public office as a result, with the integration of the church into the state at the end of the fourth century secular severity was increasingly accepted as compatible with Christianity. Later, Aquinas justified the death penalty on the grounds that it alone could protect society when it was under threat. In contrast, and continuing in the way of the early church, radical heretics such as the Waldensians in the thirteenth century and the Anabaptists and Mennonites in the sixteenth opposed the imposition of capital punishment. For such opposition to civil and ecclesiastical orthodoxy they were often put to death themselves. Orthodoxy, Reformed as well as Catholic, identified itself closely with the secular power, supported the sword of the secular arm, and benefited from it. God and the gallows together kept society secure, anarchy at bay, and heresy suppressed. The Protestant Reformers especially, living in an age of social disintegration, espousing a theology of original sin, and believing in the inherent depravity of human beings, feared that without the threat of death in the here and now, and of hell in the hereafter, mankind would run amok, and the fragile fabric of society would be rent asunder. Martin Luther attacked the custom of the executioner asking forgiveness of the felon whom he was to kill. No apology need be made for performing a necessary function. The executioner, like the magistrate, was an instrument of God.[7] Acting through secular instruments it was God himself who exacted punishment and took life.

The first recorded execution in England was in AD 695. It was for theft, and its effect was to be exemplary: to discourage the others.[8] Throughout English history the vast majority of the victims of the gallows-tree were those convicted of property offences. The full flourishing of the capital code was a relatively late development, however, and was roughly coterminous with the Protestant ascendancy. The three most distinguished lawgivers of the Anglo-Saxon, Danish, and Norman lines were 'tender of human life'. Alfred the Great repealed many capital offences as being incompatible with the Christian dispensation, and 'for the mercy that Christ taught' made restitution rather than retribution (except for treason) the hallmark of his code. Legend has it that in one year Alfred hanged forty-four of his own judges for errors they made in their over-eagerness to hang others. King Canute forbade that 'Christian men should be condemned to death on any slight cause'.[9] William the Conqueror abolished the death penalty for all crimes (although his substitution for it of castration somewhat devalued the quality of his mercy). With these notable exceptions, however, capital punishment was a constant and growing part of English criminal justice. For centuries its scope expanded, especially as crimes came to be seen not merely as matters between individuals but as offences against the state. Its limited use had not deterred crime, perhaps its more extensive deployment would have greater effect. If a single hanging failed to have the desired result, a general dispatch might prove more efficacious. In Leicestershire, in 1124, for example, forty-four thieves were

hanged on the same occasion. The forms of judicial death were varied –
hanging, beheading, burning, and even boiling – and it could be accompanied
by other bodily indignities such as drawing and quartering.

Throughout the late Middle Ages hangings were a normal if irregular and
infrequent occurrence in most years. Although homicide far from invariably
attracted the death penalty it did so much more regularly than any other
offence. It struck directly not only at the human but at the divine order. Man
was made in God's image, and life was God-given. To kill was both to mar
the creation, and to usurp the prerogative, of God. In East Anglia in the early
fifteenth century, for instance, over a third of those convicted of homicide
were hanged compared with a fifth of those guilty of other violent offences
and less than a sixth of those convicted of property crimes. There were, of
course, far more such offences, and so those who witnessed executions were
five times more likely to see someone suffer for housebreaking or theft than
for murder.[10]

Hanging, so tradition has it, fared especially well under Anglican monarchs.
Sir Thomas Buxton stated that in the reign of Henry VIII, the Defender of
the Faith and reformer of the Church of England, up to 72,000 people were
executed, although this figure may be grossly inflated.[11] He was the only king
to permit Sunday executions, and he even prescribed boiling as an appropriate
alternative to hanging when the felon who was to be dispatched was a cook
who had poisoned his master's guests. His daughter Elizabeth, the Supreme
Governor of the Church of England, continued in his mould, and some
estimates indicate that over five hundred people a year were judicially put to
death in her reign, though this again is likely to be an exaggeration. An
indication of the temper of the time is given in a letter to the Queen's Chief
Justice from a Somersetshire magistrate who called the statute for the execution
of gypsies 'that godly edict'.[12]

Mercy, however, was initially allowed to season justice. The church by the
mid-seventeenth century had managed to mitigate the full rigours of the
common law by extending benefit of clergy to all felons. To be deemed a cleric
was to remove the malefactor from the jurisdiction of the civil authorities who
would execute punishment without mercy, and place him under that of the
bishop who would merely ensure that his sin was 'purged'. It had been
extended to women in 1692, and the definition of literacy was an increasingly
lax one including all who could read, or merely recite, the first verse of Psalm
51, aptly known as the 'neck verse'.[13] Benefit of clergy thus operated as a kind
of automatic reprieve for convicted literates.[14] The pen was mightier than the
sword. In 1705 the literacy requirement was abolished and the privilege
became available to all.

Despite this miracle of discrimination, by the end of the eighteenth century
the English criminal law provided the most extensive capital jurisdiction
Europe has ever seen. The Bloody Code, as it was known, was not a universal

growth, but a peculiarly English phenomenon, the product of a nation of Protestants and property owners, and of the triumph of Parliament. In the two centuries prior to the death of the last Roman Catholic monarch, Henry VII, the number of capital crimes had increased by a mere six. In succeeding reigns as hanging was extended, so mercy was restricted. During Henry VIII's reign, for the first time, certain offences were declared 'unclergyable'. The years after the Glorious Revolution in 1688 saw the systematic removal of benefit of clergy from many existing capital statutes, and the introduction of many more non-clergyable capital offences. Parliament, relishing its undisputed supremacy, was flexing its legislative muscles. In 1688 there had been only fifty capital offences in England, over forty of which were statutory additions to the small common law quota of treason, murder, arson, robbery, and grand larceny; a hundred and thirty years later there were over two hundred and twenty.[15] All felonies except petty larceny and mayhem (maiming) were capital. In other European nations during the same period the number and severity of punishments declined markedly, a consequence of the changed intellectual climate of the Enlightenment.[16]

The opposing trend in England was largely due to the political, economic and social changes accompanying the rise of Parliamentary supremacy and the early days of the Industrial Revolution: 'much liberty, great cities, and the want of a punishment short of death, possessing a sufficient degree of terror' as Paley summed it.[17] The anxiety of the commercial and landed classes, at once wealthy and insecure, jealous of their freedoms yet fearful of their subordinates, was the impetus for the growth of 'Albion's fatal tree'. The opportunities for crime, and the temptations, were growing commensurate with the expansion of commerce and the consequent burgeoning of middle-class prosperity. Contemporaries testified that the fear of violent crime against property and the person soared in the first half of the eighteenth century (despite the rapid decline in homicide in the same period),[18] fuelling the clamour for more draconian measures to deal with the issue.

Harnessed with the increasing vulnerability of the propertied portion of society was a system of law and order which seemed designed to aid the criminal. Apprehension was unusual since there was no regular police force. The gentry, still mindful of the pretensions of monarchs, would not tolerate such an idea. In a nation where law was respected, where liberty was safeguarded, and where the judiciary were independent of the executive, the rights of the individual were better protected than anywhere else in Europe. Under a system of criminal procedure which was rigidly formalistic and allowed many an acquittal on technical grounds,[19] from which torture was banished, and which in its day and compared with continental standards was considered to be of unparalleled liberality, the conviction of those who were caught was no foregone conclusion. Thus, the argument ran, where liberty precluded preventive policing, and where the rights of the accused were so well defended the punishment of those found guilty should be exemplary.[20] Colonel William Frankland asked in the House of Commons why 'our laws are severe', and straightway gave the orthodox answer:

It is because we love freedom and happiness; because we are jealous of previous restraint and control of our actions; because we wish to avoid the teasing vigilance of the perpetual superintendence of the law; because we would not purchase exemption from crime, by the loss of virtue . . . Such sanctions are the price we pay for our liberties.[21]

Parliament and the law courts, whose members represented the legislative and judicial aspect of the ruling class, accepted the maxim that where there was 'little preventive justice there must be much penal'[22] and put it into effect. To secure Colonel Frankland's freedoms and protect his property the poor felon had to die.

The notorious Waltham Black Act of 1723[23] was brought in as an emergency measure to deal with the deer-stealing, and other activities in the royal forests, of men who disguised themselves by blacking their faces. It was sweeping in its scope, making more than fifty distinct offences capital for seven different groups of offender. Thus this single statute possessed more capital provisions than other countries' entire criminal codes. It was intended to be temporary but it lasted a hundred years, spawning many other similar statutes. It has been accurately described as 'the source from which the great river of eighteenth-century deterrent justice flowed'.[24]

Alternatives to death were deemed inadequate. Gaols existed but no prison system; transportation to the colonies was sometimes seen as a positive encouragement to crime, 'a summer's excursion, in an easy migration, to a happier and better climate'.[25] Hanging alone, or so it was thought, would be sufficient to restrain the unbridled concupiscence and criminality of the lower orders. Hanging was not to be the ultimate deterrent for the most serious crimes but the usual deterrent for almost all crimes. Virtually no capital statute provided any alternative to the death penalty; practically all capital offences were created more or less as a matter of course by an unreformed Parliament, spurred on by the lobbying of landowners, banks and other commercial interests, more anxious to protect their own property than to preserve others' lives. A leading Whig accused his fellow MPs of 'culpable negligence' in allowing this 'mushroom growth of modern wantonness of legislation'.[26] Another, appalled that 'statute Law . . . was the fertile parent' of the Bloody Code, denounced its enactments as 'the weeds of the Statute Book [which] showed the corrupt soil from which they sprung, a Legislature which represented not the wants and wishes of the people'.[27] A perceptive critic from the Bar sorrowfully observed that custom had supported error, and the many-headed legislative monster had been unleashed by hasty and careless legislators to run amok.

I do not know any greater error that legislators ever committed than mistaking cruelty for efficiency of punishment. It was originally the error of feeble and unreflecting minds, legislating under the dictation of passion, not of reason, and mistaking intemperance for energy. Afterwards the frequency of executions, for inferior crimes, degraded the awful example of judicial death into a familiar occurrence. This engendered a corresponding carelessness in the minds of legislators, as to the sacrifice of human life. Passion first made revengeful laws, and revenge once incorporated within the system of justice reproduced its own image, after passion had expired. Legislators looked only to what their predecessors had done, without recollecting the circumstances which palliated errors that could not be justified. Instead of examining the merits of the artificial system of penal morality which they found established, whose source was indignation, and whose object vengeance, they guided their conduct by its example, and went on habitually multiplying these inhuman enactments, which justice and reason equally renounced.[28]

There was little attempt to schematize capital legislation and acts proliferated in a haphazard manner to deal with individual crimes as they arose. 'If a country gentleman', said Edmund Burke, 'can obtain no other favour from Government, he is sure to be accommodated with a new felony without benefit of clergy.'[29] Destroying Westminster Bridge was the same kind of offence as destroying Fulham Bridge, but each offence had a separate capital statute. Hanging was prescribed for impersonating a Chelsea Pensioner. At a single assize thirteen people were hanged for associating with gypsies. Forgery of birth certificates, or of baptism or marriage registers, were capital offences. Owing to the promiscuous plethora of capital statutes inconsistencies were rife. To commit arson, or to make an attempt on the life of a parent, were mere misdemeanours, while to pick a pocket of more than a shilling was a felony.

> To steal fruit ready gathered is a felony; but to gather it and later to steal it is only a trespass; to force one's hand through a pane of glass at five o'clock in the afternoon in winter, to take out anything that is in the window, is a burglary – even if nothing is actually taken; though to break open a house with every circumstance of violence and outrage at four o'clock in the morning in summer, for the purpose of robbing, or even murdering the inhabitants, is only a misdemeanour; to steal goods in a shop, if the thief be seen to take them, is only a transportable offence, but if he be not seen, that is, if the evidence is less certain, it is a capital felony.[30]

In theory felons were rarely too young to die. No child under seven could be punished for a capital offence. Those aged fourteen or over were presumed to possess a complete capacity for discerning between good and evil and thus they could be executed. Between seven and fourteen they were *doli incapax*, but strong evidence of malice might 'supply age'. In practice children under the age of fourteen were hardly ever hanged in the nineteenth century, and even in the eighteenth century such executions were rare.[31] The threat, nonetheless, was considered to be worth retaining. In 1748 William York, a boy of ten, was sentenced to death at Durham Assizes for the murder of a five-year-old girl. The execution was postponed by the Chief Justice, Sir John Willis, so that he could consult with his brother judges on the propriety of hanging someone so young. In a judgment in which they all concurred Willis ruled that the child was 'certainly a proper subject for capital punishment and ought to suffer; for it would be a very dangerous consequence to have it thought that children may commit such atrocious crimes with impunity'. Although the judges recognized that 'the taking away of the life of a boy of ten years old [might] savour of cruelty', they considered that 'the example of this boy's punishment [might] be a means of deterring other children from like offences'.[32] He was, however, reprieved. On the same basis Andrew Brenning, aged thirteen, was condemned in 1801 for burgling a house and stealing a spoon, but his sentence was commuted to transportation. The only documented execution of a child in the nineteenth century is that of John Bell, a thirteen-year-old murderer who was hanged at Maidstone in 1831.[33] Two years later nine-year-old Nicholas White was sentenced to death for poking a stick through a cracked shop window and stealing two pennyworth of paint. Once again he was reprieved.[34] Almost invariably those under fourteen convicted of property offences could count on a reprieve.[35] Although it was not until 1908 that the death penalty was abolished for those under sixteen, 1833 was the last year in which a juvenile was to be hanged, when a fourteen-year-old boy was executed for stealing. Nonetheless, some 90% of those hanged were under twenty-one years old.

All this was done in the name of deterrence. For some exponents of the Bloody Code hanging alone was not deterrent enough. Although by the mid-eighteenth century most of the more grisly accompaniments to capital punishment had fallen into dissuetude, as late as 1789 a woman called Christian Bowman was judicially burned for petty treason (coining) and it was only in 1790 that such punishment was abolished. From then on women would receive the same deserts as men, and be hanged. With the extension of the death penalty to the most paltry property offences it was thought necessary to distinguish the punishment for murder by some further refinements. The anonymously authored pamphlet *Hanging Not Punishment Enough for Murtherers, High-way men, and House-Breakers*[36] argued for the reintroduction of torture both to mark the greater heinousness of some crimes now that so many were capital, and to provide an effective deterrent which hanging clearly was not. Severe as this policy would be, ultimately lives would be spared because deterrence would work. Although, despite this plea, torture was to be introduced, Parliament decided that savage indignities could be perpetrated on the corpses of hanged murderers. The Act of 1752 'for the better preventing the horrid Crime of Murder'[37] gave judges the discretion in murder cases to substitute dissection for gibbeting. The Preamble stated that it 'had become necessary that some further terror and peculiar Mark of Infamy be added to the Punishment'. Public dissection, representing as it did the '*ne plus ultra* of punishment', was the fitting and usual solution.[38] The Act further stated that 'in no case whatsoever the Body of any Murderer shall be suffered to be buried'.[39]

As may be gleaned from their diaries and letters, continentals genuinely admired the English criminal justice system which forbade torture, and which in its procedure and practice provided at least some protection for the accused, but marvelled at a code whose penalties could be so extensive and so extreme.[40] The American attorney, James Sullivan, pleading on behalf of some Massachusetts' rebels, urged that mercy towards them would be shown even in England 'whose sanguinary disposition daily gluts the grave with legal consignments'.[41] Eighteenth-century London was known as the City of the Gallows. Since it had received full legal recognition in the 1752 'Murder Act' the practice of 'infamous exposure' – hanging the carcases of executed criminals in chains from gibbets – increasingly added to the macabre effect. Gallows and gibbets were designed to be prominent, to such an extent that they served as landmarks for travellers who were instructed to enter the suburbs of York 'by the gallows and three windmills', and to leave 'Frampton, Wilberton, and Sherbeck all on the right' and go over a stone bridge 'by a gibbet on the left'. The Statute Book regarded the hangman 'as a kind of Universal Medicine, applicable to men, women, and children of every age and variety of criminal constitution . . . and for his sake England stood single and conspicuous among the civilized nations of the earth'.[42]

The 'innovatory process' which gave rise to the plethora of capital statutes caused Sir Thomas Buxton to castigate the Bloody Code in the House of Commons:

> Men there are living, at whose birth our code contained less than seventy capital offences; and we have seen that number more than trebled . . . there stand upon our code one hundred and fifty offences made capital during the last century . . . and a great proportion of those executed were executed on statutes thus comparatively recent.[43]

Although he was right that the extension of the scope of the death penalty was the result of innovatory statutes and was not the ancient tradition of Common Law, the majority of those actually executed during the eighteenth century had offended against statutes passed in the time of the Tudors and Stuarts rather than 'freshly-minted' ones.[44]

The execution of the full severity of the law for most capital crimes remained rare. In practice the eighteenth-century criminal law claimed few lives in comparison with some earlier periods. In London and Middlesex about fifty-six people a year were hanged at the end of the eighteenth century, compared with one hundred and forty at the end of the sixteenth.[45] Few of the capital statutes were regularly employed: between 1749 and 1819 there were only twenty-five sorts of felony for which any individuals were executed and about one hundred and seventy capital felonies for which no one suffered death.[46] Only a small and declining proportion of those capitally condemned were actually executed. Between 1749 and 1758 more than two-thirds of the capitally convicted were executed. Less than a third died in the last decade of the century. By 1810 it was about one in seven, and half that proportion again by the mid 1830s.[47] Thus in the early nineteenth century the number of those hanged nationally was reduced to about seventy a year, and those were mainly for offences against the person.

The number of executions for offences against property remained stable, especially after 1750. Shop-lifters were usually pardoned, as were many others. Sixteen men and one woman were condemned to death for property offences at the 1818 Reading Assize, but only one died. The only property offence for which the capital sentence was regularly executed and rarely commuted was forgery. Between a half and three quarters of those convicted of forgery were hanged in the years 1775 to 1815. They had struck at the very basis of the newly-devised system of exchange and paper credit, the lifeblood of a commercial nation. Despite 'intercessions from many respectable quarters' Dennis Daly was hanged at Reading in 1803 for the crime of forging a cheque for £10. As a local newspaper observed, 'in the case of forgery death follows the stroke of the pen'.[48] Only the proportion of those convicted of murder who were hanged exceeded this.

Various factors reduced the potential death toll. The citizen's feeling of morality, justice, proportion, and fair play led to 'pious perjuries' whereby juries would acquit the obviously guilty or deliberately underestimate the value of the stolen property to remove petty thieves from the shadow of the gallows. While victims were slow to prosecute (prosecution was a private not a public matter) and juries were reluctant to convict minor offenders, judges were prone to pardon. A penal policy which permits hanging for theft does not demand it, and a judge who may hang children is not a judge who must.

Perhaps more essentially, mercy was increasingly incorporated into the execution of the criminal law by the system of reprieve. The power of the deterrent was supposed to lie in the uncertainty of the threat, not in its constant implementation: the basis of the law was *metus ad omnes, poena ad paucos*; its perfection would be 'that it should never be executed, that the terror alone should be sufficient to prevent the evil, that the fear should be so operative on the minds of all, that the punishment should extend to none, that the result should be *poena ad nullos*'.[49] The regular use of the prerogative of mercy was essential and intrinsic to a system where so many offences were capital.

Yet the threat of death hung over all, and in times of public disquiet about certain offences, or if a crime wave were feared in a particular area, the full terror of the law could be imposed and dreadful examples made of both men and women, young and old. After the end of the American Revolution the crime rate soared as a result of the return of many discontented ex-servicemen. No longer could criminals be transported to the New World. The gaols were full. Crisis threatened. The authorities reacted by a more sustained use of hanging than had been evident since the 1720s.[50] Again in the dangerous years after the end of the Napoleonic wars the average annual execution rate increased to more than a hundred.[51] At a more parochial level, during a spate of shop-lifting offences in the Ludgate area, nineteen-year-old Mary Jones, whose husband had been pressed into the navy and whose children were starving, was executed for stealing some coarse linen from a shop counter.[52] After one girl convicted of daytime housebreaking had been reprieved, Judge Hardinge condemned another, Mary Robert, to set an example. She was to die 'to enforce a law, which aimed not at [*her*] death, but at the *death* of her crime'.[53]

In the execution of justice, the enforcers of the moral order had to make enough examples to 'inculcate fear, but not so many as to harden or repel a populace that had to assent, in some measure at least, to the rule of property'.[54] They also had to square their practice with their consciences. Occasional exemplary punishment, 'a system full of mercy though seemingly severe', could be justified on the basis that it would deter crime, and thereby produce 'less suffering and more happiness than other systems apparently more lenient'.[55] An indiscriminate 'judicial massacre', as Dr Johnson termed it,[56] could not.

Underpinning this approach to criminal justice was contemporary philosophy, secular and Christian. Since the days of the jurist, Sir Matthew Hale, the dictum of the judges had been that 'Christianity is part and parcel of the Law of England'. With the rise of rationalist thought, however, morality, and thus the criminal code, was no longer the exclusive demesne of religion. Philosophers increasingly developed the theory of the natural right to self-preservation. That this natural, universal, and inalienable right did not prove a moral or intellectual barrier to the spread of the death penalty in England was largely the result of the work of the leading apologist of the new Protestant order of constitutional monarchy, John Locke. For Locke the right to secure property was the chief end of civil society. In his *Second Treatise of Government*, published in 1690, political power was defined as the 'right of making Laws with Penalties of Death, and consequently all less Penalties, for the Regulating and Preserving of Property', and maintaining peace and security, 'and all this only for the Publick Good'. He emphasized again and again that the state had 'no other end but the preservation of property', and could employ whatever punishment it would in its protection without infringing the civil rights and liberties of its people.[57] Although every citizen had an inalienable right to life this right could be 'forfeited' if he committed a criminal act that threatened the fabric of the social compact and so 'deserved' death.[58]

This doctrine of forfeiture proved to be very influential in English law, and could and did justify the infliction of the death penalty for the most trivial of property offences. Under Locke's patronage, the protection of property, without unnecessary regard for the lives of the poor or interference in the liberties of the prosperous, was to be the hallmark of English justice. In its practice it was to exemplify the philosopher's ideal: no prying state, no police force, no peremptory justice, but when a culprit was caught and convicted then no punishment was too severe. Indeed so literally were his dicta taken that the view 'that our laws are made to maintain property, not at all to keep up religion' was attacked from the pulpit.[59]

The interests of property and religion were not usually depicted as being in conflict. R. H. Tawney has characterized the eighteenth century as the age in which religious thought was no longer 'an imperious master' in the arena of politics and ethics, 'but a docile pupil'. Certainly in that era the Church of England brought no distinctive contribution to social ethics, and, 'except by a few eccentrics, the very conception of the Church as an independent moral authority, whose standards may be in sharp antithesis to social conventions', had been abandoned.[60] Its leading voices echoed the intellectual arguments of their age and buttressed the severity of the criminal code with scriptural authority. A Scottish contemporary of Locke, Gilbert Burnet, who had been elevated to the See of Salisbury for his support during the Glorious Revolution by a grateful William III, in his influential commentary on the Thirty-Nine Articles, defended the infliction of capital punishment in the protection of property. God had set a precedent in the Mosaic code and so provided 'a full justification of such punishments under the Gospel', for 'the charity of the Gospel does not take away the rules of justice and equity by which we may maintain or regain our possessions from violent aggressors, only it obliges us to that in a soft and gentle manner, without rigour or resentment'. Thus biblical exegesis leant religious sanction to obligations under the social contract: 'we owe to human society and to the safety and order of the world our endeavours to put a stop to the wickedness of men; which a good man may do with great inward tenderness to the souls of those whom he persecutes'.[61] There was one further benefit to be taken into consideration, a view echoed by Anglicans down the years until final abolition: hanging was positively good for the recipient:

It is highly probable that as nothing besides such a method could stop the progress of injustice and wickedness, so nothing is so likely a means to bring the criminal to repent of his sins, and to fit him to die as a Christian, as to condemn him to die for his crimes. If anything can awaken his conscience, and strike terror in him, that will do it. Therefore as capital punishments are necessary to human society, so they are often real blessings to those on whom they fall.[62]

A quarter of century later an even more distinguished bishop, Joseph Butler of Durham, developed another aspect of the argument in his *Sermons*. He expounded the advantages of vindictiveness. Echoing Luther he declared that vengeance was an attribute of God himself, and the civil magistrates were instruments of divine wrath. Exemplary punishment satisfied legitimate public outrage. The indignation raised by cruelty and injustice, and the desire of having it punished, was by no means malice. Rather it was 'resentment against vice and wickedness: one of the common bonds, by which society is held together; a fellow-feeling, which each individual has on behalf of the whole species, as well as of himself'. Legitimate outrage was necessary for justice to be done. Too great compassion for the offender would render 'the execution of justice exceedingly painful and difficult and would often quite prevent it'.[63]

These early philosophical and episcopal proponents of the imposition of the death penalty in the protection of property and of society itself helped to undergird the great expansion of capital statutes in the eighteenth century. Once in place, however, the Bloody Code in the latter half of the century was facing censure from most secular thinkers, while still attracting widespread clerical approbation and even occasional admonition that it was in practice too merciful. The year 1785 saw the publication of two works by Anglican divines, one bestowing on the English system of criminal justice the laurel of perfection, the other berating the moral cowardice of its practitioners and their unwillingness to inflict punishment with due severity.

The first of these was Archdeacon William Paley's *Principles of Moral and Political Philosophy*, dedicated to the Bishop of Carlisle, the father of the future Chief Justice of the King's Bench, Lord Ellenborough. A former Cambridge don, and a stylish if self-confessedly unoriginal philosophic theologian,[64] Dr Paley was widely looked upon as 'an oracle both in politics and in morals' in his own day and for decades to come.[65] Unburdened by the tortuous ingenuity so common among continental thinkers, in his blunt North country way he expressed 'native common-sense' with clarity and concision. He seemed always to have discerned clearly what the age wanted. So wisely did he calculate on the popular need that all his publications were eagerly welcomed by the middling sort – the educated rather than the intellectual – who lacked time or talent for more ponderous study. Above all, his famous textbook on moral and political philosophy provided the conservative consensus in Parliament, on the bench and in the pulpit with an authoritative justification for their criminal code.

Combining an easy complacency with a condescending patriotism, Paley viewed the English criminal code as perfect in design, though the product of serendipity. He elaborately vindicated the haphazard plethora of capital statutes, finding a virtue in the unpredictability of their enforcement, and commending the paucity of actual executions. He set out by observing that there were two methods of administering penal justice. The first assigned capital punishment to few offences and inflicted it invariably; the second assigned it to many kinds of offences, but inflicted it only upon a few examples of each.[66] England had developed the latter. In so doing it was introducing considerations distinct from that of guilt. Paley accepted that it would be natural 'to demand the reason why a different measure of punishment should be expected from God, and observed by man'.[67] He distinguished the here and now from the hereafter. From the Divine Judge we would receive our just deserts; the human judge, however, should punish us above our offences in order that our fate might deter others. Punishment was to serve a utilitarian purpose; it was no longer linked to justice.

> The proper end of human punishment is not the satisfaction of justice, but the prevention of crimes. By the satisfaction of justice, I mean the retribution of so much pain for so much guilt; which is the dispensation we expect at the hand of God . . . this demand is not the motive or occasion of human punishment.[68]

The main consideration in assessing the degree of punishment was not the severity of the crime, but the ease with which it could be committed. Thieves must be hanged simply because 'property being more exposed requires the terror of capital punishment to protect it'.

> This severity would be absurd and unjust, if the guilt of the offender were the immediate cause and measure of the punishment; but it is a consistent and regular consequence of the supposition, that the right of punishment results from the necessity of preventing the crime; for if this be the end proposed, the severity of the punishment must be increased in proportion to the expediency and the difficulty of attaining this end; that is in proportion compounded of the mischief of the crime, and of the ease with which it is executed. By how much detection of an offender is more rare and uncertain, by so much the more severe must be the punishment when he is detected.[69]

Thus the English system of criminal justice corresponded perfectly to Paley's ideal. It was as humane as it was lenient. To deter crime it was necessary to make many crimes capital but not to exact that penalty very often. No prospective criminal could act without knowing he could hang for it. And so 'the wisdom and humanity of this design furnish a just excuse for the multiplicity of capital offences which the laws of England are accused of creating beyond those of other countries'.

The charge of cruelty is answered by observing that these laws were never meant to be carried into indiscriminate execution . . . it is enough to vindicate the lenity of the laws, that some instances are to be found in each class of capital crimes, which require the restraint of capital punishment; and that this restraint could not be applied without subjecting the whole class to the same condemnation.[70]

Nor would this best of all solutions to the crime problem be vitiated by the execution of the innocent. His philosophy allowed for, and even incorporated that difficulty. The good of the whole was more important than the suffering of the few, even if, sometimes, they were innocent. They could die happy in that they died for England: 'he who falls by mistaken sentence may be considered as falling for his country, whilst he suffers under the operation of those rules, by the general effect and tendency of which the welfare of the community is maintained and upheld.'[71]

When Paley and his followers were talking so glibly of punishment it was almost entirely the punishment of the poor to which they were referring. The rich, after all, did not need to steal. Thus the poor would suffer to protect the rich, and an innocent poor man dying at the hands of the hangman nonetheless served the same good cause of protecting his betters. Paley's easy assertion was merely a refinement on what a Scots judge, addressing the protestations of a condemned convict, put more bluntly: 'Innocent or not, ye'll be nane the waur for hanging for a' that.'[72] When James Villette, the Newgate Ordinary in the 1770s, attended a young boy at the gallows, another confessed to the crime for which he was to die. Villette, it is alleged, was infuriated by the delay occasioned by attempts to get a reprieve (ultimately successful), and told the executioner to get on with the job, as it was now too late 'to worry about details of this kind'.[73] If punishment were primarily to deter it made no difference whether the guilty were hanged or the innocent. The lesson of the scaffold would be the same and just as effective.[74]

Paley's theological utilitarianism – this 'somewhat ingenious and amusing apology for existing abuses' as Hazlitt characterized it – is a most notable illustration of Tawney's strictures. It was 'not an attempt to show what [was] right, but to palliate and find out plausible excuses for what [was] wrong'.[75] It was, therefore, very influential with the large number of unpretentious middle-brow clergy and others who absorbed it at Cambridge and saw no reason to question it either then or thereafter.[76]

One contemporary who did question Paley's justification of the criminal code, however, did so on the basis that the code was not imposed with sufficient severity. A barrister and Surrey magistrate turned Calvinist cleric, the Revd Martin Madan, feared that present practice taught the wrong lesson.[77] So many were reprieved that none was deterred. He expressed his concerns in a widely-read pamphlet on *Executive Justice*. Echoing, as Paley had done, earlier assize sermons,[78] he maintained that the lenity of the law, and the squeamishness on the part of juries and judges to put their duty before their humanity, was the reason for the failure of the Bloody Code to prove an effective deterrent, and thus more 'dangerous and atrocious crimes' were committed in England than in any other civilized nation. The problem could be solved, Madan believed, by a vigorous application of the existing laws, of whose severity 'no one but the criminal' could reasonably complain. Punishment should be both severe and certain, and its full rigour executed in every case. He thought that ultimately this severity would save lives being wasted on the gallows since most criminals would think again if they knew for certain they would die if they were caught. His Calvinist theology, holding all sins as equally damnable in the eyes of God, found no difficulty in applying the extreme penalty of the law to the most minor offence.

His tract particularly reproved judges and ministers for a neglect of duty, and was very much read and discussed. He had dedicated it to the assize judges and sent each of them a copy. Whether his advice was followed by those in authority is more doubtful. The abolitionist Sir Samuel Romilly believed that it was, and cited in support of his contention statistics which showed almost a doubling in hangings in London the year after its publication, and the fact that mass executions were reintroduced.[79] The predictable denial by the Chief Justice, Lord Ellenborough, that it had had any influence on policy may not be thought sufficient to negate this impression.[80]

Faced with such eminent authorities, and encouraged with the minatory opportunities that the gallows provided, it is not surprising that clerical practitioners should rarely show any trace of doubt that executions were other than for the greater good. Eighteenth-century assize sermons, an excellent barometer of clerical opinion, saw the gallows as all the more vital in an irreligious age. Ease and affluence had undermined dependent faith. With a diminution in the fear of God went an increasing lawlessness which could only be restrained by the unremitting execution of capital sentences. With irreligion came 'unwarranted tenderness' towards criminals which would undermine the stability of society.[81] John Fletcher, the saintly vicar of Madeley, when approached for help in winning a reprieve by the sister of John Wilkes, a teenage robber, wrote to him pointing out that his crimes were 'of the most capital nature', and that instead of desperately seeking a reprieve he ought fervently to seek repentance. Once before Fletcher had successfully saved a young man from the gallows but he had had no thanks but 'many upbraidings' for his pains, and the recipient of his assistance had 'turned out very bad'.[82] He would not make the same mistake again. Rather than write a petition for Wilkes, he prepared a prayer for his and the public's edification which acknowledged the justice of his condemnation and which ended 'Let me not from the gallows be turned into hell . . . let the hands of human justice push me into the arms of divine mercy'.[83]

Occasionally, however, a voice was raised in protest against this Anglican unanimity. The Revd Dr Bronlow Forde, the much-maligned Ordinary of Newgate from 1799 to 1814, risked censure by writing to Jeremy Bentham in 1803 urging the total abolition of the death penalty for all crimes. A deeply humane man, he had learned from everything he had witnessed 'on these melancholy occasions' that executions managed as they were at present, answered 'no end whatsoever, either of punishment or example'.

When the criminal is dead, both the crime and the punishment are forgotten. Let him live and labour and the public may benefit from his example whilst he himself is making some atonement for his crimes by his industry, and humbly endeavouring to make his peace with God. I have often reflected, and as often wondered, with what small degree of devotion or right frame of mind certain persons have joined in the second prayer in our Church service: 'Almighty God, who desirest not the death of a sinner, but rather that he may turn from his wickedness and live.' Strange it is that our religion is so mild and our laws so sanguinary. Instead of sparing the life of a criminal in order that he may turn from his wickedness and live our criminal code nips him in the first bud of his sin, cutting off all hope of reformation, and destroying the possibility of atonement to the injured party. I hear some one say, What is to be done with criminals? Would you execute none? None.[84]

Although in educated circles at least this was no longer a solitary voice crying in the wilderness, at the close of the eighteenth century, England could still be cruelly typified by the story of shipwrecked sailor who when washed ashore, and seeing a body swinging from a gibbet, thanked God that he was in a Christian country.[85]

2 The Ripened Fruit

The Preparation for Punishment in Georgian England

I have talked to you hitherto as a Judge. But look up to me! I can give
you comfort; and can tell you, without impairing the weight of your
doom in this world, that you can turn away your eyes to the Judge of us
all, whose mercy has no limits, and whom no sinner can implore in vain,
if the tears of penitence and remorse are deep and sincere.

Mr Justice Hardinge[1]

Depend upon it, Sir, when a man knows he is to be hanged in a fortnight,
it concentrates his mind wonderfully.

Samuel Johnson[2]

Bishop Burnett extolled the benefits that the threat of the noose could produce
on the impenitent thief. Certainly the death penalty gave an urgency to
Christian evangelism. For a few souls the hour of ultimate decision had come.
Chaplains and others who saw themselves as pioneers of penitence found in
those about to die the perfect vehicles for this expression of their faith.
Concomitant to that it was vital for a society which decreed death for a myriad
of property offences to believe that the penalty was justified, that the
condemned were contrite and compliant to their fate, and that a deterrent so
terrible was uniquely effective.

The trial judge was the first who had the opportunity, and, besides that, the
duty to lecture the condemned malefactor and draw out the moral lesson of
his fate. A graphic and approving picture of a typical scarlet-robed assize judge
is given by the Revd Martin Madan, the vitriolically pro-hanging Calvinist
cleric:

Methinks I see him with a countenance of solemn sorrow, adjusting the cap
of judgment on his head . . . His Lordship then . . . embraces this golden
opportunity to do most exemplary good. He addresses in the most pathetic
terms, the consciences of the trembling criminals. He vindicates the *mercy*,
as well as the *severity* of the law, in making such examples, as shall not only
protect the innocent from outrage and violence, but also deter others from
bringing themselves to the same fatal and ignominious end. He acquaints
them with the certainty of speedy death, and consequently with the necessity
of speedy repentance – and on its theme he may so deliver himself as not

only to melt the wretches at the bar into contrition, but the whole auditory
into the deepest concern – tears express their feelings – and many of the
most thoughtless among them may for the rest of their lives, be preserved
from thinking lightly of the first steps to vice, which they now see will lead
them to destruction.[3]

Such secular sermons were seen to be vital to the whole didactic theatre of
punishment, linking human justice with divine, Christianity with capital
punishment.

Judge, cleric, and hangman each had a specific but integrated role in this
morality play. The Newgate Ordinary – the official chaplain to the condemned,
or 'the great Bishop of the cells' as he was often called[4] – dominated the
second act, and played a leading part in the finale, justifying the sentence of
the court, and lending religious sanction to the gallows. Others, equally
sensible of the importance of their performance, nonetheless saw this trinity
in a less hallowed light. John Bright, the Quaker MP, confessed that he 'never
read these accounts of the clergyman and Calcraft[5] performing on the same
scaffold without feeling that if it were possible for the Apostles to witness such
scenes they would not recognize the clergyman as one of their descendants,
or as a teacher of the religion which they taught'.[6] Edward Gibbon Wakefield,
the cousin of the great Quaker philanthropist Elizabeth Fry, and a leading
abolitionist pamphleteer, lampooned judges, clergy and executioners as
the business 'partners' who imposed, sanctified, and performed monstrous
punishments. The judge provided 'the animals for the slaughter'; and the
Ordinary 'broke their hearts, so that they [might] stand quiet, without kicking
or bellowing', while Jack Ketch 'butchered them'.[7] The chaplain came to be
considered as 'an adjunct of the executioner' and it was generally thought that
the 'main business of the Ordinary [was] to break the spirits of capital convicts,
so that they [might] make no physical resistance to the hangman'.[8] Some clergy
would resort to almost anything to get the required end. It was by ruse that
two clergymen in 1810 induced 'contrition and penitence' in an obdurate child
killer, Richard Faulkner, who was incarcerated in Norwich Gaol. After all
usual means had failed – he had even threatened to murder them when they
had tried to minister to him – they dressed a little girl in the dead child's
clothing and led her by twilight into the condemned cell. Faulkner, who was
only fifteen himself, was so startled and terrified by the apparition that he
trembled and sweated and begged the clergy to stay with him, confessing his
crime and imploring divine forgiveness. 'In this happy transition he remained'
until his execution two days later.[9]

Wakefield had been converted to abolitionism partly by the doctrines of
Romilly, Buxton and Bentham but even more by his own experiences, for he
had been in prison himself. In 1826 he had begun a three year sentence in
Newgate for his abduction of and duplicitous marriage to a Miss Turner. At

first he had had 'not a doubt of the efficacy of public executions as deterring from crime', but as time went on he had come to believe 'just the contrary'. 'Newgate' he said, was 'the very best place to form a second opinion on the subject.'[10] There he chronicled aspects of the existence of the condemned. 'A batch of convicts [was] sentenced to death every six weeks in London' for crimes other than murder. The average age was twenty. Not all would perish, and in the condemned cell they would await the decision of the Privy Council. When it had come to a conclusion, the condemned were assembled together in one ward and made to kneel down while the chaplain communicated to each his fate. Now the penitential work would really begin:

> As soon as a man is ordered for execution, the great increase of his danger produces extraordinary exertions on the part of those who administer the offices of religion to the inmates of Newgate . . . the Ordinary and his assistants visit the press-yard frequently every day, and indeed almost live with the condemned men, exhorting them to repentance, prayer and faith.[11]

Such concern was not yet usually shown to those convicted of murder. Under the Murder Act of 1752 they were rushed to their doom within forty-eight hours of being sentenced. While awaiting death they were shunned and 'if visited at all, it is only by a clergyman, and that by stealth, as it were, since it is understood that the offices of religion are denied to the murderer'. In the same stark way they were led to the scaffold 'without any religious ceremonies or other formal observances',[12] a mode of treatment wildly at variance both with that accorded those condemned for other crimes, and with that which would be lavished on their Victorian successors. Burial too was denied them, their corpses being given over to the ultimate indignity of the gibbet or the surgeon's knife.

The other condemned felons were generally allowed between five and seven days to prepare for death. In about half of these cases the exertions of the clergy to mediate reassurance were successful, or so even Wakefield estimated. He did not doubt that a considerable number of those who were executed died 'with a firm expectation of happiness in another world'.[13] Death was better than some lesser penalty for the spiritual well-being of the criminal classes. The Revd Horace Cotton, at the time chaplain of Newgate for more than a dozen years, could not remember one instance of what he would consider to be a 'sincere conversion to religious sentiments except in prisoners who were executed'.[14] Cynicism or naivety could diminish or amplify the number 'saved'. The author of *Old Bailey Experiences* said that 19 out of 20 showed no true repentance while another Ordinary of Newgate, John Davis, giving evidence to the Royal Commission in 1866, recorded a higher success rate, except with foreigners. In his opinion 'the condemned ministered to for a fortnight are in a condition of much more apparent penitence than is often the case with those who die a natural death'. In his experience only one had professed no belief in God right to the end, and he was French.[15]

Before the slaying itself, a purificatory liturgy had to be performed. On the Sunday before the execution the Ordinary preached the condemned sermon, an opportunity to appal those about to die, and admonish those who had so far escaped the noose.[16] On the following morning the bells of St Sepulchre's church tolled twelve times with double strokes, in accordance with Robert Dow's charitable bequest, as the grim procession left Newgate and wound its way through the expectant crowds to Tyburn. In the whole procedure the priest or chaplain had an essential and vital role: 'the processional to the gallows and the execution itself were supposed to be a carefully stage-managed theatre of guilt in which the offender and the parson acted out a drama of exhortation, confession and repentance before an awed and approving crowd.'[17] The scaffold was both an altar and a stage. The chaplain was high-priest and impresario. As the men stood with the nooses round their necks he would admonish them and the spectators:

> Sad is the state, deplorable the condition you have brought yourselves to; adjudged by the laws of your country; and by them accounted unworthy any longer to live, unworthy to tread this earth, to breath this air; and that no further good, nor further benefit to mankind can be expected from you but only the example of your death, and to stand like marks on fatal rocks and sands to warn others from the same ruin for the future.[18]

Their one hope lay in this death. Their repentance could transform their executions into an expiation. Their suffering would be their penance. The state was thus portrayed as both punitive and benevolent: the punishment was severe but was not merely for the present benefit of society but for the everlasting welfare of the criminal.

The ideal, if ambiguous, moral example was that given by the 'Macaroni Parson', the Revd Dr Dodd, a cleric for long fashionable in high society, who had himself published a sermon urging the restriction of capital punishment. In 1777 he became, as far as Dr Johnson could recollect, the first Anglican priest to suffer 'publick execution for immorality',[19] being hanged for forgery. That such a fate should befall a prominent clergyman of the Established Church could undermine popular respect for Christianity.[20] Yet some good could come out of the evil. His deportment, as depicted in the Ordinary's *Genuine Account of the Behaviour and Dying Words of William Dodd, LLD*, partially compensated for the bad example he had set. He was the sincere penitent, perfect in contrition, acknowledging his guilt, praying for his fellow sufferers, and being 'launched into eternity, imploring mercy for his soul for the sake of his blessed Redeemer'.[21] But for the rope around his neck, he could be mistaken, as one Dutch visitor wryly observed, for a minister in the pulpit.[22] Nothing should be done to mar the effect. All efforts to save him were frustrated.

Several leading Methodists, including John Wesley, had sought his reprieve, but few Anglican clergy had joined them, and none of any prominence. Dr Johnson attributed 'their inactivity' to 'a paltry fear of being reproached with partiality towards one of their own number'. Johnson himself laboured hard and long in his service, even composing various appeals which Dodd delivered as his own.[23] Not that he had any high regard for Dr Dodd. He 'was very willing to have him pardoned . . . but . . . did not wish he should be made a saint'.[24] A devout Anglican, Johnson disliked the prospect of a clergyman being paraded through the streets 'to a death of infamy, amidst the derision of the profligate and profane', and in addition had long believed that death was too severe a penalty for so venial an offence. The silence of the clergy was justified in the face of Johnson's strictures by Dr Newton, the Bishop of Bristol, who regretted merely that Dr Dodd was hanged 'for the least crime he ever committed'.[25] It was generally agreed that the best thing in his life was his leaving of it.

Less is known of provincial executions, at least until the advent of local newspapers, but the surviving pamphlet accounts suggest that a similar improving ritual was practised throughout the land. Particularly valuable were exhortatory confessions from the gallows when the malefactor, soon to be 'launched into eternity', would admonish his hearers neither to break the sabbath, nor indulge in drunkenness or fornication. It was hoped that young men of the lower classes in particular would take heed to these dreadful displays of the inevitable consequences of adolescent rebellion.[26] The manner in which many a young man departed this life gives rise to the strong suspicion that they had been worked upon and honed by skilful practitioners in penitence or that the accounts had been edited or even composed according to a set and edifying formula.[27] Parents were extolled, religious observance enjoined, and all blame for their misdoings was accepted by the felons themselves. Neither family background, nor social conditions were responsible for their actions, only their own wilful sinfulness. Henry Durrant and James Tilley, teenagers executed for burglary on the newly erected 'Newgate Drop' at Horsham Gaol in Sussex, had been convinced of their own worthlessness. At 12 noon on 24 August 1822 they walked from the gaol accompanied by the chaplain, executioner and other officers, and ascended the stage. Each prisoner then addressed the assembled crowd in a manner so stilted and with words so formulaic as to betray their preparation for the scene. They were 'very penitent'. Tilley spoke first. Turning left and then right to the audience below he admonished them.

Now young men, I hope you will take warning by my unhappy situation:

don't break the Sabbath, always go to Church, and beware of bad company
for that brought me to the gallows.

Durrant in his turn came forward:

Now young men, take warning. Only a week before the job happened for
which I am to suffer death, I was at a fair, out here revelling. Now you see
what I have come to. Bad company brought me to the gallows.

The following week, David Burnett, another young man condemned for the
same crime, mounted the same steps, and harangued the crowds in words
almost identical to those of his two immediate predecessors.[28] It was the
Saturday matinee performance, with the same cast but a new leading man.

Such gallows edification was even written into the curriculum of some
schools. In one near Reading, for instance, the master, a Methodist, used to
take his pupils on hanging days to witness the local executions as 'improving'
scenes.[29] All the local schools were given a holiday when a girl was to be
hanged at Horsham drop in 1824. The Master of Collier's school took all his
pupils on a picnic so they would not see spectacle, and was severely criticized
for this action by 'contemporary moralists'.[30]

As assize sermons would justify the severity of the court, so those delivered
after the execution would point the moral. Preaching the day after the execution
of Robert Avery for forgery, William Kingsbury related how he had regularly
visited him in gaol. Avery seemed to have genuinely repented and found faith
and would, Kingsbury hoped, find mercy from Jesus who had pardoned the
expiring thief. From his fate Kingsbury pointed out 'some of those striking
and salutary lessons which the execution of a criminal is calculated to teach'.
Sabbath-breaking was the beginning of a career of vice which led headlong
to the gallows.

The beginning of vice is as the letting forth of waters; it will end in infamy,
disgrace, and misery in a prison, in distant exile, if not in a shameful death
at the abhorred place of public execution.[31]

He warned his congregation that crimes would sooner or later be brought to
light. Furthermore, late professions of repentance were very uncertain, often
deceptive, easily mistaken, and were not to be relied on with confidence. In
support of this he cited an example from Scotland from the testimony of a
very respectable clergyman, where a woman infanticide was given much
attention in prison and 'not one of the ministers who attended her doubted in
the least degree the reality of a change in heart'. But the rope broke at the
execution and she was freed and returned to her old vicious ways.[32]

Foreigners, like Scotswomen, had a habit of not playing their prescribed
part in the morality play: neither Mrs Manning, a Frenchwoman, nor Franz
Müller, a German, despite the insistence of Dr Capell, the Lutheran minister

attending him, would confess.[33] From time to time even Englishmen would persist in their obduracy. Some would merely declare their innocence to the last. Others would go so far as to contest the justice of the sentence. The whole ritual drama would then flop. A morality play could become a scurrilous farce. One priest related the following altercation:

> I exhorted Anderton and Dudley to beg of God that they might be examples of true repentance and to warn the people by their sad untimely end. They did not. Anderton told his spectators that his sentence was very hard and severe. I told him that he had endeavoured to overthrow the established government. He said that he forgave his judges. I replied that they needed not his forgiveness.[34]

Similarly John Pope, a sheep stealer who was hanged outside Horsham in 1819, repudiated all religious attentions and 'would not take the sacrament for a thousand guineas', declaring that he was 'a murdered man'. His dying words echoed those of Dickens' dark creation, Hugh: 'It is impossible for me to forgive my enemies so I invoke the vengeance of heaven upon them.' With proud defiance he railed against the iniquity and inequality of the law, and asked, as Paine had done, why it was that only the poor were hanged. The laws of England, he thundered, were 'fine laws for stringing up a man like a dog. A poor man, if he had no rich friends, was 'bound to suffer by them'.[35]

Even on the verge of doom some men would vilify the chaplain.[36] Often their abusive behaviour was fortified with drink. After three young men 'who at first seemed not enough concerned' had drunk greedily of wine, they 'grew most shamefully daring and wanton'. They swore, laughed, and talked obscenely. At Tyburn 'the scene grew still more shocking; and the clergyman who attended was more the Subject of Ridicule, than of their serious attention'.[37] When the Ordinary asked Henry Marshall 'if he consider'd what a great work it was to repent for the sin of murder, so as to save his soul from ruin', he replied that 'to be sure he should take care of himself'.[38] Richard Patch, before flinging himself precipitously from the scaffold, rebuked the Ordinary with the words, 'I have confessed my sins to God. Man can give me no relief.'[39] On another occasion when a Newgate schoolmaster tried to convince a man of a further 'state of existence', he received a scornful reply:

> What you too gammon on as well as the parson! They take your life away, and then they think to make amends by telling you of another and a better world; for my part I am very well satisfied with this, if they will let me stay in it.[40]

Felons would cut the tassels off the pulpit cushion, spit at the pulpit, and shout abuse at the Ordinary during the condemned sermon, or even threaten to shoot him.[41] Sometimes the abuse was well-deserved. So thoughtless or absent-minded was Mr Swinton, chaplain of Oxford Gaol, that on breaking

off at mid-point in the sermon he told his congregation that he would give the
rest of what he had to say the following Sunday.[42] Jack Shepherd told Mr
Wagstaff, the Ordinary, that 'one file's worth all the Bibles in the world'.[43]
Bernard Mandeville was grieved by the behaviour of the condemned 'whom
for the greatest Part you'll find drinking madly, or uttering the vilest Ribaldry,
and jeering others that are less impenitent; whilst the Ordinary bustles among
them, and shifting one from another, distributes Scraps of good Counsel to
unattentive Hearers; and near him, the Hangman, impatient to be gone, swears
at their delays'.[44]

A century later Mrs Fry, the saintly Quaker prison reformer, and a stern
opponent of the Bloody Code, was grieved to admit that 'commonly the chief
thought [of a condemned woman] relates to her appearance on the scaffold,
the dress in which she shall be hanged'.[45] Their deaths were considered more
than enough to expiate for whatever crimes they had committed, and most of
the women thought their crimes petty in comparison to 'the crime of the
Government towards themselves'. Thus the moral and religious effect of
indiscriminate capital punishment was the opposite of that which was intended
for 'their persuasion is that this act of severity obliterates and atones for every
former misdeed', and so the minds of the prisoners were hardened against
repentance 'by the reflection that the pain is short, and the supposed reward
is permanent'.[46]

The satisfaction of success outweighed these failures. In terms of preparing
them to face the inevitable, Christian ministration was undoubtedly beneficial
to the condemned, and this was reflected even in their physical state. Success
was visible, salvation was made flesh:

> In nearly all such cases of religious fervour, the bodily health of the
> enthusiast is excellent, his sleep sound, his appetite good, his pulse steady
> and his skin moist; whilst, speaking generally, he who goes to the scaffold
> scoffing at religion is full of bodily disease, of which the main symptoms are
> want of appetite and sleep, a rattling or fainting pulse, and a skin hot and
> dry, as if he were in a burning fever.[47]

Another witness was astonished by the 'resignation and fortitude' of those
awaiting their deaths. He attributed this to the 'indefatigable ministry' and
'soothing conduct of the Revd Mr Cotton'. Many under his care had become
'the most sincere penitants; nay more, several prisoners, who have received a
free pardon after having been ordered for execution, have since publicly
declared that they should never again be in such a fit state to meet eternity'.[48]

So involved did some ministers become in the last days of their charges that
their own health suffered. Mrs Fry related that she had 'been deeply affected
in attending a poor woman who was executed' for infanticide. She had visited
her twice, and 'the whole affair was truly afflicting' to her. On the eve of the
execution she recorded the following in her diary:

The event has brought me into much feeling, attended by some distressing nervous sensations in the night, so that this has been a time of deep humiliation to me, this witnessing the effect and consequences of sin. The poor creature murdered her baby; and how inexpressibly awful now to have her life taken away![49]

Despite such traumatic experiences, there was no shortage of offers of outside help in this missionary work. When a batch of capitally condemned prisoners were confined in the cells of Newgate the prison was beset with applications for admittance by persons who wished 'to be allowed to administer consolation' to the unhappy malefactors. These applications 'were generally made by dissenting ministers'.[50] The work was rewarding, Methodists were particularly enthusiastic. John Wesley ministered to, among others, Dr Dodd, and was much encouraged by the resignation and godliness which he found each and every time he visited the 'evangelical penitent'.[51] His brother Charles also engaged in this great work. On one occasion he prayed in the cells with a sick negro who was to be executed for robbing his master. The following morning 'the Black [and] the other nine children appointed to die' were led to Tyburn. None showed any terror of death. When the cart drew off 'not one stirred, or struggled for life'. Charles spoke a few suitable words to the crowd; and returned, 'full of peace and confidence in our friend's happiness'. That 'hour under the gallows' he considered to be 'the most blessed hour of [his] life'.[52]

The Ordinaries did not usually welcome these attentions. The inadequate or uncaring were threatened by the influx of inexhaustible evangelists; the venal feared rivalry for the rich pickings from published 'confessions'; the more dedicated found the approach of some 'enthusiasts' crass and insensitive.

The Revd John Taylor, Ordinary from 1747 to 1755, tried unsuccessfully to obstruct the ingress of the determined Silas Told, who had been introduced to prison work by John Wesley, and regularly attended at Newgate.[53] The immediate effectiveness of his ministry and that of his master Wesley must have been a manifest and standing reproach.

On the other hand the Revd Brownlow Forde who was Ordinary from 1799 to 1814 complained of the dissenting ministers and Methodist preachers who 'haunted the gaol' and who harassed and worried his men. Forde was a wonderfully idiosyncratic and eccentric individual who was regularly to be found in a club-room of a public house, smoking a pipe, and enthroned in a superb masonic chair.[54] Yet he was a kindly man and seems to have been an outstanding Ordinary. A Parliamentary Committee of Inquiry into Newgate did not think so. He obviously offended their sense of decorum with his bluntness and candour. Shortly afterwards he resigned his office. His departure was sorrowfully marked by the *Gentleman's Magazine*, which described him as a 'very worthy man, much and deservedly esteemed by the City magistrates' who settled on him 'an annuity which provided for the comforts of his latter days'. Further, his friend, the noted reformer Basil Montagu, who had co-operated with him for many years in his work in Newgate, wrote him a lengthy and persuasive apologia.[55]

The position of many an Ordinary was weakened by the attitudes of the City Aldermen who supervised Newgate and appointed the chaplain. He held office during good behaviour and by their favour. Horace Cotton, who served at Newgate from 1814 to 1839, tried to end the practice of placing a coffin on a table in full view of the condemned during chapel services. The Gaol Committee of Aldermen insisted on its reinstatement.[56] They were themselves divided in their churchmanship between the high church and the 'high evangelics', and they severally admitted clergy of their own persuasion into Newgate. In 1773 James Townsend, the Lord Mayor, even attempted to secure the appointment of Told to the vacant post when the Anglican Ordinary, John Wood, retired. The 'evangelics' were particularly prone to such interference since they considered that the salvation of the condemned could not be left to the tepid ministrations of the Ordinaries. Both Forde and Cotton recorded how with scant ceremony these 'enthusiasts' would demand entry to the cells when they were ministering to the men.[57] Mr Baker, a gentleman who regularly attended Newgate to pray with and give religious advice to the prisoners there, even accompanied the malefactors into the condemned pew for their final sermon.[58] On one occasion those in his care complained of the unorthodox views of another visitor. Baker used his influence to have him barred from visiting.[59] The ministrations of some less scrupulous visitors were sometimes followed by the publication of a detailed account of all that transpired. One minister, on leaving a man who was to be executed the following morning, went home and wrote a full account of his crimes, confession, and death, and of the author's participation in the fatal catastrophe. This he sent the next morning to the papers. The subject of his literary endeavours had, however, been reprieved, unbeknown to the divine who had thus prematurely penned his obituary.[60]

Concern for the condemned transcended the boundaries of sex. The most celebrated penal reformer of the day was Elizabeth Fry. Nor was she alone among women in preparing the condemned for death. Saving the souls of the most wretched appealed to women of influence and religious enthusiasm.[61] Miss Richards, Miss Unwin and Miss Tomlinson worked a miracle of salvation on the distraught and inconsolable Mary Voce who was awaiting execution in Nottingham for the murder of her child. After her condemnation at least two of the young women were always with her. After hours of agonizing prayer with her, she suddenly pronounced that God had saved her, prison had become her Bethel, and her fate was the happiest conceivable, a brand plucked from the burning.[62] Such work was not confined to women of station. Two servant girls, Sarah Wilkes and Elizabeth Childers, were despatched by John

Fletcher to Stafford Gaol with the purpose of inducing the brother of the former to acknowledge his guilt and confess his sin. Despite the ridicule of the gaoler, this they did with complete success, working day after day on the hapless youth, and reporting that he went to his fate 'exceeding happy, and employed in breathing out prayers and praises to God'.[63]

Sometimes the assistance of these enthusiastic young women, like that of their male colleagues, was often more appreciated by the convict than by the prison chaplain. In a work dedicated to the female members of the Royal Family, in which she inveighed against the inadequacies of the fox-hunting clergymen who did not rebuke error but rather stood in the way of female ministry, Mrs Elizabeth Lachlan gave a remarkable account of two such evangelical 'feminists', a Miss Payne and a Miss Owston. They had visited a young man called James Cook, a Leicester bookbinder who had been condemned to death for the most brutal murder, dismemberment, and incineration of a creditor, Mr Paas.

The women had bought a tract about him and embarked upon a correspondence with him, thus beginning 'the mighty work for this grievous sinner's conversion'. They sent religious tracts and handbills, including a little verse book called 'Sunbeams'. The reply from Cook fell on 'the holy Bible which lay open before my friend – she pushed it off the book with horror, exclaiming – "What! a dreadful murder's letter on the Bible" '.[64] But the letter invited her and the other lady to go to visit him in prison and they agreed. Armed with a 'new large Bible, having marked some hundreds of verses, peculiarly suited to such a wretched criminal's case', they went to Leicester Gaol. There, to their obvious surprise and pleasure, they encountered a youth of 'most interesting, handsome countenance, heavily ironed, leaning over a table, on which was placed a writing desk, and on this lay the little book, "Sunbeams" '.[65] Miss Payne assured him that one drop of Christ's blood would wash him clean, but first he had to repent, 'the first proof of which is, your open and full confession of your crime. This is what I am most anxious to procure.' She pressed him hard:

> – I did confess when I was examined before the magistrates . . .
> – Yes, I did see it; but that confession was false, you know it was.

He remained silent. She earnestly continued:

> – Are you not wretched? . . .
> – I don't enjoy myself as much as if I had nothing on my conscience, certainly.
> – Enjoy yourself! You know that there does not breathe in existence a more miserable creature than you are at this moment.

He was again silent. Miss Payne's persistence finally paid off. A few days later he was 'much improved'. He prayed and then confessed to her in full. She consoled him with the thought that she believed him worthy of death and, through death, of eternal life:

> Be assured you will suffer; that you must stand before an earthly tribunal, and that it is impossible you should be found other than guilty and worthy of death. But though the justice of man absolutely requires your forfeited life, the mercy of God offers you eternal life and pardon, if you can believe.[66]

What more could they want than to be able to worship God with their young protégé, but the gaol chaplain, Dr Fancourt, refused them permission to attend the communion service in the prison chapel. He would not let them usurp his role. They had failed to observe the usual courtesies. On their first arrival at Leicester, they had not been aware that it was customary to inform the chaplain of any intentions of visiting the gaol, 'in order to speak the truth as it is in Jesus, to such poor famishing souls therein, as might feel desirous of the same'.[67] Even when they were told of this, since they would visit willynilly, they declined to ask his permission, but agreed to inform him of their intentions.

> We accordingly went: but, alas! instead of beholding the calm and unruffled meekness which shone forth so brilliantly in the character of the great pattern of all excellence, we were ushered into the presence of one whose age might have commanded respect, but whose irritability of temper was strikingly perceptible even after a few words only had escaped our lips.[68]

He said that the soul of the prisoner was admitted to his charge. This they doubted, firmly believing that they were the instruments chosen by God for Cook's conversion. He forbade their entry; they withstood him. Mrs Lachlan reflected at length on 'the unholy jealousy that exists too often in an unregenerate priesthood towards the exertions of woman in the cause of Christianity'.

The newspapers shared the chaplain's opposition. Five days after the hanging, on 15 August, a Leicester paper criticized Miss Payne for pampering 'the murderer with all sorts of delicacies'. She would, they considered, 'have been much better employed, and greatly more to her credit, if she had waited upon and commiserated the poor widow and orphan children, instead of spending her time with the foul villain'. Her conduct betokened 'nothing but a pompous desire to have her name talked and spread about'. The editor thought that 'three clergymen of the Established Church were quite sufficient to convince, if not convert, a murderer without the interference of females'.[69] Along similar lines, *The Age of Sunday* found something 'infinitely disgusting in the interference of some women in the case'. 'What', they asked, 'have women to do with a beastly murderer who was not a degree above the New Zealanders?' Cook had had enough spiritual advice without their voluntary assistance. They might have left the business to the chaplain. In court, the article pruriently insinuated, Cook had looked up 'to ogle Miss Payne' and on leaving the dock kissed hands to her. They supposed that she had a lock of his hair as a memento.[70]

Two evangelical Anglican clergymen, on the other hand, who had witnessed the trial, seen Cook plead guilty to the charge, and continue to read the New Testament while in the dock, wrote commending the women and their ministry. Specifically mentioning the same incident in court criticized above, their interpretation was very different: 'never, perhaps, did a child look up to his parents in an hour of difficulty with more interest than Cook did to you, at that awful time'.[71] One wonders whether it was the press or the clergy who more accurately interpreted the relationship between the young man and his two ladies. Yet the trial judge, Mr Justice Parke, wept openly while commending the youth's soul to God's mercy and his body to the gibbet, and other contemporary accounts also witness to the sincerity of his contrition.[72] In his sermon on the Sunday following the hanging, even Dr Fancourt acknowledged the penitence of the late James Cook.

In these varied means of caring for the condemned the interests of state and church coincided exactly. Confessions induced by cajolement or caress were an essential adjunct to the whole process of punishment in Georgian England. They were also an essential prelude to penitence and salvation. The judge in the court and the minister in the cell were servants both of the temporal kingdom and of the heavenly. Some, less charitably, saw them as Pilate and Caiaphas.[73]

3 Narrowing the Noose

Sir Samuel Romilly and the Reform of the Criminal Law: 1808–1840

We have no right to shed a criminal's blood, because he has shed the
blood of another man: we have no right in reason to do this: we have
no warrant from religion. It is doubtless a great evil for a man to be
murdered; but that, in reason, is no argument for inflicting death upon
the murderer, except that it is necessary to check the crime of murder.

Lord Brougham[1]

Lawgivers, beware,
Lest, capital pains remitting till ye spare
The murderer, ye, by sanction to that thought,
Seemingly given, debase the general mind;
Tempt the vague will tried standards to disown,
Nor only palpable restraints unbind,
But upon Honour's head disturb the crown,
Whose absolute rule permits not to withstand
In the weak love of life his least command.

William Wordsworth[2]

Not all opinion, philosophical or Christian, endorsed the English way of
punishment. In centuries past, Henry VIII's Lord Chancellor, Sir Thomas
More, and the Restoration bishop, Jeremy Taylor, had urged a merciful and
just contraction of the infliction of the death penalty for minor offences.[3] Coke
and Bacon both believed that 'the acerbity of the law' deadened its execution.
The illness might be diagnosed but a cure was not yet forthcoming. The
intellectual turning point came in 1764, when the Bloody Code was at its
height, with the publication of the first systematic study of the principles of
punishment, *Dei Delitti e delle Pene* (On Crimes and Punishments) by the
Italian Cesare Beccaria. He argued that since man was not his own creator,
he did not have the right to destroy life either individually or collectively.
Capital punishment, he said, was justified in only two circumstances: if it
would prevent a revolution against a popularly established government, or if
it were the only way to deter others from committing a crime. On the latter
point, in contrast to Paley, he concluded that it was not, and gave compelling
reasons for this assertion. His main thesis, and one that was to hold sway right

Dr Dodd's Last Interview, 1777

Newgate Chapel on the Eve of Executions, c.1800
From a drawing by Rowland and Pugin

Elizabeth Fry at Newgate, late eighteenth century

Execution of Mary Ansell at St Albans, 1899

down to the present day, was that the prevention of crime and not its punishment should be the prime aim of an enlightened society, and that crime was prevented not by the severity but by the certainty of punishment. Despite being denounced by the Inquisition, these ideas rapidly swept the continent. Their influence was felt particularly in England where Parliamentarians like Edmund Burke, William Eden and William Wilberforce, jurists such as Blackstone, and such literati as Samuel Johnson, Oliver Goldsmith and Jeremy Bentham, began to set forth arguments against indiscriminate capital punishment similar to those of Beccaria.[4] Nonetheless it is somewhat of an exaggeration to claim, as one recent historian does, that 'by the 1790s the overwhelming intellectual response to the Bloody Code was that it was untenable'.[5] Although a strong current, it was not yet a flood, and its force was stronger among lay thinkers than among clerical or judicial. Coinciding with this disdain for the Code went a decline in the rate of violent crime between 1780 and 1820, an increasing rejection of violent non-capital punishment, a greater emphasis on the reform and rehabilitation of the criminal, and the institution of the penitentiary.

Various moves were made in Parliament to replace the death penalty with some secondary punishment for a range of property offences. Bills passed the Commons in both 1750 and 1770 only to be rejected in the Lords.[6] In 1777, as a result of a *cause célèbre* – the condemnation of the Revd Dr Dodd for forgery and the grave public disquiet his subsequent execution had aroused[7] – the proposal to enact yet another capital statute was opposed by the Whig Member for Liverpool, Sir William Meredith. He made an impassioned plea that enough was enough.[8] New capital offences multiplied and yet crime was not deterred.

> The argument was always the same: 'If you hang for one fault, why not another? If for stealing a sheep, why not a cow or a horse?' . . . The Shoplifting Act had been to prevent the actual robbery of bankers, goldsmiths, and shops where there were goods of great value; but it was used to make it death to lift anything off a counter 'with an intent to steal'.

Sir William, citing the case of Mary Jones, declared that he did not believe 'a fouler murder was ever committed against law, than the murder of this woman by law'. Under 'our good old common law' only treason, murder, rape, and maliciously burning a dwelling house had been capital offences, and even with these four, if recompense were made 'life would not be touched'. Next he turned to the contemporary case of Dr Dodd:

> So fatally are we deviated from the benignity of our ancient laws, that there is now under sentence of death an unfortunate clergyman who made satisfaction for the injury he attempted; the satisfaction was accepted; and yet the acceptance of the satisfaction and the prosecution bear the same

date. There does not occur to my thoughts a proposition more abhorrent from nature, and from reason, than that in a matter of property, when restitution is made, blood should still be required.

Although the Bill, which had passed on its first reading by thirty-nine votes to ten, was later quietly dropped, the issue would not go away. Despite the temporary reversal of reforming zeal occasioned by the French Revolution and the fear of social change that it induced, by the beginning of the nineteenth century the time was ripe for a major reform of the criminal code.

Radical ideals had already been enunciated and even put into practice by the Quakers. As early as 1659 George Fox petitioned Parliament that 'no man be put to death for cattle, for money or outward thing'. Society should 'mind the law of God' and 'let the thief live to restore for his theft – neither Moses nor the Apostles saith hang him'. In 1699 his disciple, John Bellers, decried the death penalty as a 'stain to religion'. William Penn, in the Pennsylvania experiment, endeavoured to apply Quakerism to the law of the state, and only one execution is known there between 1682 and 1700. Penn rejected 'the wickedness of exterminating, where it was possible to reform'. He made the law as difficult as possible to enforce in order to reduce capital punishment to its lowest limit, and required two witnesses, proof of clear premeditation to kill, and the sanction of the executive before the death sentence could be passed on murderers.[9] When these laws were sent to England for approval they were repealed, without exception, by the Queen in Council. Pennsylvania gave in, and in 1718 yielded its own code for that of the mother country. With the Revolution in 1786 the former colony substituted hard labour for death for the crimes of robbery, burglary, and sodomy. The following year Dr Benjamin Rush of Philadelphia read a paper at the home of Benjamin Franklin advocating for the first time the complete abolition of capital punishment.[10] Like Beccaria he rejected the deterrent argument, not on the utilitarian grounds established by the Italian, but for political and moral reasons. Republican ideology and liberal theology were the bases of his denunciation of the death penalty. It was 'the natural offspring of monarchical government', a hangover from the tyrannical *ancien régime* disowned by the new Republic. Republican strength lay in virtue not in coercion. Humanity was the foundation of virtue; in its inhumanity the death penalty eroded virtue 'without which the American Republic would fall'. Republican governments would consider 'human sacrifices as no less offensive to the sovereignty of the people', than to 'the majesty of heaven'. 'An execution in a republic', he concluded, was 'like a human sacrifice in religion': it was 'an offering to monarchy'.[11]

Seven years later Pennsylvania introduced a penal code abolishing the death penalty for all crimes other than first degree murder. Here then was a code of penal law built upon the Christian principle of the reformation of the offender. The Act 'For the Better Preventing of Crimes and for Abolishing the

Punishment of Death in Certain Cases', limiting it to murder in the first degree, laid this out specifically. On the one hand, neither the follies nor crimes of our fellow creatures cancelled the Christian obligations of benevolence to them; on the other, since 'the design of all punishment is to prevent the commission of crimes, and to repair the injury that hath been done thereby to society, or the individual, and it hath been found that these objects are better obtained by moderate but certain penalties, than by severe and excessive punishments . . . the punishment of death ought never to be inflicted where it is not absolutely necessary for the public safety'.[12]

This experiment in enlightened penology won widespread praise from reformers. An American Universalist clergyman pointed to the wholesome and practical example of the Quakers as one of the several influences that had been at work to bring about a better condition of society: 'the community have seen a whole denomination living in peace and quietness, who have protested against the punishment of death'.[13] In another remarkable tribute they were praised for 'prying into and alleviating' society's evils:

> If you see one of them come into a bookseller's shop, it is not to enquire for Campbell's 'Pleasures of Hope' or for Roger's 'Pleasures of Memory', but for Buxton on 'Prison Discipline' or for the last account of the 'State of Leicester Gaol'. These are their delights, their luxuries and refinements. They do not indeed add new grace to the Corinthian capitals of polished society, but they dig down into its dungeon glooms and noisome sewers . . . They have, and will have their reward.[14]

It was this example that inspired in 1808[15] the formation of the first abolitionist body in England, *The Society for the Diffusion of Knowledge upon the Punishment of Death and the Improvement of Prison Discipline* (SDKPD). It advocated the abolition of hanging for all offences other than wilful and premeditated murder. Not surprisingly its leading lights were Quakers, one of whom, the scientist and philanthropist William Allen, along with Basil Montagu, was the co-founder. Montagu became its most prolific and able propagandist and over the next decade published a number of well-argued and temperate tracts.[16] Other members were Peter Bedford and Samuel Hoare, both Friends whose creed had taught them to abhor cruelty and respect the sanctity of life. The Quakers were not entirely alone. Numbered among the membership of the London Committee of the Society were six Anglican clerics, including such prominent figures as Samuel Wix, vicar of St Bartholomew's, London, and author of *Reflections on Punishment*, Archdeacon Wrangham of Hunmanby and Daniel Wilson, 'a noble character' as one Quaker called him,[17] who afterwards became Bishop of Calcutta. Anglican clergy were also well represented on the Dublin Committee.

The same year saw the first attempt in Parliament to get a hanging statute repealed. Throughout its history the campaign for the abolition of the death penalty involved a conjunction of extra-parliamentary activists and their parliamentary sympathisers, often only a few hundred of the former and a mere handful of the latter. Though few in number they were often passionately and always selflessly dedicated to the cause.[18]

What Parliament had done only Parliament could undo, and thus the first step, as the final triumph, of the abolitionists took place within the Palace of Westminster. It fell to Sir Samuel Romilly to bring the ideas of Beccaria and Bentham to the British political scene. Romilly, a man of exceptional gifts, and a friend of William Wilberforce in his campaign against the slave trade, fulfilled a similar role to his mentor in the crusade against capital punishment, devoting his whole life to this humane work. He rarely attended church services but when he did it was those of the Established Church he chose. He was no Christian in the orthodox sense that would have been understood by Archdeacon Paley. The scion of an exiled Huguenot family, he was brought up in a very religious but not very austere household. His father looked to the substance rather than the forms of religion, and the substance, he thought, consisted in doing good to his fellow creatures.[19] Under the influence of the French *philosophes* Romilly later became a believer in a Supreme Being, the immortality of the Soul, and in a practical 'Christian charity which might have put bishops to the blush'.[20] His concern extended to the unnecessary suffering of animals, but his life-work was to alleviate the suffering of his fellow human beings, and to attack both slavery and savagery wherever it was found. As a small child the gruesome illustrations of Fox's *Book of Martyrs* had repelled him. At school he had observed that the more severely boys were punished the worse they became.[21] These early lessons were to inform his life's work. A barrister by profession, he made the criminal law very much the special object of his study, and it was in this area that he was to make his indelible mark.

The Bloody Code was at its height as he grew to maturity. The triumph of the hangman seemed total. Yet he had overreached himself, and from now on his would be a decreasing domain, yielding inch by inch to those who would make him redundant. Romilly would not go that far, and in this he differed from Beccaria. He wanted the restriction, not the abolition, of the death penalty. He confessed to his close friend the Revd John Roget that it was 'absolutely impossible, even if it were to be wished (of which I am not quite sure), to omit death in the catalogue of human punishments'; for if the criminal refused to submit to the punishment imposed, or escaped from prison, or committed new crimes 'he must, at last, be punished with death'.[22]

While still in his twenties Romilly had become publicly involved in the issue of capital punishment. Anonymously, he had taken up the pen to counter the influence of Martin Madan's intemperate pro-hanging tract[23] and had attracted favourable attention in influential Whig circles. It was not until 1806, however, when he was nearly fifty, that Romilly finally entered the House of Commons as a Whig member. He soon began to agitate for the repeal of the death penalty for offences against property, and the campaign for the abolition of capital punishment can be dated 18 May 1808 when, at his bidding, Parliament abolished an obsolete statute which had made stealing 'privily' from a person a capital offence.[24] Only one offender to Romilly's knowledge had ever been executed under it. Not without demur, however, was this mitigation brought about since some saw it as a 'dangerous innovation'. The French Revolution and its attendant horrors did not assist the process of reform.

In 1810 he further tried to get Parliament to abolish capital punishment for three minor property offences including the theft of five shillings from a shop. In his speech to the Commons[25] he analysed the dangerous failings of the existing law in arguments that owed much to Beccaria, arguments that were to be repeated by his fellow Whigs for the next fifty years. At the purely pragmatic level the policy of terror was not working. Pragmatism had been Paley's main justification, yet here Paley's argument was turned on its head. It had made no allowance for the tender consciences of jurors and judges. Romilly pointed out that thieves often escaped punishment altogether owing to the reluctance of juries to convict, and the propensity of judges to reprieve. The gibbets and corpses paradoxically weakened the enforcement of the law rather than terrifying criminals, hanging terrified prosecutors and juries who feared committing judicial murder on the capital statutes. Convictions would become more numerous when that fear was removed. Certainty of detection rather than severity of sentence was the best deterrent of crime.

> It is the desire of a supposed good which is the incentive to every crime; no crime, therefore, could exist, if it were infallibly certain that not good, but evil must follow, as an unavoidable consequence to the person who committed it . . . All that can be done is, by a vigilant police, by rational rules of evidence, by clear laws, and by punishments proportioned to the guilt of the offender, to approach as nearly to that certainty as human imperfection will admit.[26]

> Punishment, he argued, should be proportionate to the offence, and it should be deserved. Judicial discretion could produce wide anomalies, some condemned felons being executed, others being spared depending on what were considered to be mitigating or aggravating circumstances. Capital punishment could only be justified by necessity not by desert.[27] Property crimes neither merited nor warranted death as a punishment. He pointed out that many heinous sins were not punishable with death, though morally and in their effect they were far worse than some capital crimes. Compared with bigamy, for instance, he was sure that stealing a few yards of ribbon or of lace from a shop was an offence far lower on the scale of moral guilt.[28]

Again he subjected Paley's rejection of the notion that it was better that ten guilty men should go free than one innocent man be punished to withering condemnation. For Romilly the very purpose of punishment was to protect the innocent and the guilty were punished only to that end. When the guilty escaped the law had done no good but also no harm, but where the innocent were condemned the law had injured those it was meant to protect; it brought the law into disrepute. If the innocent were convicted the guilty went free.

> Perhaps amidst the crowd of those who are gazing on the supposed criminal when he is led out to execution may be lurking the real murderer who reflects with scorn upon the imbecility of the law and becomes more hardened.[29]

His argument, like that of Paley, could be termed 'utilitarian'. The great difference between them was that he wished to protect people before property. Thus the innocent must never be condemned.[30] Innocent or guilty, however, Romilly asked if there could be any circumstance when theft from a shop of goods worth five shillings merited death.[31]

One aspect of his speech caused great offence: his attack upon 'the venerable Dr Paley'. This was necessitated by the reverence with which his views were held by Romilly's opponents. His word was Holy Writ. Thus Mr Windham rose, not to oppose Romilly's Bill, but to defend the reputation of a 'great and good man' whose work was 'a great national blessing', and to recommend to the House that all its members read 'the excellent observations upon criminal law made by this celebrated divine, and to judge for themselves'.[32] Yet for Windham to concur with Romilly in thinking that it would be 'extremely proper to revise many of our laws' was to undermine the very basis of Paley's position which was that the English criminal law was as near perfect as could be.

Scathing and effective as Romilly's rhetoric was in the Commons, the second reading of his Shoplifting Bill failed to impress the Lords who rejected it by thirty-one votes to eleven. The sages of bench and woolsack were the Scylla and Charybdis between which he could not navigate. That the lawyers opposed him did not surprise him: he knew them to be of an inveterately conservative turn of mind. Lord Ellenborough, the Chief Justice, whose stalwart defence of Christianity resembled that of the Inquisition and whose own religious faith was typified by Shelley as 'bloody, barbarous, and intolerant',[33] ventured the opinion that the judges had been too lenient, and it was this fault on their part which had encouraged these attempts to alter the law. He warned against a measure 'pregnant with danger to the security of property'. That the bishops opposed him occasioned Romilly little more surprise but still angered him. The Archbishop of Canterbury, Charles Manners Sutton, and six other prelates voted with Ellenborough and the Lord Chancellor, Lord Eldon, against the bill. An acerbic entry in his Journal for 30 May 1810 reveals Romilly's scorn for those who, he hoped, had prostituted their principles:

I rank these prelates among the members who were solicited to vote against the Bill; because I would rather be convinced of their servility towards the government, than that, recollecting the mild doctrines of their religion, they could have come down to the House spontaneously, vote that transportation for life is not a sufficiently severe punishment for the offence of pilfering what is of five shillings value, and that nothing but the blood of the offender can afford an adequate atonement for such a transgression.[34]

This was to overstate the case. Though none of them spoke in the debate, the bishops were neither quite so supine nor so accommodating as he made out. The Church of England, it is true, was largely a department of state responsible for religious affairs, it was bound hand and foot by acts of Parliament, and its office holders were appointed for political reasons. They were complacent and conservative, and were expected to vote for the Government. But to do so was their delight as well as their duty. They were certainly not prostituting their principles. They voted according to them. They shared the common morality of the day. Their latitudarian Christianity lent them nothing distinctive or disturbing. In an age when sin and crime were indistinguishable, the bishops, like the judges, believed in the existing system of criminal justice, a system which mitigated terror with mercy. They never intended that capital punishments should be generally imposed for trivial offences. They were persuaded by the argument for deterrence. They believed that without such a threat hanging over it, unregenerate humanity in an unstable age would resort all too easily to criminality or insurgency – activities which arose out of vice and depravity, not out of necessity, or deprivation. Curbing sinners – holding the lower classes in check – was a task which law and gospel could perform together. They, of course, shared the same class and property interests as the judiciary and the legislature, and it was easy to confuse self-interest with national interest. But to attribute their compliance with the status quo entirely to selfishness or servility is to deny the moral investment that the ecclesiastical establishment had in the criminal justice system of the eighteenth century.[35]

Undaunted by their wrecking of his bill, Romilly campaigned ceaselessly to ameliorate the rigours of the law so beloved by judges and bishops. He several times urged the formal abolition of disembowelling and quartering for high treason, eventually compromising on the issue of quartering to win the consent of the Lords 'that it should no longer be the law that the heart and bowels of a man convicted of high treason should be torn out of his body while he was yet alive'.[36]

England's way of judicial death, while a relatively recent innovation, was already hallowed by tradition, and buttressed by a xenophobia which was antipathetic to learning lessons from foreigners on how best to conduct English affairs. Romilly was given a stout warning by a doughty patriot in the House:

Sir, our system has formed the character of the people. And what a people! Those can best speak of them who best know them. If our system of laws is different from other more admired systems, so also is the character of the people. And may it continue different! Oh! let us pause before we introduce changes, founded on new maxims, derived from other sources, applicable to other states of society, and supported by doctrines avowedly calling in question the whole frame and policy of our criminal jurisprudence.

To question the Bloody Code and to do so on the basis of foreign precept and example was, in Colonel Frankland's eyes, well-nigh treasonable.[37]

Alongside the resistance to any attempts to contract the scope of the death penalty, moves were still being made to increase its demesne. In angry response to one such attempt, Lord Byron entered the abolitionist lists in 1812. His maiden speech on the occasion of a reading of the Framework Bill, which was to make the destruction of machinery a capital offence, was a model of controlled anger and moral indignation. He asked his astonished peers:

Is there not blood enough upon your penal code, that more must be poured forth to ascend to Heaven and testify against you? . . . Will you erect a gibbet in every field and hang up men like scarecrows? . . . Are these the remedies for a starving and desperate populace? Will the famished wretch who has braved your bayonets, be appalled by your gibbets?

To condemn some poor starving wretch to death would require more than a law, it would need 'twelve butchers for a Jury and a Jeffries for a Judge!'.[38] Yet, as late as 1816 a statute making the destruction of machinery at a colliery a capital offence was passed almost on the nod,[39] and the following year saw a resurrection of the sentence of hanging, drawing and beheading carried out on three half-starved rioters in Derbyshire.[40]

Every year Romilly introduced bills for the abolition of capital punishment for a variety of petty property offences. The Commons repeatedly passed them, the Lords turned them down every time. The extent of the opposition he was up against was revealed when on one occasion he approached Lord Stanhope to test whether the Lords were any more favourably disposed towards his Shoplifting Bill. Stanhope considered that 'it was a bill to screen the greatest villains upon the face of the earth, men who were much worse than murderers'. He went on to explain that he meant those men who employed boys literally to risk their necks in their nefarious service. Even so, it left Romilly's astonishment 'not much diminished'.[41] Faced with such attitudes, progress was slow. Romilly did not live to see even the abolition of capital punishment for shoplifting, and it was not until the two decades following his suicide in 1818, shortly after the death of his beloved wife, that hanging for crimes other than murder were progressively excluded by Acts of Parliament. If others would reap the harvest, it was Romilly who had sown the seeds and nurtured the young plants in often hostile terrain. It was for this life work that his successor, Sir James Mackintosh, posthumously apotheosized him: 'While private virtue and public worth are distinguished among men, the memory of Sir Samuel Romilly will remain consecrated in the history of humanity'.[42]

Once again the Quakers took the lead. At the instigation of the leading evangelical Friend, Joseph John Gurney, who was both Elizabeth Fry's brother and Wilberforce's close friend, the subject of capital punishment was 'solidly considered' by the Yearly Meeting in 1818 and the Meeting for Sufferings was asked to prepare a petition for presentation to the House of Commons. The frequency of this punishment, they contended, extended as it was to crimes of very different degrees of guilt, was 'repugnant to the mild and very benevolent Principles of the Christian Religion'. Were these principles acted upon wholeheartedly, were 'the genuine spirit and precepts of the gospel implicitly obeyed', then the way would be open for the total abolition of this penalty. Thus the penal code, whilst securing the ends of justice, should be changed so as to imprint upon it 'the characters of Christian Mercy, Righteousness and Love, – the firmest bulwarks of Society and Government'.[43] 'Mercy, righteousness and love', not 'retribution and terror' were those qualities which, in the light of the Friends' more positive view of human nature, sustained society.

The petition from this 'highly meritorious and examplary body of men' was presented by Wilberforce himself, and was mentioned with warm approval by Mackintosh[44] during the debate on a motion of his for the setting up of a Committee on Criminal Law. Another petition – significantly from the Corporation of London itself – echoed its sentiments, and rejoiced that harsh laws were being overcome by a 'tenderness for life, which originating in the mild precepts of our religion is advancing and will continue to advance as these doctrines become more deeply inculcated into the minds of the community'.[45] This Christian sentiment from the commercial community of the metropolis was surely not the foreign thought Colonel Frankland had complained of! Others warned that the English were making commerce their God, bowing down before it 'like the worshippers of Juggernaut to their grim and bloody idol'. The moral character of the nation was crushed beneath its wheels while they offered human victims as a propitiatory sacrifice.[46] Mackintosh's motion was carried against the advice of the Government.

As a result a Commons' Select Committee on Criminal Law relating to Capital Punishment was set up in 1819. The membership of the Committee was unanimous in the direction they should go, differing only as to the distance. Along with the chairman, Mackintosh, it included Russell, the future Whig Home Secretary, and the seconder of the motion, Gurney's brother-in-law, Thomas Fowell Buxton. Buxton noted that although no one on the Committee, including its chairman, went as far as he in wanting total abolition 'all [went] a very great way'. He was content that 'if [they] merely made forgery, sheep stealing, and horse stealing not capital it [would be] an annual saving of thirty lives which [was] something and satisfied [him] in devoting [his] time to the subject'.[47] Gurney was among those called to give evidence and he was quite satisfied by his examination and the contribution he was able to make.[48] The report provided a careful and comprehensive view of the state of the criminal law, and recommended the abrogation of capital punishment in many cases.

The Quakers this time petitioned the Lords, recognizing that it was in the Upper Chamber that opposition to change would be fiercest. While reiterating the practical arguments against hanging they believed it 'right to plead on the highest grounds' that could be assumed. They were 'conscientiously persuaded that under the Christian dispensation the punishment of death ought to be unknown', and that a Christian state was 'obliged to be guided in its legislation by the principles of the gospel'.[49] Never daunted by an awesome setting, this tiny Christian association was prepared to point out their Christian duty to the legislature and judiciary alike. This was a soaring language seldom heard from the larger churches, and never from the Church of England. In the satirical broadside *The Hangman and the Judge*, 'Jack Ketch', worried for his livelihood, blessed the bishops for not taking part against him, and relished the hanging of a Quaker as 'the most exquisite pleasure in life'.[50]

In accordance with the Select Committee's recommendations Romilly's three bills relating to shoplifting and theft were enacted in 1820 and, in 1823, on its hundredth anniversary on the Statute Book, the Waltham Black Act was virtually repealed.[51]

This latter measure had been successfully steered through Parliament by the recently appointed Tory Home Secretary, Sir Robert Peel. His advent was initially viewed with cautious optimism by the reformers. He was known to have reformist notions, and with his connections in the church and state had the power to effect reforms which others hardly dared propose.[52] He had earlier complained that the Tories had lagged behind public opinion which was more liberal than their policies.[53] He had privately and in part sympathized with Mackintosh and Buxton, who now relinquished the task of taking the reforms forward into his hands. Nonetheless, in office, he recognized that the fuller implementation of their aims would take time, and believed that they would be best secured by specific measures and not by general propositions. Under his cautious guidance other statutes, though not yet repealed, were slowly but surely modified, and their application meliorated. In this guise they with greater ease passed through the Lords who were more prepared to raise the minimum limit of goods stolen from a dwelling-house from forty shillings to five pounds than to abolish capital punishment for larceny completely.[54] With a reforming but cautious and Conservative Home Secretary it was hoped that 'the citadel of legislative inertia' had at last 'been finally outflanked'.[55]

Others, more radical and impatient, termed Peel's reforms 'superficial and delusive'. The law had been consolidated and tidied up, obsolete statutes had been excised, and anomalies removed, but its severity had hardly been mitigated. Above all the death penalty remained for forgery. The criminal code was still based on Paleyan, not on moral, principles. He had made laws practicable but not just. Where, they asked, was a code of morality which taught 'the doctrines proclaimed in his "amended" legislation' to be found? To forge a note for so much money was death, to forge a receipt for the same amount was not. Neither the light of Nature disclosed it, nor the authentic Word of God revealed it. Conscience revolted at 'the monstrous confusion of principles which such a system of justice' displayed, and religion broke 'in pieces upon the altars of a merciful dispensation the tablets of sanguinary law'.[56] So half-hearted and amoral a compromise could not stand. As with the Homicide Act of 1957, so with Peel's reforms, a settlement based solely on the principles of deterrence proved unworkable and immoral. His critics were proved right. Public opinion, increasingly disquieted by the workings of the criminal law and influenced in considerable measure by the brilliant propagandists Edward Gibbon Wakefield and J. Sydney Taylor,[57] was moving fast away from the old certainties, and Peel had fallen far behind it. Taylor was right in stating that neither reason nor the Christian religion allowed an enlightened public 'to reverence a vindictive system of justice' which attempted 'the suppression of crime by a violation of those moral distinctions which are more firmly established by God and nature than the foundations of the universe'.[58] Within four years of their enactment Peel's major statutes were repealed and replaced with far more radical measures, measures which he opposed. The going, however, remained tough.

The new Whig administration which came to power in 1830 might have been expected to hasten and broaden the process towards abolition since both Grey, the Prime Minister, and Brougham, the Lord Chancellor, had been stalwarts of the anti-hanging campaign while in opposition. As Labour Governments were to do a century later, so the Whig disappointed expectations. Criminal law reform was not high on the Government's agenda, and thin arguments for leaving things as they were were now propounded by those who had earlier derided them. The time was not right. Machine-breaking was endangering economic progress, and sheep-stealing was rife. In 1831 a moribund statute was revived when two men were hanged for larceny in a dwelling house. The *Morning Herald* marvelled that a law which the House of Commons under a Tory Government had pronounced a disgrace should be 'deemed a sufficient warrant for the shedding of blood by a Whig ministry'. So long as such laws remained on the statute book there was no guarantee that similar sacrifices should not be deemed expedient and 'that Mercy, pleading with all the powers of Reason on her side, [might] not be too weak to save, while ferocious laws say – "destroy" '.[59]

Petitions asking for further restriction of the capital code poured into Parliament, and on two occasions were presented by Anglican bishops.

Increasingly victims were reluctant to prosecute and jurors to convict. The Lord Chancellor, who had earlier approved and presented a petition of jurors in London, now rebuked those who violated their oath and found contrary to the evidence. It was, he said, for Parliament to change the law, not for juries to undermine it.[60]

Once again it was left to private Members to pressure Parliament into doing just that. Rising to the challenge, William Ewart, the Liberal Member for Dumfries, who had displaced the increasingly quiescent Mackintosh as the spiritual heir of Romilly, introduced bills repealing the death penalty for burglary, horse-stealing, and sheep-stealing.[61] Peel opposed him, on these reforms in particular, and on further revision of the criminal code in general.[62] Before further progress along abolitionist lines could be dared, the Government set up a Royal Commission on Criminal Law which met between 1833 and 1836.

The Commission was to consider whether it would be expedient to reduce the whole of the criminal law into one digest. The Government and the Commissioners were reluctant to 'go too fast', fearing a reaction if a crime wave succeeded the abolition of capital punishment. The real reason, but one not openly stated, was the lack of an alternative to the death penalty, but 'such an avowal – that men must be hanged because we did not know what else to do with them – could not be made by any government – either in decency or because no man could be hanged after such an avowal'.[63] In the event, just as the Select Committee had done before, the Royal Commission concluded that many capital statutes could be repealed without danger to public security and with benefit to public morality. As a result of their Report and its recommendations the Home Secretary, Lord John Russell, the following year sponsored a bill in the Commons to abolish hanging for twenty-one of the thirty-seven offences still subject to it, and for restrictions in its use in the sixteen remaining instances. Ewart proposed an amendment abolishing it for all offences other than murder. His argument merged the practical with principle: abolition in other countries had been a success; while capital punishment was, he urged, 'opposed to the principles of true religion and right reason'. The amendment was lost by seventy-three votes to seventy-two, Russell, Peel, and Gladstone voting against it. However, although hanging was retained for sixteen other offences it was thereafter applied in peace time to one crime only, murder.

In her first Queen's Speech the young Victoria hailed 'this mitigation of the severity of the law as an auspicious commencement' of her reign. The *Morning Advertiser* praised Ewart for his efforts in reducing the number of death penalties, but rebuked him for his moderation, and argued that he should have pushed for total abolition. Thus admonished, in March 1840, he introduced the first Parliamentary motion to abolish capital punishment and got over ninety votes in the Commons. Again he was praised by much of the press.

The ageing Wordsworth, however, worried that the continuing restriction would lead to the ultimate abolition of the death penalty, penned a series of fourteen sonnets on the subject which reflected both a considerable empathy with those condemned to die on 'Weeping Hill' and a concern that legislators might be tempted to abrogate their duty to the nation to maintain deterrent measures by their tenderness for the suffering of their fellow human beings.[64]

Over the next twenty years agitation continued in the Commons and in the country. Prominent and indefatigable members of the Society for the Abolition of Capital Punishment visited the main towns and cities of the kingdom, holding meetings where the merits of total abolition were expounded, publishing pamphlets and soliciting 'Prize Essays' to the same effect.[65] In the House, under Ewart's guidance, the erosion of the number of capital offences continued: by 1841 they were reduced to seven, by 1861 to four: murder, treason, piracy with violence, and arson in Her Majesty's dockyards.[66]

Thus far and no further. Restriction was not abolition, though it was enough to satisfy many of the reformers who were opposed not to the death penalty for the most serious offenders but to its promiscuous execution on the undifferentiated mass of petty criminals.[67] At least in part Whig opposition to the plethora of capital offences and the concommitant large number of reprieves was based on their belief that this conduct undermined the law and threatened stability. Justice was a lottery, the power of the state vacillating.[68] From then on murderers and traitors alone would be subjected to the ultimate penalty of the law, and the penalty would be exacted inexorably. The full majesty of a confident criminal justice system would be maintained. The defenders of limited capital punishment had merely withdrawn to higher ground and a narrower front.

In the development of a tenable middle ground between the reactionary perpetuation of the Bloody Code and the radical option of outright abolition[69] the Established Church again leant invaluable support.[70] During the debates, in 1832, a leading if eccentric Anglican Divine justified the preservation of hanging, although allowing for some restriction. In arguments that would be echoed by Christian retentionists for over a century, Richard Whately, former Oxford philosopher, and recently created Archbishop of Dublin, while acknowledging with Beccaria that prevention was the prime aim of the criminal law, deprecated the 'false tenderness' towards punishment so prevalent in the world:

> Merely excessive and misplaced compassion is, indeed, as much to be respected as any error can be, but when compassion is withheld from the deserving and bestowed only on the undeserving, the error is as odious as it is practically noxious. It seems to me one of the worst features of the character of a great part of the nation that very little sympathy, comparatively, is felt, except for the guilty.[71]

He argued, as Fisher of Canterbury was to do over a century later, for the restriction of the scope of the death penalty in order to preserve it from abolition. To threaten to hang all and sundry for every offence and then reprieve most of them was a nonsense. The death penalty should be restricted but certain. The most effectual method to prevent crime was not 'to trust to the severity of the punishments, which are threatened merely, and seldom inflicted; but to establish as close a connection as we are able between the ideas of crime and punishment.[72]

In the same year as Whately produced his tract, and to similar effect, though from a different standpoint, the Revd Samuel Wix published his *Reflections*.[73] A long time and early supporter of Romilly, Wix argued that the 'spirit of the gospel' was fundamentally opposed to capital punishment for any crime other than for murder. Conscious, however, that an appeal to the teaching of Jesus might not persuade all Christians of the validity of his case, he resorted to the old argument of expediency. It was not the punishment of vice that was complained of but its ineffectiveness. The severity of the law militated against its execution:

> Unremitting execution of sentence, on the clear proof of guilt, is, indeed, the life of all law; and would tend more to prevent crime, under any supposable leniency of punishment, than can reasonably be expected from the severest system, in which the minds of the community do not concur, and which the executive power will not, cannot, carry into effect; nor ought.[74]

The restriction of the scope of the death penalty had to be coupled with provision for its better execution. If murderers had to die then an amelioration of the present practice was called for 'on the benevolent principles of the gospel'. By the 'Murder Act' of 1752 condemned killers had been allowed only one whole intervening day between sentence and execution, except when the sentences were passed on Friday, when the hanging was to be on the Monday. Wix wanted a 'longer time than ordinary, between sentence and the gallows' so that they 'might have more space for salutary reflection, for improving under the offices of a spiritual adviser, and for praying and preparing for that pardon which . . . will never be denied to the truly penitent and faithful'.[75] He got his wish in 1836 when the forty-eight hour provision of the Murder Act was repealed and a period of between fourteen and twenty-seven days substituted.[76]

Thus, by urging the limiting of hanging to murder alone and by providing for the spiritual welfare and eternal salvation of the condemned, the arguments of religious writers like Wix played a crucial part in squaring capital punishment with Christianity and in assuaging qualms about the cutting off of God's creatures in their sin. The Anglican *via media* was at work. Paley's justification for, and the bishops' stalwart defence of, the English way of death was no longer tenable. Then it could be given up. All was not lost. By agreeing to the narrow restriction of hanging, indeed by welcoming it, Christians could retain capital punishment. Even Penn allowed for that.

The official voice of the Church of England, as represented by its teachers and bishops, had consistently leant moral support first to the Bloody Code, and then, when that was being irretrievably revoked, to the retention of the death penalty for serious offences. In the cause of abolition it was left to prominent families of Friends, aided by a few maverick Anglicans, and their Parliamentary allies to do all the running. It is an indication of how small and interrelated a circle it was that campaigned against the death penalty that both Thomas Fowell Buxton and Samuel Hoare were the brothers-in-law of Joseph John Gurney and Elizabeth Fry, and that Hoare was also related to William Allen by marriage.[77] With so many successes behind them, and with that eternal optimism which accompanies moral conviction, they remained over-confident of achieving their final goal:

In the light of advancing progress, limb after limb of that old tree, the gallows, has been dropping away, till only its central trunk, as it were, remains, on which the murderer, and the murderer alone, can now be fastened; and there are symptoms which seem to indicate that it, too, shall speedily be overturned.[78]

4 Technicians of Guilt

Chaplains and the Condemned in the Early Victorian Prison System

There can be no question whatever that the most hopeful means of
working the reformation of the murderer – and by reformation I mean
the conversion of his will from bad to good – is supplied by the certainty
of impending execution.

   When condemned criminals have entirely lost hope they show actual
goodness and purity of disposition, true abhorrence of committing
any deed in the least degree bad or unkind; they forgive their enemies . . .
and die gladly, peaceably, and happily. To them the last secret of life
has revealed itself in their excessive pain.

Arthur Schopenhauer[1]

A few months in the solitary cell renders a prisoner strangely impressible.
The chaplain can then make the brawny navvy cry like a child; he can
work on his feelings in any way he pleases. He can . . . photograph his
thoughts, wishes, and opinions on his patient's mind, and fill his mouth
with his own phrases and language.

John Clay[2]

With the restriction of capital punishment to the single crime of murder, and
the great prison building programme of the early Victorian age, the role of the
amateur evangelists declined while that of the increasing number of prison
chaplains grew. Penitence became a profession.

   This was not always to the advantage of the condemned. Daily contact with
criminals could lead to cynicism and contempt. Joseph Kingsmill, the full-
time chaplain of the new model Pentonville Prison, was another Dr Fancourt.
In his account of his prison ministry[3] he combined the usual arguments about
the right of the state to self-preservation, the unique deterrent which the
gallows were to 'the wicked and semi-insane', and the authorization for capital
punishment given by scripture. Certainly not an ardent evangelical, but a
biblical literalist nonetheless, he saw no difficulty in applying biblical precepts
directly to contemporary society. He was contemptuous of those who showered
more mercy on murderers about to be hanged than on those about to be
murdered. He thus dismissed the abolitionists as 'wholly in error', since 'death
punishment for murder is perfectly consistent with the New Testament,

necessary for the prevention of crime, and humane, in the largest sense, that is, as regards society at large'. The question is simply 'will you deter murder or permit many innocents to be slaughtered and society kept in perpetual fear?'

With the likes of Mrs Lachlan in mind, he criticized the efforts of 'philanthropic persons, friends, clergymen, and legal advisors' who buoy up hope till the last moment and so the malefactors' policy 'must be not to confess or to do so only partially, and to assume the garb of penitence and religion'. The chaplain should have no qualms. His duty was plainly, from the very first, 'to assume, as a thing settled beyond all question, the guilt of the condemned, and accordingly to direct the sinner to confess to Almighty God all his sins . . . and next, to acknowledge his crime'. Confession could be induced by the chaplain, conversion was far more dubious. Kingsmill opposed the private administration of communion to the condemned as a violation of the principles of the Church of England. He viewed the whole practice of celebration of the Lord's Supper under such circumstances and 'the admission of the foulest criminal to its participation on a few weeks of very doubtful repentance as nothing short of profanation and gross abuse of the Divine Ordinance'. He wished to ensure that the sacrament would be administered to the condemned only with the express sanction of the diocesan bishop. In this way many a wretched criminal would be 'saved from going down to the grave with a lie on his lips', the chaplain would be protected from 'painful importunities' (by the likes of Miss Payne perhaps), and 'one of those pictorial features of the horrid drama, which serve to defeat the moral effect of the whole exhibition upon the public mind' would be removed.

In contrast to Kingsmill's scepticism both as to the reality and necessity of the conversion of the condemned, some chaplains spared no efforts to 'save' their charges. The 'most irritable and ungovernable anxiety' beset many a chaplain if the prisoner betrayed 'no symptoms of repentance and no emotions of shame and regret'.[4] Sometimes their concern for confession led them into trouble. Mild indeed was the manner of Mr Cotton who had merely to be rebuked for preaching a sermon to the condemned which was considered too harrowing to their feelings.[5] More desperate were the methods of the Revd John Davis, Ordinary of Newgate in 1845. He was rebuked in the Russell Report of that year for encouraging 'the Convict Hocker' after he had been pinioned and just before his death to make a final confession to the 'Gentlemen of the press present', a confession hitherto withheld and to which they would have given publicity. Hocker fainted and had to be revived by the surgeon before his execution could take place 'with due Order and Solemnity'.[6] If a convict made a voluntary confession, Russell concluded, such a confession might be so far regarded as satisfactory 'inasmuch as it confirms and thereby strengthens the public Confidence in the Verdict of the Jury, and as it exhibits the penitent State of Mind to which the Convict has been brought'; but if such a confession were sought for, if its attainment was 'plainly made a Matter of Importance the very fact of its being so sought for implies a Doubt of the Completeness of the Case, and of the Justice of the Verdict and of the Sentence and public Confidence in the Verdict, which ought to be final and satisfactory, is thereby shaken'.[7] Despite this stern admonition, four years later in 1849 the Revd Richard Chapman of Coventry Gaol caused a serious scandal by his treatment of a condemned woman called Mary Ball. One day he visited her cell and called for a lighted candle. For what he said was a matter of seconds, but the assistant matron said was two minutes, he held the prisoner's hand over the flame. 'If you feel this pain so much', he said, 'do you realize what you will suffer in the torments of hell, where your body will burn for a hundred years?' He believed that to save her soul he had to give her a foretaste of her eternal fate. An inquiry was held by the local magistrates and he was suspended from prison duties.[8]

As the century wore on confession and conversion remained dominant issues for those who had to carry out the death penalty. It was no easy thing for decent men to send another soul into eternity. It put them more at ease if the condemned admitted their guilt, agreed in the justice of their punishment, and repented of their sinful ways. When John Tawell handed a written confession to Mr Cox, the Aylesbury Prison chaplain, an attempt was made by a section of the magistrates to compel him to hand it over to the visiting justices. The chaplain would do no more than assert that Tawell had made a full confession of guilt. The document itself he would not deliver up. It had been made under the seal of the confessional and on condition that it should not be published.[9] Asked in evidence before the Royal Commission in 1864 if he was relieved when a person convicted on only circumstantial evidence confessed, the Revd John Davis of Newgate replied that it was a great relief 'and to no man so much as to the culprit himself . . . but they almost always confess. I never saw but one who died without confessing, a woman . . . of whose guilt there was no doubt.'[10] Davis himself, however, had been earlier accused of putting the appropriate words into the mouths of the condemned.[11]

Were all chaplains so sanguine? Chaplains' and gaolers' journals from the mid-nineteenth century, laconic in the extreme about all else, mention the ministrations to condemned prisoners in considerable detail. A refrain echoed again and again is the comment in the Gaoler's Journal for York Prison in 1833 referring to each man who was hanged as 'Penitent and ever since conviction own[ing] the justice of his sentence'. It was a sorrowful chaplain who had to record of another that although he was attended by Mr P., the Wesleyan minister, during most of the time he was under sentence of death, 'he died without making any confession, paid no attention to any religious instruction, was never heard to utter a prayer during his imprisonment and had no belief in a future state of rewards and punishments'.[12] The gaoler echoed the sense of failure but tried to glimpse some hope at the end:

Mr P. has been very attentive to him and has done all he could to bring him to a proper state of mind but all in vain, he refused to the last to make any confession of his guilt but did seem to pray when the rope was round his neck.

After the execution of an impenitent highway robber who to the last had protested his innocence, the chaplain of Lincoln Castle seemed to console himself with the observation that, once the man had been condemned, not a soul had come to visit him, though he had several living relatives. Even his own family has spurned someone so steeped in sin as to know no repentance.[13]

In a lengthy communication, Mr Mowley, the chaplain of Lancaster Prison in 1857, recounted the efforts made to induce a confession from Richard Pedder, a wife murderer who even in a last letter to his children, which the chaplain preserved, claimed that her shooting was accidental. Mr Mowley did his best to ease a confession out of him by alluding to the prevailing view that his wife had been an adulterer and a drunkard. These charges he utterly denied. Accompanied by another cleric, Mr Wright from Manchester, he again visited Pedder after the Sunday service and 'conversed with him on his awful state and particularly the necessity of his making a full and candid acknowledgment of his guilt, to which he made an evasive reply'. Later that afternoon they again visited him but to no greater avail. The following morning Pedder accompanied them to the chapel at 11 o'clock where he received the sacrament of the Lord's Supper. He rose from the table with a thankful heart for the comfort he had received in complying with the commands of his blessed redeemer. At 12 o'clock he met his death with great composure and firmness. Happily for him, concluded Mr Mowley, he had employed his time prior to his trial in reading and reflecting. He was happy to say that he had seldom met with anyone more tractable and teachable in all his long experience in the gaol. It must have come as a great relief to the chaplain to hear from the warder who had spent the previous night with Pedder that the condemned man had confessed that he had intended to alarm his wife but not injure her. It was probably confession enough to put the chaplain's mind at rest. Whether it was true or proffered by a sympathetic warder to soothe a troubled priest we do not know.[14]

The most detailed and dramatic account we have comes from the Lancaster Castle Chaplain's Journal for 1862.[15] Beginning on 14 August the chaplain regularly visited Walker Moore, yet another domestic murderer, in the condemned cell. Although he made good progress from the start, it was not until after all hope had gone that he became most pliable. On 17 August the chaplain came to the gaol to see him.

I found that he did not sleep so well last night as previously. I suppose that what took place yesterday and the notification to him of the day of his execution will have caused this. From the chaplain's point of view, however,

his demeanour is becoming more and more what it should be. He joined
and followed me in prayer with great though quiet earnestness tonight and
expressed his thanks to me with every appearance of deep feeling.

From then on this 'reserved seriousness of manner' began to 'pervade all his
daily deportment'. However, on 21 August, speaking to him of the crime, he
was 'somewhat disappointed by finding him still dissatisfied with his trial'. He
had previously been given to understand that there would be a Queen's
Counsel specially appointed to defend him, and he thought that the judge had
been precipitate and unfair towards him.

I read and expounded to him some selected passages of scripture, and
prayed for him for the graces of conviction of sin, penitence, and confession
of sin. Concluded with B. Wilson's short prayers for a criminal under
sentence of death, in all of which he joined with much apparent fervour.

The following Sunday, despite his attentiveness and respectful attitude, the
chaplain found him hard going as he would insist on palliating his offence. He
began to get an inkling that Moore's enthusiasm for seeing him and his
respectful demeanour may have had to do with something other than religious
instruction. He was convinced that he harboured some feeling of hope and
had the impression that the chaplain could do something yet to save him. The
latter feared 'that this hoping to the last may operate unfavourably towards
Moore's best interests'. He left the gaol 'thoroughly used up'.

Nonetheless he continued to see him frequently and for long periods, often
leaving the prison exhausted, culminating in preparation for holy communion.
A relieved chaplain recorded after this interview that 'his manner tonight was
very quiet and thoughtful, and Warden Ellison thinks that, during these last
two days, a considerable and favourable change has been observed in him'.

The following evening, the eve of his execution, Walker Moore climbed up
a water closet in the chapel yard, and plunged head first into a cistern a little
more than a yard deep. Self-murder had compounded, rather than judicial
sacrifice expiated, his sin. The distraught chaplain could 'not describe the
pain which this calamity to the gaol caused' him. He did 'not recollect a more
painful day in [his] lifetime'. The investigation into this affair lasted for three
days and resulted in the chaplain being severely reprimanded for failing to
consult with the visiting justices about the care of the prisoner. The gallows
had been cheated of its prey.

Of course, purely pastoral attentions had always been a major part of their
role, and the ministrations of the more sensitive chaplains were received by
many prisoners with great and moving gratitude. The Revd T. W. Franklin,
the prison chaplain of Hertford Gaol, was much appreciated by John Thurtell,
a murderer in whom he had encouraged a contrite heart. When at the execution
Thurtell thanked him for all he had done, the good chaplain burst into tears.[16]

When Martha Brown went to the scaffold in 1856, the prison chaplain, Dacre Clemetson, was too distressed to go with her. His compassion, however, had its price, since he left her to be accompanied by her local vicar, Henry Moule, who was a passionate advocate of capital punishment.[17] The chaplain of Winchester Gaol took his duties so seriously that he hurried to London in a vain attempt to intercede with the Home Secretary (who was at Balmoral at the time) on behalf of a boy who was shortly to die for a murder committed aboard ship. One of his accomplices, also condemned to hang, had confessed to the chaplain that he had compelled the lad, under threat of death, to take part in the killing.[18]

As always, the ministrations of prison chaplains helped the condemned go to their deaths bravely, though sometimes they laboured in vain. A notorious case, searingly portrayed in a speech in the Commons by John Bright, was that of Sarah Thomas, hanged in 1849 for the murder of her brutal mistress. She refused to co-operate in her demise, and had to be dragged, struggling and screaming, by half a dozen warders to her public execution, the clergyman in vain 'coaxing or exhorting her to walk quietly to the scaffold'.[19]

In this increasingly professional world 'amateurs' – outsiders to the prison system – still had a role to play. When one his parishioners, James Rush, was sentenced to death for the murder of a neighbour in 1849, the Revd William Andrew paid regular visits to him in the condemned cell at Norwich Castle. He had been asked to come by Rush himself who would have nothing to do with Mr Brown, the prison chaplain. With the latter Rush had always been impassive, but when Andrew arrived he 'began to tremble, and then a wave of emotion and grief swept over him and he sank down on his bed'. They sat thus, almost silent, for two hours. On subsequent visits Rush professed his innocence, and Andrew despaired of bringing him to confession, although perhaps something could have been done had he been allowed to visit alone, without Brown in attendance. It was not allowed. Rush went to his end impenitent. Andrew explained why in a two-and-a-half hour extempore sermon to an immense congregation. Rush had hardened his heart by wild profligacy and sensuality, and God had left him in his sins.[20]

An account of such 'amateur' ministry, remarkable for the depth of its compassion and sensitivity, was given by the Revd C. B. Tayler in his autobiography.[21] Many years before, in 1826, he had gone to Bury to visit John M. who was condemned to death for robbery. At the request of the old chaplain Tayler agreed to take his place in the cell and on the scaffold with his former parishioner. Having sat up all night with the condemned man 'it was impossible not to feel an intense and agonizing sympathy with that poor condemned prisoner – impossible not to identify oneself, in some measure, with his wretchedness; and what should I have done, how could I have attempted to support and comfort him, without that Book of Books, that Word of life'. He preached the condemned sermon in the chapel where a coffin was displayed and all the prisoners were assembled. Afterwards the prisoner asked to bid farewell to his fellows, and, true to the customary homiletic paradigm, he admonished and warned them, especially one sixteen-year-old, of 'what Sabbath breaking, poaching, and thieving' had brought him to: 'I began as you have done; and now I am going to be hanged like a dog.' As the end approached Mr Tayler was overcome by his feelings. He was deeply affected by the sight of that 'fine young fellow, in the very prime of youthful manhood, his finely developed form, and firmly-knit limbs, his fresh healthy countenance, in all the vigour of life – he was but six and twenty – before me; and to know that in a few minutes he would be a motionless and bloated corpse'.

Tayler continued beside the man until the end, saying the words of the burial sentences and dropping a handkerchief to indicate to the executioner to do his work. He watched until he was dead. He was shocked by the ribaldry and jokes of the crowd. Later he thanked the executioner for his merciful application but, like many later chaplains, found it difficult not to recoil from his proffered handshake. Twenty-three years later he saw a letter written by John M. to his mother, telling her of his heavenly hopes and the great kindness of the chaplain. Despite this compassion, and close identification with the suffering of the young man, nowhere does Tayler even hint at dissent from such a punishment for such a crime.

Another semi-professional, the Revd J. Young, chaplain pro tem at York Castle, regularly visited Taylor Whitworth in the condemned cell. On their first encounter he 'found him much dejected and had a long conversation with him on the sin laid to his charge. He seemed very much pleased to receive religious instruction. After prayer I left him in better spirits.' The better spirits continued and his interest in religion grew, fed by tracts and many conversations and much prayer with the chaplain. As the end fast approached, Mr Young was more and more convinced of the sincerity of Whitworth's penitence and conversion. On the last day they 'talked for some time on the great change that should soon take place'. He spoke freely on the subject. His faith in Christ seemed strong. He 'turned to many passages of God's Holy Word containing the promises of pardon and support to sinners'. His hope of salvation seemed well-formed. A little before 11 o'clock Young administered to him holy communion 'from which he said he felt great strength to his soul'. Just before he was led away to execution he prayed 'most fervently'. Young accompanied him to the scaffold reading the usual service, and took his 'parting leave of him in good hopes that he was about to exchange a life of pain and suffering for one of joy'.[22] The gaoler again noted that Whitworth was 'very penitent and acknowledged the justice of his sentence'.

Gratitude to the chaplain for his ministry and 'happiness' in the acceptance of their fate are common expressions used of condemned criminals in the prison journals. One records the daily visits of a chaplain to a man called Ryley who had killed his wife. On the day before the hanging the chaplain found him 'still happy and cheerful'. He had a good hope through Jesus Christ, expressing his gratitude to the chaplain for this, and saying God would repay him. At 6.45 the following morning the chaplain again visited Ryley and 'found him still calm and happy'.

> I read to him and prayed with him until nearly 11 when I administered the sacrament, the Governor, and the schoolmaster being present. He afterwards prayed aloud and privately said he should be happier than he was then. At ten to 11 he was pinioned and I talked to him until the signal to move to the scaffold. He walked firmly and knelt down before me until I read the service. He looked peaceful and firm. I shook hands with him and he kept hold until he was drawn away. He was praying aloud until his last breath and I had reason to hope he was happy in his death as he said he had no fear but God could and would pardon him through Jesus Christ. He was very attentive and very affectionate and very grateful. He died in less than two minutes.

Happiness is an odd but dominant expression in the York Journals. Later that year, on Christmas Day, the same chaplain preached the condemned sermon for another man about to be hanged, on the text 'The end of all things is at hand.' Afterwards, like any good churchgoer, the condemned made appreciative remarks about the service to the priest, and like any priest the chaplain basked in them. The man 'was still happy and cheerful and hoped all his sins were pardoned as he put his trust in Jesus Christ and was not afraid to die'. He had 'enjoyed the service of the day, he said, very much'. The chaplain hoped that he would die in peace.

It was not hard for *Punch* to ridicule such set pieces. On the eve of being hanged a felon might be terrified by such ghostly exhortations, but could hardly be 'pleased' with them; 'like a serious gentleman at large sitting under Mr Spurgeon'. It concluded that the attention paid by the convict to the discourses of his spiritual adviser 'was about equal to the pleasure which he derived from them'.[23]

In all the surviving accounts of the work of mid-nineteenth century prison chaplains, not once do we hear any cavil about capital punishment, even when it was still being inflicted for crimes other than murder, although the Parliamentary abolitionist, Lushington, related an earlier incident in Newgate when the Ordinary secured the life of a boy forger by refusing 'to administer the sacrament to him, upon the ground of his youth, and that was considered a sufficient ground to let him off'.[24] In contrast, the famous Brighton preacher, Frederick Robertson, who never attended a condemned person, but had to witness a murder trial in 1852 as chaplain to the High Sheriff of Sussex, found that the experience reversed all his 'intellectual convictions of the need and obligation of capital punishment'. He was horrified by the brutal murder but then related what occurred at the sentencing of the murderess. Baron Parke put on the black cap. The poor woman 'with burning cheeks and eyes as brilliant as fire with excitement', was held up between two turnkeys to receive her sentence. In his haste to get the distasteful business over, the judge omitted to say by what death she was to die: 'So the fainting thing was held up again, and the last sentence of the award repeated with the words, "Hanged by the neck".' Robertson confessed that he felt as if he were 'a guilty man in sitting by to see a woman murdered'.[25] This is more than any prison chaplain acknowledged.

With exceptions such as Kingsmill, and extremes such as Chapman, the chaplains were increasingly concerned with the evangelistic opportunity that the death penalty provided, and the urgent duty which it imposed upon them. Good, compassionate men with urgent business to attend to, they accepted, in spite of, or perhaps because of, their personal experiences at the scaffold, the prevailing views on capital punishment. If pressed they might have opted for refinements, they might have favoured the ending of hanging in public, but not of hanging itself. It was simply too valuable, 'the most efficient means of reformation'.[26] It also ensured the centrality of their role.

5 A Sentence of Scripture

Capital Punishment and Biblical Exegesis in the Early Victorian Age

Those who believe in the Christian religion believe also in the Jewish religion, and under the Jewish religion, abundant was the application made of death-punishment; and thus may be seen authority-begotten prejudice operating in support of it.

Jeremy Bentham[1]

The Law of God is clear: the murderer is always positively excluded from any and from all mitigation of punishment . . . 'He shall surely be put to death'.

William Cobbett[2]

We appeal, not metaphorically, but literally, from the 'letter that killeth, to the spirit which giveth life'. We derive from the tenor of the Gospel two principles: the condemnation of the spirit of revenge, and the encouragement of the spirit of repentance; and both these principles we believe to be against the punishment of death.

William Ewart[3]

A Christian country which maintained capital punishment for murder was always anxious to secure scriptural authority and ecclesiastical support for so doing. Man was made in the image of God, and life was God-given. Only on divine authority could that image be marred and life extinguished. Thus the proponents of capital punishment asserted not only that the Bible authorized judicial killing for murder but indeed it enjoined it on all Christian states. The philanthropist Anthony Ashley-Cooper, afterwards seventh Earl of Shaftesbury, along with many other extreme evangelicals, had very strong feelings on the subject, being certain that 'the Word of God does not permit but commands "He that sheddeth man's blood, by man shall his blood be shed" '.[4]

As the incarnation of justice in a Christian country, it was the regular practice for the trial judge to quote the proof-texts of scripture when the sentence of death was passed. Condemning one young murderer to death in 1832, the judge said

It is impossible for an earthly judge to consign you to any other fate than that which the law of God decrees, when it says, 'Whoso sheddeth man's blood by man also shall his blood be shed', and also, 'The land cannot be cleansed of the blood that is shed therein, but by the blood of him that shed it'.

He continued to admonish him at considerable length with gospel precepts, before additionally sentencing him to be hung in chains, despite an appeal by relatives and others.[5]

When hanging had been the indiscriminate punishment for a whole host of offences there had been little attempt to justify it on biblical grounds, let alone to urge that the Bible commanded it. Paley's argument was philosophical and utilitarian, not scriptural. This inability of the proponents of the Bloody Code to found it on a biblical basis was eventually exploited by reformers in their attempts to restrict its scope. Although in the same year that Paley's *Principles* was published the Revd William Turner in his *Essay on Crimes and Punishments* touched on the biblical arguments for and against capital punishment, and in 1807 Beccaria Anglicus devoted a letter to them,[6] it was to be another half century before the publication of the first major work in England on the biblical authorization of capital punishment.[7] Its author, Samuel Wix, seemingly ignorant of the above, knew of no others who shared his view that the Bible was incompatible with capital punishment.[8] The longer he lived, the more confirmed he was in the inefficiency of capital punishments; and the more maturely he became acquainted with the scriptures generally, and with the New Testament, especially, the more his belief was strengthened that the spirit of these punishments was at variance with the spirit of the gospel of Jesus Christ.[9] Although under the Mosaic law offences other than murder were capital they were repealed by the law of Christ. Jesus had intended to ameliorate the old law (Matt. 5. 38ff.), but 'we, however, have a Criminal Code, very far more severe in its exactions and inflictions'.

> Instead of an eye for an eye do not our laws demand death for an eye? That precept of the Christian law giver; of Jesus Christ, which forbids the requiring 'a tooth for a tooth' or 'an eye for an eye', cannot be supposed but, in its principle, to prohibit the requiring death for an eye; for theft; for forgery; and for numerous other crimes, not mentioned in the Mosaical law, as subjecting to death.[10]

Perversely, although English law had more capital crimes than the Mosaic Code, of the crimes enumerated in that code – impiety, witchcraft, bestiality, blasphemy – only an unmentionable crime (buggery) was then capital in England.[11]

Despite his earlier close association with Quakers in the SDKPD, he was anxious that no one should misrepresent his views, calling them 'Quaker notions'.[12] Indeed they were set at the heart of Anglicanism in that the Prayer Book began with 'When the wicked man turneth ... he shall save his soul alive', and God 'desireth not the death of a sinner'. Commenting on the 37th Article which asserted that 'the laws of the realm may punish Christian men with death, for heinous and grievous offences', Wix averred that 'a mild government, formed on principles of Christian justice, [would] confine them within the smallest possible number, consistently with public order, and general security; and even should it be thought proper not to extend the punishment beyond cases of personal violence, or to confine it to the single offence of murder, in all its varieties, such mildness would not be at variance with the Article'.

> Under the Mosaic dispensation, a mildness of punishment, so far as relates to the number of capital offences, compared with that, at present, prevailing under the British Government, is most striking. Yet the British Government professes itself a Christian Government, and should, therefore, be governed by laws founded on Christian principles.

Christian magistrates, he concluded, should not punish with death any crime for which they did not have scriptural mandate. Effectively this reduced the legitimate range of the noose to those guilty of murder.

With the more or less contemporaneous restriction of the death penalty to homicide, however, battle was joined between those pushing for complete abolition and those who wished to retain it for murder. The latter feared that 'the doctrine of expediency' had superseded 'the authority of the scriptures' which, of course, clearly demanded the death penalty for murderers.[13] They need not have feared. The abolitionists, while resorting to utilitarian arguments about deterrence, and the effect hangings had on the moral fabric of society, were nonetheless largely inspired by their Christian faith and were ready to state their beliefs when necessary. Both sides regularly cited scripture for their purpose, and were to do so with little change in emphasis from the mid-nineteenth to the mid-twentieth centuries.

Although the arguments at times involved different interpretations of specific texts the two camps were readily divisible into those on the one hand who interpreted texts literally and uncritically and gave equal authority to the commands of the Old Testament as to the teaching of Christ, and those on the other who spoke of the 'tenor of the gospel' by which all else must be interpreted, or the 'spirit of Christ' under whose authority all else fell. The former were particularly reliant for their justification on the two passages cited by the judge above; the gospel passages were used only for the secondary purpose of inducing penitence and encouraging hope. The latter countered the citation of Old Testament proof texts by referring to the gospels where Jesus refused to condemn the woman taken in adultery and where in the Sermon on the Mount he transcended the *lex talionis* of the Mosaic law. In addition the Old Testament provided the stories of Cain, and Lamech, and David to counter any rigid adherence to an ancient code.

The command given by God to Noah in Genesis 9.2–6 ('whoso sheddeth man's blood by man will his blood be shed') was vital to the advocates of capital punishment. The Revd George Barrell Cheever, a prominent Calvinist divine from New York City, whose writings were influential in England as well as in America, confessed that the scriptural proof for the death penalty was 'somewhat limited, though plain and powerful'. Consequently he was forced to ascribe to the Old Testament an authority equal to that of the New, calling the Genesis passage 'the citadel of the argument, commanding and sweeping the whole subject'. The God of mercy had given this 'comprehensive element of law to Noah', and would 'never suffer it to be blotted from human statute books by the presumptuous tampering of a single generation'.[14]

This 'champion of the Sacred Cause of Hanging'[15] went to extraordinary lengths to demonstrate the folly of mercy. Even God blundered at first since 'in consequence of the divine lenity in the case of Cain, the crime of murder had become frightfully common, the earth being filled with violence'. God had not fully appreciated the psychological dexterity with which his creature would exculpate his crimes:

> The assurances that his own life would not be taken, with which Lamech, whether a murderer or a homicide, comforted himself and his wives by the example of Cain's preservation, shows how men reasoned from that lenity; and that the consequence of it would be a great cheapness in the estimate of human life, a great freedom in the indulgence of violent passion, unrestrained by consequences, and a perfect carelessness and recklessness in bloodshed.

The Almighty did not make the same mistake twice, however, and after destroying almost all of his first creation, which a contemporary polemicist typified as 'capital punishment in the superlative degree',[16] he gave strict orders to Noah to extirpate all murderers in the future. Thus it seems, according to Cheever, that God himself had tried the experimental abolition so often advocated by the reformers only to find that it had not worked. If it had not proved a success under the governance of God, all the less was it possible for human rulers to govern mercifully and yet curb lawlessness. It was as ingenious an argument as it was absurd. Yet, in a pre-critical age of biblical scholarship, such efforts were necessary to reconcile apparent inconsistencies between the policy and practice of the Almighty, and to dispose of the abolitionist paradigm offered by his actions as opposed to his decrees.

The Quakers, unsurprisingly, had always been to the forefront of those seeking 'the spirit of the gospels' to confront and refute the advocates of the law. To such an extent was the Society of Friends identified with the campaign against the death penalty that all 'morbid philanthropists' were ridiculed as being 'spiritual Quakers'.[17]

One such was the Revd Henry Christmas, librarian of Zion College, who in 1845 produced perhaps the most effective English refutation of the biblical argument for capital punishment.[18] Christmas had been a convert to abolition. At one time he had thought that capital punishment was of divine appointment, and of universal obligation, but he had gradually changed his mind. Of course he shared with his opponents a literalist view of the biblical material. Thus he agreed with them that God spoke directly to the patriarch Noah in Genesis 9.6, and that this was the most important proof text. So far they were in accord, but no further. He concluded that the phrase was a prediction not an injunction, meaning no more than Jesus' comment that 'those who live by the sword will perish by the sword'. He contended that 'by man' was a pleonasm: 'Whoso sheddeth the blood of man that is in man, his blood shall be shed.' Thus he maintained that there was no command before Moses demanding capital punishment. He referred to Cain and Lamech, murderers yet not put to death, and the treacherous murder of the men of Shechem by Simeon and Levi which went unpunished, but he did not attribute this to divine error. The law given to Moses had been repealed for Christians, and even if it had not, to follow the Levitical law would necessitate killing people for the same crimes as Moses had lain down, an action which would be unconscionable. Drawing on a potent and obvious contemporary analogy, he pointed out that the negative biblical testimony for slavery was not enough to sustain it and it was abolished; so too should be the death penalty at least for a trial period.[19]

Christmas' book was very influential, Dickens himself being convinced by the arguments employed therein. His exposition of scripture both undermined the sanction for hanging, and implied that the Old Testament was not as authoritative as the New. Thus the infallibility of scripture was under attack. One respectful opponent hurried into print and, while admiring Christmas' scholarship, lamented that 'his mode of meeting Holy Scripture would lead to consequences which he, equally with myself, would utterly abhor'.[20] Ironically this same author was forced later to argue that the teaching of Jesus could not be taken literally, and that the citation of proof texts (as he himself had done) was futile and lent alarming weight to 'the infidel's boast' that 'you may prove anything from scripture'.[21] A less respectful opponent castigated those who denied or invalidated the authority of the Old Testament as the 'subtle enemies of truth', and their arguments as resting on 'Infidel and Rationalist principles'.[22]

A decade later Charles Phillips argued a similar case in a lengthy work[23] which was much admired and roundly abused by the effervescent foe of sentimentality, James Stephen. He recognized that behind the arguments about dubious statistics, alleged miscarriages of justice, and the mythical social contract, the real ground on which Phillips, and indeed most opponents of capital punishment, relied was founded on what he conceived to be 'an entire misconception of the whole character and purpose of Christianity'. They were as selective in their use of scripture as their opponents, and as tendentious. He ridiculed the argument advanced by Phillips that 'whoso sheddeth man's blood, by man shall his blood be shed' is prophetic or denunciatory rather than imperative. This contention Phillips supported with the fact that Moses, David, Ehud, and Jael were all murderers and yet were not put to death. 'The cases of Ehud and Jael', observed Stephen sarcastically, 'have been put to strange uses enough but surely this is the strangest of all: a Divine command has been disobeyed, but can a Divine prophecy be unfulfilled or a Divine threat come to nothing?' For Stephen the Genesis passage was as clear as it was conclusive. Thus he was content to 'leave the criminal to God's judgment, after treating him as we believe God would have us treat him – that is by hanging him'.[24]

Many other attempts were made to iron out the difficulty of the Genesis text,[25] but in a pre-critical age never was there a more convincing argument as that which simply countered the Old Testament with the gospel. Some early abolitionist contributions along these lines were merely soppy.[26] More impressive was the contribution of Edward Webster. In 1856 he turned to the subject in a paper published by The Society for Promoting the Amendment of the Law.[27] For him the very 'first question was a religious one: did God demand the death of a murderer?' He found no mandate in the New Testament, but only in the Old. However the examples of Cain, Moses, David, and Paul as murderers who were not only not killed, but who actually served God's will, and the fact that the Mosaic law was for a peculiar people at a particular time and not for all men everywhere, undermined that supposed mandate. But more important was the gospel, the gospel of repentance. The greater the crime a man committed, the greater the right he had to save his soul by repentance. Considering the enormity of murder, he averred that a whole life's repentance could not be too long for expiation.

William Tallack, the Quaker Secretary of the Howard Association, argued that any form of wrong or injustice could be authorized by the quotation of isolated texts, apart from 'the spirit and scope of scripture', and thus 'the Devil could cite texts to tempt our Lord'.[28] The Revd Lord S. G. Osborne in his evidence to the Royal Commission in 1866 put the matter succinctly. He began by denying the Old Testament exegesis:

> As for the arguments taken from the bible to enforce or justify capital punishment, I never could for one moment admit their validity. Murderers, when God especially ruled his own people were not always put to death.

But even had they been, from Cain downwards, it would not have altered his opinion. It was a question of the spirit and not the letter.

I take the four Gospels and the Epistles not relying on this or that passage but on the spirit of mercy which breathes throughout as their common life; in that spirit I read forgiveness to all on repentance and faith in the common Redeemer . . . [29]

Intellectual opponents of the death penalty, many of whom held 'liberal' views for their day, declared that 'to meet the scriptural objection . . . is to slay a dead giant', and that 'whether from a more intelligent spirit of criticism abroad, a deeper and wider piety, or a more uncompromising scepticism, the argument from scriptural warrant has now few serious or respectable supporters'.[30] Their 'infidel' approach to the Bible was not so popular with the general public, few of whom were aware of such critical scholarship, while those who were usually preferred the more obvious and literal interpretation of the orthodox clergy.

Across the Atlantic a parallel conflict was taking place, along markedly sectarian lines: Calvinist versus Unitarian and Universalist. Most impressive and passionate in his advocacy of the 'spirit of the Gospel' was the secretary of the Massachusetts Anti-Gallows Society, the Revd Charles Spear.[31] Spear was a Universalist minister, and his Universalism undoubtedly fed his social activism and informed his exegesis. A reaction against the Calvinism so prevalent on the East Coast at the end of eighteenth century, Universalism was a benign faith, stressing the salvation of all – even the most reprobate, the rejection of eternal punishment, and the benevolence of the Deity. Such beliefs sat easy with support for the abolition of the death penalty. Spear was a theological liberal who would not confine himself to a literalist interpretation of scripture. Although dealing thoroughly with the Old Testament passages, he believed that it was the teaching and example of Jesus that were crucial. Jesus had enjoined us to love our enemies. He commented most powerfully on that solitary incident in Jesus' life when he encountered someone under the shadow of a capital offence: the woman taken in adultery (John 8. 3–11).

Jesus turns the thoughts of these accusers inward. Would it not be well, when we look upon the miserable culprit, to turn our thoughts in upon our hearts? A certain divine used to exclaim, when he saw a criminal carried to execution, 'There goes my wicked self.' And when the advocates for blood come forward in their zeal, would it not be well, to pause, and remember the words of Jesus? 'He that is without sin among you, let him cast the first stone.' Let those who cry for blood, erect the gibbet and place the halter! How many would then be executed?

A writer very feelingly remarks, that when we see one on his way to the gallows, we should say, 'There goes my father, my brother, or my son.' How many executions would take place if the whole community possessed such a feeling?[32]

Again and again he pointed to the totally different spirit of New Testament from that of the Old:

> Moses addressed the injurer, Christ the injured. Moses said 'eye for eye', Christ says to the injured person, 'ye have heard that it hath been said of old . . . but I say unto you . . .'. Moses made his enemies die for him, Christ died for his enemies.[33]

A member of the Senate of Massachusetts, the Revd Charles Hudson, in a report of 1838, had pointed out that when Christ was crucified he was crucified between two capitally sentenced criminals. One of them said he was justly punished and Jesus did not demur. Hudson had argued that he would have taken this opportunity to oppose this punishment if it were against the will of God. This silence in the gospels was to be cited again and again by the proponents of capital punishment.[34] Recognizing the danger of this tack, Spear countered that to argue thus was to commit a grave error.

> Too much reliance has been placed on mere phrases, and cold, unmeaning criticisms. Jesus himself never stopped by the way to controvert mere words. He began by laying the axe at the root of the tree. The law of retaliation stood in his way. He said at once 'love your enemies'.[35]

Christ had not spoken out against capital punishment on the cross because he had already laid down principles that would subvert every cruel law. With an iconoclasm which would seem perfectly in place today Spear berated the church which had for centuries engaged in discussing 'mere words and trifling ceremonies' while 'humanity has been suffering, human rights disregarded, and prisons and gibbets strewn over the earth'.

In the United States, as in England, the fact that the majority of the champions of abolition were also biblical liberals, and frequently dissenters – Universalists, Unitarians and Quakers – and some were atheists such as Bentham and Shelley, put them in bad odour with the more orthodox Calvinist and Anglican clergy who, believing in retribution, innate depravity, and eternal punishment, supported the necessity of hanging and the infallibility of scripture. They rallied to defend the literalness of the biblical text and the moral imperatives that such a reading endorsed.[36] There was open warfare.

Abolitionists returned time and again to the cross to nail their opponents' arguments. Christ the innocent victim of capital punishment; Christ who died for his enemies but did not kill them; Christ who was gibbeted before jeering crowds, and yet called down forgiveness on his murderers. They were at their impassioned best when reflecting on his sacrifice, and they seem mystified that any calling themselves Christians could see any different or could speak otherwise:

> So far from Christ countenancing the death infliction, even for his murder,

his own dying supplication was the pardon of his murderers. Yet under judicial forms, and a sanguinary code, was this monster murder plausibly committed. Surely, surely, the pure, and innocent, and sacred blood which stained Mount Calvary, should have been the last which earth's tribunals ever shed! But alas, it was not – and many a scaffold's guiltless martyr has since told erring man, that in assuming God's prerogative – 'He knows not what he does.'[37]

Their opponents, not to be outdone, retorted that although on earth Jesus came as a saviour, now he reigned as a king, and he would come again as a judge. And he would be a hanging judge, consigning the unrighteous to everlasting punishment.[38]

Between the two sides a great gulf was fixed. Their respective approaches were irreconcilable, and their understanding of the ways of God as revealed in the Bible were unintelligible to each other. Blake put it exactly:

The Vision of Christ that thou dost see
Is my Vision's Greatest Enemy . . .
Both read the Bible day and night,
But thou read'st black where I read white.[39]

In the capital punishment debate, as in so many others where the biblical witness has been in question, the same arguments were to be repeated, the same passages cited, the same ingenuity in exegesis shown for another hundred years. Few converts were made by the arguments though much effort was expended. There was considerable truth in the frustration expressed by one commentator:

Men too often study the scriptures, not so much for the discovery of truth, as to find support for the prejudices which have already gained possession of their minds.[40]

6 An Open-Air Entertainment

Publicists and Public Executions: 1840–1850

Executions are intended to draw spectators. If they do not draw
spectators; they don't answer their purpose. The old method was most
satisfactory to all parties; the publick was gratified by a procession; the
criminal was supported by it. Why is all this to be swept away?

Samuel Johnson[1]

The good old laws were garnished well with gibbets, whips, and chains,
With fine old English penalties, and fine old English pains,
With rebel heads and seas of blood once hot in rebel veins:
For all these things were requisite to guard the rich old gains
   Of the fine old English Tory times;
   Soon may they come again.

Charles Dickens[2]

This is, in truth, our circus . . . our gladiatorial arena. We Christians,
who talk of Rome with measureless pity and contempt . . . as a nation
of angels might do . . . here prepare our feasts of blood. We do not fill
our theatre with wild and famished animals, to gloat over them while they
tear each other to pieces; but we only give another direction to the
cannibal instincts of our people, and gratify them after a fashion
peculiarly our own. The scenes enacted in front of Newgate disgrace
us in the eyes of Christendom.

W. Hepworth Dixon[3]

In July 1840, drawn by compelling curiosity, two men in their late twenties
who had already established themselves in the literary circles of the capital
joined the vast throng outside Newgate Gaol. They had come to witness the
execution of one of the most celebrated murderers of the time, François
Courvoisier, a French valet who had killed his master, Lord William Russell.
It scarred both onlookers, and resulted in the publication of two of the most
passionate and influential assaults on capital punishment.

William Makepeace Thackeray had been persuaded to attend the hanging
by the abolitionist MP Richard Monkton Milnes who doubtless hoped to win
a novelist's pen to the cause. In this he was successful. The effect of the
hanging on the sensitive Thackeray was profound, and the depression it

induced could only be relieved by the purgative of composition, depressing as that was.[4] Within a month he produced an article, 'Going to See a Man Hanged', for *Fraser's Magazine*.[5]

He had been revolted and outraged by what he had witnessed, and was not ashamed to admit that he had closed his eyes at the awful moment of execution. What he had seen had been traumatic enough, leaving on his mind 'an extraordinary feeling of terror and shame'. It seemed to him that he had been 'abetting an act of frightful wickedness and violence performed by a set of men against one of their fellows'; and he prayed that such a hideous and degrading sight would soon be out of the power of any Englishman to witness. For Thackeray, the intricate arrangements made to secure Courvoisier's eternal future merely compounded the blasphemy and contributed to the torture. The state 'commits the criminal's soul to the mercy of God, stating that here on earth he is to look for no mercy; keeps him for a fortnight to prepare, provides him with a clergyman to settle his religious matters (if there be time enough, but government can't wait) . . . My Lord in the Black cap especially prays that heaven may have mercy on him, but he must be ready by Monday morning . . .'

> The horrid gallows is perpetually before him; he is wild with dread and remorse. Clergymen are with him ceaselessly; religious tracts are forced into his hands; night and day they ply him with the heinousness of his crime, and exhortations to repentance. Read through that last paper of his; by Heaven it is pitiful to read it. See the Scripture phrases brought in now and anon; the peculiar terms of tract phraseology; one knows too well such language is learned – imitated from the priest at the bedside, eagerly seized and appropriated, and confounded by the poor prisoner.

He rebutted the 'biblical' justification of capital punishment by an appeal to reason and 'Christian law' (we shall hear the contrast often again):

> Murder is such a monstrous crime (this is the great argument), – it is natural he should be killed . . . it is natural. That is the word, and fine philosophical opinion it is – philosophical and Christian. Kill a man, and you must be killed in turn, that is the unavoidable sequitur. It is natural and therefore it must be done. Blood demands blood.
>
> Does it? The system of compensation might be carried on ad infinitum – an eye for an eye, a tooth for a tooth, as by the old Mosaic law. But (putting the fact out of the question, that we have had this statute repealed by the Highest Authority) why, because you lose your eye, is that of your opponent's to be extracted likewise?. Where is the reason for the practice? And yet it is just as natural as the death dictum . . . Knowing however that revenge is not only evil, but useless, we have given it up on all minor points. Only to

the last we stick firm, contrary though it be to reason and to Christian law . . .

His hitherto quiescent imagination was roused by what he had seen, and it was his own personal experience of what it was to slaughter a man that converted him. He came away 'with a disgust for murder, but it was for *the murder I saw done*', and felt 'ashamed and degraded at the brutal curiosity' which had taken him to that sight. Hanging was no less than a 'disgraceful sin', and he prayed that Almighty God might cause it to pass from us, and 'cleanse our land of blood'.

This essay, at once an act of confession and catharsis, was Thackeray's means of coping with the melancholy effect which the hanging had had upon him. It was enough for him once to state his horror and never allude to it again. He neither attended another hanging nor, apart from the occasional allusion,[6] wrote further on the subject.

Watching the same scene from a convenient balcony rented for the 'entertainment', and spotting Thackeray among the crowd below, had been Charles Dickens. Unlike his rival he had not averted his gaze when Courvoisier had been killed. He had been fascinated as much as repelled by what he had seen, and immediately put it to good use in his prolonged description of hanging, that 'obscene presence', in *Barnaby Rudge*, published in November 1841. As for Thackeray so for Dickens, Christianity and capital punishment were ill-juxtaposed. Brutalized by his upbringing, Hugh, in his 'Dying Speech', could not make much of the 'faith and strong belief' urged on him by the chaplain. Rather he who had never raised a hand in prayer called down the God of wrath on all his oppressors: 'on that black tree, of which I am the ripened fruit, I do invoke the curse of all its victims, past and present, and to come'.[7]

It was not, however, until five years later, after he had witnessed a beheading in Rome which he had found no more edifying than a hanging in London, that Dickens wrote explicitly and at great length about the Courvoisier hanging in four letters to the *Daily News*.[8] Unlike Thackeray he did not express any regret at going, but he too had been disgusted. His fascination as well as his revulsion was perfectly obvious from his description of the 'dismal contagion'. Despite his and his friends' abhorrence of the murder and its perpetrator, 'if any one among us could have saved the man . . . he would have done it'. Unlike Thackeray, Dickens made little of the cruelty done to the criminal. He always shared the common assumption that murderers were all vicious brutes, the Bill Sikeses of this world. Hangings such as these inverted the usual sympathies and so were more corrosive of the public good than the crimes for which they were the punishment: 'it was so loathsome, pitiful, and vile a sight, that the law appeared to be as bad as he, or worse'.[9]

More unequivocally than in *Barnaby Rudge*, Dickens in these letters advocated the 'total abolition of the Punishment of Death, as a general principle, for the advantage of society, for the prevention of crime, and without the least reference to, or tenderness for any individual malefactor whatever'. He had been influenced by the numerous papers that had flowed from Nugent's Aylesbury Committee.[10] He had been convinced by the Revd Henry Christmas' interpretation of the crucial biblical texts,[11] but even so it was not the interpretation of one text or another that signified, but the character of Christ, for 'if any text appeared to justify the claim, I would reject that limited appeal, and rest upon the character of the Redeemer, and the great scheme of his religion'.[12] This is Dickens speaking almost like a Quaker. His view here, exalting mercy and forgiveness towards the malefactor as the ground for abolition, is aberrant, and was not to be turned to again. He had been persuaded by foreign experience that abolition did not cause an increase in capital crimes. He adduced examples of miscarriages of justice. But it was the ill-effects on others, a brutalizing contagion he had felt personally, that most exercised him.

Disquiet about public executions and the 'low-lived black-guard merry-making' that accompanied them had been voiced long before Thackeray and Dickens. 'Hanging Days' were macabre public holidays observed along with Easter, Whitsun, and Christmas.[13] Bernard Mandeville, as early as 1725, was warning that they were 'exemplary the wrong Way', and encouraged where they should deter.[14] They were 'void of that decent solemnity that would make them awful', and the demeanour of the condemned indicated to the populace that there was 'nothing in being hang'd, but a wry Neck, and a wet pair of Breeches'. In 1816 the Quaker Joseph Gurney was distressed to find that so many of the vast throng attending a triple execution in London were possessed of 'a feeling of pleasure in the excitement itself' with 'a stupid indifference to the sufferings of others'.[15] Three years later George Sinclair complained in the Commons of 'the revolting emotions which might be traced in the countenances' of all those who had surrounded him at a recent hanging: 'the impatient curiosity of some, the brutal apathy of others, the thoughtless levity, the indignant horror, and even the savage satisfaction which the features of the different spectators exhibited'.[16] Ewart condemned 'the profligacy and impiety; the ribald jests, the profane oaths' at what he styled 'the Saturnalia of the gallows'.[17] In Nottingham so dissolute and drunken was the crowd that twelve spectators – chiefly women – were crushed to death at the execution of William Savile.[18] When Mrs French was hanged at Lewes this 'open-air entertainment', as *Household Words* described it, attracted a crowd of ten thousand people 'screaming, fighting and roaring with gypsy jollity'. The public houses and beer shops were mobbed.[19] At the execution of William Palmer at Stafford, much to the distress of middle-class moralists, the town assumed the appearance of a fair, hostelries did a roaring trade, and singing and dancing went on in them all night by merrymakers come to watch the hanging.[20] The chaplain of Stafford Gaol, Mr Buckeridge, deplored the 'moral debasement' exhibited on the occasion of the execution of Anne Wycherley. The country, for the space of twenty miles around, had been 'overrun with persons of both sexes, of the most abandoned, debauched, and dissolute characters'. Crimes were committed in the streets, blasphemies uttered in the beer shops, and obscene jokes made in the presence of the dying woman.[21]

The lower orders attended executions in droves, while the increasingly 'good and respectable' Victorian middle classes shunned them, or if they went made some embarrassed apology.[22] Concern that working-class women should enjoy them was allied to a desire that the more genteel should be protected from them. In 1840 Stephen Lushington, the ecclesiastical lawyer and radical MP, declared that 'not a single execution now ever took place in a provincial town in England that every respectable individual resident in it, or its neighbourhood, did not remove their wives and daughters and families lest they might be disgusted by that horrible and awful exhibition of the extreme penalty of the law'.[23] 'Unmitigated horror on the well-disposed, unmitigated mischief on the brutal' was how *The Spectator* summed up the direct effect of public executions.[24]

The more earnest devotion to the Christian faith that typified many early Victorians and the increasing influence of the Evangelical Movement were undoubtedly major factors in this change in attitude on the part of the educated and influential. Their perception of executions was diametrically opposed to the accepted wisdom of the previous century. No longer could public hangings be depicted as moral, judicial, and religious dramas. Rather they had become, or were revealed as no more than, popular festivities, orgiastic carnivals, melodramas of deplorable bad taste. It was not that they had changed their nature[25] but that people of influence and rectitude were revolted by them, and had concluded that any virtue a public hanging might have was greatly outweighed by its potential for vice.

If the genteel were increasingly disgusted by the spectacle, the vulgar, it was feared, would be dangerously corrupted. Lord John Russell defended the institution of public punishment by assuring the honourable Members that had they attended an execution their feelings would have been very different from those of the common multitude whose lack of religious and moral education – not the public hanging itself – produced the spectacles that they all deplored.[26] The audience just would not react to the performance in the way intended. In rebuttal, an abolitionist MP, Sir Fitzroy Kelly, conceding that 'men of right-thinking minds and virtuous habits' might suffer no injury from the sight of a hanging, pointed out the obvious, that it was not on those classes that the spectacle was intended to operate. The effect was to be produced on the minds of 'the vicious, the uneducated, and all those most open to evil impressions'.[27] Reformers had long observed that far from being a deterrent this public sport merely habituated the onlookers to such sights, rendering the terrible commonplace, and provoking ribaldry and sympathy for the felon rather than didactic terror.

The show complete, the pleasure past,
The solid masses loosen'd fast:
A thief slunk off, with ample spoil,
To ply elsewhere his daily toil;
A baby strung its doll to a stick;
A mother praised the pretty trick;
Two children caught and hang'd a cat;
Two friends walked on in lively chat;
And two, who had disputed places,
Went forth to fight, with murderous faces.[28]

It was notorious that it was the worst thieves and felons who were the most constant attenders, 'drawn by a fascination or attraction for scenes of blood, or strong excitement'. They came 'to see their late associates die, as they call it, manfully, and to learn how to die in like manner themselves'.[29] It was well documented that many of those hanged had witnessed others hanged before them. 'Let it be remembered' Mrs Lachlan had enjoined us, 'that [the murderer] Cook was present at the last execution in Leicester'.[30] Cope, a Governor of Newgate, had said that 'in his fifteen years experience he had never known but one criminal hanged for murder who had not witnessed an execution'. Dr Lyford of Winchester Gaol said that thirty-eight of the forty men he had seen executed had previously attended an execution.[31] Dickens cited the already much-quoted figures of the chaplain of Bristol Prison, John Roberts, who had attended 167 prisoners under sentence of death and found only three who had not been spectators at other men's executions. So far from being a deterrent, Dickens feared that hanging might even have been an incentive to crime.

Present this black idea of violence to a bad mind contemplating violence; hold up before a man remotely compassing the death of another person, the spectacle of his own ghastly and untimely death by man's hands; and out of the depths of his own nature you shall assuredly raise up that which lures and tempts him on.[32]

But beneath Dickens' fear of the brutalizing effect on others lurked a more insidious but subconscious doubt. It was not just the lower orders who might be corrupted by this public savagery. The characters of even the most intelligent and literate members of society might be injured by it too. Robert Dees had observed that it was a fact as perplexing as it was indubitable 'that in the minds of many the sight of one execution only arouses an intense desire of beholding another; and that a taste is thus gradually formed, which is strengthened by every fresh gratification of it, and which becomes more and more urgent for the repetition of the spectacle by which it was originally excited'.[33] It looks as though Dickens himself was one of those attracted to the sight of seeing people hang, and at the same time repelled by his own fascination. To attend one execution might be put down to experience, to attend four looks more like voyeurism. Other men of eminence reflected this dichotomy.

Such a 'horrid eagerness' to witness the slow death of the young and healthy was made quite explicit in James Boswell's Journal. He had been struck by the firm and manly vigour of a 'young Macheath' whom he had seen one Tuesday when he attended the chapel in Newgate specifically to observe those who would die the following day. He could not sleep for thinking of him. The following morning his 'curiosity to see the melancholy spectacle' was so strong that he could not resist it although he was sensible that he would 'suffer much from it'. Accompanied by a friend he got a grandstand view of the 'dismal scene'. He was so terribly shocked by what he had seen that he was thrown into 'very deep melancholy' and could not sleep for a second night running.[34] Yet he never thereafter missed the opportunity to attend an execution, compelled by 'an irresistible impulse' to be present. This sadistic addiction he disingenuously took to be 'a proof of sensibility, not callousness' since the greatest proportion of spectators were women.[35] On one occasion he visited Dr Johnson, 'after having been present at the shocking sight of fifteen men executed before Newgate'.[36]

George Augustus Selwyn, the politician, was another habitué of executions, taking the most macabre interest in every detail of the crime, and the criminal, while the sight of a disfigured corpse or of an acquaintance lying in his shroud 'afforded him the deepest and most unaccountable pleasure'. He even travelled to Paris specially to see Damien being broken on the wheel for trying to assassinate Louis XV.[37] His friends shared his compulsion. The Earl of Carlisle attended the execution of the Revd Mr Hackman on Selwyn's behalf 'and from no curiosity of [his] own' so as to give him a good account of it. 'Everybody there', he wrote, enquired after you.' Dr John Warner, Rector of Stourton in Wiltshire, wrote to him after viewing the body: 'he is now a fine corpse at Surgeon's Hall, where I saw him yesterday; a genteel, well-made young fellow of four and twenty.'[38]

Similarly Dr Shephard Taylor, despite delineating the first execution he attended as an 'awful' and 'revolting' spectacle, attended three others in as many years. The victim of one of these he described as 'falling beautiful'.[39]

That such a fascination had sexual undertones is even more obvious in the writings of Thomas Hardy. He was only sixteen in August 1856 when he witnessed the hanging of Elizabeth Martha Brown who had killed her adulterous husband, but as an old man seventy years later Hardy could still vividly recall the way in which her 'fine figure . . . showed against the sky as she hung in the misty rain, and how the tight black silk gown set off her shape as she wheeled half-round and back'.[40] Calcraft, the executioner, had forgotten to tie her dress so that she should not be exposed as she swung, and had to reascend the scaffold to do this. One morning two years later Hardy rushed from breakfast to climb a nearby hill so that with the aid of telescope he could watch the hanging of James Seale in Dorchester. He was disturbed not by the event nor the moral questions associated with it, but, like Dickens, by his own sensations and fascination: 'He seemed alone on the heath with the hanged man, and crept homeward wishing he had not been so curious.'[41] In his notebooks Hardy detailed the shocking strangulation and burning of Mary Channing in 1705 when, to stop her shrieking, one of the constables 'thrust a swab into her mouth & the milk from her bosoms (she had lately given birth to a child) squirted out in their faces "and made 'em jump back" '. Other macabre details, such as the smell of roast meat, were also recorded by the octogenarian author.[42] Days before the execution of Edith Thompson in 1923, having read her love letters and been impressed by her looks, Hardy penned a lyric on 'this thing of symmetry, seemly to view,/ Brought to derision!'.[43] This life-long erotic fascination was surely the sort of 'contagion' that Dickens inveighed against.

The year in which Dickens' letters were published, 1846, marked the high-point in the abolitionist crusade. Like the prison reform campaign which it paralleled, it was international. Several countries had recently abolished capital punishment or public executions and various great literary men, Goethe and Victor Hugo among them, had lent their pen and prestige to the abolitionist cause.[44] In the United States the 1840s saw the rise of many Anti-Gallows Societies sponsored by prominent and influential members of American society, including two former Vice-Presidents. Again the plebeian circus entertainment was deplored.[45] In 1847 Michigan became the first jurisdiction in the English-speaking world to abolish capital punishment for all offences other than treason. Even in England, and even among the Tory shiresmen lampooned by Dickens, few regretted the passing of the gibbet and the Bloody Code. The abolitionists were becoming more militant, as was indicated by the replacement of the more moderate Society for the Diffusion of Information on the Subject of Capital Punishment (which in turn had replaced the older SDKCP in 1828) with the uncompromisingly named Society for the Abolition of Capital Punishment (SACP), founded by Frederick Hill and Thomas Beggs and the MPs Charles Gilpin and William Ewart. Although the Bench of Bishops was not conspicuous in the abolitionist cause,[46] many other Christians were. The Secretary from 1854–63 was a Quaker, Alfred Hutchinson Dymond, and as usual other Quakers, such as John Barry (who was to promote Charles Phillip's *Vacation Thoughts* in 1856), had an active share in this Society. The leading Anglican member was the Revd Henry Christmas who, it seems, much to the disgust of a fellow priest of the Catholic Party, represented another 'one hundred and fifty brother clerics'.[47] The abolitionists held meetings, organized petitions, sent deputations to the Home Secretary to plead for reprieves, and bombarded the press with letters. 'Educate, proselytize and agitate' was the formula they used. The issue was exhaustively debated in sermons, treatises and tracts in the mid and late 1840s when the pamphlet-war was at its height.[48] Therefore Thackeray and Dickens were in a strong stream of educated opinion in the 1840s when they condemned the noose.

Although the second report of the Lords' Select Committee on Criminal Law in 1847 recommended that for offences of the gravest kind capital punishment be retained, a major difference of opinion was revealed in that those who had most contact with the convicts were the least sanguine as to the deterring or exemplary effect of penal infliction, and leaned the most to making punishment reformatory. Thus at the end of the decade, abolitionist organs were still confident of hanging's speedy and complete demise. The *Eclectic Review* cited the profusion of both domestic and foreign books and articles on the subject as evidence of widespread and growing concern about the question of capital punishment which had 'penetrated into every class of the civilized community'. A monarch, a nobleman, a doctor of divinity, two Edinburgh bailies, a popular novel writer, a theological tutor, a chartist and a country gentleman were among the writers who had presented themselves for review. In contrast 'the defenders of the pain of death are daily becoming fewer, and only a very limited portion of the community can now be found to maintain it, even for the extreme crime of murder'.[49] Douglas Jerrold, the leading contributor to the abolitionist organ *Punch* (so named after the puppet who hangs the hangman) since its inauguration in 1841, attributed what he confidently predicted would be the imminent demise of the death penalty to the efforts of men of letters: 'the gallows is doomed, crumbling, and must down – overthrown by no greater instruments than a few goose-quills'.[50]

Something which to begin with may have seemed as no more than a distraction was the suggestion that executions be removed from the public gaze, that they be made private affairs behind the new prison walls. From the early years of the eighteenth century there were calls that felons should be put to death in private.[51] Various piecemeal attempts had already been made at placing limitations on the spectacle. The actual killing had become quicker and the ritual had been deprived of the display of the malefactor through the streets beforehand and the exhibition of his corpse thereafter. A speedy dispatch using a drop was said to have been first used for the execution of Lord Ferrers in 1760, and had come into general use in London in 1783 when the Tyburn processions had been abolished, hangings in future taking place outside the walls of Newgate Gaol. In due course, 'the Newgate Drop' had spread from the capital to the provinces.

Gibbeting had also been discontinued. Hanging in chains upon the gibbet, practised since mediaeval times, was first legally sanctioned for murder as late as 1752.[52] Even then it never formed part of the sentence – as it did in Scotland – but the Act allowed the judge in special circumstances, or on the application of a relative of the murder victim, to direct that the body be hung in chains to induce terror in the hearts of the wicked and provide 'a comfortable sight to the relations and friends of the deceased'.[53] This formalized what had been, in any case, the practice. For instance, in 1741 the Revd Dr Penny, chaplain to the Duke of Newcastle, asked the court to order that his brother's murderer be gibbetted.[54] The deterrent effect of this demeaning exposure was aimed at the lower classes. When John Swan was executed in Epping Forest on the site of the murder of his master, and within view of some gentlemen's houses, the gibbeting was moved elsewhere on the orders of the trial judge. The whole business was designed to be as degrading as possible. The body, saturated with tar for preservation, was suspended from a gibbet which had been erected on a position of prominence near the scene of the crime or in sight of the offender's home. It was left to rot, exposed to the ravages of the weather and carrion. To prevent the cadaver's removal the post was studded with thousands of nails, a precursor of barbed-wire. To prevent the post being burnt down it was often coated in lead. Despite John Wesley's desire to extend it to suicides, gibbeting was too barbaric even for the English, ran clear counter to the express words of scripture,[55] and had already fallen into disuse by the end of the eighteenth century, its demise hastened by the distaste for this 'nauseating practice' shown by George III.[56]

In 1832, however, there had been an attempt to revive it, when the Anatomy Bill, which dispensed with the dissection of murderers as part of their punishment, had been before the Commons. A clause had been inserted to the effect that 'the bodies of all prisoners convicted of murder shall either be hung in chains, or buried under the gallows on which they have been executed, or within the precincts of the prison in which such prisoner has been confined, according to the discretion of the court before whom the prisoner may be tried'.[57] Despite much hostile press comment,[58] gibbeting had been put into practice in two provincial towns, Durham and Leicester.

In the former it had been William Jobling, a minor accomplice in the murder of Mr Fairless, a justice of the peace, who had met this fate. The perpetrator of the murder, Armstrong, having made his escape, the hapless abettor had been hanged in Durham and displayed at Jarrow Stake on Tyneside. Great crowds had visited the spot, some approaching by boat the post on which the body was suspended. Compassion mingled with curiosity, and a subscription for the felon's family had been got up at the very foot of the gibbet. His friends had finally stolen the body for burial. Public disquiet had been aroused over this case as it was to be a century and a quarter later over that of Craig and Bentley.[59]

The second case was that of James Cook who had been gibbeted a few days after Jobling. His body, dressed in the clothes in which he had died, his face covered in tar, had been placed in an iron cage with specially constructed shoes to prevent the legs falling off, and raised on a thirty-three foot pole. Mrs Lachlan recalled how on the Sunday a vast crowd of people had lined the road to the gibbet, and, taking advantage of the opportunity, 'several ranting preachers were busily engaged the whole of the day, in singing, praying, and preaching'. The 'saints' were also engaged in giving tracts away, and the place 'throughout the day seemed like a fair'. With a touch of sarcasm she added that she was glad to see a notice 'cautioning every person from selling beer or liquor on the ground'. In her opinion, this was no way for a Christian land to carry on.

> To teach examples of vengeance to the people in the name of justice, to sanction the indecent treatment of the dead, although the memory of that dead be stained with crime – to cover the beauty of the land with abominable nuisances shocking to the sight and feelings of women and children, odious to the masculine sense of all enlightened minds, and only brutalizing to the vicious and profligate – is no evidence of wisdom in government – no proof of a judicious and discerning zeal for the moral training and mental cultivation of the people.[60]

Parliament, urged on by the indomitable Ewart, had taken Mrs Lachlan's strictures to heart. Jobling's and Cook's were to be the last gibbetings in England. Ewart's Bill 'to abolish the practice of hanging of bodies of executed criminals in chains' had easily passed both Houses and had become law in 1834.[61] Perhaps financial considerations also eased its passing. The apprehension of Anthony Lingard in 1818 had cost Derbyshire £31 5s 5d, but the expenses incurred in his gibbeting had amounted to £85 4s 1d. The iron suit had cost £75 to make and the lead cladding had also been expensive. A further ten guineas was charged by the gaoler to convey the body from Derby to Wardlow.[62] From now on the corpses would be buried within prison walls, and with full funeral rites if the chaplain so wished.[63] Inadvertently, Ewart had taken the first step to the sequestration of capital punishment: if the corpse could be decently buried inside a prison, could not the criminal be decently killed there?

Indeed, further refinements were made in the whole process of executions. In 1845, after complaints in Parliament,[64] a Home Office Departmental Inquiry had been carried out by the Revd Whitworth Russell, the former chaplain of Millbank Prison, then the Inspector of Prisons, into the practice of admitting visitors into the chapel at Newgate to hear the condemned sermon. This had been initially prohibited in 1825, but the prohibition had lapsed and 'Old Bailey Ladies', as *Punch* styled them, regularly swarmed to the condemned service to have 'their Christianity and their morals mightily refreshed by the discipline'.[65] This voyeuristic attendance had been deemed 'highly injurious, with respect to the Visitors and the Public at large, to the

Prisoners generally, and to the culprit about to undergo the extreme Penalty of the Law'. It was injurious to the public inasmuch as it ministered 'to the Indulgence of a morbid State for Spectacles and Sensations which [had] a prejudicial Tendency'.[66] It was injurious to the prisoners whom it distracted from the religious service and from their contemplation of the fate of the condemned. It was injurious to the felon in question who, if penitent, should not become an object of the 'gaze of idle Curiosity', or, if impenitent, should not be granted a stage for his bravura. Exactly these arguments could be used against public executions themselves. Russell also deprecated the admission of journalists into the prison to witness 'the pinioning and preparing the Convict for Execution'.[67]

Despite such refinements in procedure, and the greater privacy they afforded, the executions themselves had remained public. Many of the objections to gibbeting could equally well be made of these open-air rituals. They were excuses for the worst excesses of vice, and the display of the worst aspects of human nature. Yet for the moment the majority of both sides in the argument, retentionist and abolitionist, feared that private executions would turn into a 'small tea-party selected from certain official circles'.[68] The abolitionists went further, terming them 'private strangulation' and 'secret murder'. In 1841 the first attempt to abolish public executions was made by the moderate reformer Henry Rich in the House of Commons. He had been as appalled as others by the demeanour of the working classes, especially the women, who flocked to hangings. His motion was not that hangings should be performed in secret but before a restricted and invited public: members of the felon's family, the press, ministers of religion, the public authorities. In addition all the convicts in the prison would be compelled to attend. The execution as proposed would be 'formal and solemn . . . unexposed to the interruptions and crowdings of curiosity . . . It would be decorous'.[69] Peel, then leader of the opposition, remained opposed to 'this most dangerous proposal'. Only one other member supported it. The motion was withdrawn. With prescience, however, *The Spectator* argued for a modified sequestration, in a hall added to Newgate and conducted 'with the solemnity of an act of religion and only in the presence of a clergyman, a surgeon, and a body of witnesses especially admitted to testify to the identity and to the fact of death, and the absence of all cruelty'.[70]

An alternative means of amelioration was proposed by the 'precisians of Rochdale', two thousand of whom petitioned the Commons to preserve the public nature of the performance but to change the cast. In future, they urged, executions should be celebrated 'as a religious ceremony, and by a clergyman of the state church'. Such an officiant would add a greater degree of decorum and decency to proceedings than the 'hireling of the sheriff'.[71] *Punch* took this proposal to its logical extreme and suggested an honorary canonry for 'the church's son, the religious hangman, Jack Ketch'. His pew would be immediately under the bishop's throne, and he could process in the Cathedral bearing a mace before the Dean.[72] It was more in shock than in surprise that the same journal later reported that William Kalabergo had actually been 'hanged over the chapel of Oxford County Gaol, after having been pinioned in front of the communion-table'. Thus in 'the very seat of orthodoxy, Authority had declared the execution of a criminal to be a holy solemnity'.[73]

Such wilder eccentricities aside, however, there seemed much to commend to more sober and serious minds the notion of a solemn act of religion, a human sacrifice conducted in an inner sanctum, beheld only by the high priests of hanging and a select congregation. This was a rich possibility, not of compromise with the abolitionists, but of transcendence over them. Judicial killing could be sanitized, even sacralized. It could finally become what it had long meant to be.

In 1847, 1849, and 1850 William Ewart, aided by John Bright, a Quaker, and fellow Liberal Member of Parliament, sought abolition in vain. Ewart played on the fears of his fellow members that hangings had a deleterious effect on the labouring classes whom they had a duty 'to elevate and refine not demoralize and debase'.[74] He ended his speech in the 1850 debate with words which sounded the knell of his campaign rather than, as he hoped, of 'this last vestige of barbaric punishment'. He may indeed never have been more convinced than he was then that 'the reform which we support is founded on sound principles of punishment, on the lasting interests of humanity, and on the genuine spirit of the Bible',[75] but others were less convinced that society could afford to lose the noose. The tide was ebbing both in England and the United States.

The hanging of Mr and Mrs Manning in 1849, the first execution of a married couple for a century and a half, revived flagging interest. Another Quaker wrote that 'the disgusting eagerness of the people to witness the execution of Manning and his wife has again turned public attention to the question of capital punishment'. The entrepreneurial energies of those living in the neighbourhood of Horsemonger Lane knew no bounds. A scaffold stadium was erected in the front gardens of nearby houses frustrating attempts by the chaplain of the prison, the Revd John Rowe, to get the magistrates to stop its construction. On the eve of the execution a crowd of some thirty thousand people assembled in festive mood in front of the prison, including among their number many 'respectable' people.[76] Despite his earlier revulsion Dickens not only attended the hanging but, as he had done when Courvoisier had been dispatched, sought out the best view, paying two guineas as his share in the renting of a nearby roof. Again it had a powerful affect on him; again he wrote to the papers, this time to *The Times* denouncing public executions but not raising 'the abstract question of capital punishment'.

When the two miserable creatures who had attracted all this ghastly sight about them were turned quivering into the air, there was no more emotion, no more pity, no more thought that two immortal souls had gone to judgment . . . than if the name of Christ had never been heard in this world, and there was no belief among men but that they perished like the beasts.[77]

The execution of the Mannings had singularly failed to produce the desired effect. Had any portion of the crowd been 'moved to sentiments of fear, repentance, or natural horror by what they had seen upon the drop' it would have been a 'great comfort' to Dickens. But none was so moved.

Feeling no sympathy for the malefactors, but appalled rather by the public spectacle of their demeaning deaths, he found a solution in advocating private executions. As one perceptive commentator had observed, the argument of his earlier letters had borne 'exclusively against the publicity of executions, and not in the least against executions themselves'.[78] He had diagnosed the illness and thought there was but one cure. Now he realized that there was an alternative and less drastic a treatment:

> I simply wish to make some account for the general good, by taking the readiest and most public means of adverting to an intimation given by Sir George Grey in the last session of Parliament, that the Government might be induced to give its support to a measure making the infliction of capital punishment a private solemnity within the prison walls.[79]

Under this strategy of concealment 'the obscene and odious crowds of onlookers' would be banished, and the condemned killer would be taken out of the heroic limelight and dismissed to 'dread obscurity'. No visitors would be allowed to attend him, no newspapers would carry report of his 'sayings and doings'. Above all 'we should not return to the days when ladies paid visits to highwaymen, drinking their punch in the condemned cells of Newgate'.[80]

Dickens' more cautious attitude to hanging was conditioned by his desire to escape the stigma of having 'effeminate feelings', a charge which the great Whig historian, Thomas Babington Macaulay, had levelled at the proponents of abolition in a Commons speech in 1846. The more Dickens tried to avoid the taint of effeminacy the more punitive became his attitude to crime. The mental picture he had of murderers remained a caricature and a stereotype. They were irredeemably wicked, and never in themselves deserving of compassion. The danger of hanging or at least of public hanging was that it engendered pity for those who were contemptible. Dickens was always quick to point out that he had no 'Quaker feelings', and he was anxious to dissociate himself from those who might appear 'soft' on criminals. Thus he invoked the virile aid of the novelist and crime-fighter, Henry Fielding, who a century before had urged the incarceration of executions. Although at this point he still remained in principle opposed to capital punishment, he was prepared to accept the possible rather than the ideal.[81]

Not all agreed with Dickens by any means. Some found virtue in the very things he deprecated. Sir Francis Head asked if Maria Manning should have been spared what Dickens described as 'the whistlings, imitations of Punch, brutal jokes, indecent delight of thieves, low prostitutes, ruffians and vaga-bonds' since those were the most fearful aspects of the punishment, and 'under Providence these coarse ingredients' might have effected 'that momentary repentance which the mild but fervent exhortations of the chaplain had failed to produce'. *The Spectator* commented that 'of all the machineries for conversion, surely this was the most extravagantly conceived'.[82]

Others still advocated hanging's total suppression. On 19 November a meeting was held to call for the complete abolition of the death penalty. Dickens declined to attend. Charles Gilpin deplored the conduct of the crowds at the Mannings' execution, and praised Dickens whom he felt sure shared the convictions of those in the hall even though he differed from them in thinking the abolition of public executions was a step in the right direction. This view he countered by reading communications from Douglas Jerrold, Richard Cobden and John Bright. William Ewart and the Revd Henry Christmas, whose writings undermining the biblical basis for the death penalty had previously so powerfully persuaded Dickens, then condemned capital punishment as being opposed to Christianity. The former further deprecated the press for its melodramatic depiction of Mrs Manning as a Clytemnestra or Lady Macbeth, while the latter pointed out that neither of the Old Testament's most notorious murderers, Cain and Moses – the Mannings of their day – had been put to death. Ewart's motion was carried and the Revd Horace Richards moved that a petition embodying its sentiments be presented to Parliament. The mood of the meeting was considered by *The Times* to be as much in bad taste as the deportment of the crowd had been at the Mannings' execution. The *Morning Post* criticized the contribution of Henry Christmas in particular, quoting a joke of the 'Reverend but not very reverend gentleman – a joke which told with such amazing effect on the risible faculties of the audience that we have no doubt the worthy parson, encouraged by this essay, is even now agonizingly labouring at a Comic Pentateuch'.[83]

Such behaviour on the part of the abolitionists could only make the alienation of Dickens more acute. In another letter he publicly split with them, condemning them for being willing to prolong public executions rather than jeopardize total abolition. In this move he reflected a widespread change of educated and influential opinion. The cantankerous essayist Thomas Carlyle, a reluctant abolitionist in 1842, by 1850 was no longer content to 'protect scoundrels', and, denouncing the 'tumultuous frothy ocean-tide of benevolent sentimentality', asserted the existence of a religious right and duty to take revenge on murderers as enemies of God.[84] The philosopher J. S. Mill was an abolitionist in the 1840s but opposed an abolitionist bill in the Commons twenty years later. Thackeray, it is alleged,[85] relented, and even *Punch* changed its mind.

The issue now was how to refine capital punishment, not how to abolish it. An outward veneer of respectability, the hallmark of the Victorian age, was to apply also to hanging: not in front of the children. In this process the church had a major role to play.

7   The 'Scare-Crow Deity'

The Imprisonment of Punishment: 1850–1868

> The murder that is depicted as a horrible crime is repeated in cold
> blood, remorselessly.
>
> *Cesare Beccaria*[1]

> The Gallows Tree, what is its plea
> What lesson does it teach,
> That it should stand on every land
> Where Christ's message preach?
> Your tolling bell, what does it tell
> Of death's solemnity
> To that fond crowd, who laughed aloud
> Beneath the gallows tree?
>
> *The Morning Herald*[2]

Moses Hatto was hanged outside the new county gaol at Aylesbury on Friday the 14 March 1854, before a concourse of 'the lowest of the people, a large proportion of whom [were] females'. Some had come as much as twenty miles, and many of them had already frequented one of the seventy or so 'public houses and beer shops' of the town before walking up Bierton Hill for the day's entertainment.[3]

Occurrences such as these had long occasioned concern, but little effective action. In contrast Hatto's execution or, more accurately, the attendant merrymaking, resulted in two petitions, one asking for the abolition of capital punishment entirely, the other seeking the abolition of its public form. Christian pressure was brought to bear on the organs of government which were in effect colluding with the basest instincts of the crowd rather than bridling them.

Aylesbury was particularly good ground for activism on this issue. In 1809 the leading inhabitants of the town had petitioned the Grand Jury about its decision to move hangings from their convenient location outside the town to a more central one in front of the county hall. This new departure, they complained, would 'exhibit before our doors and windows, for upwards of an hour, a Spectacle, at which Human Nature must shudder, whilst we lament that it is necessary such Punishments should be inflicted'.[4] With the new prison built in 1845 on Bierton Hill, it was thought that a more appropriate venue had been found. It merely allowed for greater crowds with less congestion. John Tawell had been the first to suffer at the new gaol, and his fate had already prompted Douglas Jerrold to begin his series of tirades in *Punch* against 'the moral lesson of the gallows'.[5] In the same year an Aylesbury Committee on Capital Punishment had been formed by its radical-Whig MP George Nugent Grenville, who was both a criminal law reformer and an abolitionist. It was this group which organized the abolition petition.

In addition the spiritual leader of Aylesbury and Archdeacon of Buckingham, Edward Bickersteth, a member of an influential Evangelical family, had already spoken out against public-execution spectacles. This affair brought back all the memories of a hanging he had previously witnessed in Shrewsbury, and of the accompanying 'drunkenness and debauchery'. This time he determined to do something about it. Bickersteth, however, did not want to be associated with either popular radicalism or with the abolitionist cause. Consequently he made no attempt to get signatories from the lower classes, who might be unduly influenced by the self-interested publicans, while in the framing of his petition he made it quite clear that it was the abolition of *public* executions only that was at issue. The petitioners specifically assented to the doctrine that 'the laws of the realm may punish Christian men with death for heinous and grievous offences'; and while they rejoiced 'in the relaxation which the wise policy of late years [had] made in the penal code of this country', they were convinced that 'the interests of society and the claims of justice alike required that the crime of murder should be visited in death'.[6]

The petition was presented to the 'High Tory' Bishop of Oxford, Samuel Wilberforce, son of the great William, who in turn took it to the House of Lords. There he asked the Government to consider the propriety of changing the practice of hanging in England. This they could do since it was under their control that the mode of execution lay. He reminded the Lords that moralists had condemned public executions for a century or more; he cited the example of America which had moved in this direction in the New England States especially; and he claimed that 'intramural executions' would enhance rather than detract from the awful effect of the occasion.[7] His trump card, however, he saved until last. He firmly believed, he told a reassured House, that the continuation of hanging was essential to the highest principles of justice. It was precisely because he felt that the present system of capital punishment was threatened by the continuation of public executions that he sought their abolition. Further gruesome hangings and the appalling public behaviour associated with them would make decent men recoil from inflicting the death penalty. The abolitionists would have their way.[8]

His fears were justified. Two years later concern was expressed in the Lords that women were escaping the death penalty because of qualms about executing them publicly. Lord St Leonard argued that it was better 'to execute women in private than to let it be understood that they were not to be executed at all'.[9]

Lord Redesdale feared that 'the non-execution of women for the murder of their children' would encourage such crimes among women 'of a certain class'. The recent rash of infanticides documented in the press could clearly be attributed to this policy.[10] That was enough. On 9 May 1856 the bishop asked for a Select Committee to be formed. Every year, he told the attentive peers, there had been an increasing resistance to carry out hanging in cases where it ought to have been carried out, and thus the deterrent effect of capital punishment was compromised. He too was particularly alarmed that recently there had been very few executions of women even for the highest offences. If the hanging of women ceased, the hanging of men would not long continue thereafter.[11] He was appointed to chair the Select Committee. Its membership included both St Leonard and Redesdale, and Anthony Ashley, the seventh Earl of Shaftesbury. He was a close family friend of the Bickersteths under whose influence he had become a fanatical millenarian evangelical. A noted philanthropist, the same Christian zeal which made him pity the exploited also directed him to punish the sinful. In his opinion the word of God did not permit but commanded the execution of murderers.[12]

In the Commons Ewart was understandably worried that the Lords' Committee might make inroads into the efforts for total abolition. Under the guise of setting up a rival Commons' Committee, he hoped to win the House over to the abolitionist side. He told the House that he had long been convinced that the 'repeal of the punishment of death' was in strict conformity with 'the precepts and spirit of the gospel'.[13] Privy executions would merely veil the evil, not remove it.[14] He contended that the myriad problems of capital punishment could only be resolved by abolition altogether. His peroration was a passionate appeal:

> We ask you no longer to pass an irrevocable doom, but one which, if erroneous, may yet be recalled. You banish, by the present system, or you greatly tend to banish, the solemn, yet consolatory spirit of repentance. We ask you to revive it in the holy ministrations of religion, and in the solitude and silence of the cell. Finally we adjure you to remove from your courts (if I may borrow a phrase from Cowley) this 'scare-crow deity' which has so long dishonoured and deformed them; to replace it by the unstained effigy of justice; to substitute for the last vestiges of a barbarous code, the precepts of a milder wisdom; and to breathe into the laws of your country, the pure and peaceful spirit of the Gospel.[15]

However, on 10 June 1856 his motion was overwhelmingly defeated by 158 votes to 64.

In less than a month the Wilberforce Committee delivered its report.[16] It concluded that the great preponderance of evidence represented the sight of capital executions as by no means generally deterring in its effect. It was a spectacle which, if anything, diminished the awfulness of the effect of the punishment. It tended to harden those who witnessed it. It made martyrs and heroes out of brazen criminals who were encouraged to make shows of bravado and protestations of innocence, and drunken holidays out of what should have been the most solemn and awesome occasions.

Bickersteth himself had been one of the most influential witnesses. He referred to two public hangings of his own knowledge, the latter of which he had witnessed himself, the former having been related to him by a correspondent. This was of a Methodist local preacher in the 1820s on the clearest evidence of murder. He had addressed the crowd, said he was going to glory, and led hymn singing. Such a scene, thought the Archdeacon, 'must either have diminished the crowd's respect for the laws of man, or have weakened their fear in God'.[17] The second, in 1841, was of Josiah Misters, a Shrewsbury man, convicted of attempted murder. The whole thing was like a fair, with women and children of the 'labouring class', many of whom had walked for miles, constituting the greater part of the attendance. As an evangelist he had been frustrated in his attempts to point morals from it. He had been 'anxious before the day came, if possible, to use it as a day upon which some moral effects might be produced, but [he had] found it was quite in vain [and] . . . the event was a source of great evil'. He treated it as of no consequence that as a vicar in Shrewsbury at the time, he never visited the prisoner and 'had nothing to do with the gaol'. He had, however, consulted Mr Winstone, the chaplain of Shrewsbury Gaol, about the hanging and his view concurred with his own.[18]

Of Aylesbury Gaol he did know something, and feared that the worst offenders, including Moses Hatto himself, had been frequenters of public hangings, three of which had been held in Aylesbury in the previous decade. He read a letter from the Revd G. A. Cuxson, chaplain of Aylesbury Gaol who considered the effect of a public execution on the spectators 'to be generally very demoralizing, though there may doubtless be exceptional cases where it is wholesome and deterring'. The audience, alas, was so often unworthy of the performance.

> I have only once, in the exercise of my office, had to attend a criminal left for execution, and I then observed that the breathless silence which had prevailed during the short time intervening between the culprit's appearing on the scaffold and the moment of his death immediately afterwards followed, as it had always been preceded, by the most incongruous sounds of low jesting and indecent ribaldry. The brief silence originated in the morbid curiosity of the crowd to catch the expected words of the hero of the moment.[19]

He had formed the impression during his intercourse with criminals that a disproportionate number of them seemed to have witnessed executions on several occasions, and this had been 'remarkably confirmed' when he made it his business to question all his prisoners serving six months or more upon that point, for he found that the great majority of those of them who had had the opportunity, and amongst them 'all the worst characters in the prison', had frequented executions. So also, only a few months prior to his own execution had Hatto, and it had become 'a subject of deep regret and bitter remorse to him that he had gone to it as to a holiday fair, and had returned from it without perceiving any warning'.[20]

Bickersteth had also asked what happened to the prisoners in Aylesbury Gaol on the day of the execution and found that they were left entirely to themselves without labour, 'so that they had nothing but their own reflections to employ them'. That was a salutary effect. Any increase in the solemnities attending an execution would be an improvement. He would have private executions with black flags, bells tolling, church services being held at the time with prayers for the criminal and improving sermons. The day should be a day of humiliation not merriment. 'A certain mystery and uncertainty about the actual extinction of life creates greater solemnity upon the mind than public witnessing of the act.' This sentiment was echoed by other witnesses, and was specifically quoted and approved by the Select Committee.[21]

Almost as an incidental aside the Archdeacon recommended that it 'should depend upon the confession of his guilt afterwards whether [the hanged man] should be interred with Christian rites or not', even though he admitted that innocent people might sometimes have been hanged. Although he accepted that the extraction of confessions was vitally important, Wilberforce maintained that such a distinction was a 'dangerous principle'; Lord Somerhill, on the other hand, thought it better to bury murderers without Christian rites.[22]

Bickersteth's fears were shared by the Revd John Clay, chaplain at Preston House of Correction for thirty-five years. He referred to the noxious effect of the hanging of the Pendleton Murderers.

> Those men protested their innocence up to the last moment; just before they were turned off they sang a hymn together; and this double fact of the protestation of innocence, and the singing of a hymn, created a very grave sensation among intelligent persons, who had some doubts whether the men were really guilty or not . . . if those men had been executed within the walls of the gaol, such a scene would not have taken place . . . I think their firmness, so to call it, would have given way.[23]

There was no hint of a doubt on the part of Mr Clay that a miscarriage of justice might have taken place, merely that the suspicion of it could have been suppressed.

He went on to recall his own experience of an execution. He had wondered if his nerves would stand it. They did triumphantly. He had expected that he should faint or feel very unwell, and to his own great surprise, and in some measure to his own disgust, he felt nothing of the kind. He had seen 'a couple of murderers hung', but the effect upon his nerves had been nothing compared with what he had expected. He was quite sure, however, that had he been told that the men had been 'executed with certain circumstances of solemnity and so forth', he should have thought a great deal more of it.[24]

He favoured retaining the bodies, and burying them under sombre grave-stones with short, didactic inscriptions carved on them. Prisoners in passing could not but notice them. These would 'have ten times more effect upon evil doers as find their way into a gaol than the sight of a public execution', although he admitted that he had never talked to criminals on the subject of public executions.[25]

The Committee recommended that public executions be abolished and private ones substituted, and that a black flag be hoisted to indicate to those assembled outside that all had been accomplished. This latter measure was 'in earnest compliment to the Bishop of Oxford, under whose pastoral care the Committee had been appointed'. *Punch* commented that a bishop had been 'better employed in the vineyard of his master, than in the ropeyard of the Judges'.[26]

Not all church leaders seemed to share the Bishop of Oxford's dedication to the subject. Other matters detrimental to public morals occupied their minds. Holyoake, an abolitionist propagandist, and the last person in England to be imprisoned for blasphemy, indignantly asked why the then Archbishop of York, William Thompson, condemned 'sensational novels' but did not 'utter one word against this vile, this real, this villainous sensation provided by the government in every country of the kingdom?'.[27]

Nor did all chaplains agree with the evidence given to the Select Committee. Kingsmill of Pentonville believed that public killing had a peculiar deterrent value, the great and necessary precautions taken in the prisons to prevent the suicide of the condemned indicating 'that public exposure by so ignominious an end as the gallows has its peculiar horrors'.[28] *All the Year Round*, the weekly journal published by Dickens from 1859, included an article by an anonymous author (probably a clergyman) who had attended an old man called Giles on the scaffold. From this, his one and only experience, he denied the accuracy of reports of executions: 'I have never yet read what has impressed me as a truthful account of any such scene.' He went on to describe the executioner Calcraft as a very different sort from the popular perception.

> Calcraft entered. A mild gentle-faced man . . . I can see him as I write – his eyes full and grey, though small, and sweet in their expression. He does not 'shamble' as he walks; nor does he talk coarsely . . . His walk, his voice, his expression, and his manner, are in fact, completely reassuring.

The 'mild man with grey hair' pinioned Giles, remarking 'that doesn't hurt you, my good fellow?'. Giles agreed that it was 'very comfortable'. Assuring him that he would not be tortured, Calcraft asked and received his victim's forgiveness, the old man offering 'his poor pinioned hands like fins' to the hangman to shake. Processing with the chaplain intoning the burial service and the bell tolling, they mounted the scaffold. There Calcraft 'fixed the rope with long pains to arrange the knot in the most merciful place'. Then with a 'God bless you for it is now!' he launched the sinner into eternity: 'Cr, *chunk!* And there was a fall and something swaying to and fro, till at last it became steady.'[29] This enthusiastic portrayal of the 'delicacy' of public executions was, however, almost unique among practitioners.

Initially the weight of opinion from all quarters operated against any action towards the abolition of public executions. The Chief Justice and the Home Secretary both opposed change. The Lords took no action to implement the Wilberforce Report. Radicals and Conservatives (including *The Times*) were united in opposing its recommendations but for entirely different reasons. Abolitionists hoped that if judicial killing remained public then public opinion would inevitably demand its abolition. To secrete it away would dangerously delay its final demise. The experience of the United States gave grounds for their fear. After an initially strong start, leading to the abolition of public hangings in a number of states, the abolitionist movement was moribund by the mid 1850s and remained so for a further half century. Sequestration 'had subtracted much of the fire from the anti-gallows campaign'.[30] The reformers at home trusted that the Englishman's love of liberty and fair-play and distrust of the authorities would ensure that hanging would remain public. Lord Hobbart, indeed, thought that outright abolition was far more likely than that capital punishment would ever be inflicted except in the full face of day.[31] Thomas Beggs, then Honorary Secretary of the SACP, with considerable foresight doubted whether private executions would indeed remove the evils complained of in public hangings since 'so long as a large portion of the press have an interest in finding aliment for the lovers of sensation, so long will the morbid appetites of the people be fed by reports of the daily conduct of the criminal'. He was certain that accounts of the executions, 'with all their ghastly accompaniments would find their way out, and the apparent mystery by which they were attempted to be concealed would add to the interest in the minds of the people'.[32] Almost a century later Archbishop Fisher was to express dismay that this prediction had come true. Retentionists, on the other hand, feared that to remove hanging from the public gaze was to diminish its deterrent effect and thus hasten its abolition.[33]

That it did not is in some way attributable to the contribution made by the Church of England. The effect of the evidence of both Archdeacon Bickersteth and the prison chaplains to the Select Committee was that capital punishment would continue to have a deterrent effect, indeed that effect would be enhanced, if it were carried out with due solemnity, mystery, and awe. It was the beginning of a dramatic change in the procedure of hanging. From being a painful, agonizing, demeaning, and slow death, in the full gaze of a deriding public, it was to become a highly formalized, technically exact, and wonderfully speedy extinction, attended only by a handful of witnesses. From being a holocaust upon the high places, the death penalty was to become a sacrifice within the holy of holies. The outward accretions were to be purged away, the essential virtue was to remain.

Many recent commentators[34] have attributed the demise of public executions to the fear which the authorities had for the untamed multitudes that attended them. The authority of the sovereign, which should have been enhanced in this display of power over life and death, was in fact endangered. All the evidence which I have adduced suggests that it was not fear but disgust which was the primary motivating factor. The crowd was not so much a terror to the upper classes as a reproach. As Henry Fielding put it in the eighteenth century, 'instead of making the gallows an object of terror, our executions contribute to make it an object of contempt in the eye of the malefactor; and we sacrifice the lives of men, not for the reformation but the diversion of the populace'.[35] And the dignity which was compromised by the sordid deportment of the lower orders on such occasions was not so much that of the king as of God himself. It was not a cabal of revolutionaries who gathered outside Newgate but the 'synagogue of Satan' come to partake in 'the Saturnalia of Sin, Death, and Hell'.[36] Executions were religious rituals more than secular ones. Similarly these commentators maintain that with the sequestration of capital punishment went a decay in the ritual.[37] It was not a decay but a transformation. From now on street theatre – a mediaeval mystery play – before an untutored and dissolute audience was replaced by a private performance before invited and appreciative guests. As one clerical writer put it, 'the very imagination of death inflicted upon the criminal in the privacy of a prison, in absolute isolation from all his fellows, – the awe and mystery which would be associated with that terrible and silent scene' would more powerfully effect the populace than 'the heterogeneous reminiscences of a public execution.'[38]

Thus a coalition of public opinion began to form around this Christian compromise of the imprisonment of capital punishment. Sometimes abolitionists like Dickens, who yet felt no pity for murderers, opted for a solution to all they had criticized in the public display attending executions. Perceptive retentionists, led by the Established Church, realized that to retain the penalty, they had better retreat with dignity behind prison walls. Public disquiet over capital punishment had been largely aroused by the indiscriminate nature of its use for all and sundry crimes, and by the evils attendant on open air hangings. By 1861 capital punishment had been restricted to four offences, and effectively to one, and with the creation of the great Victorian prison system well under way, the ideal setting for the solemn execution of murderers, hid from the gaze, but yet in the presence of, their fellow criminals, had been provided. Thus sanitized or sacralized, capital punishment had shed many of its most obviously objectionable features, and so abolition was no longer necessary or even desirable except to that minority who opposed hanging on principle, and not just as it had been practised. By the 1860s the abolitionist cause was moribund. In 1862 the Society for the Abolition of Capital Punishment was so diminished that it had to suspend its operations several times owing to lack of support.

This growing conservatism and changed attitude to hanging was reflected in the change of view of such erstwhile abolitionist organs as *Fraser's Magazine*. One of its most distinguished contributors would even espouse views which many must have thought – and prayed – were almost extinct. The eminent jurist Sir James Stephen wrote a hard-line retentionist article which harked back to the views of Bishop Butler on the 'pleasure of vengeance'. As a young columnist for *The Saturday Review* he had anonymously authored a whole series of articles defending capital punishment from its detractors and denouncing their attribution to Christianity of sentiments which in his opinion were not only not Christian but were distinctly traceable to an unChristian source. The supposed 'mild temper of Christianity' was really no more than 'the sentimental indulgent spirit of Rousseau'.[39] From the loftier heights of this prominent journal he expressed his views with even greater ferocity. Capital punishment was the only deterrent, and it alone gratified the 'vindictive sentiment'. In the 1840s Lord Macaulay had ridiculed the 'effeminacy' of the abolitionists, now Sir James belittled their sentimentality: they were 'too soft and pitiful'.

> There is as much moral cowardice in shrinking from the execution of a murderer as in hesitating to blow out the brains of a foreign invader. A mind which feels this shrinking and calls it a Christian feeling must have a strangely partial and one-sided view of Christianity . . . The Sermon on the Mount stands in front of a background on which is the worm that never dies and the fire that is not quenched . . . This is no doubt imagery but what does the imagery represent? This must be coupled with the Old Testament history and the character of the law that was to be fulfilled and not destroyed, before the spirit of vengeance is called unchristian . . . Will Mr Bright tell us that Quakers alone have been Christians? Have not all the constitutions and most of the legislation of modern Europe grown up under the auspices of Christianity, and have they no stern side?
>
> The plain truth is that Christianity has two sides. A gentle side up to a certain point, a terrific one beyond that point. It says 'Love one another; but you will be damned if you do not.'[40]

Such blunt views were extreme for their day, but the fact that they came from so eminent a legal source, and could be published in so influential a journal suggests that they struck an increasingly popular chord. Most educated opinion, however, still preferred to go along with Bickersteth in holding that capital punishment was justifiable on Christian grounds as the appropriate penalty for murder, that it was a necessary and effective deterrent, but that it should be accompanied with as much dignity and solemnity as possible, motivated not by vengeance, but by justice and decorum. It should be out of sight but not out of mind.

A number of controversial executions in 1864 brought the issue to a climax. Samuel Wright, a man of doubtful sanity, was refused a reprieve despite the fact that a richer man had succeeded in gaining one in a less venial case. The execution of the Five Pirates became the occasion for a party, and on the day after they were hanged John Hibbert unsuccessfully moved in the Commons to abolish public executions.[41] In May that year Ewart once again urged the appointment of a Select Committee to inquire into capital punishment, that 'great question of civilization and religion'. Confident that the statistical evidence supported his cause, he declared that the decisive argument could not be religious, since both sides could cite scripture for their purpose, but practical, since the interpretation of empirical data was more objective and less contentious.[42] John Bright, supporting the motion, congratulated the House on its increasing maturity since the last debate on this question. They had advanced so far that nobody had brought forward the argument from Genesis, and everyone had discussed the issue 'in terms of proved experiments, of facts, and of reason'. Yet his most telling point was not verifiable by any of those means: it was that the security of human life did not depend on ten or twelve people being publicly put to death every year but 'upon the reverence for life', a veneration in the minds of the people 'for that which God only has given'. Every public hanging did far more to weaken 'the security which depends upon the reverence with which human life is regarded' than it did to deter from crime.[43] Ewart's motion this time received considerable support, as a result of which the Home Secretary, the devout evangelical Sir George Grey, suggested that a Royal Commission would be preferable. Reluctantly, Ewart and the House agreed, and a Commission was set up under a leading Conservative peer, the sixth Duke of Richmond, its scope being broadened to inquire into the matter of public executions. On 29 July the Grand Jury for South Lancashire petitioned for the abolition of public executions. On 14 November Franz Müller's execution just fourteen days before the first session of the Royal Commission further exacerbated attitudes.[44]

The Royal Commission spent two years deliberating and taking evidence from a wide variety of sources, though not from the SACP. Its members, comprising as they did a wide spectrum of opinion, were often very thorough in their interrogation of witnesses. Most effective and most knowledgeable were the four overt proponents of abolition: William Ewart, John Bright, Charles Neate, MP for Oxford, and Stephen Lushington, who had been involved in the abolition campaign for over fifty years and who was later, in ripe old age, to be active in the Howard Association.

The judicial witnesses all favoured capital punishment but were unsure as to the method. They feared that public executions might alienate the public. The prison governors were unanimously in favour of sequestration. Even those like Henry Cartwright, Governor of Gloucester, who favoured total abolition, were prepared to accept intramural executions as an alternative 'as being more deterrent . . . for greater solemnity, and more humane'.

Four of the witnesses were Anglican clergymen, three being prison chaplains, of whom only one was pro-hanging. The Revd John Davis, Ordinary of Newgate for almost twenty-two years, was the first of the three, the most experienced, but easily the most confused witness before the entire Commission, an easy prey for the abolitionist interrogators. He had not done his homework nor, in comparison to the other clergy, had he learnt much from all his vast experience.[45] On the basis of having attended to twenty-four men who were executed, he concluded that it was 'quite impossible to avoid capital executions'. Only thus could recidivist 'incorrigibles' be restrained from committing murder. Yet he had no evidence on ticket of leave men (his 'incorrigibles') committing murder. From conversation, and overhearing remarks of criminals, he had got his notion that hanging had restrained them from murder. While acknowledging the dread long sentences could induce, he insisted that 'there is nothing like death'. Again he characterized murderers as *sui generis*, and usually first offenders. 'They rush into the crime', he volunteered, and 'murders are committed in mad passion', a view which fitted ill with his previous opinion on the necessity of the death penalty. He was forced to agree that it had no effect on the criminal when committing the murder. Asked if any criminal had told him that he would have killed but for hanging, he weakly replied that he could remember one case when a man had said he would not have killed had he thought he would have hanged, but who had thought he would get off on the grounds of insanity.

When he said that the taking of human life required a punishment of equal dimension, Bright inquired sharply whether he really believed that reverence for human life was not impaired by hanging a man before 100,000 people. His affirmative reply was somewhat belied by his admission that, although he had been sick for three days after his first hanging, custom had soon acclimatized him to it.

Unable to withstand their onslaught, he reverted to a particular view of the meaning and effect of scripture, a view we have encountered before. Scripture was both plain on this point and mandatory: 'the scriptures are commands to us, and therefore we must obey them; and they give the command "Whoso sheddeth man's blood by man shall his blood be shed".'

Nonetheless he was quite pleased with the number of reprieves: 'the Old Testament gives us reasons why we are not to take life. It is quite in conformity with scripture that those sentences are not carried out. There is nothing in scripture at all contrary to it.' He was not to be let off easily on this point either. Asked whether he was inclined to scriptural argument or expediency, he replied that experience was the great thing and that if capital punishment were abolished it would be renewed after a year or two. Yet pressed on the point as to whether he would revert to the Old Testament argument if the murder rate did not rise, he was reduced to saying 'we shall not see that state of things'. Despite his reliance on experience he admitted to knowing nothing of the experience of foreign countries in this matter.

A more impressive witness, one who appeared to have given considerable thought to the matter, and to have benefited from his experience, was the Revd John Jessop JP.[46] He had been chaplain of Horsemonger Lane Gaol for nearly ten years, during which time twenty-eight felons were tried for murder and four were executed (all of whom he believed to be guilty). He held that 'religiously, politically, and socially' capital punishment was quite 'indefensible'. It was contrary to the tenets of the Bible; it depraved the most depraved of the population who were those who attended; it lowered the estimation of the sanctity of life; it demoralized and was no deterrent. He had made great efforts to ascertain the effect of executions on prisoners by asking them and their warders. It seemed to have had none.

His understanding of murderers was much more profound than that of his senior colleague. His views, now perhaps commonplace among criminologists at least, must have seemed surprising in his day. Murderers for gain, he believed, were usually of a higher class than ordinary thieves, and planned their murders with a view to avoiding detection. If they knew that prison would result that would put them off as much as hanging. Other murderers act under impulse or emotion. He indicated that the greater portion of criminals do not think of the consequences, and those who do would be as deterred by life in prison as by hanging. He dismissed the often repeated argument that the lives of warders would be endangered if life replaced death, by pointing out that lunatics were already imprisoned for life in Bethlem and now in Broadmoor, and no warder or inmate had ever been killed.

Jessop argued for the division of murder into first and second degree. Murderers of the first degree would be those guilty of premeditated killing, poisoning, murder with rape, and some others. They would be considered morally and politically dead and would be imprisoned for life without hope of release. They should be isolated, without visitors. 'They should be civilly dead, and no longer heard of in society.' Such incarceration was not to deter others but to protect society from that offender. Those of the second degree would have committed more venial crimes and could hope for eventual release.

An equally interesting witness was the third prison chaplain, and another abolitionist, the Revd William Cook Osborn, who had been for twenty-two years chaplain of Bath Gaol during which time there were no executions.[47] It held remands awaiting capital trials but received no capital sentences. He objected to capital punishment on all the usual grounds but again it was his experience of murderers which gave him so different a view of how they should be dealt with.

> A careful observation in my official position has produced the conviction in my mind, that it is possible and probable that persons may be hung who, if the extenuating circumstances of their lives were known, would have their sentences commuted to imprisonment for life, if not even for a limited period.

Murderers were 'not great criminals'. As a rule they did not belong to the criminal class. The few great criminals who committed murder would be better deterred by a life sentence which they can envisage than death which they cannot, especially since so many remissions had destroyed whatever deterrent value capital punishment may have had. At a pastoral level the current practice of carrying out the death sentence did not allow for sufficient time to bring the man to repentance. We tampered with God's dispensation.

The evidence of the Revd Lord Sidney Godolphin Osborne, the rector of Durweston, Dorset, was particularly perceptive. He was a philanthropist of a militant and ferocious type who lashed abuses and relished controversy. He had often in the past proclaimed his abolitionist views in letters to *The Times*, and as counsel had participated in a number of murder trials. The irrevocability of capital punishment particularly concerned him since even the best of legal systems was capable of error.[48] This was an argument not often made. In support he cited the case of a boy called Adams charged at Aylesbury with murdering his father. It was felt that in the struggle between the two, who did not get on, it was as likely the father would have shot the boy as vice versa. The prosecution deliberately failed to produce vital evidence to avoid a death sentence.

He shared with two of the chaplains a very deep and profoundly unpopular insight into murder, asserting that it was not always the most heinous crime, nor were its victims always 'innocent'. Murder, 'all-awful crime as it is, is not in all cases the crime which proves the criminal to be the worst man'. Jealousy, or some other provocation, was often the main cause, not gain.

> However dreadful the crime of murder may be committed under this provocation, in my poor opinion there are worse crimes, crimes showing a condition of mind more deliberately wicked. In dealing out capital punishment to all criminals convicted of murder, I hold that we confound every principle of justice, for we call all perpetrators of the crime as of equal guilt ... There are many degrees of guilt which led to [the victim's] destruction; sometimes he himself by his own guilt had led to the very deed causing his own end.

Robbers and burglars knew that death might be their end, and accepted it: it was an occupational hazard. They tried not to get caught. Nothing, on the other hand, would deter the crime of passion. Again he pointed to the paradox of murder. He would not say that all murderers were criminals because it was 'a very curious fact how few positive criminals commit murders'. Murders were usually committed under other feelings, such as lust or jealousy; 'by persons, however, chiefly of the class in life of our criminals, though not known to be themselves criminals'. He would have preferred penal servitude, but if capital punishment were to be retained it should be behind prison walls. If men and women were to be hanged their execution should be as solemn and dignified as possible.

The Royal Commission took two years to report but when it did it recommended the division of murder into first and second degree and, by seven votes to five, the abolition of public executions. All four abolitionist members, recognizing that sanitizing executions would weaken their case, dissented from this, urging instead that capital punishment be abolished. One other member, O'Hagan, agreed with this in principle but thought public opinion would not sustain it.

In this he was a fair judge, and his view was more realistic than the wishful thinking of the abolitionists. Rather misjudging its effect, the Abolition Society welcomed the report and the publicity surrounding it as contributing to what they thought to be 'a growing public opinion in favour of total abolition'.[49] With considerable prescience Lord Osborne dissented from this view. He had never doubted that 'before long we should have private executions – very few of them – murder better defined – only the most atrocious capitally punished'. If something like this were to come about, he would wait for the rest, which would surely eventually follow.[50] He would, however, have a long wait.

Although, as a result of the Commission's recommendations various bills were debated in Parliament, the major one, the Law of Capital Punishment Amendment Bill (1866), to introduce degrees of murder, was withdrawn because of a tied vote in the House of Lords. When the Duke of Argyll spoke there of society being a minister of Divine Justice in inflicting punishment for the crime of murder, the Bishop of Oxford added a loud 'Hear, Hear'.[51] The intellectual and Parliamentary dominance was passing firmly to the retentionists. In 1867 the indomitable Ewart died, and although Charles Gilpin, as usual a Liberal MP, and a Quaker, succeeded him in Parliamentary leadership, supported by Bright, there were no other abolitionists of stature in the Commons. The Lords, of course, remained a dead loss.

The next year saw the introduction of the Richmond Commission's second recommendation in the Capital Punishment within Prisons Bill. It was a great blow to the abolitionists when during the April debate John Stuart Mill, the nation's leading political philosopher and one who had interceded for some condemned Fenians the previous year, rose to oppose an amendment which, if passed, would have done away with the death penalty entirely.[52] The philanthropists had done a fine thing in so restricting the death penalty, he told the House, and their only mistake was in 'not perceiving the right time and place for stopping in a career hitherto so eminently beneficial'. Hanging for some murderers should be retained for humanity's sake, he contended. Capital punishment was far more humane than immuring the culprit in a living tomb. Oblivious to the glaring inconsistency, however, he went on to insist that nothing other than death would do as a deterrent. With a complacency which was to be generally emulated for almost a century, he asserted that miscarriages of justice could not take place under our system which if anything was 'too favourable to the offender'[53] (begging the question, of course, of whether a particular defendant were an offender). Abolition, he said, in terms reminiscent of Lord Macaulay, would have a degenerative effect on the fibre of England, bringing with it as it would 'an enervation, an effeminacy in the general mind of the country. For what else but effeminacy is it to be much more shocked by taking a man's life than by depriving him of all that makes life desirable or valuable.'[54] Capital punishment showed a regard for human life by adopting a rule that whoever takes life will lose it.

Some members of the House spoke of his speech afterwards 'in most exalted terms, as if some new light had suddenly arisen'.[55] *The Times* applauded his 'rare courage' in disregarding 'the sentimental and showily benevolent view'.[56] *Punch*, now a renegade, was mightily impressed. With advocates of his calibre there was no doubt that the Bill which satisfied the misgivings of so many would pass unamended.

The last public execution was a controversial one, that of the Irishman, Michael Barrett. The case had caused considerable disquiet. An attempt with explosives to free some Fenian prisoners in Clerkenwell House of Detention had led to considerable civilian loss of life, and feelings against the Catholic Irish ran high. Barrett alone was convicted but many felt that his involvement was peripheral. Despite the pleas of Bright and Mill for clemency, the consensus in Parliament was that even if Barrett were not guilty, he was a self-confessed nationalist, a Catholic, and a Fenian, and so should die. Others petitioned for a reprieve. Several, including William Smith, vicar of Overbury, wrote to the Home Secretary, Gathorne Hardy, accusing him of murder. It was well-known that Barrett's was to be the last public hanging in England, and the price for a room with a view of the Newgate drop was as high as £10. Yet only about 2,000 spectators attended, and though a few were drunk, there was little sign of the levity and vulgarity many expected. At 7 am on 26 May, 1868 William Calcraft entered Barrett's cell, pinioned him, and led him to the scaffold. The hood was quickly placed over his head, the noose adjusted, and the drop fell. He died without any mishap.[57]

Three days later the Capital Punishment Amendment Act[58] received royal assent, and so ended public executions for ever. On the morning of Thursday 13 August 1868 at Maidstone Gaol Thomas Wells, aged eighteen, was the first person to be hanged behind prison walls. Present were sixteen reporters from the Metropolitan press.[59] Hanging might be secluded but the public were represented by proxy, and over breakfast could read in lurid detail of the final moments and death of the condemned.[60]

The sequestration of hanging was an idea whose time had come. In 1853 an attempt to get up a petition in Aylesbury on this issue raised only six signatures, a year later Bickersteth 'with no particular effort' could get sixty of the more influential inhabitants to sign.[61] Fourteen years later, the gallows, like the gibbet, a landmark of the English countryside for centuries, was gone for good. *The Times* in a leading article on the Act marvelled at the remarkable advance in public opinion:

> If we go still further back, though not beyond the reach of living memory, we find eminent judges solemnly protesting, in the name of religion and on behalf of society, against the substitution of any secondary punishment for offences now considered almost trivial . . . The labours of the Society for the Abolition of Capital Punishment may perhaps have contributed to it.[62]

The arguments of the abolitionists had helped to prepare the Government and the authorities to accept private executions, not the abolition of capital punishment. The abolition of public executions, as its most recent chronicler has observed, 'was a linear descendant of a long line of criminal reforms' instigated by Beccaria and Bentham, and initiated by Romilly. As such, and in the same way as the earlier efforts to curtail the Bloody Code, 'it was an independent movement, not just a subordinate part' of a larger campaign to gain total abolition.[63] Indeed many of its advocates were firm retentionists. They had stolen the thunder from the abolitionists, and answered many of the peripheral arguments against the death penalty. The crusade for total abolition would have to continue in far less favourable circumstances, and with far less support.

Indicative of the change in mood was the effective replacement of the SACP by the Howard Association. The former had always been a very small society which had been compelled on several occasions to suspend its operations owing to lack of support. After the Royal Commission had finally reported in favour of the retention of the death penalty, the Executive Committee of the Society again decided to suspend active operations and to resume, as during some previous periods, a watching and waiting role. Some influential members, however, thought it desirable to continue to collect and diffuse information on capital punishment, but in the context of the much wider question of how best to deal with crime in general. The Secretary, William Tallack, complied with their view by inviting the formation of a new committee for this more comprehensive object. Thus the Howard Association was founded in 1866 in the Stoke Newington Friends' Meeting. Tallack was appointed secretary of the new society, and many of the leading members of the SACP, including Bright, Ewart, and Lushington, became its supporters, although the older emaciated organization, led largely by Quakers, continued until the First World War. The Howard Association wanted abolition, but agreement with this was not a *sine qua non* for membership, and it had a wider scope in advocating criminal rehabilitation and penal reform (its committee included the governors of Gloucester and Bedford gaol, and the former deputy-governor of Chatham). A society solely dedicated to abolishing hanging could no longer sustain itself.[64]

8 Hanging in Limbo

From the Abolition of Public Executions to the First World War: 1868–1918

> Then shall ye do unto him, as he had thought to have done unto his brother: so shalt thou put the evil away from among you. And those which remain shall hear, and fear, and shall henceforth commit no more any such evil among you. And thine eye shall not pity; but life shall go for life.
>
> *Deuteronomy 19. 19–21*

> There sleeps in Shrewsbury jail to-night,
> Or wakes, as may betide,
> A better lad, if things went right,
> Than most that sleep outside.
>
> And naked to the hangman's noose
> The morning clocks will ring
> A neck God made for other use
> Than strangling in a string.
>
> *A. E. Housman*[1]

No longer did the shadow of the gallows hang heavy on the land. Hanging had been removed to a discreet distance behind high prison walls. Efforts to restrict it further through the revision of the law made no progress: the attempt to get a new felony of infanticide failed thrice to get through Parliament between 1873 and 1875 (and a further three times before the First World War, finally succeeding in 1922); and the establishment of degrees of murder failed in seven separate bills between 1867 and 1874. No more successful were attempts to abolish it altogether. From 1868 until the first Labour administration over half a century later the agitation to abolish the death penalty was sustained not primarily by Parliamentary activism but by a thin thread of dedicated abolitionists, grouped in the Howard Association, who by organizing meetings, publishing and distributing pamphlets, letter-writing on a large scale, and petitioning for individual reprieves, tried to win public support, or failing that, at least to arouse public interest.[2]

Sometimes such agitation was successful. Of the seven capital sentences passed at the Winter Assizes in December 1871, six were commuted as a result of popular pressure. Only in one of these cases, at Cheltenham, did a number of clergy interpose on behalf of the condemned man. He was hanged.[3] Such a high success rate was exceptional, and took place before the full anaesthetizing effect of sequestration had sapped abolitionist energies. As the years went by, it was not always so easy to maintain such support.

Particularly galling and frustrating for the late Victorian reformers after the abolition of public executions had taken place was the attitude of the Established Church. Sermons extolling 'the sanguinary code, engraven on man's heart and uttered by his conscience which is the voice of God', such as that preached in Westminster Abbey by Christopher Wordsworth, William's nephew, then an archdeacon but shortly thereafter to be Bishop of Lincoln, were still typical of the attitude of church leaders, high church (as he was) and low.[4] William Tallack, himself a Quaker, bemoaned the fact that the abolitionists lacked the support 'with some noble exceptions, of one important section of the public – the clerical and ministerial body'.[5]

It had been the same in the United States where the strongest supporters of abolition had been the Quakers, Unitarians and Universalists, while the staunchest retentionists had come from the ranks of the Calvinist Churches, especially the Presbyterian and Congregationalist, who effectively constituted the American Church Establishment in the nineteenth century.[6] It was this grouping that had both sustained slavery, and later during the Civil War demanded the total defeat of the South.[7] In England the ecclesiastical powers that be had been the most reluctant to support any moves for social reform. Tallack, on the basis of this comparative evidence, concluded that the 'organized ecclesiastical leaders of Christendom' had been 'peculiarly characterized by a lack of certain forms of moral courage', a reluctance to share their privileges with others, and an arrogance that precluded any dialogue on the interpretation of scripture.[8]

A short interlude in the Buckinghamshire countryside reveals the problems faced at the local level by those individuals intent on keeping up the pressure. The Anglican clergy were content with the status quo. Aylesbury, that erstwhile fertile ground for abolitionist sentiment, had been satisfied with the success of its archdeacon's proposals. A local worthy, a prominent supporter of the Howard Association, and an abolitionist, Robert Gibbs, feared that private executions had led to an increase in death punishments: whereas in 1870 only six people had been executed in England, and three in 1871, in 1881 the number had risen to eleven, the following year to thirteen, and by 1883 it was fifteen, 'whereas, according to the annual diminution in public executions there should have been none'.[9]

Gibbs set about to win reprieves where he could. His correspondence shows that he tried to rally the clergy to help win a respite for a condemned murderer called Mobbs. The curate of his parish, the Revd Martin Smith, and the Primitive Methodist Preacher both attended the court to speak on his behalf for a reprieve but their depositions were not taken. Yet even Mr Smith, who would have been glad if he had been spared, considered that 'an undeviating practice of carrying out the capital sentence would be for the good of the community'. Gibbs, he knew, thought differently on this matter.[10] He made even less headway with the Revd John Spencer, a local rector, who replied to Gibbs' entreaties that he knew nothing of the parties concerned and did not see what he could 'consistently do in this sad affair'. The guilty should be punished and death was merited for murder. The sentence was both just and scriptural, and mercy, although misplaced on earth, was available at the feet of Jesus to all who would prostrate themselves there in penitence and faith. Such was Spencer's hope and prayer for the condemned man.[11]

To return to the capital, pamphleteering on the issue had more or less dried up. One of the few tracts on the subject during these fallow years was W. A. Copinger's *Essay on the Abolition of Capital Punishment*[12] which repeated the old arguments about the interpretation of Genesis and the Mosaic Code. He was arguing a case in which no one was any longer interested. Christian sentiment to a very large extent had been satisfied with the abolition of public hangings, and with the concomitant extension of time between the sentence and its execution which was now set for the Monday following the third Sunday after the sentence was passed. 'Common sense' sermons, such as those of the leading proponent of 'muscular Christianity', Charles Kingsley, decried the 'softness' and 'atheistic cant' of those who hesitated to usher murderers into the presence of their Maker, and to let him decide whether indeed they could be amended.[13]

In Parliament interest flagged during the late 1860s and the 1870s, and even the irrepressible Bright conceded that there was little point in bringing up the issue again. The abolition of public hanging had made it more difficult to procure the abolition of hanging altogether. More pressing concerns, such as massacres in the Balkans, were occupying Parliamentary minds, and 'just now when they are discussing the murder of thousands, the killing of half a dozen in a year will not excite much attention'.[14] The observation was astute. In time of war or rumours of war hanging never had a high priority.

Such attention as it did excite centred round the pragmatic question of whether hanging were necessary. As time passed fewer and fewer proponents of capital punishment advocated it as the fitting punishment for murder. Both sides grew ever more reluctant to argue on biblical or theological grounds. Increasingly the argument for and against the death penalty was narrowed to this one question: did hanging deter? There was growing agreement that hanging was abhorrent, and could be sustained only if its abolition would remove a unique deterrent and lead to the loss of innocent lives. The burden of proof, however, fell on those who would abolish what common sense seemed to dictate was such a deterrent. One of the problems Victorian abolitionists faced was the lack of reliable data, and the difficulty of transposing the experience of other countries to their own. Comprehensive statistics were hard to obtain, especially from the continent, difficult to interpret, and almost impossible to apply convincingly or persuasively to an English context.[15] All else was opinion. One man's moral certainty against another man's sincere conviction. When opinion clashed the status quo was rarely shaken.

The issue was again debated in the Commons in 1872. Gilpin was rightly criticized for adducing the beneficial effects of the abolition of the Bloody Code as evidence of the likely benefits to accrue from the abolition of hanging for murder. As *The Times* pointed out, the vice of the old code lay in the enormous disproportion between offences and penalties, a disproportion which no longer subsisted now that the ultimate penalty was reserved for the ultimate crime.[16]

The debate was tired and so were the debaters. There it rested for a further five years until yet another Quaker MP, Sir Joseph Pease, who had taken up Gilpin's mantle, brought it again before the House. He argued on the basis of other countries' experience using material provided by the Howard Association. Some was frankly ambiguous. Italy, for instance, had abolished the death penalty but had a high murder rate: 'Italy is where people kill the most and hang the least; England is where they kill the least and hang the most.' In the 1870s Italy had 588 murders per million, and hardly any executions, while England had 8.8 murders per million and 56% of those were executed. It was not the strongest abolitionist case. Although the veteran Bright continued to argue that hanging corrupted the nation, and poisoned the minds of the people, the main issue was summed up by Sir William Harcourt's simple question, 'was hanging a deterrent?'. If it were, he would vote for it and support it to the last, 'for the life of the man murdered was better worth defending than that of the man who murdered'. This was the position of most MPs; not one Tory voted for abolition. Even as he spoke, Pease felt the mood of the House and recognized his failure. He abandoned the deterrent argument which was not what really motivated him. In his peroration, the only passionate rhetoric in a dry speech, he bravely looked beyond present vicissitudes to ultimate success in this Christian cause:

> If I have failed tonight in inducing [the House] to vote that capital punishment ought no longer to exist in the England of the nineteenth century, I am persuaded still that the arguments which I have used will be taken into consideration, and, feeble as my attempt has been, I shall rest satisfied for the present in having added another to the efforts that have already been made to purge laws from our Statute Book which are doomed at no distant day to perish before the tide of an ever-advancing civilization, and because they are at variance with the sublime spirit of Christianity.[17]

Principled sentiments such as these, and an undying hope that abolition would one day be a reality, kept alive a small flame that had to flicker unfanned by public or Parliamentary favour for half a century.

The following year the abolitionists were again routed, being defeated by 263 votes to 64. *The Times*' Leader commented that 'the storm which once seemed to be gathering has subsided and had been followed by a great calm'. Abolition had 'ceased to have a place among the real questions of the day'.[18]

Undeterred Pease tried again in 1881, this time under a Liberal administration. During the arguments about deterrence, the safety of prison officers and the alternatives to capital punishment, one Tory MP, Mr Warton, referred to the Bible in an attempt to bolster the more secular arguments. He 'trusted they were all Christians'. He 'was content with the Divine notion of human justice, as it was shown in these words (Gen. 9. 6) at that most important crisis in the history of our race', and rested his case on 'the Divine command which was older than Christianity'. The argument for the unique deterrent effect of capital punishment was buttressed by the Bible itself: 'God was acquainted with the human heart, and he knew by what means men were deterred from crime'.[19] In riposte, Mr Anderson, the MP for Glasgow, said that he was not surprised that Warton should go back to the Ark because 'he was an antediluvian Conservative in all things'. As had so often been done in the past, and as would be done in the future, he reminded the biblicists that Christians believed their creed had superseded that of the Old Testament.[20] Mr Firth pointed out that modern biblical scholarship could well undermine the traditional argument based on Genesis 9. 6 since, when the Revised Version of the Old Testament was published, it was likely that the words 'by man' would be removed from the text 'and therefore the argument founded on this passage, and which had done great service in the past, would entirely be lost'.[21] According to Mr Newdigate all the agitation on the subject could be blamed on 'a class of persons whom he might describe as "humanitarians" ', a small and troublesome minority who had not managed to cloud the reasoning of the British people.[22] In riposte Mr Sergeant Simon pointed out it was due to the exertions of the humanitarians that the Bloody Code had been repealed and the slave trade abolished.[23] Pease lost by 175 votes to 79.

Sir William Harcourt devoted much attention to the old problem of degrees of murder when he was Liberal Home Secretary in 1881–2. For him the question was one which should be settled entirely with reference to convenience and expediency, and the Bible should be left out of it.[24] He proposed a bill confining murder in the first degree to murders committed 'with intent to kill', but after consulting with the judiciary and Bar he abandoned the attempt, concluding that it was impossible to frame a definition which did not include cases that ought not to be included and exclude cases that ought to be included.

Despite the greater precision of private hangings, and greater refinements in the mechanics of hanging,[25] mishaps occurred on several occasions that we know of. John Lee testified to the triple failure in his own case since he had thus survived. Others, however, did not profit by the errors. In 1883 James Burton was hanged by Marwood in Durham Gaol, but the slack of the rope caught under his elbow and he had to be drawn up alive. While Burton twice muttered 'O Lord, have mercy on my poor soul', the executioner made good the fault and pushed him into the cavity again. This time there was no hitch. Questions were asked in the House. Articles urging the employment of a professional salaried hangman, or the devolution of the duty to prison staff, or even the adoption of alternative methods of execution – the guillotine or the garotte – were published.[26]

Several other instances of imperfection were recorded in the 1880s including one in which the executioner, Berry, pulled the man's head right off.[27] As a result, in 1886, the Conservative Home Secretary, Sir Richard Cross, fearful that capital punishment would be brought into public disrepute and thereby endangered, appointed a confidential Departmental Committee under the chairmanship of Lord Aberdare, a former Liberal Home Secretary, to look into the existing practice and to ensure that in future 'all executions might be carried out in a becoming manner'. It reported two years later, concluding that if the drop were too short the victim would suffocate slowly, if too long decapitation could result which, though the lesser of the two evils, was both 'revolting in itself and affecting the public imagination;.[28] To obviate these problems it recommended the adoption of a uniform scaffold apparatus, a standard length and thickness of rope, and a method of securing the slack. In addition a table of 'drops' was appended. If these measures were put into practice, accidents would still happen, but, Aberdare observed, 'this shock to public opinion [would] be of extreme rarity'.[29] Once again it was necessary to sanitize the process to keep the practice.

The behaviour of hangmen had long given cause for concern. Anything that tended to bring capital punishment into bad odour would. The Committee heard evidence of how some executioners had been known to hold levees in public houses in which they regaled their fellow guests with stories of the executions, displayed their apparatus, and even upon occasion sold portions of the rope.[30] They were generally a 'low class of men prone to take stimulants'. On the other hand, how many men of character would want such a job? Indeed, the Committee knew that men with families would not be employed on such work 'since the consequences might be very injurious to any children'.[31] Marwood had been frequently drunk in the latter part of his career, and Binns was once drunk during a hanging. Both were dismissed.[32] As a result of such behaviour the Home Secretary made the suggestion to Sheriffs and the Prison Commissioners that from now on executioners should reside in the prison itself on the eve of the execution and that the amount of drink they be allowed should be strictly rationed to one pint of ale at dinner and supper, and a quarter pint of spirit.

Although he was exonerated before the Committee, Berry, about whose conduct rumours had already been circulating, soon fell from grace. His Home Office file is enormous and details the many transgressions that he committed. These included swearing, holding public house 'levees', accepting bribes to take unauthorized persons into the prison to act as his 'assistants', and 'generally acting in a manner calculated to discredit capital punishment'.[33] Eventually in 1891, after the near decapitation of Conway at Kirkdale Gaol, Liverpool, Berry was dropped from the official list and never employed again, though he regularly wrote appealing for work right up until 1902.[34] During that period, and even after his death, he caused his erstwhile employers much embarrassment by alleging that under a Roman Catholic Home Secretary and Lord Chief Justice reprieves were more readily granted to those of their own confession than to Anglicans, and by fabricating the claim that he had resigned after discovering that he had hanged two innocent men. The lengths that the usually reticent Home Office went to rectify this mis-statement are an indication of the concern they felt that the public might believe that innocent men had died.[35]

As a result of Berry's indecorous behaviour at Kidderminster in 1889 when he gave lectures in public houses on 'Morality' and 'Phrenology' and referred to those whom he had recently executed, the Home Office was petitioned by the local Mayor and Visiting Justices and by the Grand Jury of Worcester to the effect that public executioners should be placed under the direct control of the Secretary of State. Questions were asked in Parliament. There was much discussion about how best to proceed. Should the Home Office take over all aspects of the execution, including the provision of the hangman, from the Sheriff, whose responsibility to execute the death sentence it was, or should responsibility be left with him? It was decided that potential hangmen would all be interviewed, and successful applicants trained, by the Home Office. As death sentences were passed so the Sheriffs would be notified that so-and-so was available and recommended, but the final decision as to whom to employ would remain a local one. Records on each executioner would be held at the Home Office and Governors would be asked to comment on their deportment at the execution. Those who proved unsatisfactory or whose conduct was in 'any way objectionable so as to cast discredit on him either in connection with his duties or otherwise' would be removed from the list. This compromise would regularize matters, and reduce the risk of unprofessional conduct, without adding to the public responsibilities of the Secretary of State, and without increasing the risk to him of public opprobrium in the event of mistakes.[36] For in spite of all endeavours, the Home Office privately confided, miscarriages would take place 'for experience [had] shown that hanging [was] apt often to fail'. Therefore the most careful provision had to be made ' for it being carried out in the most decorous and efficient manner since repeated miscarriages would certainly strengthen the hands of those who advocate the abolition of capital punishment'.[37]

The morbid curiosity of the crowd was gratified, despite the removal of executions from public view, by those who wished to do so being able to congregate outside the prison on the day of a hanging, and by fulsome newspaper accounts which appeared the day after. Just as in the earlier days of public hangings, ribaldry, obscenity, and blasphemy still at times typified the behaviour of those who waited on the streets for an execution which although out of sight was not out of mind.[38] The paraphernalia of private executions helped the public imagination to find a focus. At the execution of John Conway, a middle-aged child murderer, a crowd of people, numbering quite 2,000, assembled outside the prison to witness the hoisting of the black flag. Soon after seven o'clock the people began to congregate on the waste ground opposite the main entrance of the gaol where a full view of the flagstaff could be had, and by a quarter to eight the crowd had swelled to one of large dimensions, completely filling the wasteland enclosure. The early comers passed the time by discussing Conway's trial in all its phases. A hush came over the crowd when it was observed that someone was untwisting the line of the flagstaff, preparatory to hoisting the black emblem when the signal should be given. The clatter of the voices among the people then went on again until the prison bell began to toll, denoting that the procession of death had begun inside the prison. The crowd 'uttered almost simultaneously "There's the bell", and eagerly waited for the dread signal'. At three minutes to eight the black flag was slowly hoisted 'giving the fact to the world that the death sentence had been meted out to John Conway'. The expressions among the crowd on seeing the signal were numerous, but 'the one chiefly heard was "He's away now" '. The people then rushed to the prison entrance to witness the departure of anyone leaving the gaol, 'gazing with a kind of awe and curiosity at the Under Sheriff and the reporters as they left the building'. Acting Inspector Stowell, Sergeant Cowman, and a large staff of policemen kept order amongst the crowd.[39]

Of the execution itself, reporters, who were present, could be shockingly explicit:

> Fr Bonte, the Roman Catholic Chaplain, celebrated mass with Conway. Members of the press were admitted. Conway wanted to speak, and Berry grudgingly allowed him to after the priest intervened. He was an old man, it was a long drop, and his neck nearly severed. After the execution Fr Bonte read out a statement in which Conway confessed to the crime. All considered Berry had behaved badly to the victim.[40]

Such reporting was endangering the very purpose of private executions. The solemn ritual of the inexorable denunciation of church and state was being reduced to the macabre titillation of the breakfast table. Secrecy

increasingly joined privacy. The entry of the press, allowed for in the Act of
1868 as part of its attempts to reassure the public, was gradually restricted,
1934 being the last year in which a reporter attended an execution.[41] In 1901
the tolling of the bell before, and in 1902 the hoisting of the black flag after
the execution was abolished. Language, too, became increasingly formulaic.
In 1925 the Home Office instructed Governors to keep comment brief and
stereotyped: every hanging from then on 'was carried out expeditiously and
without a hitch'. The camouflage was complete.

These further refinements had the desired effect. Reviewing the position
in 1891, the Howard Association indicated that hanging was being increasingly
restricted to 'homicides of great enormity'. That, coupled with the sequestration of executions which had removed the 'horrible spectacle', and the
many more pressing matters claiming notice, had lessened public concern.[42]
Two years later, it was considered 'inexpedient' to bring the issue again before
Parliament.[43]

A factor which was to have an important underlying bearing on the debate
about capital punishment was the increasing acceptance in the latter half of
the nineteenth century of the critical approach to the scriptures. In 1885 the
English translation of Julius Wellhausen's *Prolegomena to the History of Israel*
was published, a work whose effect on the understanding of the Pentateuch
was to be as profound as that which Darwin's *Origin of the Species* had had on
the creation stories in Genesis in 1859. At the same time the first 'biographies'
of Jesus were being produced. These were novel attempts to treat the man
Jesus of Nazareth as a historical human figure. As the divine authority of the
Old Testament was being called into question so the human Christ was
becoming more dominant. Christians were reminded of what had always been
true in theory if not in practice. Christ was central, the beginning and end of
all interpretation. He and not the Bible was the Word of God, and the biblical
text, especially that of the Old Testament, had to be understood in the critical
light that he shed upon it.[44] To cite Genesis in support of hanging and to rest
the case on that alone was no longer tenable. Although some Parliamentarians
might remain 'antediluvian Conservatives' for many years to come in their
simplistic quotation of the biblical texts, it was much less easy for the churches
to remain so blinkered. In the light of Darwin and Wellhausen an unalloyed
appeal to Genesis was rendered impossible for those church leaders who
wished to maintain their intellectual integrity. From now on, at the episcopal
level at least, the argument over capital punishment had on the whole, with
the exception of the conservative evangelicals,[45] to be conducted in a more
sophisticated and variegated way.

The full effect of these developments was little felt at the time since the
majority of ordinary Christians were not aware of them, and most of the
church, like most of the nation, was still not interested in the case for abolition.
Articles on the subject took a retentionist stance or else admitted exceptions

to total abolition.[46] One such temperate abolitionist was the Revd Harry Jones who wrote two articles for the diversion of the church-going middle classes.[47] Only very occasionally was the possibility that an innocent man might be hanged alluded to. One who, because of his youth, escaped the noose but nonetheless spent several years in prison before his innocence was demonstrated was William Habron, an Irishman convicted on flimsy evidence of the murder of a policeman.[48] His case, however, was considered to be the exception that proved the rule. The authorities nonetheless remained as sensitive on this issue as they did on malpractice in the execution of the sentence of death.

Thanks to Dr Josiah Oldfield, the chairman of the moribund Society for the Abolition of Capital Punishment, around whom agitation on the subject of capital punishment at the beginning of the twentieth century very largely centred, we have a snapshot of influential, and mainly clerical, opinion at the turn of the century. In 1900 he wrote to all the judges, bishops, Free Church leaders, and prison chaplains and governors throughout the United Kingdom asking for their opinion on an experimental suspension of capital punishment.[49] One judge joked that the murderer, not the penalty, 'should be suspended', and only two replied seriously: Mr Justice Grantham, and the former Lord Chief Justice, Lord Russell of Killowen, who was opposed to capital punishment.

He got a greater if no more encouraging response from the Anglican bishops, though he had anticipated better. He knew that 'the exponents of God's will in the early church had spoken with no uncertain voice upon the sanctity of human life, upon the wrongfulness of all violent murders, and upon the great function of the church to convert men's souls before they died, and to make them better rather than to kill them'. He had been further encouraged to approach the bishops by the example of 'the Master withdrawing a woman from the penalty of death which she had incurred by the Judaic law, by the opinions given by the early fathers, by such examples as those of Clement XI, who insisted that penalties should be established in such a way as to tend to improve the moral character of the criminal'. However not a single reply 'took up any other position than that hanging should be perpetuated'. There were no novel arguments put forward. Gloucester, Wakefield, Llandaff, Truro, Rochester, Worcester, and Southwell, agreeing with the secular wisdom on the subject, all believed it to be a unique and necessary deterrent to murder. Only one bishop cited the Old Testament texts as the reason for his support for hanging. The conservative evangelical, Bickersteth of Exeter, the cousin of the former Archdeacon of Buckingham did 'not wish to see the abolition of capital punishment', which was in accordance with Genesis 9.6. George Chadwick, the Bishop of Derry, thought it analogous to killing in war, where death was inflicted on 'deadly enemies of society'. He attacked the abuse of scripture by the abolitionists. In his opinion it could only be maintained 'that

Christianity has interdicted the exercise of this natural right of society to defend itself' by such 'a slavish interpretation of our Lord's words as would forbid a child to call his father "Father", and would oblige a sentinel and jailer to go two miles with a Boer and a felon who pressed them'. Thus literalism, so often the ground of the retentionists, was charged against their opponents. The bishop, in tone reminiscent of John Davis thirty years before, went on to speak of his conviction based on 'observation' but not, one suspects, on experience.

> Of course that which is lawful in the abstract would not be allowable in practice unless it were advantageous also. I can only say that, after a long and interested observation of the facts, I am convinced that there is a brutalized section of society, whence comes the greatest peril of violence to society, which is not as much impressed – not nearly as much impressed – by any other penalty. For my part, I am in favour of capital punishment.

The Anglicans, however, were outdone in their deference to Caesar by the Roman Catholic bishops. Admittedly only two answered, but both gave the same opinion. Leeds saw an increased danger to the community if murderers got life instead of being hanged. In his view capital punishment was supremely deterrent, and he would go back to hanging publicly. Nottingham by no means regarded capital punishment as one which should be inflicted only as a deterrent or in order to prevent a danger to the community. In rare ecumenical consensus he believed that 'the state, as a "power ordained by God" [had] the right and duty to exact punishment, as *punishment*, strictly adequate to the offence'. The adequate punishment for murder was clearly indicated by the Almighty in Genesis 9.6 as death. The approach of death gave every opportunity and incentive to repentance. He was satisfied with the present mode of execution. Experiments would have been 'useless, misleading, and mischievous'. Cardinal Vaughan was also known to favour the retention of the death penalty.

The replies of the Free Churchmen, on the other hand, revealed that not one advocated perpetuating capital punishment. Several did not see their way to abolition, but as Christians they were not satisfied for the situation to remain as it was, and they would gladly hail its abolition the moment it were possible to sweep it away. The Baptist leader, and President of the Christian Socialist League, Dr John Clifford, believed that 'the community would gain in security if society said that human life was too sacred to be taken away by its express act. The progress of civilization has made it possible to at any rate experiment by suspending the penalty for a period.' Dr Newman Hall thought that certainty of conviction and a life sentence was more of a deterrent than the gallows. He would have kept murderers 'alive humanely, while dead socially'. From a Christian perspective, 'if the criminal is sincerely penitent his continued existence is a benefit; if he is not penitent, he is not fit to die'. The Quakers, of course, were resolved to fight to end capital punishment.

Oldfield commented that the division between those church leaders who favoured retention and those who did not was no mere difference of opinion, but sprang from differences in their respective theologies.

> When one contemplates the attitude of the Anglican and Roman Catholic bishops and the attitude of the leaders of the Free Churches, one is struck with the fact that the difference of opinion upon doctrines creates a similar difference of opinion upon humane progress, and one thanks God for 'Dissent'.

The only prison chaplains who replied both advocated capital punishment as the best deterrent, while they confessed that murderers were no worse than other criminals. Every prison governor replied but most said they could not answer without Home Office permission. This was refused. However, Oldfield could reveal that only one favoured capital punishment, and all the others were opposed. One wrote: 'I do not consider hanging a deterrent. As a rule, those who commit murder never think of the penalty.'

Oldfield was obviously very concerned to have clerical support. His Council included several prominent nonconformist clergy,[50] but no Anglican. Once again he tried to win the support of the Archbishop of Canterbury, Randall Davidson, writing to him in fulsome tones asking for a word of guidance to bring before a public meeting on capital punishment:

> It is constantly thrown in the teeth of advocates for the sacredness of human life and advocates for the conversion instead of hanging of those who are spiritually diseased that the bishops are always opposed to progress – in that they fought against the abolition of slavery and in that they persistently voted against the abolition of capital punishment for the theft of 5/– – that I should be glad to be able to reassure them that the bishops of today are guides and helpers to all reformers that make for hope in man's destiny and that they would not exclude the most degraded and most spiritually diseased from the sanctuary of the Church which shields from death all who claim its protection.[51]

He struck a chord, but this merely led to the Archbishop going on the defensive about his episcopal precursors. He replied three days later in a letter marked 'Private'. He admitted to not having studied the subject in depth, but in so far as he had he could at present see no reason to believe that the abolition of capital punishment would be 'other than detrimental to the highest interests of the community'. Nor could its present administration in England 'be regarded as a harsh and thoughtless exhibition of the state's supreme power'. Rather patronizingly he reminded Oldfield that 'many of the wisest, the most thoughtful, and the most Christian of modern philanthropists have been strong opponents of the movement for abolishing capital punishment', though he failed to name any, and he rejected the analogy 'between this question and such reforms as the abolition of slavery'. He took particular exception to the mention of the episcopal opposition to Romilly, since, 'as a matter of fact', a gross injustice had been done to the reputation of bishops in Parliament upon that subject.[52] He concluded by fearing that he could not support abolition, *'although of course I am most anxious that the subject should be quietly and temperately considered in all its bearings and it is, I agree, quite possible that some day a different view may be taken of what is necessary in the public interest'.*[53] To his horror *The Tribune* reported that Oldfield had read out the italicized passage at the public meeting. Again the Archbishop wrote rebuking him for this breach of confidentiality and for quoting him only in part.[54] Oldfield apologized but defended himself by saying he had been misrepresented by the press.

The Lambeth archives before the First World War provide merely these snippets of an archbishop who is not particularly interested in the subject, except where he thinks his predecessors have been criticized, the reputation of the bench imputed, and his own views misrepresented. Propriety was very important to Davidson as was indicated the only time in which his signature was sought for a petition of reprieve. Neither he nor the then Dean of Durham, Hensley Henson, would support the efforts to save Roger Casement, the Irishman condemned for treason, once they had discovered that he had been a practising and promiscuous homosexual.[55] In the hanging debate, as in so many other areas of social reform, the stricture is justified that 'it is clear, if not edifying, that Davidson gained much of his prestige with the statesmen by refusing to join most of the agitations which attempted to bring moral pressure on them'.[56]

These were fallow years indeed for the reformers. Their influence in, and the interest of, Parliament was at its nadir. Solitary and increasingly bizarre pamphlets issued by the Society for the Abolition of Capital Punishment, such as one suggesting that the vengeful spirits of unrepentant murderers dispatched by the hangman would seek to frequent their old haunts and incite others to sin, did nothing to enhance its repute, despite the attribution of this argument to 'the Spirit of a high class Hindu in conversation with a well-known Anglican cleric'.[57] By the outbreak of the First World War the Society had faded away.

Even the Children Act of 1908, which prohibited capital punishment for those under sixteen years of age, was merely making statutory what since 1887 had become the standard practice of reprieving all those under eighteen. No further progress was to be made until the 1920s. One campaigner wrote that whereas a few years before she had 'believed that there was a strong and growing popular feeling in favour of the abolition of capital punishment', now she was less confident that this was so. Nonetheless she would labour on, seeing the task ahead as being the arduous one of preparing the ground and sowing the seed 'in anticipation of the day when we shall see the general apathy disperse and our country freed from the shame of a state-paid executioner'.[58]

9   Sentiment and Salvation

The Conversion of the Condemned in Late Victorian and Edwardian England

And he of swollen purple throat,
   And the stark and staring eyes,
Waits for the holy hands that took
   The thief to Paradise;
And a broken and a contrite heart
   The Lord will not despise.
Oscar Wilde[1]

It is all very pretty and sentimental for a chaplain to say 'he's in Glory now' when the drop falls, but it means precisely nothing, and the large majority of padres have too much wisdom to make an assertion which is tantamount to the declaration that the crime of murder is punished with a sentence of eternal bliss.
Major Wallace Blake[2]

Apathy or indifference to what was at most a peripheral issue; acceptance of a procedure which if not always decent and dignified was at least out of sight behind closed doors; and outright support for capital punishment as the just desert for certain offences: all these factors help to explain the attitude of clergy and bishops to the death penalty in the second half of the nineteenth century and the beginning of the twentieth. One other motive was equally potent: the evangelical opportunity, the unique setting that hanging provided for the sacrament of God's grace. It was precisely among the most religious clergy, not the most arrogant or the least sensitive, both Evangelical and Anglo-Catholic, that the opportunities afforded by the imminence of death were so valued, and for decades were to cloud the issue of the morality of the death penalty.

Opinion was divided as to the merits or demerits of hanging in this respect.[3] Confession was seen as a prerequisite of regeneration. To die with a lie on your lips was unthinkable. It was also unthinkable that an innocent man might be hanged. Repentance was sometimes signified by no more than a brief declaration of guilt extracted by the chaplain on the scaffold. Sir Samuel Romilly's fourth son, Henry, vainly attempted to sap the credentials of such a traditional function.[4] Was a last minute repentance, he asked, sufficient to atone for a life of crime?

> Why should a minister of the Gospel be placed by the law in such a position as to be compelled publicly to use language which implies the possibility of a life of immorality, irreligion, and crime of the very worst kind, being atoned for, in the eyes of a perfectly wise and just judge, by half a dozen words of supplication forced from him by the urgent entreaties of a clergyman during the one or two minutes immediately preceding his being suddenly deprived of life?

The injury was two-fold: to society by suggesting to the public mind that the perpetration of a great crime was by no means an insurmountable bar to happiness in a future life; to the criminal by suggesting to him 'hopes of pardon in another world, on grounds which, judged by the fundamental doctrines of our religion, we can scarcely deny to be delusive, at the same time that we deprive him of the opportunity of establishing that hope on grounds which, judged by the same doctrines, we believe to be effectual'. A death-bed repentance was 'immeasurably less likely to avail you than a repentance proved by years of amended life and sorrow for past sin'.

This was rather to caricature the contemporary role of the clergy in the care of the condemned. The ministrations of chaplains and others had always been intrinsic to the whole business of executions, but slowly, with the passing of the years, and especially after the abolition of public hangings, the emphasis had been changing. As a result of the Capital Punishment Amendment Act (1868) the Secretary of State was empowered to make rules about the conduct of executions, and the first such, in August of that year, increased the period of time between the capital sentence and its execution from a matter of days to several weeks. Less and less did chaplains see their primary job as securing a confession of guilt on the brink of the drop, but rather a deep-rooted repentance, schooled over time. Scaffold confessions yielded to condemned cell confirmations. Increasingly chaplains would spend many hours alone with the prisoners under sentence of death, nurturing whatever flicker of faith they had, and nursing them to accept their fate with calm confidence. Their caring work was undoubtedly responsible for the resigned manner in which so many in the end went to their deaths, making things easier for the prisoners but also for their killers. Such a pastoral role had its allure, but the danger attendant on it was that it would cloud the issue of abolition.

For most people the argument of Henry Romilly could be dismissed when such living saints as Edward King, Bishop of Lincoln, refuted it by his practice. The bishop spent much time counselling the condemned in Lincoln Castle Gaol, but never once did he condemn the punishment. The records of his involvement are moving and show how powerful and effective such ministry could be; they also reveal complete satisfaction with the existence of the death penalty. His interest in those awaiting execution began in 1887 with an invitation from a hard-pressed prison chaplain for the bishop to visit a young fisherman from Grimsby who had deliberately killed his lover, though under strong provocation. King took the case into his own hands, visiting him daily. He was worried since the youth seemed to be 'as ignorant as a South Sea Islander, knowing nothing of God or sin, or of right and wrong'. Teaching from the story of the Prodigal Son, the bishop instructed him in the unseen realities of life and death, sin and forgiveness. He confirmed him, heard his confession, and prepared him for holy communion. The youth asked him to sign a petition of commutation. King was reluctant to comply with the request. He thought the sentence just and that it was all-important not to let the youth think hardly of the law.

> He must not think that it is unjust. He must be made to know that he has incurred the just punishment for an awful crime. Yet the supreme object is to save his soul, and can I expect him to listen to my ministrations if I refuse to attempt to save his life?

Therefore, it was on the grounds of expediency that he wrote to the trial judge who affirmed that it was appropriate for him to do this. The petition was turned down.

On the morning of the execution, King celebrated holy communion but before the service said 'let us say a little prayer to consecrate the hand which did the sad deed, before it holds the body of the Lord'. He accompanied the boy to the scaffold, grateful to have been with 'the poor dear man'. The bishop thought him 'most beautiful'; and 'his last (and first) communion on Sunday morning put [him] to shame'. He felt 'quite unworthy of him'. And then, according to the hagiographer, the double miracle: a warder, a nominal Roman Catholic, seeing the earnestness of King's ministrations, became an Anglican, and a relative of the victim likewise found God.[5]

From that time on the bishop made it a practice to visit prisoners in the condemned cell and to spend long periods with them in private devotion. He missed on one occasion only, and that owing to ill-health.[6] Whenever he passed by the gaol he was silent and took off his hat.[7] In a letter to Archdeacon Stow, chaplain of Lincoln Gaol, who had asked him to see an impenitent murderer, King wrote that when confronted with such a life so 'very dead to spiritual things, perhaps this sharp knife is the only pruning that could save the little life that remains from complete death'.[8] O happy noose!

King's experiences could be shadowed by that of other bishops and chaplains. In November 1893, Edward Henry Bickersteth, Bishop of Exeter, visited a youth who had killed his girlfriend out of jealousy. The boy had been receiving twice daily visits from the chaplain, John Pitkin, and had shown a gratifying interest in religion. The bishop instructed and confirmed him in prison a few days before his execution. On the day itself the youth took leave of Pitkin in 'a very affectionate manner'. After the execution the mother wrote to thank him and to inquire if she could lay a wreath on the body. He replied that her son was truly penitent and felt obliged to remind her that 'William's death was not unjust, and that he felt he merited it at the hands of his country in atonement for his guilt'. Her request to visit the grave, while understandable, was contrary to the prison regulations.⁹ Pitkin averred that condemned prisoners especially valued the chaplain's visits. Very often, he noted, the spiritual progress such prisoners made was 'marvellous', and this 'extra-ordinary development in a short time' showed 'how vastly different their lives might have been if they had, in earlier years, given themselves to the principles of moral and religious instruction'.

An example of this transformation given by the Revd J. Stott, chaplain of Maidstone, was that of George Smith, the 'Brides in the Bath' multiple murderer who was executed on 13 August 1915. At first Smith disavowed all religion and contemptuously handed the chaplain the Bible and Prayer Book which, according to rule, had been placed in his cell. This bravura shortly evaporated and soon he attended every evening the simple service conducted for his benefit. He took to reading the scriptures, and asked to be confirmed and to receive the sacrament before his death. Archbishop Davidson was consulted, and he sent his suffragan Bishop of Maidstone to talk to Smith and ultimately confirm him. On the eve of his execution several clergy came to visit him. While the chaplain and bishop believed in the sincerity of his conversion, one of the warders referred to it as a 'religious dodge'.¹⁰ A fellow inmate relates that he was both craven and cowardly and had to be dragged from his cell to the scaffold beside the main gate.¹¹

The experience of the condemned cell was able, according to one account, to convert an abolitionist into an advocate of capital punishment. Bishop Seaton of Wakefield, when appointed vicar of Armley in 1905, as part of his duties had to minister to condemned men in Leeds Gaol. We are told that he began that task in full belief that the death penalty was contrary to Christian principles 'but his experience led him quite definitely to the opposite view which he continued to hold for the rest of his life'. He had found that in a surprisingly large number of cases the convicted men 'recognized the justice and appropriateness of their sentence, and were in many cases unwilling to live'.¹²

Just as in earlier times, Christians outside the walls took an eager interest in the spiritual welfare of prisoners sentenced to death. Pitkin complained of those who involved themselves with the condemned and sent in 'books and large bundles of tracts and letters it would take three months to read if two-three hours daily were devoted to them to poor men awaiting execution, who had perhaps only eight or ten days to live'.¹³ When John Lee continued to profess his innocence as he awaited execution, he received a vast correspondence from all parts of the country, urging 'the dear brother' to confess.

Several clergymen came to prison on the Saturday before the execution to see Lee, but on the advice of the governor he saw only one. Such a congregation of clerics around one convict was an unnecessary concentration of resources, especially since Pitkin himself was an able and compassionate pastor, being 'much affected' as he accompanied Lee to the drop. Lee's own account is the only one we have which testifies to the steadfastness of the chaplain in what was always a most traumatic experience, since 'thrice-hanged' Lee survived three botched attempts to hang him and was afterwards reprieved. 'The chaplain', he observed, 'seemed to be on the verge of collapse.'[14]

Evangelical piety stretched even to the hangman. In contrast to their mainly brutish eighteenth-century predecessors, later Victorian executioners, though often of indifferent character, tended to display a cloying religiosity. Calcraft went to church regularly, and received regular visits from the vicar of Hoxton church prior to his death. Another hangman informed a chaplain that he felt he was 'helping the Lord by removing the weeds from God's garden'.[15] Some even portrayed themselves as having a vocation to minister to the condemned. Contemporary with Pitkin was John Berry, a Wesleyan Methodist, who between 1884 and 1891 hanged over a hundred people. He liked to meet his victim beforehand to comfort and reassure where he thought him penitent. On one occasion, finding John Hill, who had murdered a young girl, not merely unrepentant but boasting and laughing in his face, Berry warned him:

> Wait until morning when you stand on the edge of doom with the rope round your neck. If I had my way I would not use a rope but kill you like a beast of the field with a hammer.

Berry claimed that this admonition terrified the recipient of it into a more suitable frame of mind for meeting his Maker and he ended as truly penitent as his type of man could ever be. His co-defendant, John Williams, was worried about what he would suffer. Berry asked, 'Why should I bother if you suffer? Did you worry about what the girl suffered.' But, nonetheless, he felt he could 'be saved' and urged him to prayer. This had the desired effect and Berry recalls that he felt a certain exultation, that he, the despised hangman, had been used as an instrument of grace.

He always prayed before an execution and was inclined to usurp the role of the chaplain. At this execution, as at some others, Berry brushed with the clergyman concerned. He had his hand on the lever when the cleric asked for another word. Berry refused him with 'no, you're too late' and pulled the lever.[16] The amateur pastor in the cell was the professional technician on the scaffold.

Ever careful of the soul of the felon he was about to dispatch, Berry was wont to send the chaplain a copy of a sentimental poem entitled 'Lines for One under Sentence of Death' to use for the edification of his charge. This practice continued until a chaplain complained to the governor who reminded

Berry that the soul of the prisoner was the chaplain's concern.[17] He stopped sending the poems but remained bitter against chaplains who, he thought, treated him stand-offishly. He found it extraordinary that they refused to discuss with him the character or behaviour of the prisoner.

Although long after his resignation he was 'born again' at a Free Church Mission, and as a result became an abolitionist, during his period of service he put great weight on the scriptural injunctions and argued that the abolition of capital punishment would be a defiance of the divine command. After his conversion, however, he spoke with more understanding on the lines that murders were the reflection of the sins of society which were not absolved by a second killing. In 1913, just before he died, he wrote, 'my experiences have convinced me we shall never be a civilized nation while executions are carried out in prison'.[18] These 'confessions' must, however, be treated with some scepticism given the disreputable conduct that led to his being dropped in 1891 from the post of executioner, his attempts to get reinstated even as late as 1902, and his consequent grudge against the Home Office.

Important as the pastoral care of the condemned was, it put chaplains under a terrible emotional strain each time a man with whom they had grown intimate was killed. There was no chapel on the day of a hanging since

> The Chaplain's heart is far too sick,
>   Or his face is far too wan,
> Or there is that written in his eyes
>   Which none should look upon.[19]

One witness recalled that he would never forget 'the face of the wretched young chaplain who found himself face to face with his first encounter with sudden death, and who, poor soul, had over-primed himself with stimulant'.[20] The chaplain of Liverpool Gaol, a sincere, sensitive man, 'for days before an execution went about with pain on his face and in his bearing'.[21] Not surprisingly, given what he had witnessed, Pitkin testified that it was a great relief to the prison staff when the lever was pulled and it was all over 'for a state of anxiety and sadness nearly always pervades the prison when an execution takes place'. On another occasion 'the falling of the drop, the disappearance of the poor criminal into the pit with his neck broken' quite unnerved him. He 'was obliged to stand quite close to the pit . . . and was really afraid that [his] will-power would hardly keep [him] from falling into the pit [him]self'.[22] One of his colleagues, the chaplain of Dartmoor, not a hanging gaol, was glad to escape this ordeal during his long term of prison experience. He had gathered from Pitkin that 'nothing so upsets the nerves of all the officials as the case of men under sentence of death, the most unconcerned apparently being the condemned man himself'. Pitkin, who had attended more executions than any other man in the kingdom except the executioner, told him that 'it was always the most upsetting experience of his life, and one that was never got over by its frequency'. The only cure was a change of scene, and 'whenever possible he always made a point of getting away after the horror of an execution to some fresh scene abroad . . . even with this change it took him a week to ten days to rally and become his normal self'.[23]

Again not a word opposing it. Occasionally, to other members of staff, chaplains would admit to doubts about the morality of capital punishment.[24] One confessed to the Governor of Pentonville that he 'felt a bit of a murderer' himself.[25] Others, such as the Revd J. W. Horsley, who in the 1880s had all the murder remands in Middlesex and Surrey under his care, advocated degrees of murder.[26]

The evidence of callous or unsympathetic behaviour on the part of chaplains is very slight. The 1921 Labour Party Prison Enquiry recounted an unattributed story of 'a penitent negro' who had killed his girlfriend and handed himself in to the police. After conviction the chaplain saw him daily but 'was cruelly inhumane'. He used to order the man to kneel down, 'gabble off' some prayers, curtly ask if he had anything to say and then depart. His substitute was entirely different, being 'brotherly and humane and quite melted the negro, addressing him by his Christian name'. It was the chaplain himself, however, who attended the execution. Immediately the man was dead the chaplain turned to the warder and said, 'Well, we have got rid of a rare rascal there.' The warder could restrain himself no longer and told him that 'the negro was a gentleman and he had treated him scandalously'.[27] Sometimes prisoners recalled chaplains being so lacking in sympathy or so insensitive as to preach in the presence of the condemned sermons on the text 'the wages of sin is death'.[28]

Abolitionists continued to express concern about the involvement of chaplains in the whole hanging process. The extraction of confessions, and the insensitive ritual were particularly criticized. Occasionally killers would willingly tell all to the chaplain. Charles Pease, for instance, under sentence of death, admitted to another murder he had committed and for which an innocent youth was serving a life sentence.[29] As late as the turn of the century, however, the occasional chaplain was still prepared to take quite desperate measures to secure a confession from a reluctant subject. In Chelmsford Prison in 1903, just as the executioner was going to pull the lever and drop the Moat Farm Murderer, Samuel Dougal, the chaplain, the Revd J. W. Blakemore, stopped him and asked the hooded prisoner whether he was guilty or not. Three times he asked without an answer. Finally the man muttered 'guilty' and was dropped. The chaplain explained his conduct as due to the 'intense spiritual anxiety' he felt for Dougal. He had prayed with him during the previous quarter of an hour, and not knowing what else to do 'under strong impulse, and quite on the inspiration of the moment' he made 'the strong appeal on the scaffold'.[30] For this he was criticized in the press and the incident was raised in Parliament. Some MPs pointed out the danger that even an innocent man, anxious to get it over might so reply; others argued that it was a clergyman's duty to save a man's soul even if he suffered. The issue was ostensibly resolved by the Home Secretary giving an assurance that instructions to chaplains would prevent a future recurrence.[31] From then on chaplains were to be concerned not with questions of guilt or innocence, nor with public confessions, but solely with preparing the condemned person to meet his end with courage and dignity.

The edict took time to gain universal acceptance, at least in Scotland. Among the few papers relating to hanging in Archbishop Davidson's pre-war correspondence is a letter from Carl Heath, the Quaker Secretary of the Society for the Abolition of Capital Punishment, asking for the Archbishop's opinion on the issue of these gallows' confessions, an issue about which they were going to protest. Although admitting that *private* confession to a priest might well be helpful to the condemned in some cases, it was, he told Davidson, strongly objectionable that such confessions should be publicly demanded and that the condemned should be pursued with appeals to the last moment as had recently been sensationally reported in the press in connexion with an execution at Inverness.[32] The Archbishop replied by return that he could not recall of any complaint ever being made to him nor did he know of the Inverness case to which Heath had referred, where in any event the chaplain would be a Presbyterian and so not under his jurisdiction. He remained non-committal on the issue. If such a case came before him he would consider it carefully upon its merits and he would always be ready to offer advice to prison chaplains.

The Archbishop's assistance was again sought over the use of the burial sentences at hangings. A persistent campaigner, J. W. Wenham, was seeking its discontinuance since the priest was conducting not a corpse to the grave but a living man to the gallows. The Archbishop, having consulted the chaplain of Maidstone Prison, was satisfied that the words used, as laid down in the 'Form of Service to be used at an Execution' issued in 1897 under the authority of G. P. Merrick, the Chaplain Inspector, were entirely appropriate. Wenham was bitterly disappointed that the Archbishop would not provide the necessary lead and said that he would lobby MPs and endeavour 'to get lay and secular effort to do what I strongly held to be the duty of the church to help to do'.[33] In his appeal to secular and lay support, though described by civil servants as 'a crank', he was more successful since the Form of Service was withdrawn in 1927 and an instruction issued to prison chaplains that audible prayers should be said only at the prisoner's request and that they should never be from the burial service.[34] A few months later, again after ponderous Home Office discussion, it was decided that chaplains need not lead the dying man to his fate but could instead accompany him or follow up the procession.[35]

Such small victories had to sustain the abolitionists through years of snail-slow progress.

10 Great Expectations

The Post-War Decade: 1919–1929

Then within a prison yard
Faces fixed and stern and hard.

Ah! it is the gallows-tree
Breath of Christian charity
Blow, and sweep it from the earth.
Henry Wadsworth Longfellow[1]

While the First World War inspired considerable public indignation over the imposition of the death penalty for military offences, it temporarily killed all agitation for its abolition under civil law. With the life of the nation at stake and with millions of young men being mown down on the battlefield it could hardly have been otherwise. As the war receded, and as the 1920s progressed public interest in the subject of capital punishment, and the energy of activists, revived.

The year 1921 saw the amalgamation of the Howard Association and the Penal Reform League to form the Howard League for Penal Reform. Neither of the older organizations had much money and they probably had less than 500 members between them. Neither had been concerned solely with abolition, and the new League itself was at first doubtful about the attitude of its members. Nor did it wish to jeopardize its close links with the Home Office and prison officials, and its wider penal reform work, by too close an identification with a fringe concern or with 'cranks'. There was nothing about abolition in its initial statement of policy. Similarly a Labour Party report left aside the question of the justifiability and expediency of capital punishment while recommending that if the practice were to continue it should no longer happen within prisons where it degraded the whole prison population.[2]

Attention began to focus on abolition the following year when an eighteen-year-old boy, Henry Jacoby, was hanged despite a jury recommendation for mercy, while the better-connected, more vicious, but certifiably insane Ronald True was reprieved. The passing of the Infanticide Act, removing this offence from the category of murder in recognition that no woman had been executed for the killing of her baby since 1849, led to a revival of interest in capital punishment within Parliament, but permission for an abolition bill was withheld in the Commons by 234 votes to 86.

In January 1923 Edith Thompson was hanged when the Home Secretary, William Bridgeman, broke with seventeen years of tradition and refused a reprieve. Her lover, Freddy Bywaters, had killed her husband. Her letters to Bywaters suggested some conspiracy, but many thought then, as they do now, that she was being hanged for adultery as much as for murder. Her execution was seen 'to have been without other than merely legal justification; and to have been the result of a kind of frozen moral inertia which seized those whose business and responsibility it should have been to avoid an act that . . . was in the considered judgment of sober public opinion as essentially unjust as it was inexpedient'.[3] Rumours soon circulated that her 'insides had fallen out' during the execution, and it is possible she had miscarried.[4] Her death caused considerable concern, as a direct result of which the Howard League took a referendum of its members, almost three-quarters of whom wanted rid of capital punishment altogether.[5]

Capital punishment was still an issue alien to most of the Christian churches who were not yet able to ask large questions of the new society which was emerging. The First World War had revealed the churches as shallow. Faced with the greatest ethical challenge of their history they had provided pastors at the Front, but no prophets at home. The Free Churches withdrew further into themselves. Evil was personal rather than corporate. Morality was to do with individual sin, not social. The avoidance of alcohol, dancing and gambling were the ethical imperatives paramount to the Methodists; the avoidance of hell and the assurance of personal salvation were the farthest boundaries of their doctrine.[6] The Church of England remained the church of Empire and immersed itself in triumphalism. Its leaders still reflected in their politics and clubs the old cosy consensus between church and state. In 1918 Archbishop Davidson refused to intercede for a conciliatory peace, and even failed to criticize the anti-German hatred expressed on the hustings. On Advent Sunday the Bishop of London, Arthur Foley Winnington-Ingram, preached on the necessity of stern punishment 'to deter the wrongdoer and maintain the moral standards of the world'.[7] He was talking about the Germans, but what he said would apply with equal force to native criminals. Moral issues such as the continuation of the death penalty were peripheral, and few in the church hierarchy wished to challenge the settled order.

A rare and rather ghoulish contribution to the debate was made by the Very Revd William Inge, the 'Gloomy Dean', in his weekly newspaper column. A noted Anglican apologist and polemicist, as Dean of St Pauls he was also an 'Establishment' figure who moved in the same circles as senior politicians and judges. Although he styled himself a liberal, he was well-known for his outspoken – even bitter – attacks on the new-found socialism that motivated some of the younger church leaders.[8] In an article for the *Evening Standard* he offered a brief ethical contribution to the issue of capital punishment. He began by assenting to the old position that there was 'nothing immoral or unreasonable in regarding the criminal law as the instrument of the outraged conscience of the nation'. In his view it was 'incompatible with Christianity to hold that God had no wrath and did not punish retributively'.[9] However, estimating moral culpability was a difficult business for mere human beings. The term 'murderer' did not define a man. Some killers were not without virtue; others were not fully responsible for their actions.[10] The mandatory death penalty for murder should be abolished.

On the other hand, there were criminals who were worse than many murderers and they too should be liable to a discretionary death sentence. Inge here showed the influence of the neo-Darwinian eugenics movement of which he was a leading spokesman. Eugenicists argued that criminals were constitutionally deficient in the evolutionary scheme and would ultimately be rendered extinct. After 1900 they sought to purge the race of genetic impurities by, amongst other measures, the sterilization, incapacitation, and even elimination of criminal incorrigibles.[11] When Lady Margaret Professor of Divinity at Cambridge, Inge justified this policy on the theological ground that since human beings had been allowed to know the 'divine' laws of heredity it was in order that they might put them to use.[12] Later he even went so far as to call eugenics a religion and equate it with Christianity.[13]

Thus he was not entirely alone in arguing that the state had the right to protect itself against its enemies, and to take the life of a criminal if it were 'fairly certain' that he was 'irredeemable', and that 'he must be, as long as he lives, a pest and a danger to his fellow-citizens'. The infliction of death should never follow automatically upon conviction; it should be decided by careful investigation and observation of the character and tendencies of the convict, the crucial question being whether he was curable or not. 'Experts', it seems, were not subject to the frailties of 'mere humans' noted above: according to Inge's prescription, potential incorrigibles should be detained for a year or more, putting them under 'moral and religious discipline supervised by experts in morbid psychology' who would, in some cases, be able to certify that they were apparently 'cured and fit to be at large'. But there were some habitual criminals, not murderers, whom it would be much better to 'put out of the way'.

Hanging, however, was macabre and degrading, and so a better way of execution should be considered: one that would not expose 'the criminal to any unnecessary disgrace'. The criminal ought to be 'humanely extinguished in a lethal chamber with as little publicity as possible'. It should not be a punishment 'any more than the killing of a mad dog [was] a punishment', nor should it involve 'any moral judgment upon the character as apart from his actions'.[14] Humane extinction whereby the morally neutral rejects of creation were put down should, in the view of the Dean, replace the death penalty which imposed the ultimate punishment on the worst offender. A scientific had replaced a moral universe.

Another eminent Anglican, on the opposite side of the spectrum from Inge, and whose politics had been publicly deplored by him, was also about to make his first contribution to the debate. At an abolitionist meeting in Manchester, two weeks after the execution of Edith Thompson, the chairman, the Revd Canon Dorrity, read out a letter from Dr William Temple, then Bishop of Manchester. A radical intellectual, Temple managed throughout his life to criticize sharply the social elite (of which he was a prominent member) and to be applauded by it. He had been simultaneously Headmaster of Repton School and President of the Workers' Education Association. He had always, even in childhood, emotionally identified with the under-dog, and since 1918 he had been a member of the Labour Party. His letter revealed that he believed that the state had the right to kill its own citizens, but only in the most exceptional circumstances. As an example he gave the 'outbreak of murder on such a scale as to create a general sense of insecurity of life', which would legitimate hanging as an emergency measure. He thought that capital punishment was probably 'slightly more effective as a deterrent in the moment of temptation than any other form of penalty'. But for Temple, harking back to an old argument of Dickens, this was more than outweighed by the dangerous glamour that the existence of capital punishment had 'for unbalanced minds working as a persuasive suggestion'. It added an enticing thrill to crime. Furthermore, he thought that Bentham was certainly right in his contention that callousness in the state produced callousness in the citizens and so 'another influence is set going by the existence of capital punishment tending to undermine belief in the sanctity of life which that penalty exists to safeguard'. It also created 'a peculiarly vicious sort of sympathy with criminals'. Thus on balance Temple concluded that 'abolition would be found to result in fewer murders in the long run'. However, so long as death remained the penalty for murder, Temple held that it should be inflicted on all those who are found guilty of murder, since 'nothing does so much harm as to prescribe a severe penalty and then in practice inflict a lighter one'.[15]

The Manchester Guardian, commenting on the Bishop's statement, correctly observed that the real question for him was one of expediency, and the greatest objection to capital punishment as presently practised was that its grim details 'surround the criminal with an unholy interest, if not a glamour, which is so inexpedient that it deserves to be described as wholly evil'. Disdainfully distancing itself from its step-brothers in the gutter it feared that 'assisted by some unscrupulous sections of the press our deterrent [was] in danger of becoming a debauch'. The pillorying of condemned murderers in the newspapers was to the early twentieth century what gibbeting them had been to the early nineteenth.

Thus the leading mind of the Church of England, while not yielding on the issue of the justification of the state's right to take life in its own protection, was opposed to capital punishment in practice or at least as it was then practised. This was a theme that Archbishop Fisher was later to develop as the bulwark of his argument for modified retention. Though so different in temperament and expression, both these bishops shared a similar basis for their differing conclusions.[16] Again it was only the Quakers who consistently and constantly denied outright both Temple's justification of the right of the community to take life and Inge's contention that some individuals were past redemption.[17]

In April 1924 socially concerned Christians of all denominations met in Birmingham under Temple's chairmanship for a Conference on Christian Politics, Economics and Citizenship (COPEC). It was an abortive attempt to set a social and political agenda for the churches. Although the members of the executive committee were divided over the issue of capital punishment, the full conference passed by a large majority a resolution calling for its abolition. Their report pointed out that Christ prayed for his murderers, that his mission was redemptive, and that Christians should try to prevent murders which would render discussion on the penalty superfluous. To cut short a life where there was no opportunity of remedying the mistake or reforming the criminal was, in their opinion, incompatible with Christianity. Redemption was the method of Christ and punishment was only permissible when it served the interests of love.[18]

With the advent of a minority Labour Government under Ramsay MacDonald in January 1924, hopes had been raised that such resolutions would at last be embodied in legislation. Almost all Labour politicians had a religious element – usually a nonconformist one – in their socialism. It was said that the Labour Party owed more to Methodism than to Marxism, and Keir Hardie, its most prominent founding father, had claimed that socialism was 'the embodiment of Christianity in our industrial system'.[19] As a rebuke and warning to the existing denominations which had proved reluctant to criticize the status quo, over fifty Labour churches were established in the 1890s to direct a Christian perspective on the great social issues of the day. Keir Hardie frequently preached in them, and William Temple said of a Labour church service that he had 'never felt so near the real presence of true religion'.[20] Within the orthodox tradition several socialists – including Philip Snowden, the first Labour Chancellor – had been members of the Free Church Socialist League or the Society of Christian Socialists. It was thought likely that this radical Christian background would influence them in power to implement the policies they had hitherto espoused.

To encourage them on this way the Howard League and the Penal Reform Committee of the Friends (set up at the behest of the Yearly meeting in 1920) swung into action. A Bill was prepared, a petition got up, a pamphlet published, and a deputation sent to the Home Secretary, Arthur Henderson.[21] Their reception was lukewarm, and in any case Labour lost office in November of the same year.

The main result of all this activity was to show the need for a central body representing the organizations concerned, and able to conduct a sustained campaign over an extended period to convince the public and Parliament of the ineffectiveness and immorality of the death penalty. The main inspiration behind this move was the young Quaker, Roy Calvert, who organized a Central Consultative Council for the Abolition of Capital Punishment, composed of representatives of ten religious and reform societies. Optimistically anticipating complete abolition within three or four years, this council in turn founded the National Council for the Abolition of the Death Penalty (NCADP) in November 1925. Subscribers to this new body were few but dedicated, and membership never rose above 1200 in its twenty-three year history. The members were of varied political, social, economic, and religious backgrounds. 'Dissenters' were particularly well represented, including the Penal Reform Committee of the Quakers, and the Free Church Council. Temple was one of the honorary Vice Presidents. So too were Canons Adderley and Donaldson of Westminster, and the Dean of Chester.

Calvert became its first secretary from 1925 until his premature death in 1933. He soon proved to be the most able, dynamic and influential abolitionist of his time, combining passionate commitment, moral seriousness and scientific rigour. He never said anything which he could not support with evidence or logic. His research provided the abolitionists with more accurate, more comprehensive, and more convincing statistical material than any their opponents could muster. Thus his work for the National Council and the publication in 1927 of his influential book *Capital Punishment in the Twentieth Century* were major factors leading in the following year to a Private Member's Bill on abolition which was passed by one vote in the Commons but failed to get a third reading. It indicated, however, that Parliamentary support for abolition had increased dramatically in the previous five years. For the first time ever the Commons had voted in favour of complete abolition.

Despite its disappointing first term of office, and the fact that it remained in a minority, the second Labour Government of 1929 again raised abolitionist hopes, but again prematurely. Labour was unprepared for office, and was soon to suffer a failure of moral nerve. Nonetheless the first full debate on capital punishment in this century was instigated by a Labour MP, W. J. Brown. Although practically all the arguments centred on deterrence, miscarriages of justice, and the quest for a viable alternative, there was a tendency on both sides to cite scripture and seek the support of Christian doctrine. Captain Eden quoted the sixth commandment, and three Labour MPs referred to Christianity in their speeches against the death penalty. Mr Clarke appealed to the House as 'a Christian Assembly' to support abolition. Two members who had had considerable contact with murderers put forward a sympathetic picture of many of them, far removed from the tabloid caricature of the psychopath or 'villain', and having established their humanity, went on to pray the gospel in their defence. Mr Lang, a practising Christian, who had attended scores of murder trials, and visited many prisons, informed the Members that prison governors and warders would tell them that they had 'learned to pity and love some of the most extraordinary murderers who have been placed in their charge'. He witheringly depicted 'the whole duty of the chaplain' as to persuade the condemned man that 'it is a much happier thing for him that he should die than that he should live'. For Lang this was a perversion of the gospel. The Opposition had quoted the Old Testament, now he would quote the New. He reminded the House that 'the wisest Teacher of all, who made no legislation and did not enter into politics – I have never made the mistake of calling Him a Socialist – when He had to decide, His decision was that His own precious life might be given in order that the least might have a chance'.[22]

Sitting impatiently throughout the debate on the Conservative backbenches was Viscountess Astor, the first and at that time the only woman MP. Of Irish-American stock, and a recent convert to Christian Science, she had very pronounced views on moral issues. Dressed strikingly in a black coat and skirt, with a tricorn hat and a gardenia in her lapel, she could hardly fail to catch the Speaker's eye. In her forthright manner she rose to inform her male colleagues that the worst crimes – child abuse and rape – were not punished as heavily as murder. And why? Because men made the laws. In her experience, murderers were not the worst men, sometimes they were the best, and everyone who had had anything to do with murderers, as she had, knew that they are not the worst sort of criminals. She explicitly urged the House to pass beyond the Mosaic law and 'think of this in the Christian sense as far as possible'.[23] Reform rather than punishment ought to be the basis of the criminal law. The Christian message was one of hope 'even to the vilest human being that ever lived'. This dynamic ethic had replaced the older punitive tradition. She warned her Honourable Friends that sometimes when 'we stand up for tradition we forget that great saying when our Lord was told the disciples had transgressed the tradition of the Elders and he said "You, by sticking to the traditions of the Elders, transgress the laws of God".'[24]

Irritated by her speech, Rear Admiral Sueter, another Tory backbencher, commented in an ironical aside: 'If we are going to be defended in this Empire by Sermons on the Mount then God help us.' The debate culminated in a compromise: a House of Commons Select Committee on Capital Punishment.

11 This Son of York

William Temple and the Select Committee on Capital Punishment: 1930–1939

The principle which lies at the root is really that reverence for man which recognizes his kinship with God, which perceives the Divine Image within him. It is this which makes human life sacred and herein lies the justification for the dread punishment of death . . . He who forgets that his fellow-man is more than a brute, who ignores his kinship with God, he must be sent away to meet God . . . He must be sent and sent swiftly, before the only tribunal really competent to deal with his case. The Death Penalty is really the assertion of man's kinship with God, his real greatness and absolute value.

Revd J. Trevor Lewis[1]

Surely this is the strangest way to God, to plant scaffolds at the gates of heaven. It is true Christ saved the dying thief on the Cross; but an old divine strikingly said: 'There is one record in the scriptures of a dying repentance that no one may despair, but only one that no one may presume'. And the dying thief's repentance does not justify the Roman crucifixion.

Revd James Barr MP[2]

The House of Commons Select Committee on Capital Punishment consisted, as select committees always do, entirely of MPs in numbers proportionate to their respective party's strength, the chairman being a member of the ruling party. This chairman was the Scots Presbyterian minister, and Labour MP, the Revd James Barr. That a minister of the Christian religion should chair a Commons' committee and that a weighty part of a Commons' report should be on 'scriptural considerations'[3] is indicative of the central part religion played in the history of hanging. It is hard to think of any issue today which would induce a Parliamentary committee to look seriously and in depth at Leviticus and Lactantius. It is hard to think of many MPs today who would be capable of doing so. The Report's religious sections were of course drafted by Barr who was knowledgeable not only about the biblical but also the patristic background. His discussion with one of the witnesses, William Temple, by then Archbishop of York, indicated that he was every bit as thoughtful and well-informed on the subject as the Archbishop himself.

Temple was the only bishop at that time who was really interested in the issue of capital punishment, and equally he was the only one who had given it considerable thought. Others, like Davidson, would voice opinions if pressed, but their correspondence reveals that this was always in response to the initiatives of others, and they had to seek advice on how to reply. They accepted the status quo and considered that the Church of England was playing a responsible role within it by providing chaplains to counsel the condemned. Temple, in this as in so many other areas of social concern, was disturbingly activist. The personal experience of this deeply sensitive man also played its part. When Bishop of Manchester, he had been asked by the chaplain of Strangeways to come down and speak to a young man who was about to be hanged. 'Poor Billy Temple', the chaplain recalled, had entered the condemned cell, 'got hold of the young man's hand, and broke down into tears and had to leave the cell.' The chaplain observed that 'perhaps the murderer was more affected by the obvious affection and love of the bishop than he would have been by any words he had said'.[4]

Since that encounter with the raw end of the issue his views had developed in depth and range, and he had become increasingly active in the campaign for abolition, lending his name to the establishment of the NCADP, and agreeing to speak on its behalf on a number of occasions.

The death penalty, in his view, could not be divorced from the wider issue of punishment in a Christian society. When invited to preach the John Howard Anniversary Sermon in St Martin-in-the-Fields in January 1930 he chose as his subject 'The Ethics of Punishment'. Concentrating first on the biblical basis of the Christian view of punishment he pointed out that not only had the Old Testament law set limits on retaliation, but Christ had gone further and said that there should be no retaliation. It was law versus spirit: throughout his discourse Jesus was 'inculcating not that man should obey certain injunctions imposed upon him by rules and laws, but that he should be possessed by the spirit which is here illustrated'. This for Temple constituted the very essence of the contrast between the new order which Jesus was founding and the existing order based on rules and regulations. The whole aim of Peter's question on the number of times he should forgive was not to be stimulated to forgive his brother seven times but to be freed from the duty to forgive him at all, when he had done so the seven times demanded of him by the law. 'The religion of the spirit' said Temple, required 'forgiveness for evermore because the spirit is love, and love will always want to forgive'.

Forgiveness was at the heart of Jesus' teaching and 'relentless' divine severity was 'not directed against those things towards which men are normally severe: it [was] directed always and only against failure to forgive'. Thus for punishment to be ethical it must be 'the action of the community towards its own criminals . . . not a limited form of individual vengeance'. Once society had repudiated the crime of the offending member by his punishment, when the standard has been upheld, then 'the whole energy of those responsible for the penal system must be bent towards devising treatment most conducive to the effective restoration of the offender according to the standard which has been accepted, to strengthen first the humanity and then the distinctive personality of the criminals whom they desire to restore to the life of full citizenship'.

Turning specifically to the death penalty, he reiterated the arguments he had used in 1923, that capital punishment in effect did the reverse of what its proponents intended in that it devalued the worth of human life rather than protected it. Christians, he concluded, should not oppose the death penalty on the ground that it put the criminal out of existence which (with belief in eternal life) it did not, but on the ground that it rendered impossible 'the effective maintenance of the standard which the law demands of the Christian'. In this way Christians could legitimately assert 'to those who in the past have upheld and enforced this penalty because they believed that it engendered a reverence for human life' that they were not destroying but fulfilling their law. Thus once again Temple opposed capital punishment not on principle but in practice, in that it devalued rather than defended human life, demonstrating that the strongest argument of the retentionists could be turned on its head. This, however, was merely his opinion. He produced no evidence to support his contention that capital punishment had the effect on the popular psyche which he claimed.

For the Select Committee he prepared a paper along these lines, and appeared in person in July 1930. In his written submission he developed more fully his understanding of punishment.[5] Examining the traditional tripartite nature of punishment (retribution, deterrence, and reformation) he pointed out that retribution alone was punishment in the strict sense. The others are not essentially penal elements. In so far as a man was made to suffer that others might be deterred he was 'being used as a means to social welfare, but not necessarily as a moral agent at all'. In so far as he was treated in whatever way might conduce to the improvement of his character, such treatment was medical rather than penal. He was unhappy, however, with the misleading term 'retribution' for the essentially penal element since it suggested 'the radically false view that punishment is a kind of regulated vengeance'.

> Vengeance is the reaction of an offended person to another person who has injured him. Punishment is the reaction of the community through its representative to the law-breaking act of its own member . . .
>
> What morality here requires is that the community should repudiate the evil action and the evil person in so far as he is identified with it. Death or outlawry are only appropriate if the person is wholly evil – as no person ever is.

He considered that the only modern instance of precise retaliation, capital punishment, could not be legitimated by recourse to Genesis since that instance of the law of retaliation obviously came under 'the treatment accorded to that law by Our Lord in St Matthew 5.38–39'.

Society's repudiation of murder could be morally satisfied by imprisonment, thus it was only the question of social and moral expediency that remained. If capital punishment were uniquely deterrent this would be decisive 'since the state has the right to take life to protect something as fundamental as the general security of life', but Temple was convinced that the death penalty was not a specially effective deterrent. The reverse, in fact – it brutalized.

Beyond all such considerations, said Temple, was the Christian emphasis on the reformation of the criminal. This he put very strikingly:

> It is worse to be a murderer than to be murdered . . . The prospect of execution does not infallibly lead to penitence. A Christian society must seek the opportunity of evoking penitence through the remaining years of the criminal's life even if the state does not require the loss of liberty for the whole of his life. Christianity itself requires that punishment, as an effective repudiation of wrong, be inflicted; for the community can only exert a moral influence on the wrong-doer, if it manifestly repudiates his crime. But it calls for such sort of repudiation as does not hinder but rather facilitates its supreme interest of effecting a moral restoration.

Under questioning by the chairman, Temple developed his theme that 'from the Christian point of view vengeance is entirely illegitimate'. The whole spirit of the Sermon on the Mount eschewed vengeance.[6] The law of retaliation in the biblical books was neither static nor uniform. In its earliest form ('an eye for an eye') the law of retaliation was a limitation of vengeance not a licence. Later, by the time of Deuteronomy, it had hardened to the rule 'thine eyes shall not pity but life shall go for life'. It was the earlier form that the New Testament had taken up and taken further.[7]

Asked how he would reply to the argument that the life taken by the murderer was sacred, and the sanctity of life was still further emphasized by the community taking the life of the murderer, Temple replied that the reaction of the individual to the behaviour of the community as a whole was so largely imitative, rather than argumentative, that the effect of the state taking life tended to lower the general conception of the sanctity of life.[8]

He casually dismissed points raised by two retentionist members. Mr Herwald Ramsbotham talked of the murderer cutting off his victim without time for repentance. Temple was not impressed by this sort of evangelical argument. In a world of accidents it was 'quite impossible to believe that eternal destiny depend[ed] in any degree on the frame of mind that you were in' at the particular moment of death 'rather than on the general tenor of your life'.[9] This was also, though he did not say so, an argument against death-sentence-induced repentance and an argument for prison sentences for murderers to provide them with an opportunity to amend the 'general tenor' of their lives.

He then countered the suggestion put forward by Mr Philip Oliver that the early church countenanced death for some offences, by pointing out the obvious, that the case of Ananias and Sapphira, to which the MP had erroneously referred, was not a judicial execution at all.[10]

With that he withdrew. The strength of his testimony was two-fold, deriving from his personal authority as the leading churchman of his day and from the fact that he was arguing on his opponents' own terms. They could not ignore him, or write him off. The weakness of his well-thought-out position was that it rested so heavily on his beliefs and contentions, buttressed by no hard evidence. Since he still allowed the state the right to take life, his unconfirmed views on the effect of capital punishment on the public in general, and the criminal classes in particular, could be dismissed for lack of supporting evidence. Even worse from an abolitionist point of view, they might even one day be proved false. He himself had conceded to Mr Ramsbotham that should there be an overwhelming case that there would be a really serious increase in murder as the result of abolition he would be disposed to retain the death penalty.[11]

No other bishop gave evidence. The papers of Cosmo Gordon Lang, Archbishop of Canterbury from 1928 to 1942, contain no mention of the Select Committee, or indeed of capital punishment.

Prison chaplains were represented before the Committee by the Revd William Cottrell, the Senior Chaplain, and chaplain of Wormwood Scrubs. Since 1906 he had served in several hanging prisons. Despite this experience, however, he was not an impressive witness, sentimental and clichéd in his expression, reiterating old assertions without evidence, and often contradicting himself.

In the interests of the community, he said, punishment should be retained since it was a deterrent especially to the underworld criminal who might otherwise carry a gun and shoot to maim.[12] Yet he later conceded that a long term of imprisonment would also deter the professional criminal equally well.[13] Shifting ground he said that hanging 'might deter the really dastardly, thought-out foul murderer', or 'men of really violent dispositions'. On 'sentimental grounds' alone he opposed the hanging of women.

In all he had witnessed about fifteen executions and a similar number of reprieves, and he had never felt that an innocent man was hanged. All had ultimately confessed.[14] On one occasion he was called in by the Home Secretary because he had doubts as to a man's guilt, and the man was respited.

But distinctions should be made. Some murderers were the 'best of fellows'.[15] Chaplains often got 'very intimate with these men before they die', and he felt that many of them, as so many reprieved murderers had proved to be, would really have been 'quite decent, honest citizens'.[16] Up to a half was his estimate. Many murderers were genuinely penitent as they went to the gallows.

> Sometimes people would imagine that they are – I have heard the word used – callous. In the public newspapers all sorts of things which are absolute lies and falsehoods, that a man went to the gallows more or less in a callous way, and that sort of thing, when the man really has been very, very penitent, and has gone to meet his death as a man should.[17]

In his opinion, if the really penitent were allowed to live they would make decent citizens. He knew of many such cases since he had kept in touch with many reprieved murderers who were 'splendid fellows'.[18]

Although he thought that the time between sentencing and execution (up to fifty days) was too long, the method he considered to be as quick and humane as possible, and 'everybody is exceedingly kind to him as could be'.[19] Despite a phraseology which strikes us as trite and dated, and an attitude which reveals a man of limited ability and little independence of mind, Cottrell at least had actual first-hand experience of murderers, an experience which showed him that it was not the most brutal or least likeable who went to the gallows, but often people of considerable quality of whose lives something could be made.

A more emotional and very different contribution came from the Revd S. R. Glanville Murray, a former chaplain with twenty-eight years experience. Although he had been present at only two executions, one was that of Edith Thompson, an event which disturbed him so greatly that he had suffered a serious nervous breakdown and had been forced to resign the service. He was an out-and-out abolitionist, but he spoke for himself. He did not know if other chaplains shared his views, although he suspected that many did. His arguments echoed those of Temple: capital punishment destroys the reverence for human life; it is contrary to 'the whole spirit of Christianity'; penalties should be based on reformation. As many other Christians with actual experience of criminals had said before, he maintained that murder was not the worst possible crime; rape, incest, blackmail, cruelty were graver moral offences, and had more damaging effects on society: 'there are worse things that can befall the individual than death'.[20]

As for the effect of an execution on the participants, he provided some evidence for Temple's view on the deleterious effects of hanging.

> An execution is a moral shock of such a nature that it is impossible to say what may be its ultimate effects on mind and body. The final scene must always be a haunting and imperishable memory . . . no one can leave the slaughter-house without a deep sense of humiliation, horror, and shame.[21]

As for its deterrent effect, from his experience he knew that a great many persons when they committed offences hardly considered the penalty at all, and 'certainly not in the majority of murder cases' he had had to deal with. The murder was either on the spur of the moment or carefully planned so as to avoid detection.

A dramatic altercation then took place when the Conservative MP, Edward Marjoribanks, asked him for evidence for his claim that capital punishment was 'contrary to the whole Christian faith'. He replied.

– The central doctrine of the Gospel of the Incarnation is forgiveness.

Marjoribanks expressed surprise that he should take such a view.

– I should have thought that the actual infliction of death would not have been of such moment to you, as a minister of the Christian faith, as it would have been to other people, because you regard death as only . . .

He was interrupted

– I do not see, because I happen to be a Christian Minister, why I should regard what I consider judicial murder as less offensive than a layman, rather more so.
– Do you regard the sentence of death as judicial murder?
– Yes I do.
– Then again I am so opposed to you that I cannot continue.[22]

Retentionists might disagree with Temple's conclusions but at least they were arguing from the same premises and on the same ground, which was what made him so effective. As an archbishop he could not be dismissed, but nor could his arguments. Now from a less eminent, but more directly involved witness they got the angry confession of outright opposition which would ultimately allow them to withdraw from the whole process of the Select Committee.[23] Murray's passion sprang from direct experience as was revealed when he was interrogated further on this issue by Major Milner:

– Have you always been of that opinion?
– Since I came to consider the matter seriously. Of course up to the time of my being Chaplain I suppose I had taken the ordinary view of the general public. Then when I had to deal with individual cases, I came to think the matter out, and as one result of my many years experience of prison work I have certainly learnt not to judge and how precarious it is to judge another, and it seemed to me that precisely the same principle referred to the State.
– What was the principle factor in making you come to that view?
– I had at Warwick prison, a lad of about 18 who was charged with murder; he was sentenced to death and subsequently he was reprieved on the ground of masked epilepsy. That was the first case; and when I found out all the facts of the case it made me realize how very precarious the position is.[24]

Such an unequivocal position was also taken up by two members of the

Society of Friends, Carl Heath and Barratt Brown. Although their argument was very different from Temple's, they shared his approach to the exegesis and authority of scripture. It was no law book; it must not be understood literally; nor must any precepts or commands be followed literalistically. It must always be interpreted in 'the spirit of Christ'. They refused to be bound by particular proof texts or even portions of the teaching of Jesus, but claimed that their opposition to the death penalty was a 'fundamental religious principle' gleaned from the 'spirit of Christ' which they believed was still present and inspiring them. Everything had to be ajudged in the light of what they felt 'to be the whole spirit and consequence of his teaching and example'. Consequently, although the Sermon on the Mount could not be taken literally it could be taken seriously and could be observed loyally in the spirit.[25] Where they differed from Temple was in their outright and unconditional opposition to the death penalty. Thus even if the murder rate were to rise as the result of abolition the Quakers would still advocate it.[26]

Twenty-one one of the twenty-nine British witnesses favoured retention, including the large majority of official witnesses. The most influential of all, the Prison Commissioner, Alec Paterson, declared for retention on the 'humanitarian' basis that the only alternative, lengthy imprisonment, under the conditions then pertaining was less humane than capital punishment. His comments were particularly telling since his Christian compassion for prisoners was well-known and utterly sincere. It had been awakened by the case of one of the young men whom he had known in his early days working in the Oxford Settlement in Bermondsey, and who had been sentenced to ten years for killing his wife. Paterson had regularly cycled to Dartmoor Prison to visit him.[27]

Despite this weight of informed opinion, the majority of the Select Committee recommended an experimental abolition for five years, the use of the prerogative to reprieve all murderers until this was brought into effect, and the alternative to be 'the penalty now attached to reprieved murderers, interpreted and administered in the same way as at present'.

The body of the report, of which Barr himself was the sole author, cited both Temple and the Quakers in their understanding of scriptural authority,[28] and concluded that its proposals were 'not in contradiction with Christian faith and doctrine', nor did they 'offer any affront to the Christian conscience'.[29]

The membership was divided on party lines between abolitionists and retentionists. The Conservatives, believing that the report conflicted with the bulk of the evidence, pressed for major revisions. Yet within three months of the conclusion of the taking of evidence in July 1930 they had failed to produce an alternative draft to that prepared by Barr. The Select Committee met in November and again in December, and only then did the dissident members propose an adjournment for two months to give them the opportunity to compose a riposte, threatening to resign if this adjournment were not granted.

Recognizing the perpetually precarious position of the Government, and knowing that the Committee would die with the Government that appointed it, the Labour members, on the casting vote of the chairman, turned down the request. All six Tories walked out.[30] Their defection made it very likely that any change of government would be the death blow to the Committee's recommendations. Even the then Government, while not actually rejecting the report, made no effort to give the Commons an opportunity to debate it. The Home Secretary prevaricated for months.

The Barr Report was criticized in many papers as being sentimental rhetoric,[31] and a poetic apology for abolition. *The Times* disparaged the quality of the Committee's composition and doubted the worth of their conclusions[32] Some Christian newspapers praised their findings, however. The *Church of England Newspaper* hoped that 'the public would become so articulate' that Parliament would be compelled to take action along the lines proposed. *The Christian* said 'the continuance of capital punishment was a practice intolerable in a country even nominally Christian'. The *Baptist Times* said the recommendations would be generally welcome. The *Methodist Recorder* pronounced the report 'a long overdue step in the right direction'.

In an article on the Committee's presentation of the biblical evidence, Mrs Lewis Donaldson, the wife of a canon of Westminster, asked why intelligent people took the Old Testament passages out of context. She drew an apposite analogy with the attitude of those opposed to women's suffrage who appealed to the older and more primitive story of the creation of Eve (Gen. 2.21ff.) but ignored the later egalitarian account where God made female as well as male in his image (Gen. 1.26f.). So with the question of the death penalty. In her opinion the supporters of capital punishment left Christ out and sought to prove their case by appealing to a Jewish law of very early times – 'Whoso sheddeth man's blood by man shall his blood be shed' – or they quoted the later *lex talionis* as if it were the last word for the world. Referring to Oldfield's survey she concluded with regret that 'many of our bishops and clergy' did not know the New Testament, and 'require[d] conversion'.[33]

In April 1931 the Annual Assembly of the Congregational Union in Glasgow, in urging the Government to implement the report, said that it regarded the death penalty as 'an antiquated form of punishment inconsistent with the Christian belief in mercy, redemption, and the value of human personality'. The following month the General Assembly of the Presbyterian Church of England passed a resolution expressing its approval of the recommendations and urging the Government to give effect to them with the least possible delay.

To these entreaties the Government was deaf. John Paton of the NCADP in a series of letters to the Home Secretary from April to June 1931 tried to badger him into keeping faith with his 'moral obligation' at least to let the

House consider the report. He was not to be budged and refused even to meet with a delegation led by Lord Buckmaster.[34]

The Labour Government fell on 24 August and the new Conservative Government refused to grant time for discussion of the report in the House of Commons. The hopes of abolition were extinguished yet again. The glorious summer of promise had gone. The two acts which were passed merely confirmed existing practice,[35] while any attempt to implement the Committee's proposals got nowhere.

Little more of significance occurred during the period up to the Second World War. Pamphleteering continued on the abolitionist side, while the memoirs of prison officials, as had their evidence to the Select Committee, emphasized the necessity, and extolled the benefits, of capital punishment. Colonel Charles Rich, a former governor, a nostalgic conservative, and an ardent evangelical Christian, had no truck with abolitionists. Abolition would be a positive calamity. The law was such that it was 'practically impossible' for an innocent man to be put to death. Degrees of murder would be an improvement, but 'the robber murderer should be killed'. For such as he the death penalty was a positive boon:

> By all means give him ample time to repent and make his peace with his Maker, for if he does not make it in the condemned cell he never will. Indeed, he is likely to be a good deal less fitted to leave the world after a life-time of penal servitude than he would have been at the time of his execution.[36]

Indeed such felons had a better chance than their victim: with apparent approval he recalled that one murderer at Wakefield had expressed sorrow that he would not meet his victim in the next world as she had gone unprepared. Temple's liberal rejection of this notion had left him unmoved.

His colleague, the much-loved humanitarian Captain Clayton, believed that capital punishment had to be kept as a deterrent and as retribution in the case of the 'determined callous killer'. And this despite his physical revulsion to executions, his distaste for the 'calm, cold deprivation of life' so different from the battlefield, and his worry about the statistical evidence from abroad.[37]

The Howard League and the National Council for Abolition of the Death Penalty continued to carry on a propaganda campaign. Joint meetings were organized and conferences were held during which capital punishment was usually the major item on the agenda. The churches in general, and the Church of England in particular, were earmarked for evangelization. In January 1932, a NCADP supporter, Canon Percy Dearmer, urged abolition from the pulpit of Westminster Abbey. The following year there was a public meeting at Caxton Hall presided over by Temple at which the speakers were the President of the Methodist Church, the Revd J. Scott, and the Secretary of the National Free Church Council, the Revd S. W. Hughes. Later that year the National Council of the Evangelical Free Churches passed a motion urging abolition. Public lectures were another way of carrying the campaign into the Christian church. An annual lecture had been established in honour of Roy Calvert who had died in 1933, the theme of which was often the religious objections to capital punishment. Delivering the Memorial Lecture for 1936,[38] James Barr blasted what he considered to be an abuse of the Bible.

> Crude notions of inspiration, and authority, and application of scripture have aided and abetted some of the greatest scandals of the Christian ages. Slavery has been condoned. War has been upheld. Witches have been burned alive.

The following year's lecturer, the minister of South Place Ethical Church,[39] Dr Stanton Coit, declared that Calvert's book 'should be included among the sacred scriptures of English literature'.[40] It was 'a baptism in moral sanity by the Spirit of the most ethical of all the denominations which confess Christ as Master'. He argued that we had transferred our desire for vengeance and blood lust to the state. This was no moral advance but, on the contrary, 'the more sophisticated and veiled vengeance becomes the more insidious are its evil effects upon character'. As the missionary wrote home about the cannibals among whom he worked, ' "their diet is still the same; but they have now learned to use knives and forks", likewise we have learned to use the state and the hangman, and are pleased to think that there is no stain of human blood on our hands'. He too emphasized the importance of the way in which we look at the scriptures. He could not, finally, opt for external authority. Like the Quakers, his views had been fixed beyond argument:

> In the last resort our very interpretation of these various external authorities must rest upon our intuitive moral judgment within ourselves. We cannot prove; we know.

Still the Anglicans were lagging behind the non-conformists and so in 1936 the NCADP offered to supply speakers for deanery chapter meetings, an offer which only half a dozen took up.[41]

Their trump card in the Church of England was, of course, William Temple. They asked him to contribute yet again to the subject by writing what was to prove to be the most noteworthy abolitionist article of the 1930s, published in 1935 in *The Spectator*, republished by the NCADP as a leaflet, and widely distributed by them.[42] In it he attacked the morality of the deterrent argument. In so far as punishment was purely deterrent it treated the criminal as a means to an end. So far as this was true it was non-moral; and 'if there were no other element in any instance of punishment, it would be immoral'. No punishment is 'so purely deterrent as the Death Penalty', and so no punishment is nearer verging on the immoral than that penalty. Under the measured phrases and almost academic exposition of his theme, this was the most provocative he had ever been.

Nor was he convinced by the alleged virtue of capital punishment as being the one shock needed to induce repentance in the most obdurate criminal. Yet although unconvinced by this argument, his refutation did not dismiss it out of hand, as later bishops were to do, as irrelevant:

> Perhaps sometimes it is so. But there does not seem to be much evidence that in practice sentence of death has this tendency. Of course it is only on the hypothesis of immorality that the death penalty can be regarded as reformative at all; and it is doubtful whether many of those who incur it have a sufficiently vivid faith in a future life to accept the sentence of death as a temporary discipline.

It was his last and most trenchant word on the subject, since the coming of war once more put an end to any possibility of change in the law, and his death in 1944 prevented his involvement in the immediate post-war campaign. Had he lived to lead that campaign it is quite possible that hanging would have been abolished in 1948. His successor, Geoffrey Fisher, was to be a Primate of very different temper.

Finally, in 1934, the NCADP, in conjunction with the Howard League, had launched an abolitionist journal, the *Penal Reformer*, under John Paton, Calvert's successor. It ran until the outbreak of the war, giving details of all those who had been hanged, and providing articles from a variety of abolitionists, including Chapman Cohen, the President of the National Secular Society, and Dr Eric Strauss, a leading Roman Catholic layman. The former attributed the strength of retentionist sentiment to the trammels of religion, while the latter confessed 'with shame' that he could think of no Roman Catholic counterparts to William Wilberforce, Elizabeth Fry or Roy Calvert.[43] Several of the articles called for the reintroduction of public executions since if such dirty work were to be done it should be done openly, without any attempt to sanitize the process.[44]

Despite the professionalism and perseverance of the leadership and their efforts at recruitment, membership of the National Council declined to 750, they had to abandon their London offices, and the work continued in the sitting rooms of its members.

It was indicative of the marginalization of the issue that the NCADP came to be overshadowed by the eccentric figure of Mrs Van der Elst, a woman of considerable means and indomitable perseverance who in March 1935 began a campaign of street protests against hanging. She engaged professional publicity agents and proceeded to develop her crusade on sensational lines beloved by the press. First she procured over a 100,000 signatories for her petition urging the reprieve of Brigstock, a condemned murderer. She then persuaded Major Attlee (the future Prime Minister) to present it to Parliament on her behalf. It was to no avail. So, on 2 April, as Brigstock was being hanged in Wandsworth Prison, she hired two aeroplanes to fly over the gaol trailing black flags, while dozens of sandwichboardmen patrolled outside the gates. At 9 am ranks of women knelt in prayer as the men bared their heads. She promised that she would get 'worse and worse'. Two weeks later on the morning of the execution of the twenty-one-year old Percy Anderson her sandwichboardmen and loudspeaker vans were prevented by a strong contingent of police from approaching Wandsworth. Undeterred, Mrs Van der Elst, dressed in full mourning, drove her lemon Rolls Royce through the police cordon to the gates of the prison, going over one officer's foot in the process.[45] On another occasion she stopped a lorry and offered the driver £200 to ram his vehicle through the gate of a prison. The driver agreed, the attempt failed, but the door of publicity was opened to this odd little woman. Buoyed up by this, she capitalized on the attentions of the press – who dubbed her ' V. D. Elsie' – by paying £1000 to address a mass meeting at Queen's Hall, Langham Place in June 1935. The evening began with a one-and-a-half hour concert of music composed by Mrs Van der Elst herself. She then regaled the large audience, asking for volunteers but not for money since all expenses would be paid by her. She took full credit for the recent reprieve of Stoner, and claimed to have received 'three million letters worldwide in support'. She declared her intention of getting into Parliament 'by fair means or foul'.

So concerned at her activities had the Home Office become that Special Branch was asked to investigate her origins, since her name suggested she might be an alien (in fact she had married a Belgian). Attempts were made to deal with her presence outside prisons, but her aeroplanes had committed no flying offences, and all that could be done was to prosecute her van drivers for 'sounding a noisy instrument and calling persons together'.[46] At the request of the Home Office the Commissioner of the Metropolitan police detailed two police officers to report on the Langham Place meeting. They too came up with disappointingly little. They had been poorly briefed, confusing her campaign for that of the NCADP. They noted that all those attending were 'respectably dressed', and that the chairman was a colonel. Although at the end someone shouted 'Red Front', no obvious extremists were present, other perhaps than two Salvation Army officers in uniform. Even a discreet perusal of the petition forms revealed the name of no known communist. It was noted with relief that Mrs Van der Elst was not 'too well educated and sometimes used bad grammar'.[47]

Unperturbed by official disapproval and surveillance, after the execution of Charlotte Bryant, Mrs Van der Elst announced that she was setting up a £50,000 fund for the children both of murder victims and of those hanged. Two years later, frustrated by the leaders of the Church of England, and determined to stimulate public interest, she launched a new religion in which lives would be changed by hypnotism, criminals cured, and the campaign against hanging regalvinized.[48] From now until the late 1950s she was to be seen with her supporters keeping vigil outside prisons on the eve of an execution and singing hymns on the morning of it. Her self-publicity knew no limits. She even commissioned a pastiche on the crucifixion. On a hill several people hung from the gallows. On the left stood a red-robed judge, on the right a group of weeping figures, between them, with arms outstretched, both guardian angel and Christ figure, was Mrs Van der Elst.[49]

The NCADP, which could neither match her means nor approve her tactics, advised their members against participating in these displays.[50] There was considerable danger that the two campaigns might be confused in the public mind. It had been the great virtue of Roy Calvert to rescue the abolitionist movement from 'the futile emotion and sentiment which originally surrounded it, and place it on a sound basis of statistical fact and rational argument', and the NCADP considered that it would be very unfortunate 'if, through well-meaning but misguided activities, the case for abolition should become associated in the public mind with hysterical emotionalism'.[51]

Of lasting value, however, was the correspondence Mrs Van der Elst carried out with the Anglican bishops, the results of which she published in an appendix to her 1937 book, *On the Gallows*. She had asked for their support. Temple, of course, replied that for a long time he had been an advocate of abolition, but in this he stood alone. Hensley Henson, Bishop of Durham, wrote from the Athenaeum that he had 'always been of the opinion that capital punishment as administered in this country is wholesome and, indeed, on many grounds requisite'.[52] The Bishops of Chester, Liverpool, Birmingham, Manchester and Norwich were not in favour of abolition, Chichester and Lincoln had nothing to say to help her, and Oxford refused to enter into a discussion on the subject. The Bishop of Peterborough had great sympathy with her humanitarian ideals but could not associate himself with her campaign. Canterbury, Bath and Wells, and Winchester would not express an opinion, and Exeter did not reply. She published their letters in full and commented acidly on how often the bishops of the Established Church had opposed reform. None had agreed with the Bill for the Prevention of Cruelty to Animals in 1809, only two out of twenty-six had voted for the Bill for the Total Suppression of the Slave Trade, not one had supported the measures to abolish the flogging of women in public, or within prison. Contemporary bishops she considered to be very much in the apostolic succession.[53]

Whatever the reservations of the NCADP, it was Mrs Van der Elst who in very lean times kept public attention focussed on what was going on in our name behind prison walls. Attlee himself later, and perhaps rather generously, maintained that she did more than anyone else to secure abolition.[54]

In contrast to the frenzied activity of this colourful eccentric, there was little interest among professional politicians. The Labour Party, exiled to the wilderness, passed an abolition motion at its annual conference in 1934, and in 1938 Vyvyan Adams, a Conservative MP, and a devout Anglican, initiated on a Private Member's Motion the first full-scale Commons debate for nearly a decade. Again the argument centred on deterrence. The strongest speech came from the Revd James Barr who pointed out the favourable reactions to the 1930 Report, especially the pro-abolitionist statements made by leaders of various religious denominations – Methodists, Baptists, Congregationalists, Presbyterians, and 'some Anglicans'. In the vote 114 to 89 favoured experimental abolition for five years (the majority of Labour MPs were of this persuasion, including Chuter Ede, a future Home Secretary, and nine other future ministers). The Government refused to move and so Adams indicated he might submit an amendment to the Criminal Justice Bill of 1938. This, however, failed in Committee. Public opinion, now tested for the first time by an opinion poll, was split down the middle: 49% wanting hanging retained, 40% wanting it abolished, and the decisive 11% undecided.[55] The war intervened and no further progress was made. But it was intended that the Criminal Justice Bill would be revived as soon as the hostilities were over. Should Labour ever again be the party of government, the omens were good for abolition.

12 Hanging on the Fence

1939–1949

Mercy but murders, pardoning those who kill.

William Shakespeare[1]

Must one kill in order to make sure there are no wicked men? That is
to produce two wicked men in place of one. Vince in bono malum
(Romans 12. 21).

Blaise Pascal[2]

The long and distressing controversy over capital punishment is very
unfair to anyone meditating murder.

Geoffrey Fisher[3]

Once again during the war years all abolitionist agitation ceased, and the
number of executions increased by over 50% from a pre-war average of over
eight a year to a wartime of over thirteen, a figure augmented by the execution
of several German spies.[4] With the return of peace, the coming to power of a
radical Labour Government with an overwhelming majority, and the advent
of a Home Secretary, Chuter Ede, who had been an abolitionist, the reformers
saw a great Parliamentary opportunity. The ember they had kept smouldering
burst into flame. Led by Sidney Silverman, the fiery young Jewish MP for
Nelson and Colne, and John Paton, the former secretary of the NCADP and
now a Labour MP, they prepared for battle. To harbour dwindling resources
and to concentrate better their efforts, the National Council merged with its
parent Howard League which took over the fight against capital punishment.
Roy Calvert's widow, Theodora, scarcely waited until hostilities had ceased
to recommence the pamphlet war with a tract which reiterated the pragmatic
arguments and the moral ones, citing the late William Temple's evidence
before the Select Committee in support.[5]

Unfortunately, Temple's premature death after only two years at Canterbury
had robbed the cause of its most influential and intellectual supporter. The
war had also denied them a sympathizer as his successor. As a result of his
outspoken opposition to the bombing of Dresden, George Bell, Bishop of
Chichester, had not been appointed to Canterbury. Instead, in 1945, the
Primacy of All England had been conferred on the former Bishop of London,

Geoffrey Fisher. Fisher's succession rather than that of Bell, even more than the premature death of Temple, had been considered to be a worst misfortune to befall the leadership of the Church of England since the Second World War.[6] Although, like Temple, he had considerable interest in the subject of capital punishment, and was to make his presence prominent in the debates in the 1940s and 1950s, his views were very different from those of his predecessor. His likely response to the issue could perhaps have been gauged by those who had endured the 'prolonged and ritualistic beatings' which he had administered while Headmaster of Repton, alternating each stroke of the cane on the bare buttocks of his boys with a drag on his pipe and a word of moral admonition, a 'slow and fearsome process' which went on until 'ten terrible strokes had been delivered.'[7]

Archbishops were not the only ones to cause disappointment. Once again the Labour leaders, once they had gained power, showed no inclination to incur electoral unpopularity over what was as they saw it a minor issue. In the first two years of office Chuter Ede continued the same pattern of reprieves and executions uninterrupted and unaltered. Even insanity could not save the sadistic double murderer, Neville Heath. As ever Mrs Van der Elst championed his reprieve and drove to the Home Office demanding to see the Secretary of State. She was sent away unheard; the law was left to take its course.[8] Mrs Van der Elst, and the other abolitionist campaigners, could afford a consistency that a serving Home Secretary, whatever his erstwhile commitments, could not.

Perhaps it should have occasioned no surprise that when at last the Government introduced its Criminal Justice Bill in 1948, it contained no abolitionist clause. Eager to get it passed, they had tailored it for all-party support. Yet they proposed no other hanging bill. Herbert Morrison, the Leader of the House, thought that the issue was too 'hot' politically, and too marginal for the Government to court losing popularity over. The first discussion on hanging took place at the second reading. Chuter Ede announced that he had changed his mind and now believed that capital punishment did deter. Although he hoped that in the long term it would be abolished, he advised the House in that well-used phrase that 'the time was not right'. The post-war crime wave made it impossible to experiment with abolition 'at this time'. The murder rate increased by 20% in the immediate post-war years from an annual total of about a hundred immediately before the war. Public opinion, he maintained, supported this view.

On that point he was undoubtedly right. The Commons was as always far more inclined to abolition than the general public. In a poll taken the previous November 65% of respondents had been retentionist, Liberal voters being 8% below the average, Conservative 10% above, and Labour dead on. There was an interesting correlation with religious opinion. Anglicans at 74% in favour were within a point of Conservative voters. Nonconformists at 65%

corresponded to the overall average and the Labour figure, while Roman Catholic opinion at 70%, and the Church of Scotland at 72% were more retentionist than average.[9] The two Established Churches of the United Kingdom, Scots and English, and the two English Catholic Churches, Roman and Anglican, (the former seeking ever greater acceptance by society) thus outran public opinion, and approached closely to Conservative opinion in their opposition to abolition. Those of no religious affiliation at all were most likely to oppose capital punishment (40%). The more conventional the religious affiliation the closer was the alignment with Conservative wisdom on the hanging question.

The abolitionists were horrified by Ede's betrayal. In their eyes he had been pressurized by the police and Prison Department into opposing abolition, and was the captive of senior Home Office officials, in particular Sir Frank Newsam, the Permanent Under-Secretary. That there was some truth in this is suggested by the fact that two years after leaving office Ede was again an abolitionist. Conversely, Lord Templewood (the former Sir Samuel Hoare), who as Conservative Home Secretary in 1938 had talked in the same terms as Ede now used, this time announced he was an abolitionist. As Silverman remarked, the same events had led the previous and present Home Secretaries to change their minds in precisely the opposite directions. This was the first sign that the issue was becoming bi-partisan, and from now on a small minority of Tories would take a prominent role on the abolitionist side of the debate.

Reformers, of course, welcomed this shift in opinion, and when at the Report Stage[10] of the Criminal Justice Bill in April 1948 an amendment for the temporary abolition of the death penalty was moved by Silverman, it was seconded by a Tory MP, and an active Roman Catholic, Christopher Hollis.[11] In the ensuing debate, another Tory, and a member of the 1930 Select Committee, Sir Ronald Ross, characterized hanging as 'revolting', but favoured retention since those close to the criminal – governors, officers, doctors, and chaplains – believed that capital punishment was a deterrent. The Conservative Quintin Hogg saw cogent arguments on both sides. He hated the death penalty, but the House of Commons would be 'clothed in dishonour' if MPs abolished it now having acquiesced in the Nuremberg executions. Not all the Labour backbenchers favoured abolition. Stanley Evans was in tune with a public opinion which he considered to be 'healthy and vigorous and free from neurosis', and which accepted 'the biblical injunction – "eye for eye, tooth for tooth" ', a sentiment he shared. In contrast the Conservative Member for Darwen, Stanley Prescott, who had organized a private poll of his constituents which resulted in a massive majority for hanging, nonetheless voted for suspension.[12]

The alternative was again a major issue. Another Conservative, John Maude KC, quoted Paterson on the inhumane effects of long-term imprisonment Sir John Anderson who for ten years had served as Permanent Secretary to the

Home Office and later as Home Secretary, asked what alternative there was. Release after a short time would be intolerable to the public, captivity for life intolerable to the prisoner and prison officers. He also quoted Paterson. Then to the delight of the abolitionists, and the consternation of their foes, Reginald Paget (Labour) announced that before his death Paterson had changed his mind and joined the NCADP (this was untrue: he had misread a note passed to him by Mr Dawtry to the effect that Paterson had told him that the conditions which existed when he told the Select Committee that a long sentence of over ten years was worse than death had changed and that he had wished Dawtry luck as Secretary of the NCADP).

The Government insisted on retention and refused to allow Ministers a free vote on the Silverman clause. Nonetheless it passed by 247 votes to 224. Of the 72 Government ministers 44 abstained (including all four law officers) thus giving the abolitionists their victory. Labour had split 215 to 74, the Conservatives 14 to 134, and the Liberals were solidly for abolition – all seven of them. For the first time since the abolition of public hanging the House of Commons had approved a major change in the law of murder. As a result, Ede immediately announced that he would commute all death sentences from then on until the future of the clause was finally resolved.

The Times, Guardian, Mirror, and *News Chronicle* had all supported abolition but the letters to *The Times* favoured retention, and the other nationals were opposed. *The Police Chronicle* said that an armed police was now inevitable; the Prison Officers' Association said they would seek special compensation for officers killed as a result of abolition.[13]

Again polls taken after the Commons vote indicated that the public were against them. A *Daily Express* poll on 29 April indicated an increase in public support for hanging. Of its readership, 77% opposed the Commons' decision; 85% of its Tory, 71% of its Labour, and 69% of its Liberal voters.[14] A Gallup Poll on 10 May indicated that two out of three people of all ages and social backgrounds disapproved of the vote, but found that over a third of Labour supporters supported the Commons compared with only a quarter of Liberals and a sixth of Tories. On 28 May Mass Observation recorded figures of 69% disapproval. Anglicans and Scots Presbyterians were more inclined towards hanging than either other churchgoers or non-churchgoers. Of those in favour of abolition over a third were so because they thought it worth a trial, 29% were so on humanitarian and ethical grounds, but only 6% on specifically religious grounds. Of the retentionists 40% were so on grounds of the safety of the individual and the community, 26% wanted revenge – 'an eye for an eye' but only 1% favoured hanging on religious grounds. From the three polls cited it is clear that the number of members of the public who were undecided on the issue was very low, there was a substantial majority in every category for hanging, and the usual difference between the sexes, age, and economic groups failed to show up. Political allegiance, educational attainment, and religious belief were the only things which differentiated people, and then only to a degree.

The religious organizations were as divided as the public at large. The *Catholic Herald* affirmed that on this issue Catholics were free to use their own intelligence and consult their consciences, although it advocated degrees of murder. The *Methodist Recorder* was mildly abolitionist, but the Church Executive had gone much further and taken emergency action, communicating a resolution to every Methodist MP welcoming the Silverman clause.[15] The *English Churchman*, an evangelical news-sheet, declared that for the 'Bible Christian' no view was adequate that ignored 'the great Mosaic principle of Genesis 9. 6'. While some of the Welsh Congregational Churches had passed a motion calling on Parliament to end hanging, the Scottish Free Kirk condemned the Commons' actions as 'unscriptural', and another Scottish Synod agreed to send letters of protest to their local MPs and to the Home Secretary.[16] Anglican comment was sparse perhaps because many churchmen were awaiting the views of the archbishops and bishops in the House of Lords. They were not to be kept in the dark for long.

For four days from 27 April until 2 June the House of Lords debated the second reading of the Criminal Justice Bill which now included the clause suspending capital punishment. So keen was their interest in the subject that the peers overflowed the division lobbies and squatted in the gangways. So intense were their feelings that the debate was characterized by considerable bitterness on both sides.[17] Of the forty-five peers who spoke on the clause, sixteen were in favour of it, twenty-six were opposed, and three favoured degrees of murder as a compromise solution. Putting forward the clause on behalf of a reluctant Government was the Lord Chancellor, Lord Jowett. Looking harassed and perspiring in the crowded chamber, occasionally shifting the weight of his wig from his brow, even as he proposed the Bill he made it clear he had no sympathy with its later accretions. Thus the leading abolitionist speech came not from a government minister but from the former Tory Home Secretary, and now President of the Howard League, Viscount Templeman. Against him, however, were ranged two other former Home Secretaries: Lord Simon, whose intervention to the effect that the Commons was too far in advance of public opinion was held by Silverman to have been decisive against his measure, and Lord Samuel who argued for an extension of the prerogative of mercy instead.

In large agreement with this approach was Mervyn Haigh, the Bishop of Winchester. A cold intellectual, dubbed 'the holy icicle' by his fellow bishops, he had been, since his days as senior chaplain to Archbishop Davidson, close to the heart of the Anglican establishment. Along with Garbett of York and Bell he had been among the front-runners to succeed Temple at Canterbury. He understood the Lords well and spoke to considerable effect, giving what to some at least was considered to be the 'weightiest and most deeply pondered' contribution to the debate.[18] He felt that the present position was satisfactory. The whole Bill was 'unfortunate in the time of its birth' and it was not reasonable now to give priority in public attention to the treatment of offenders. He deplored the present-day 'almost pathological fear' of the use of punishment and the opening of the door to psychiatrists. His view of fallen humanity was not high:

> The more we have made provisions by our prison treatment for appealing to the better nature of criminals, the more frequently we find that there is less better nature to which to appeal.
>
> We must be satisfied by the strongest possible reasons that we are not interfering arbitrarily and needlessly with so happy a balance of forces as are embodied in our administration of the death penalty at this time.[19]

Dr Haigh's argument for not interfering 'needlessly' with this 'happy balance of forces' had a disquieting resemblance to that which his episcopal predecessors used when resisting the reforming efforts of Romilly and his friends at the beginning of the previous century. Nor was the bishop finished yet in his encomium of death. The death penalty helped to educate the conscience of the whole community. His 'deepest point' was 'not simply whether there will be a few more murders or a few less, but the whole attitude of the British people to . . . the criminality of crime and the majesty of the whole system of law from top to bottom'. The death penalty had about it, he claimed, 'a vertical dimension and . . . is capable of arousing, and does in fact arouse, among an immense number of people . . . a quasi-religious sense of awe'. Here he touched on a point of immense significance, a point to which we shall return, namely the ritual, religious, sacrificial overtones of hanging.

> The execution of a murderer is a solemn ritual act and its object is not only to demonstrate that murder does not pay but that it is shameful. The penalty is not only death but death with ignominy. The death penalty fulfils this role in an unequalled way because of this quasi-religious sense of awe which attaches to it. In wantonly taking a life, the murderer is felt somehow to have invaded the sphere of the sacred and to be guilty of profanity. His impious act can only be countered by imposing on him a penalty which also has a 'numinous' character. This is a deeply rooted belief which cannot be wholly rationalized but should not be summarily dismissed.[20]

His views were echoed by Dr Joseph Hunkin, the Bishop of Truro. He contended that the maxim 'whoso sheddeth man's blood by man shall his blood be shed' has appealed to mankind 'as an approximation to justice'. The categorical statement of the English law that 'murder deserves death', he went on, encouraged people to feel that murder was so dreadful a crime as to warrant the most extreme penalty. He feared the effect on 'the ordinary mind' that any lightening of this penalty would have. It would suggest murder was not so awful after all.[21] Hanging, he went on, was a deterrent precisely because it was 'horrid and loathsome'; he could have got along 'tolerably well with a long sentence'. If he were 'contemplating murder', he was sure that hanging would deter him and 'I am quite sure that the whole criminal world agrees with me'. As so many other apologists for hanging had been reduced to saying, he would rely on his own feelings rather than on statistics from other countries. But he was not finished yet. He went further, suggesting an extension of the death penalty to crimes resulting in severe injury short of death (attempted murder or rape).[22]

In contrast to the two bishops four lay peers – the Earl of Darnley, and the Lords Darwen, Dowding and Holden – basing their arguments on their Christian belief, spoke in favour of abolition. Lord Rochester found it 'difficult to reconcile the words of the two right revd prelates with the admonition of their Master and mine in St Mark 11. 25'. Lord Pethick Lawrence attacked the long record of opposition in the Lords to ameliorating the law dealing with capital punishment. Often they had succeeded in delaying humane measures for years. In this respect, he added pointedly, the record of the bench of bishops was particularly bad, yet even so he had been 'considerably shocked at some of the things that fell from the lips' of the Bishop of Winchester.[23] Unfortunately neither bishop was present to hear this criticism. Lord Temple-wood contradicted Bishop Haigh's assertion that capital punishment enhanced the majesty of the law. On the contrary, 'it surrounds with an atmosphere of unhealthy melodrama a particular form of crime . . . and it leaves the mark of Cain on the family of the executed man'.

The bishops, however, were not without support. Most influential of all was that of Lord Goddard (or 'Lord God-damn' as Churchill styled him), the new Lord Chief Justice, who in his maiden speech argued vehemently and with great effect for retention. Appositely described as 'a compound of granite and volcanic lava',[24] he openly advocated more savage penalties than Parliament was prepared to allow. To 'beat the child with the rod', he had often opined, might save his soul from hell and his neck from the noose. Yet even he would 'not follow the right reverend Prelate [Truro] in all his bloodthirsty suggestions': logically, attempted murder deserved the same penalty as murder, but a line had to be drawn somewhere.[25] Lord Maughan defended capital punishment on the ground that 'the wages of sin is death', and the pro-hanging Lord Trenchard, explicitly approving the speech of the Bishop of Winchester, insisted that 'the state should keep to the Christian principle that life is most important'.[26]

Many Christians were appalled by the views which the bishops expressed. One, Vyvyan Adams, the former Tory MP, wrote to the Archbishop of Canterbury, Geoffrey Fisher, urging him not to oppose abolition when he spoke in the Lords. As the son of a priest Adams was 'at a loss to understand how a Christian minister can support the death penalty or refrain from condemning it when it cannot be justified on the grounds of necessity'. He fervently hoped that the Archbishop would do something to restore his grievously shaken faith in the leaders of the church.[27] Fisher assured him that although he would 'reveal some perplexity of mind', he would not oppose abolition.[28]

His assurance was less than candid. He began his speech by reasserting the traditional Anglican position that the church recognized the full right of civil magistrates to take away life whether in a just war or for heinous offences. His predecessor, Temple, had argued that it was wrong to put a murderer to death as a deterrent to other people because that was to treat him as a mere means to something else, which is always morally wrong. Fisher disagreed: the death penalty was not ultimately for deterrence but for denunciation:

> What the state does is to say this. Murder is such an outrage on society, so heinous a breach of social living and so ultimate in its effect upon the victim, that its penalty shall be death. It is not that each murderer is treated thus so as to act as a deterrent to other possible murderers. It is the proclamation of a law by which every man, if he becomes a murderer, shall be judged, and to which he shall know himself to be liable; it is the public recognition that murder is, in one sense, the worst and certainly the most irreversible of crimes.[29]

The church had always upheld dual principles in the imposition of punishment. The first – 'an eye for an eye' – was negative and limiting: that punishment must not exceed in gravity the crime. The second was positive and constructive – that the law of love must permeate and direct the state in dealing with criminals. He insisted that 'within the church always, and in the world as far as it is practicable, the law of love with its power to forgive, to convert, to reform and to refashion' ought to permeate and shape the application of the law on punishment.[30]

The church and the world were not the same, and it was only in so far as it was practicable that the statesman, as the guardian of society, should mitigate the 'preventive and deterrent methods of punishment' by the operation of the law of love: 'thus Christian opinion and judgment may differ'. He then went on to speak personally and not on behalf of the church. He believed that there was a prima facie case for the law of the state to inflict the death penalty upon murderers. That case did not rest merely, or indeed at all, upon the fact that it conformed to the Old Testament maxim. It went much deeper into 'the self preservation of society'. Quoting the Bishop of Winchester approvingly, he said that the real question was what abolition meant within the social life of the community, how far it would affect the general sense that some crimes were infinitely more heinous than others. This for Fisher was crucial. Murder struck at the community rather than merely at an individual. In this argument he was following the line of thought that stemmed from Aquinas, through

Luther, Kant, and Hegel by which society, state, and law have absolute priority over the offending individual.

Like Haigh, and like 'the rest of us', he wished that the whole matter 'had never been raised at this moment' and, rather unfairly, blamed the Government for getting 'us into trouble by well-intentioned but hasty and ill-considered action'. But since it had been raised we could not return to the status quo ante. He favoured retaining capital punishment for certain offences, for example the murder of police officers. Therefore he could not vote for the clause as it stood, nor could he vote for its mere deletion. He hoped it would be amended 'so that while it is tempered to meet the exigencies of our present situation it may still be a step forward to that goal which every Christian must desire even if Christians may still differ as to the rapidity of the pace with which it can be approached'.[31] In Fisher's view capital punishment, like capitalism, was necessary in the present state of English society, but should be made more attractive.

Nowhere had he specifically referred to the teaching of Jesus and his repudiation of the *lex talionis*. Silverman, listening to this speech, expressed his profound contempt for Fisher by calling him 'the Archbishop of Cant'.[32]

Before the debate, Bishop Bell, like Fisher, had expressed some reservations about the full abolitionist position, and had toyed with the idea of advocating the abolition of the mandatory death sentence. However, for him the arguments for the total abolition had proved too strong,[33] and now he spoke unequivocally. Like all his episcopal predecessors he could not quite persuade himself that it was never in any circumstances legitimate for the state to take human life, but the retention of capital punishment now, in peace-time Britain, was an unnecessary violation of the principle of the sanctity of human life. In addition there were grave moral objections to it 'both in itself and in the circumstances of its execution', and thirdly, the experience of abolitionist countries was unfavourable to its retention as a deterrent.

Bell believed, as John Bright had before him, that 'a deep reverence for human life is worth more than 1000 executions in the preventing of murder and is, in fact, the great security of human life'. In taking a murderer's life for violating that principle the state was merely violating it further. In a tacit rebuke to Fisher he referred to his citation of 'an eye for an eye', and reminded his fellow peers that 'when that sentiment is quoted in the New Testament by Jesus it is qualified by the words: 'It was said by them of old time, but I say unto you'.

> The Christian Church was a pioneer of the mitigation of the severity of barbarian and feudal law. In doing so it was true to the teaching of its Founder . . . It was a deep sense of the inviolability of human life and hope for the redemption of the murderer that inspired such great, eminent and representative Christian teachers . . . as St Augustine, St Ambrose, St

Bernard, John Wyclif, and William Temple, in their unceasing opposition to capital punishment.[34]

A further moral consideration was the effect that it had on the participants. He went on to cite various eye-witness accounts, and reflecting on them he found it 'difficult to discover what my brother and friend, the Bishop of Winchester, said was "a quasi-religious sense of awe" hanging about the death penalty'.[35] Here was the voice of the true heir to Temple, and had Bell rather than Fisher been elevated to Canterbury the hanging issue might have been resolved earlier.

Bell was joined in his criticism of Fisher by Lord Rochester who expressed amazement that the Archbishop had 'prayed in aid of his argument Exodus, Leviticus, and Deuteronomy . . . and omit[ed] all reference to the words of Jesus Christ himself'.[36]

Cyril Garbett, the Archbishop of York, then intervened to dispel any misgiving among the retentionists that the moral highground was being claimed by their opponents. He expressed no views of his own on the merits of the case, but made the point that it was unfair to say that those who opposed abolition were indifferent to the sanctity of human life. Both sides based their case on the sanctity of life. Lord Darwen, undeterred, condemned the death penalty as inconsistent with Christian principles: 'you cannot teach people the sanctity of human life by hanging'.

When finally put to a vote, the clause for suspension was defeated by an overwhelming 181 to 28. The Lords could claim at least that they more nearly reflected public opinion than the elected Lower Chamber. Twenty-three Labour peers supported the clause, as did three Tories, one Liberal and Bishop Bell. The only other bishop to vote, Haigh, voted against. All the others, with their archbishops, sat on the fence.

The Archbishop of Canterbury's speech was considered to be the one which most affected general public opinion.[37] The hint he had given to the Government that they might find some means of discriminating between more and less heinous murders was now adopted as a possible compromise. It pleased no one, but the abolitionists had to vote for it or get nothing. Once again the Lords threw it out by 97 votes to 19. The moral high-ground was seized by Lord Goddard who claimed to speak as the champion of the public conscience in condemning such a facile discrimination in homicide cases. Representing the views of the judiciary, the formidable Lord Chief Justice thought that the proposed capital offences were a mere hotch-potch consisting of those which were thought to arouse the greatest public apprehension or abhorrence, and that the distinction between capital and non-capital murders was not founded on any rational principle and would lead to many anomalies and inconsistencies. With a foresight greater than that of Fisher he concluded that it would prove both unworkable and immoral. Cyril Garbett appealed to the Government to abandon all attempts to deal with capital punishment in the Criminal Justice Bill which was jeopardizing its many other valuable provisions. In some desperation, on 22 July Ede promised an inquiry to look into practical means to restrict the death penalty. Thus mollified, and to prevent the whole Bill failing, the reformers finally yielded and voted for it without the abolitionist clause.

As another Labour term of office neared its close the hanging issue was again relegated to the delaying tactic of an inquiry. The Royal Commission would be restricted in its scope, would outlast the government that established it, and would take four years to report. It proved nonetheless to be of great significance, and was to make a major contribution to the ultimate demise of the death penalty.

13 Death on the Drawing Board

The Royal Commission on Capital Punishment 1949–1953

At the execution of a most obdurate murderer, a baptized and confirmed Churchman, and an old choirboy of six years standing, I administered the communion to him during the last forty minutes, as he was truly penitent and prepared to die. I had scarcely ended my ministrations when the executioners entered the cell. I thereupon blessed him and the procession at once started for the scaffold. Only 35 seconds elapsed between the entry of the executioners and the fall of the drop – this was officially noted by the Governor of the Prison with his stop-watch.

Revd A. F. D. N. Williams[1]

The Cabinet were not keen to honour Ede's promise of an inquiry into capital punishment, and discussed whether it would be possible to avoid holding one. Although it was likely that after the inconclusive debates public opinion generally would be content to leave the controversy in abeyance for the time being, it was thought inevitable that the question would be raised in Parliament. To avoid being considered weak by taking no action until forced into it, but to delay matters as much as possible, the Cabinet concluded that a Royal Commission should be set up, and announced its appointment in November 1948.

It was to be carefully restricted to practical matters, however, and was not to consider 'abstract issues of justice and conscience'.[2] It was made clear that no bishop was to be considered for membership.[3] Nor was it directly to investigate the question of abolition, an issue the Prime Minister thought should be determined by Parliament, not by Commissions.[4] The question which it was, in effect, required to consider was whether any practicable half-way house could be found between the existing law, under which every person convicted of murder, unless under eighteen or pregnant, had to be sentenced to death, and the abolition of the penalty altogether. Getting the right balance of members who had not previously expressed themselves on one side of the argument or other took considerable time and ingenuity. Nor was it easy to find a chairman, several of the most obvious candidates, including Lord Justice Tucker and Mr Justice Birkett, declining. Despite the public criticism that the delay occasioned,[5] it was not until late April 1949 that the composition of the Commission on Capital Punishment was completed under the chairmanship of the cautious, diplomatic, and wise civil servant, Sir Ernest Gowers. Not the sort of man, you might think, to rock the boat.

For over four years the Commissioners met in a stately first-floor room in Carlton House Terrace. Sitting at a horseshoe table they heard evidence from the most comprehensive range of expert witnesses, British and foreign, ever assembled on the subject of capital punishment. Although the purpose of the Commission was not to consider abolition of the death penalty *per se*, but to see whether its operation could be refined, and its scope restricted, a number of witnesses would not avoid the primary question.

The unanimity of prison officials was noticeable, and suspicions arose that they were toeing a departmental line. The *New Statesman*, commenting on the early stages, said that the newspapers had been able to report 'nothing but grim demands for executions from the Home Office, the Prison Commission, prison officers and clergy, after-care associations, the police, and of course, the judges, who are dissatisfied with the rate of hanging anyway'.[6]

The nearest thing to a chaplaincy view came from written and oral evidence given by a panel of prison chaplains.[7] The opinions were their own and not that of any official body of their respective churches, but they believed that they were 'reflecting the main stream opinion of the Christian churches'.[8] They began with a statement of the traditional teaching of their denominations. Society had the right to 'act on behalf of God . . . to check and correct any subversive elements in its midst' and, in extreme cases, where 'no alternative remedy is prudently available', it may 'remove offenders by death'.[9]

They believed that capital punishment was a deterrent to murder, and that the ignominy of hanging in the public eye increased its deterrent effect. (Would they, one wonders, have reintroduced public executions?)

> It is the public nature of the act – the law solemnly executing the man . . . we do not like this hole-in-the-corner getting rid of the man [by hypodermic]. If the man is to die, let him walk to his death cleanly . . . We are amazed at the demeanour of these men. Nine out of ten go to their death bravely. They have some special grace given to them on the morning.[10]

Hanging was 'simple, humane, and expeditious', and had no ill effects on prison staff or inmates.

Nonetheless, they urged that the number of hangings should be reduced by the setting up of a board of inquiry in every case to consult with prison officials and especially chaplains in order to look at all the relevant factors concerning the individual. Under existing arrangements there were no formal channels for getting any information which the chaplains had gleaned and considered relevant to the Home Secretary's attention.[11] A board of inquiry should examine not just medical aspects but take in all comments from officers and chaplains about the man's character and advise the Home Secretary.[12] The enhanced role they wanted stemmed from their perception of the centrality of the chaplain in the whole hanging process, a centrality which could not be gainsaid. The beneficial effects of religion in such a crisis were obvious.

> The prisoner derives strength from his religious beliefs, and the daily and personal religious ministrations of his chaplain. The comfort of religion is seen most clearly in the last days when the hope of reprieve has gone, and on the morning of the execution itself. As the days go by, the condemned man comes to depend more and more on his chaplain.[13]

No doubt they thought that if their recommendations were taken up the number of executions would be reduced, but their comments strike us as extraordinary. It looks as though the chaplains were asking that they be given the power of life and death. Those whom they considered to be morally or spiritually regenerate would live, those deemed 'subversive' would die. We have met with this suggestion before in the writings of Dean Inge. The witnesses did not flinch from such a role, assuring the Commission that if called to give evidence to a board of inquiry the chaplains 'would not hesitate to give a true opinion even if it told against the man'.[14] Unable to oppose the death penalty in principle, believing in its unique efficacy in practice, the clerical participants were hoping to 'improve' a near perfect system, and enhance the central role of the church in matters of life, death, and eternity. In the boardroom of death, church and state would mutually benefit the other, the church giving sanction to the power of the secular arm, the state, in return, making the church, through its chaplains, its chief executive.

Although some abolitionist observers of the Commission at work thought that of all the prison officials the chaplains came out of their interrogation best, with their humanity still intact,[15] the Howard League found this 'evidence' and that of the other prison officials too complacent by half. The *Howard Journal* wryly observed that 'all officials of the Home Office and Prison Service [had], with marvellous unanimity, found nothing wrong with capital punishment nor the methods of hanging nor the Home Office administration of reprieves'. The chaplains 'thought all the arrangements humane and the law of the death penalty in accordance with Christian ethics'; the doctors 'had no criticism to make on . . . the application of modern scientific knowledge in the treatment of murderers'; the After-care officials 'assured the Commission that practically all reprieved murderers made good, but they apparently were satisfied that those who were hanged were rightly hanged'. The *Journal* was forced to conclude that it was 'difficult to believe that such a perfect system could spring from the finite mind of man'.[16] The League knew that such a facade of unanimity was false; that other chaplains, doctors, or governors, if called, would have given a different picture, and that those who were called tempered their opinions to coincide with the 'departmental view'. This was particularly so on the issue of the effect of a hanging on those taking part. Discreetly the League began to suggest to the Commission that the evidence so far was one-sided, and to their friends that others should come forward to right the balance. A few members sent memoranda direct to the Commission, one of whom, the Revd Joseph Walker, former chaplain at Liverpool and Manchester, spoke of the terrible effect on all those participating, an effect that was not always outwardly visible. Other former officials, including chaplains, allowed their written testimony supporting Walker's view and discounting 'the prison-conditioned belief' of the 'established chaplains' to be included as part of the League's submission. Glanville Murray's evidence before the 1930 Select Committee was also quoted.[17]

All of this, however, was rather overshadowed by the evidence of the Church of England's chief executive, Geoffrey Fisher. Expanding and developing his earlier argument, he expressed his fears that the actual mechanics of capital punishment were undermining its status. For Fisher the primary purpose of punishment was the moral denunciation by the community of the crime. This was a quasi-religious function and should be attended by all the solemnity of a religious ritual. To denigrate this solemnity was to undermine the rationale for the death penalty. Reprieves were a particular problem since it was 'a very grave thing that the solemn formula of the death sentence' should as often as not be cancelled. It was not only the formula which was solemn:

> The whole action of which the formula is an expression is profoundly solemn. In it the community acts through the agency of the jury and of the judge. It is an action taken with a deep sense of responsibility before God and before man by which a fellow citizen, a fellow human being, is to be deprived of his life on this earth and be sent to the higher Court of God's Judgment.

For Fisher it was intolerable that 'this solemn and deeply significant procedure should be enacted again and again when in almost half the cases the consequence' would not follow. He conceded that under any system the possibility of reprieve must remain, but argued that if this act was to retain any solemnity 'it must normally mean what it says and carry the consequences which it imposes'. Otherwise it was reduced to a mere formula; and 'in such a matter a mere empty formula [was] a degradation of the majesty of the law and dangerous to society'.[18] 'As a churchman' Fisher was deeply concerned that the number of reprieves, and thus the number of cases in which the solemn act of condemnation to death was pronounced without effect, should be reduced. So long as 'the awful punishment of a capital sentence' was retained, 'it should be delivered from every circumstance which may make it anything less than what it is'. The system of reprieve deprived this solemn act of its finality and thereby of the solemn dignity which should belong to it.

xecution of Crippen, 1910

Archbishop Fisher (centre) with Bishops Haigh (left) and
Bell (right), 1953

Thus he contended that the death penalty should not be imposed in those cases where it was likely that a reprieve would result.

There was a certain irony in this view. The effect of the Bloody Code was to condemn all but hang few. The late eighteenth and early nineteenth century reformers had wanted to make the punishment correspond to the crime and the sentence, and to attain this end sought the abolition of hanging for most offences other than murder. Fisher's episcopal predecessors had opposed this change. Now the law relating to capital punishment meant that all those convicted of murder were condemned to die but half were reprieved. The reformers wanted to abolish it altogether, but Fisher advocated its curtailment to those sorts of murder in which the sentence passed was likely to be the sentence carried out. It was as though in the 1950s the Archbishop was adopting a position which would have been radical in 1810.

As to the delivery of the death sentence, Fisher was in favour of retaining 'precisely the present procedure with all it solemnity . . .' At that moment a woman clad in a black cloak with astrakhan collar and wearing a large-brimmed black hat with a veil, rose from her seat and pointed at him. It was Mrs Van der Elst. 'Are you a Christian?' she inquired. 'Do you think Christ would have said exactly what you have said today? . . . It is not the job for an archbishop to come here and say the things you have said.' Sir Ernest Gowers adjourned the sitting while Mrs Van der Elst called after them as they withdrew. When she had driven off in her Rolls Royce they resumed the session as though nothing had happened.[19]

Christian opinion, continued the Archbishop, as if commenting on the interruption, was divided over the issue of the validity of capital punishment, but there would be general agreement that if it were not abolished it should be kept within the narrowest possible limits, and a general hope that ultimately conditions would be such that without danger to society it could be laid aside. 'The Christian conscience', he pontificated, was deeply concerned that the range of cases within which the death penalty could operate should be 'as much limited and as clearly delimited as possible'. There was no necessary requirement of justice that murder should be requited by capital punishment. There was certainly no Christian principle which demanded that, and if society did not 'require it for any better reason than to pay [the murderer] back what he has given, society ought not to do it'. Once again he took the opportunity to clarify what he had said in the 1948 debate, quoting the Old Testament maxim 'an eye for an eye'. What that did, he pointed out, though people did not realize it, 'was to say that we must not exact more than the original offence. It was not an exhortation that you should exact an equivalent, it is a restraint on the passion of mankind'.[20]

Such a 'clarification' seemed more often obfuscation, and sat uneasily with his earlier statement that capital punishment served a quasi-religious function of the denunciation or wrongdoing. The effect of Fisher's evidence was once again to provide a way for perfecting and so retaining capital punishment. Even if it were no deterrent it could be justified and maintained if society thought it necessary to show its abhorrence of murder by executing the murderer.[21] Fisher was once more turning to the possibility of degrees or categories of murder. If capital punishment were to be reserved for the more heinous cases, it would be morally more acceptable and less prone to the indignity of reprieve. This was a useful and fruitful contribution for the church to make to the retentionist cause since the ground had long been slipping from under them on the question of deterrence. All the evidence tended to be on the abolitionist side, and those who believed that capital punishment was a deterrent did so on the ground of 'intuition' and 'feeling', the only backing for it coming from the very subjective evidence of prison chaplains, governors, and judges.[22] The hard statistical evidence was against them, and was well marshalled by the abolitionists every time the argument came up.

Nonetheless, Lord Samuel, when giving his evidence, 'did not think much force could be given to the Archbishop's argument'. He preferred to revert to the position enunciated by Paley: 'to maintain a degree of uncertainty as to what would happen in marginal cases may be very useful in retaining a deterrent effect on potential criminals'.

Fisher's contribution and that of the other clerical witnesses dismayed at least some of the ordinary clergy. One correspondent to the *Church Times* had been appalled by the evidence presented to the Royal Commission, but was even more concerned that no attempt had been made to determine the prevailing convictions of the clergy and laity of the church either through Convocation or Assembly. He asked the Archbishop to appoint a commission to investigate the opinions of the faithful, to call its own evidence, and to present a report 'more authoritative, more representative, and more carefully considered than the evidence so far given'.[23] His appeal fell on deaf ears.

The Gowers Report was finally presented to Parliament in September 1953, almost five years after the Commission had been appointed. Restricted as they were by its terms of reference to making recommendations limiting or modifying the liability to suffer the death penalty, the commissioners came down as near as they could in favour of abolition, but ultimately could only tinker with the edifice of the criminal law. They preferred hanging to any alternative methods of extinction. They rejected the idea of introducing 'diminished responsibility' into English law, the abolition of capital punishment for women alone or, to the surprise of many abolitionists, the division of murder into degrees so favoured by Fisher. They recommended *inter alia* the abolition of 'constructive malice' (whereby a killing committed during the commission of a felony was deemed to be murder), alterations to the law on provocation, jury discretion in imposing life or death sentences, and the raising of the minimum age for execution from eighteen to twenty-one. They noted significantly that there was no convincing statistical evidence that capital punishment was a deterrent. Few of their recommendations were to find favour, none of the major ones was to be implemented. They had looked for a compromise and found none. In so doing they had rendered the division between retention and outright abolition all the starker. Only with abolition, they seemed to be hinting, would all the anomalies and ambiguities of the present system, which the Commission had been set up to rectify, be put right. Some saw this as an abolitionist conspiracy, an attempt to whittle down the gallows by indirect means.[24] There was, however, no conspiracy; it was where the evidence led.

Perhaps the greatest importance of the Royal Commission lay in the clarity with which it mustered an enormous amount of evidence for and against the imposition of the death penalty. Such a survey had the power to make converts, the most notable of whom was the chairman of the Commission himself, Sir Ernest Gowers. He had started the inquiry without any strong feelings either way about capital punishment but ended it 'as a whole-hearted abolitionist – not emotionally but intellectually'.[25] He understood why the scope of the Commission had been artificially restricted. He had seen through the facade. He knew there was not a chance of any of its more important recommendations being adopted, but at least it would 'focus attention on the truth that the only real question is whether we want to retain capital punishment or to abolish it'. At present he discreetly kept his own council. Later he was to break silence and publish a book advocating abolition.[26] Intellectually then, the case for hanging was lost.

The Labour Government which appointed the Commission had done so with reluctance and after long delay. The Conservative Government which received the Report was no less dilatory about acting upon it. Despite vigorous campaigning by the Howard League and repeated questioning by opposition MPs the Churchill administration was unwilling even to discuss the findings until a full sixteen months had elapsed. It was as though they sensed that they had inherited a sword which had already been transformed into a ploughshare.

14 Godly Butchery

Religion and the Ultimate Sacrifice

Thy name is Love! What, then, is he,
Who in that name the gallows rears,
   An awful altar built to Thee,
With sacrifice of blood and tears?

With placid lip and tranquil blood,
   The hangman's ghostly ally stood,
   Blessing with solemn text and word
The gallows-drop and strangling cord;
   Lending the sacred Gospel's awe
   And sanction to the crime of Law.

John Greenleaf Whittier[1]

According to the views of theologians, an execution is the sacrificial
death in which the repentant criminal submits to the penalty which he
recognizes as well deserved.

Karl Mittermaier[2]

The death penalty has nothing to do with the law: it is an act of self-
consecration to crime, of the consecration of crime. A community will
always, by a majority, proclaim the need for the death penalty, precisely
because it is a consecration. The sacred, whatever it had to do with the
sacred . . . The dark pit of being, of existence.

Leonardo Sciascia[3]

Throughout its history capital punishment served a religious function.
Whether imposed in the name of the king, the representative of God on earth,
or by priests, or in the name of a society considered as a sacred body, the
infliction of the death penalty was seen not just as a punishment for a crime,
but as a repudiation by society of the evil in its midst, ridding the land of its
blood-guilt. The Mosaic code required expiation for the contaminating effects
of bloodshed: 'Ye shall not pollute the land wherein ye are: for blood it defileth
the land: and the land cannot be cleansed of the blood that is shed therein,
but by the blood of him that shed it' (Num.35. 33). The execution of criminals
among the Semites constantly assumed sacrificial forms, for the tribesman's
life was sacred even though he be a felon. He must not be killed in any common
way, out of mere human revenge, but devoted, as a sacrifice, to the God whose
will he had flouted.[4] Similarly the early Germanic tribes considered the death

of the culprit to be an expiatory sacrifice to the gods who had been offended by the crime.[5] In this way religion in societies with no firmly established judicial system strove to subdue violence, and keep it from running wild by restraining vengeance.[6]

In Christian times and in Christian states, in part because the crucifixion of Jesus had always been seen in sacrificial terms, judicial execution took the place of this overtly sacrificial disposal of criminals. The religious overtones, the transcendental qualities, however, remained. The criminal was still said to be 'sacrificed to the laws of his country'. The death penalty also allowed for the possibility of salvation, for the real judgment was not pronounced in this world but the next, and the threat of imminent death could accomplish repentance and salvation in the most inveterate sinner. Consonant with this function, capital punishment, in its trappings as much as in its apologia, over the centuries has worn the mantle of religion.

Executions were demonstrations of the power of God – and of the monarch in as much as he was God's regent on earth – against rebellion.[7] They were 'spectacles for Men and Angels'.[8] The criminal seemed to undermine the stability of society by rebelling against civil government and by disobeying the laws of God. The powers that be were ordained of God. To offend against secular authority was to sin against God himself. The most prominent jurist of the Jacobean age, Sir Edward Coke, justified and explained every detail of drawing, hanging, and quartering, the punishment for the ultimate crime of treason, on theological grounds: as the crime is the undoing of the most holy bonds between man and man and man and God, so the punishment is the undoing of God's supreme creation.

> A traitor . . . shall have his judgment to be drawn to the place of execution from his prison as being not worthy any more to tread upon the face of the earth whereof he was made: also for that he hath been retrograde to nature, therefore he is drawn backward at a horse tail. And whereas God hath made the head of man the highest and most supreme part, as being his chief grace and ornament . . . he must be drawn with his head declining downward, and lying so near the ground as may be, being thought unfit to take the benefit of the common air. For which cause also he shall be strangled, being hanged up by the neck between heaven and earth, as deemed unworthy of both, or either; as likewise, that the eyes of men may behold, and their hearts condemn him. Then he is to be cut down alive, and to have his privy parts cut off and burnt before his face as being unworthily begotten, and unfit to leave any generation after him.[9]

As we have seen, the Church of England saw the ritual drama of public execution as the perfect opportunity to demonstrate the power of the gospel. In a Christian land the state wielded the secular sword on behalf of God. Law and gospel were identical. The assize sermon was the prescribed opportunity to set the drama of human justice within the theatre of the divine. This association was immeasurably helped by the fact that the language of the law and of religion were two strands of a single thread. English criminal law had emanated from English Christian faith. Thus as one eighteenth-century assize preacher put it, 'the solemn administration of justice should commence with due and devout meditation on the proceedings of that Being, concerning whom it is said, that, as mercy and truth go before his face, so, righteousness and judgments are the habitation of his throne'.[10] Christian preachers were content to depict the Almighty in the trapping of temporal authority. In one evangelical pamphlet God was likened to a High Court Judge, and the Day of Judgment was called the 'Grand Assize, or General Gaol Delivery'.[11] The monarch was rarely mentioned as the source of judicial authority. Magistracy, as one preacher put it, 'can never be represented in a more awful, or a more venerable light, than when it is adorned with a divine Commission, and armed with Divine Authority'.[12] Magistrates were no less than the 'ministers of God; his revengers to execute wrath upon him that doeth evil'.[13]

The panoply of justice was also holy theatre, carnival. Executions were public so that the public would watch and, having watched, be warned. In chapel the condemned sat apart, and were the subject of the 'condemned sermon'. Visitors could come to view the spectacle, when the victims of the morrow underwent this harrowing experience. That which was intended to edify could so easily be debased, however, and finally the public incursion of gawking spectators was deemed to be more befitting the secular stage than this religious ritual, and after a commission of inquiry, was prohibited.[14]

Tyburn was specifically portrayed as Calvary.[15] The reality was often more pagan. The condemned would process along the three mile *via dolorosa* from Newgate to Tyburn Hill, the chaplain or another friend riding with them in the death cart. 'The Hanging Song' (Psalm 51) which the condemned and the crowd alike sang at the gallows stressed the sacrificial aspect of the execution: 'the sacrifice of God is a troubled spirit'. It was not hard to depict the role of the chaplain accompanying the condemned as that of 'the heathen priest who assisted at the slaying of the victim'.[16] John Smith was 'taken off the cross' when a reprieve arrived five minutes after the strangulation had begun. Hogarth's 'The Idle 'Prentice Executed at Tyburn', the archetypal depiction of an execution, is itself based on Breughel's 'Christ Carrying the Cross'. In both the festivity almost concealed the suffering.[17] As so often happens, sacred rite only too easily degenerated into sacrilegious revel.

Popular superstition helped to elevate strangulation into an immolation. Contact with the newly-hanged corpse was supposed to have healing properties. In 1767 'a young woman with a wen upon her neck was lifted up while [a felon] was hanging and had the wen rubbed with the dead man's hand'. In 1831 a man with a growth on his head pushed his way through the crowd attending a hanging at Lewes and rubbed the corpse's hand on his face.[18] So had the sick pressed on Jesus, if only to touch his garment (Matt. 9. 20). The rope itself was considered a lucky talisman and was preserved, along with other artifacts of an execution, with the reverence accorded the relic of a saint.[19] A rope thus venerated could fetch a guinea an inch, while pieces of tanned skin were sold for much greater sums.[20] Such 'relics' of Mary Bateman, hanged in 1809, were still on sale in Ilkley as late as 1892.[21]

With the abolition of public executions, brutal, savage, and primitive sacrifices upon the high places were replaced with an exactly ordered and perfectly performed liturgy of death in the holy of holies within the impenetrable walls of the prison. The old order was inverted: secrecy replaced publicity, a speedy dislocation was substituted for slow strangulation, decorum succeeded degradation.[22] The pagan, orgiastic celebration with all its attendant superstition had become the Christian self-sacrifice. Such was the theory; the practice, as we have seen, rarely lived up to the promise. A. E. Housman depicted the decline of the ritual as practised within prison walls. Gone is all aura of sanctity, the rope is now a 'strangling string' ensnaring a scared animal.[23]

Throughout the next hundred years attempts were continually being made to refine the procedure so as to satisfy the requirements of dignity, decorum, and religiosity. First the prisoner had to be preserved intact. The sentencing judge would ask some hard questions if the man 'cheated' his sentence by suicide, and so elaborate precautions were taken against the possibility. Two officers lived with him day and night,

> who watched him when he rose to weep,
> And when he crouched to prey;
> Who watched him lest himself should rob
> Their scaffold of its prey.[24]

There were no buttons on his clothes. He was totally separated from other prisoners, even in chapel where he arrived after and left before the other prisoners, and sat in a closed box invisible to them behind a red curtain. One witness recorded that 'the parson may preach his best, the hymns may be the liveliest and most popular, yet all eyes and attention are concentrated on two dark, immovable curtains which screen the Unknown from view'.[25] He was allowed no physical contact with relations. Both these measures were considered necessary for 'the welfare'[26] and 'the safety of the prisoner' which was 'the most urgent thing to be secured, and to guard this adequately would obviously be impossible if closer communication were permitted'.[27] Then the execution had to be carried out to perfection. Drops were very carefully measured so that the victim would neither be beheaded nor strangled. Death should be instantaneous, and the length of drop was determined by the size and weight of the person. Mrs Thompson could not understand why she had been weighed three times in one day.[28] Unblemished victims were required for this scientific sacrifice. The maimed or deformed whose perfect end could not be guaranteed were reprieved. All this comprised a 'monstrous ritual' which when displayed as such was repellent to many of those who had to partake in it. It was a sanitized and modernized hangover of a pagan rite:

> The whole monstrous ritual, the solicitous care for the condemned man's last days, the elaborate precautions to prevent him from taking his own life . . . the stealthy introduction of the hangman into the prison the day before an execution, in order that he may surreptitiously observe his victim's physique from which to make the calculations necessary for the successful performance of his hideous task – what civilized man or woman would participate in all this without a sense of degradation?[29]

It was possible even in the mid-twentieth century to be quite explicit about the quasi-religious dimension of the death penalty as the previously quoted speech of Bishop Haigh in the 1948 debate in the House of Lords made clear. The prison cell could become a Lady Chapel where the penitent waited her immolation. Glanville Murray who attended to Mrs Thompson, despite her dislike of him, on the morning of her death transformed her cell into 'a sort of *chapelle ardente* with flowers, candles, and, I think, a crucifix'.[30] It was precisely this sort of thing that others found so obscene. Cassandra, writing on the eve of the execution of Ruth Ellis, denounced 'this sickening system whereby with panoply and brutality mixed with the very dubious sauce of religion and consolation we bury our worst malefactors in the quick-lime grave'.[31] One Catholic commentator contrasted the sacrifice of Christ on the altar with 'the hideous and revolting Black Mass [which] is offered up with an unwilling victim, whenever the prison bell tolls for a hanging'.[32]

Even the victim could believe himself to be a sacrifice. Glanville Murray told the Select Committee how one man expressed despair that 'God had refused [his] sacrifice' when he was reprieved: 'I have taken life and I was going to offer my own. Now I have nothing before me but years of remorse.'[33]

If the condemned were to be sacrificed by the ritual of the state, the executioner was sometimes seen and sometimes saw himself as the high priest in this ritual. That had not always been the popular perception, however, and in the late Middle Ages the hangman was shunned by the people and by the authorities alike. They were even denied burial in consecrated ground. The Protestant Reformation brought about the rehabilitation of the executioner. Luther disapproved of the practice, common in Germany and England, of the executioner asking forgiveness of his victim. He need ask forgiveness of no one: he was a father chastising his son; he was an agent of the state and so derived his authority from God.[34]

The hand that commands the sword and judges is no longer man's hand, but God's hand, and not man, but God, breaks on the wheel, decapitates, and strangles; all this is His work and His judgment.

The executioner's sword in Freiburg bore the motto 'Lord Jesus thou art the Judge'.[35] A Scottish mid-nineteenth-century retentionist tract, echoing Luther, asserted that 'it is not the Sheriff's hand, it is not the sword of the executioner, but it is the hand of God, it is the sword of his justice that takes away the life that he himself gave'.[36] The executioner was thereby invested with a divine function in that he destroyed the body in order to deliver the soul to its divine judgment. The eighteenth-century reactionary Roman Catholic political philosopher, Joseph de Maistre, hymned the executioner as the instrument of God and the high priest of society on whom 'all grandeur, all power, all subordination rests'. He is the 'horror and cement of human association' without whom 'order gives way to chaos, thrones fall, and society is extinguished'.[37] The hangman Berry, as we have already seen, believed that he had a religious vocation. Another executioner, Baxter, an elderly nonconformist, regarded himself as the instrument of the Almighty on earth.[38]

The church, believing in divine judgment and the prospect of another reality, could justify capital punishment in the light of eternity. The French Revolution had to create a religion of its own to sustain the Red Mass of St Guillotine.[39] Secular society, however, was left with a religious residue which now bore no relationship to some deeper reality. It was a punishment and a final one. Such a society had 'forfeited the logical right to pronounce the death penalty', according to Camus, since the old religious justification now had no meaning.

When an atheist or agnostic judge imposes the death penalty on an unbelieving criminal, he is pronouncing a definitive punishment which cannot be revised. He sits upon God's throne, but without possessing God's powers, and without believing in them, he condemns to death because his ancestors believed in eternal punishment . . . society traditionally assigns a priest to the condemned man, and the priest may legitimately hope that fear of punishment will help effect the condemned man's conversion. Yet who will accept this casuistry as the justification of a punishment so often inflicted and so often received in an entirely different spirit? It is one thing to believe and 'therefore know not fear', and another to find one's faith through fear. A secularized society has nothing to gain from a conversion concerning which it professes complete disinterest: it enacts a consecrated punishment, and at the same time deprives that punishment of its justification and utility alike . . .

Society thus usurps the right of selection, as if it were nature, and adds a terrible suffering to the eliminative process, as if it were a redeeming God . . . In other words, the executioner, formerly a priest, has become a civil servant.[40]

From *carnifex* to butcher, from priest to civil servant. It was this secularization of his role, this defrocking, which so upset Albert Pierrepoint, the executioner. When compelled by the Royal Commission to divulge the 'sacred details' of his 'craft', the way he prepared, the time he took, the numbers he had dispatched, he felt that his calling had been cheapened and desecrated. Three years later he resigned for reasons he would not divulge but which are likely to relate to this experience.[41] In his remarkable autobiography he quite clearly states that he had a divine vocation which he fulfilled to the letter:

> My belief is still . . . that I was sent on this earth to do this work and that the same power told me when I should leave it. I had an ambition, I have it no longer. All the desire is quite gone.

He perceived his task as a sacred one, and never more so than at the hour of death. 'The supreme mercy I can extend to them is to give them and sustain in them their dignity in dying and death.'[42] His description of the preparation of a hanged man for burial explicitly related it to the deposition of Christ. He stripped him as he hung, piece by piece removing his clothes:

> A dead man being taken down from execution, is a unique body whether he is a criminal or Christ, and I received this flesh, leaning helplessly in my arms, with the linen round the loins, gently with the reverence I thought due to the shell of any man who had sinned and suffered.[43]

Secular society could no longer understand such sentiments. 'What mystery there should be in hanging' they, like Pompey in *Measure for Measure*, found it hard to imagine.[44] For the non-believer, like Camus, the ritual of hanging was an added offence, its religiosity in a world of unbelief was a nonsense. For the traditional believer, like Fisher, the inability of modern society to treat the death penalty with gravity, the loss of all that gave it dignity, the removal of its numinous, quasi-religious quality, was to so degrade it as to make it barbarous. For many of the chaplains such descriptions as Pierrepoint's were mawkish, even blasphemous, with more than a hint of necrophilia, and their involvement seemed to give Christian sanction to something which was inherently pagan: human sacrifice. The realization of this was another factor in many a change of heart. They had seen it for themselves, their experience had changed them.

15 Murder by Degrees

From the Royal Commission to the Homicide Act: 1953–1957

> We reject thee with a shudder of repudiation. We, not to be partakers
> in thy destructive adventure of defying God and all the universe and its
> laws . . . dare not allow thee to continue longer among us . . . He at least
> will never insult the face of the sun anymore.
>
> *Thomas Carlyle*[1]

> Lackeys are always in favour of capital punishment, those who are
> lackeys by their function and those who are lackeys in their soul.
>
> *Leonardo Sciascia*[2]

The public imagination is fired by the particular rather than the general, and capital punishment had the effect of always concentrating things on the particular. The question was not 'is there a danger of miscarriages of justice?', but 'was Evans innocent and executed?'. Not, 'should adolescent accomplices be hanged?', but 'should Bentley have been?' Not, 'should women go to the gallows?', but 'should Ruth Ellis have gone?'.

In 1949 Timothy Evans was executed for the murder of his wife and child. To the end he protested his innocence, and tried to lay the blame on his old landlord and chief prosecution witness, John Christie. The revelation four years later that Christie was himself a mass murderer, whose victims included his own wife, did more than anything to shake the popular belief in the infallibility of British justice. The Home Secretary, David Patrick Maxwell Fyfe ('the nearest thing to death in life' as the Bar jingle had it),[3] had earlier said that there was no practical possibility of an innocent man being hanged. In an attempt to quell fears he instigated a brief private enquiry under John Scott-Henderson QC who, within ten days concluded that there were, by coincidence, two psychopathic murderers living under the same roof. This conclusion carried little conviction with the educated public. For them if not for the Home Office the case demonstrated beyond reasonable doubt that the possibility of a miscarriage of justice in a capital trial could not after all be wholly excluded and that an innocent person might die as a result.[4] Victor Hugo had written that he preferred to call the guillotine Lesurques (the name of an innocent executed) not because he believed that everyone executed was innocent but that one was enough to wipe out the value of capital punishment for ever. Many would agree with him. The debate over deterrence would always be clouded in the public mind by seemingly contradictory statistics, but one demonstrable mistake was enough to shake the gallows to its foundations.[5]

Similarly the Craig and Bentley case undermined the faith of many people in the system of reprieve. Derek Bentley seemed so obvious a case for respite: a nineteen-year-old boy who had been in police custody at the time of the rooftop killing of a policeman, who did not have a weapon, who was mentally subnormal, and whose accomplice, Chris Craig, the actual perpetrator of the crime, was, at sixteen, too young to die. The murder of a policeman had enraged public opinion, but Bentley's imminent execution in January 1953, after a trial stage-managed for the prosecution by the septuagenarian Lord Goddard, generated unprecedented popular and Parliamentary agitation for a reprieve. The public sense of guilt was stronger than its desire for revenge. Maxwell Fyfe, however, was not to be moved. A dour Scottish lawyer who knew that his rise to Cabinet status had come too late for further preferment, he felt the need to stamp his authority on that office the tenure of which he presently held. Priding himself as the Minister of the Crown least likely to bow to pressure, during the attacks launched on him in the House by Silverman he sat expressionless with arms folded across his black coat. Ironically the agitation to win this youth a reprieve may merely have dried the ink on the death warrant. Derek Bentley had to die for the sins of his generation, to deter other hoodlums from hiding their murderous intent behind perpetrators too young to hang. This cold rationale did little to dispel the feeling that 'his execution was a supreme indecency'.[6] He had been executed as an example, and had become a martyr.[7]

Thus in one year, 1953, the two pillars of the infallible system had collapsed. The innocent could die, the venial might not receive mercy. Perhaps in their deaths Evans and Bentley did more to bring about the end of hanging than any agitator or activist had done or would do. It was hardly surprising that in the wake of such cases there were calls for the church to speak. Some outbursts were intemperate. The editorial of the religious publication, the *British Weekly*, castigated the Home Secretary: 'one thing can always be said for a Tory Minister, he can always be trusted to show a proper contempt for the conscience and convictions of the public'. Two members of the Board of Directors resigned in protest; the editor, the Revd Shaun Herron, apologized. The case, he said, had affected his judgment.[8] Canon Kemp of Exeter College, reflecting interest among his students and peers at Oxford, tried to get the church to make a statement on the theological and ethical issues, and asked the Social and Industrial Council to take it up. The Council was uncertain whether such a statement was 'desirable', and asked Archbishop Fisher for his views. He replied that he did not think it would be wise to attempt to produce any kind of statement on capital punishment. For any adequate survey he would have had to appoint 'a rather expert committee of moral theologians and ask them to give concentrated thought and time to the subject'. He doubted whether he would be justified in taking that course, or whether he would be successful in securing the necessary co-operation.[9] The Council expressed its relief at his response. Hanging, it seems, was not at the top of the Church of England's agenda, nor were the theological or ethical implications worth serious consideration. Fisher, after all, had it all worked out.

February 1955 saw the first Parliamentary discussion of the Report of the Royal Commission. Although the Government said that it wanted to hear the views of MPs on the matter, the new Home Secretary, Major Gwilym Lloyd-George made it clear that the major proposals for reform were unacceptable. He recognized, as had the Commission itself, that if the proposal on jury discretion in particular found little favour 'the view may well be taken that . . . we are driven back on the major question whether capital punishment should be retained or abolished'.[10] Yet Lloyd-George, an abolitionist while in opposition in 1948, now rallied to the defence of the noose. With a continued increase in crimes against the person the Government 'could not think that it would be right now to abandon the sanction of the death penalty'.[11] Silverman, backed again by Hollis, proposed an amendment to the bland motion 'taking note of the Report' which would have brought about a trial five-year suspension. He saw, as the Home Secretary himself had hinted, that the Report strongly supported the abolitionist case since it so clearly lacked faith that the changes it proposed would make an appreciable difference. Chuter Ede, again in opposition an abolitionist, supported Silverman's motion, bravely admitting that he had erred in letting Evans go to the gallows. Answering the Home Secretary's point, he agreed that at that moment the public were not in favour of abolition, but he also doubted whether at any time in the previous hundred years a majority would have supported any of the great penal reforms that Parliament had made. He believed that there were occasions when the Commons 'had to say a certain thing is right, even if the public may not at that moment be of that opinion'.[12] The debate was characterized by less emotion than that of 1948, and some took this as an indication that the House sensed the inevitability of abolition. Nonetheless, the amendment was defeated by 245 votes to 214. Most Labour members supported it, while most Conservatives opposed. The Tories, however, were turning. In the election the following May the Government increased its majority but the new MPs were largely abolitionist.[13]

Abolitionists were increasingly active and alliances were made which ranged across all boundaries, political, and religious. The momentum was quickened by the *cause célèbre* of the Ruth Ellis case. For what in other countries would be described as a *crime passionnel* in which a woman shot her unfaithful lover, this young mother was sentenced to die. Among other prominent figures, a leading Methodist, Dr (now Lord) Soper wrote to the press appealing for a reprieve, and addressed a lunchtime crowd in Manchester telling them that he believed that there was 'no person, male or female, sufficiently bad to be written off as a loss to the community'. Fifty thousand people signed a petition for mercy which was presented to the Home Secretary by Canon Collins of St Paul's Cathedral. A lengthy leader was published in the *Daily Mirror* by their influential columnist and convert to abolition, Cassandra, entitled 'Should Ruth Ellis Hang?'. He answered with a resounding 'No'. Not Ellis, not anyone should fall victim to this 'savagery untinged with mercy'.[14] On the morning of 13 July 1955, in the last minutes of her life, as Ruth Ellis prayed before a crucifix, the crowd outside Holloway Prison joined with the eccentric campaigner Mrs Van der Elst in the chant of 'Evans – Bentley – Ellis'. They were names that would haunt the hanging debate for years to come.

In the wake of the Ellis execution, the National Campaign for the Abolition of Capital Punishment (NCACP) was initiated to make a short intensive drive for abolition. Soon it had 20,000 members. The chairman was Victor Gollancz, the left-wing publisher and pamphleteer, and old enemy of Archbishop Fisher since his dismissal from his teaching post at Repton when the latter was Headmaster. Its council members, including the Quaker QC, Gerald Gardiner, Canon Collins, Christopher Hollis MP, Arthur Koestler, Frank Owen, and Reginald Paget QC, MP, were enthusiastic campaigners, although personal idiosyncrasies and differences marred their effectiveness. Gollancz and Collins in particular were notoriously difficult to work with, while Koestler, equally a maverick, was 'all brains and no boots'.[15] The unorthodox were, nonetheless, seen to have assumed the mantle which the orthodox had failed to do. In a letter to the *Church Times* the Church of England was reproached for having nothing to say on the matter of capital punishment, and having left it to 'Mr Victor Gollancz to put the Christian point of view'.[16]

With his commitment and charisma and a publishing house at his disposal, Gollancz was particularly effective as an organizer, fund-raiser, and propagandist. Orthodox Jewish in origin, and a Hellenist by inclination and training, he was a 'passionate moralist, and ardent non-denominational Christian, and a socialist of ethical rather than utilitarian enthusiasm',[17] qualities exemplified in his tract on *Capital Punishment: The Heart of the Matter*, which was written in white-hot passion in a period of four days in October while he was visiting Florence. It made the case against capital punishment on the grounds of absolute moral standards which for Gollancz were more important and more decisive than the empirical arguments about statistics and probabilities of deterrence. He began by recounting the story of the woman taken in adultery not to demonstrate the obvious parallelism but to show that Christ too eschewed every side issue, every other argument and went straight to the basic. Even if capital punishment were conclusively proved to be a unique deterrent and he were certain that abolition would be followed by a startling increase in murders 'I should still say with undiminished conviction, that the most urgent of all tasks that confront us, or would confront any people that had a care for religious or humane values, is the ending of capital punishment . . . Capital punishment is wrong and that is all there is to it.'[18] We would not deliberately kill a child even to preserve the nation. We cannot preserve civilization by negating it. There is a holiness and potentiality about human life we cannot snuff out: 'We dare not lay a hand on potentialities.' We cannot know God's purpose in respect of any human life and we may not interfere with that purpose by limiting the span. 'By killing anyone at all' we 'to that extent kill Christ'. Just as the murderer has already done, so we would do again.[19]

He prayed Dostoevsky in aid, citing the passage from *The Idiot* about a guillotining and the terrible knowledge that at a certain moment you will die. He concluded by stating his creed that 'to execute a man for murder is to punish him immeasurably more dreadfully than is equivalent to his crime' since 'a murder by sentence is immeasurably more dreadful than a murder committed by a criminal'. It was a powerful, uncompromising and passionate reiteration of what the Quakers had been saying for years but which the more conservative denominations had never countenanced. At the same time as Scottish prison chaplains were prepared to aver that even if hanging did not deter, it was deserved, so Gollancz was arguing that even if it did deter it was unconscionable. Worlds apart.

Arthur Koestler likewise employed his literary gifts in the cause of abolition. His *Reflections on Hanging*, also published in 1955, was widely read and discussed. Like Gollancz, he used passion and outrage to state his case. His approach was very unlike that of the earlier more balanced and reasoned advocates of abolition. Balance and reason alone had not won the day. An appeal to the heart, and an attempt to arouse moral revulsion might bring more success.

The council determined to attract as much attention and wield as much influence as possible. To win over educated opinion in such a matter was vital. Therefore a Committee of Honour was formed of eminent representatives from the arts and sciences, the churches and politics.[20] The young elite were coming over to the side of abolition. They had been appalled by the injustice of the imposition of capital punishment and by the intransigence of ministers and civil servants of their parents' generation: Evans and especially Bentley – their peer in age if not in any other respect – had won their support, just as Goddard and Maxwell Fyfe had earned their contempt.[21] In an Oxford Union debate in 1955 378 were in favour of abolition, and only 161 against. Two years before the majority in a similarly sized house had been only 40. Gerald Gardiner added considerable academic weight to the cause by the publication of a book putting forward the more conventional, more dispassionate argument,[22] and by undertaking a hectic round of speaking engagements. 'Tall, austere, and terribly frank', he cut a striking figure and spoke with uncompromising moral vigour.[23] The campaigning had its effect and at a meeting in Church House on 10 November 400 were turned away even from the overflow area.

In the same month the Government announced they would not act on the recommendations of the Royal Commission, thus preventing the possibility of any bill dealing with anything touching on capital punishment being debated in such a way as could lead to a division. So Sydney Silverman introduced a bill to end hanging which got a first reading. Indicating the desperate arguments the retentionists were forced to use, the mover of the rejection, Sir A. Grimston, said he '*refused to believe* that for the professional criminal, hanging was not a deterrent'. Without saying so this time, Lloyd-George did the same as Chuter Ede had done explicitly in 1948 and reprieved everyone throughout the thirteen months of debate.

In February 1956 the Government, to forestall Tory support for the Bill, was forced to bring in a motion to retain capital punishment but amend the law of murder. In the week of 10–16 February pleas for the suspension of hanging were made *inter alia* by Leonard Wilson, the Bishop of Birmingham, by both Donald Soper, the former President, and Leslie Weatherhead, the then President of the Methodist Conference, and by Kenneth Slack, representing the Social Responsibility Department of the British Council of Churches, although Fisher cautioned the Council itself against an uncritical acceptance of their recommendation that the death penalty be abolished or suspended.

On the 16th a packed Commons debated the Bill which had been introduced by the Home Secretary. Much time was devoted to the question of miscarriages of justice, an issue which had been merely theoretical in 1948. The former Home Secretary, Chuter Ede, moving an abolition amendment, reiterated that he had not met anyone who continued to think the execution of Evans, which he had authorized, was justified. Had all the facts been known at the time, public opinion, he was sure, would never have allowed it to have taken place.[24] As a result of this trauma and of a reconsideration of his Christian faith he had reverted to abolitionism. In this he was supported by a large movement in informed public opinion, shaken as it had been by the events of the previous few years. This was particularly so as regards religious opinion. Ede had himself 'received numerous letters, not from great church organizations but from congregations of the faithful of all denominations in various parts of the country assuring [him] of their feelings on the moral issues which [were] involved'.[25] A fellow Christian MP, G. H. Rogers, also spoke passionately of his personal involvement, this time in the case of Ruth Ellis. On the eve of her execution he had taken in Ellis' son to try to shield him from the full horror of what was to happen the following morning. He could not believe that 'the gentle Teacher from Nazareth would have supported capital punishment . . . It is against the basic Christian principles on which our civilization is supposed to rest'.[26] He was supported in this assertion by one of the rare breed of clerical MPs, the Revd Llywelyn Williams, a nonconformist minister. He correctly observed that *Hansard* would prove that every time a measure had been introduced to ameliorate the harsher aspects of penal legislation, the same arguments had been adduced as on this occasion. Appeals to the views of the bishops, he pointed out, could be made by both sides but not to equal effect. Speaking 'carefully and not disrespectfully', he proceeded to weigh the opinions of Fisher and 'the generality of the bishops of the Established Church' who notoriously had always been upholders of the status quo, with those of 'the greatest ecclesiastical luminary of this century, by general consent, the much-lamented William Temple . . . Upon this issue he [had] given an unequivocal lead to the adherents of the Established Church.'[27]

Fittingly the debate was rounded off by the small, silver-haired Silverman himself who, in a rousing and unscripted peroration, again focussed on the essentially moral issues at stake:

> In the end the question which the House of Commons has to decide tonight will not be answered out of the law books and the legal precedents. It will not be answered by statistics. It will not be answered by fine distinctions, nuances of legal or penal theory. In the end it is a great moral issue which the House of Commons has to decide tonight.

Returning to where the debate had begun, the alleged miscarriage of justice in the Evans case, in a generous tribute to a Conservative Home Secretary which was also a damning indictment of the system he defended, he deplored the moral calcification which the hanging of an innocent man had produced:

> The worst thing about the death penalty is that it can persuade a highly intelligent, responsible, conscientious human being like the present Home Secretary, to convince himself – because he dare not believe the contrary – that Timothy John Evans was guilty, as charged, of the crime for which he was executed.[28]

The Ede amendment was passed by 293 votes to 262. Forty-eight Conservatives voted for it, of whom eighteen were new members, and seventeen had either voted for retention or abstained a year before. The majority were 'post-war' Tories, conservative on economic matters, more liberal on social questions, and on average younger than the retentionists. It was now less unfashionable for Tory MPs to be abolitionists. Nine Ministers abstained and only eight Labour MPs voted against abolition. Koestler, Gardiner, and Gollancz were in the public gallery to savour the victory.

Prematurely sensing complete success, Gollancz set about winding up the campaign, declining further help, thanking MPs, and telling the Bishop of Middleton that there was now no point in holding a projected mass meeting in Manchester. Koestler vehemently disagreed, since the battle in the Lords would be a difficult one. The wisdom of his judgment was vindicated when the Government announced that in fulfilment of their promise to act on the vote they would merely allow the Silverman bill to proceed. To ministerial chagrin, it passed both its second and third readings in the Commons. Gollancz returned to the fray.[29]

After an initial abortive attempt by Gollancz and Collins in 1954 to galvanize the membership of Christian Action, an inter-denominational pressure group set up in 1949, into undertaking a campaign aimed at changing opinion within the churches,[30] its Council had by now unanimously agreed that they would run the Christian side of the National Campaign. Lacking both experience and sophistication they got off to a bad start. In the weeks before the February debate they rather naively distributed abolitionist tracts in the cathedrals and major parish churches asking the public to send their opinions on hanging to Canon Collins on a postcard. Such tactics could easily backfire. The new Archbishop of York, Michael Ramsey, castigated it as 'an unchristian action' encouraging the public to 'superficial thinking on a great moral issue'.[31] More successfully they organized a joint meeting with the National Campaign which was held in the Festival Hall on 24 May. When Canon Collins preached on the subject in St Paul's, he received many abusive letters from 'church people who felt that hanging was an essential safeguard of the British way of life'.[32]

The support of the Church of England was obviously still crucial, and Collins wrote offering to help Bell in the debate if he could.[33] Members of Convocation were lobbying the bishops in the Lords; a strong group of clergy was preparing a petition to present to Fisher asking him to speak strongly in favour of abolition to counter the Government's hope that the Lords would defeat the Silverman Bill. The staunch abolitionist John Wand, who had replaced Fisher as Bishop of London, had been approached for support in this, and Collins asked Bell to let him know of any other bishops in the House whom he knew to be in favour.

In consequence, Bell, the prime mover among the episcopacy, was feverishly busy trying to rally support among his fellow bishops. He wrote to those he thought most likely to respond favourably, and gathered the support of Sheffield, Manchester, and Liverpool. The Bishops of Birmingham and Chelmsford who were not yet members of the Lords were also in favour. Ramsey was wholehearted in his support, but it took some doing to persuade him to speak in the debate.[34] The Bishop of Bristol, however, holding similar views to Fisher, would not lend his weight to outright abolition.[35] Thus although once again the Bill was massively defeated in the Lords by 238 votes to 95, four of the eight Law Lords, both archbishops and eight bishops voted for it, and only one bishop, Chavasse of Rochester, against.

Despite this semblance of unity the motives of the bishops were mixed. Michael Ramsey, in his maiden speech, said that while he could not agree that

New Testament teaching was against capital punishment, nor that it was a Christian thing to remove retribution from punishment, nevertheless he would vote for the Bill.[36] In the past capital punishment had seemed an appropriate punishment for murder: it had been severe, it had deterred, it had represented the simple condemnation of the whole society of the crime of murder, and it had allowed for repentance. He did not think that there was moral absoluteness on either side of the controversy but when the total moral effects were weighed the abolitionist case was now by far the stronger, since 'the death penalty in this country no longer has the moral dignity of representing, in an absolutely sure and certain way, the will of the community to inflict an unspeakable penalty for an unspeakable crime'.[37] The activity of the popular press was largely to blame for this. His argument, if not his abolitionist position, was very similar to that of his colleague at Canterbury, and both later repudiated a suggestion from Lord Pakenham that their opinions conflicted.[38]

The Anglo-Catholic leader and acknowledged ecclesiastical expert on moral and social questions, Bishop Mortimer of Exeter, spoke next, announcing his conversion to the abolitionist cause. Tall, handsome, and dignified, he had a marked effect on the House. He agreed largely with the Archbishop of York. The atmosphere surrounding murder trials was reminiscent of that in the ancient Roman Colosseum. Additionally, he believed that nowadays crimes were being perpetrated which were worse than murder, such as child abuse or drug trafficking, and yet they were not punishable with death.[39]

This was all too much for some of the Lords Temporal, and one, Lord Chatfield, the former Admiral of the Fleet, interposed. Without a hint of irony he established his credentials by boasting that as a child he had won a religious prize in the 'Britannia'. He reminded the House of the Mosaic law and the Ten Commandments, and warned that their effect should not be done away with by Act of Parliament, even one countenanced by the bishops.[40]

Undeterred, once more Bishop Bell rose to call the attention of the House to the Episcopal Bench. In 1930 Archbishop Temple was the only bishop known to favour abolition. In 1948 the speakers from the Bench were three to one against abolition. In this debate, however, even if for different reasons, all the episcopal speakers were in favour of abolition.[41]

This unanimity was deeply shocking to Lord Teviot who had found in Lord Chatfield the real exponent of biblical Christianity.[42] Indeed it looked likely that the bishops would be aligned for once against the lawyers, a fact which disturbed Lord Elton.[43] Against the episcopal unanimity he produced the testimony of Baden Ball, chaplain of Wandsworth, that the death penalty was supremely deterrent. To buttress this Lord Elton next referred to the saintly Edward King. Had such a bishop opposed hanging that would have been enough to persuade Elton, but King remained a retentionist all his life. There were at any rate some good Anglican authorities on the other side of the argument.[44]

Bishop Greer of Manchester took up this point. St Paul, he said, had not opposed slavery, but circumstances changed. In different times and circumstances it was perfectly proper to disagree even with Edward King. Greer was a regular visitor to Strangeways, and previously as a civil servant had to deal with petitions from condemned murderers. He believed that the process of execution had a very deleterious effect on those who had to participate in it, and that psychologically it could make pathological types in society more prone to murder.[45]

Fisher, at his most pompous, indicated that he would vote for the second reading in order to permit the Lords to amend the Bill, not because he was a total abolitionist. In fact his speech indicated that he had moved further from that position, now that he could again see a solution to some of his misgivings about the procedure of hanging.[46]

He acknowledged that the death penalty had been ill used in the past to punish heresy and protect property, and asserted that it might only be used to defend society itself. In his mystical view of the body politic, crime, and especially murder, struck at the very fabric of society. It was not so much that a person was killed but that society was injured. He would have found it impossible to comprehend the older, pre-Norman view by which homicide was considered to be a wrong to the victim's family, to be expiated by a fine, not as a crime against the state. He had little idea of the reality and banality of the vast majority of murders: murderers kill individuals, they do not assail society. For Fisher, however, murder was not the sordid, drunken, domestic act of a man against his wife, or the punch up in the pub where one youth stabs another, as murders so often are; it was the contradiction and violation of 'the fundamental principal on which society rests: that every member of it will respect the life of every other member and at least allow him to live'. Murder was rebellion against society's norms, murderers were subversives. Thus, 'where murder exists it is the first duty of society to repair the damage done by it to its own integrity and to bear witness to the majesty of its own first principle'. Society would dispense with hanging at its peril since it was a witness to the sacredness of human life and so of social order: 'to require a man to surrender his life may be the greatest possible tribute to its intrinsic value'. This, he asserted was Christian doctrine and, along with Ramsey, he disagreed with 'those sincere but mistaken people who regard the death penalty as a thing altogether and always un-Christian and wrong'. His vote for the Bill would be in spite of those who held such mistaken views and for quite different reasons. He hoped that this 'terrible, irrevocable, and cleansing witness' should 'in some form' be continued.

But the present system, by 'its clumsiness', militated against what he saw as the purpose of capital punishment. The regular use of reprieves made 'the solemnity of the sentence empty', introducing uncertainty 'where above all finality should be final'. In consequence of its regular exposure to public debate and the vagaries of party politics the death penalty was no longer 'the community with one voice bearing its witness purposefully, deliberately, prayerfully to the solemn law of society and of God' but becomes instead 'a matter of controversy and thereby loses its power to speak as it should'. Further, the media had 'robbed the system as it stands of all its proper dignity and sense of eternal destiny'.[47] Thus Fisher hoped that the Lords would take this opportunity to retain 'a true place for the death penalty in the moral order of society while removing some of its features which seem clumsy or dangerous or specifically open to criticism or especially repellent to sensitive people'. Once again, despite the rejection of this notion by the Gowers Commission, he took the opportunity to argue that categories of murder would solve the problem, restricting hanging to a few designated homicides, excluding from its purview those who killed in passion, and largely removing the need for reprieves:

> A murderer would have to put himself into the reach of the death penalty by a deliberate act. He would have openly declared war thereby on the first principle of morality and society not in a moment of passion but of choice. In these cases there would be no room for self-delusion, for uncertainty or for reprieve. The death sentence would be passed with all its dreadful solemnity and would be a final and decisive proclamation of moral truth.

This would refound the death penalty on its only secure and legitimate foundation as an act expressing the general will of the community for the defence of society and the solemn vindication of the laws of God.

Almost as an afterthought, he reiterated the antique but often unspoken buttress for retention, that capital punishment provided a unique evangelical opportunity. That this was of major concern to him was not revealed in the debate, but earlier he had been in lengthy correspondence with Maurice Harland, Bishop of Lincoln. Following in the footsteps of his illustrious predecessor, Edward King, Harland had had considerable pastoral involvement with the condemned. He seemingly supported hanging on this ground alone: 'I cannot bring myself to believe in [its] abolition. I write from the point of view of ministration to the condemned to bring about his conversion and to try to fit him for eternity', and even the execution of the innocent did not dent his conviction.[48] It was an argument also used by Ramsey who cited the pastoral ministry of King as demonstrating that capital punishment was not devoid of a rehabilitative element.[49] So often in the debates over capital punishment, the hint occurs that underlying the social contract and scriptural arguments there is a powerful but hidden reason for hanging, that it provides a uniquely satisfying opportunity for pastoral ministry. Nothing like the noose can save a hardened heart; and there is nothing like such a salvation to encourage the church in its ministry: the redemption of the worst is the best.

Despite Fisher's support, or perhaps because of the reluctance with which it was given, Silverman's Bill, again savaged by the Lord Chief Justice, failed by 238 votes to 95. The Lords were once more blocking a move which had been passed by the Commons. The *New Statesman* caustically observed that 'from the hills and forests of darkest Britain they came: the halt, the lame, the deaf, the obscure, the senile and the forgotten – the hereditary peers of England, united in their determination to use their mediaeval powers to retain a mediaeval institution'. In contrast the general feeling at the Conservative Party Conference was 'thank God for the House of Lords!'.

To sustain pressure on the Government the NCACP drew up a Memorial signed by the leading educationalists, churchmen, trade unionists, scientists, lawyers and penologists.[50] No judge signed, but several prison governors did, including the chairman of their Association. Gardiner wrote to Bell about it asking him to be one of the deputation delivering it to the Prime Minister. He thought that the memorial indicated the extent of the change which had taken place among informed opinion. Seventy-five Fellows of the Royal Society had signed and he doubted whether so large a proportion of fellows could have been found to sign a public petition on any other matter. Gardiner was sure that if the present opportunity to win abolition was not seized, another would not recur for many years.[51]

The cases of Evans, Bentley, and Ellis had played effectively on the minds and consciences of the educated public. Christian support for the Memorial was considerable especially among nonconformists. Although five diocesan and ten other bishops, and ninety other Anglican clergy signed, this compared unfavourably with one-hundred-and-fifty Free Churchmen, and sixteen leading Quakers. There was no Roman Catholic signatory. Forty-one principals of theological colleges signed, but, significantly perhaps, of the eight Anglicans only one came from an evangelical College (Wycliffe Hall, Oxford), the rest being Anglo-Catholics or Liberals.[52]

The Government was compelled to do something, and the something it did was to resurrect, under Fisher's prompting, the old discredited notion of degrees of murder. A Homicide Bill was introduced which conceded some ground to the abolitionists, but which was clearly unsatisfactory to both sides. It combined in a single package the widely agreed-upon reforms of the murder law recommended by Gowers (the abolition of constructive malice, and introduction of diminished responsibility), and the more controversial provisions establishing degrees of murder. Capital murders were defined as those committed in an attempt to resist arrest or escape or during the course of theft, where a firearm or explosive was used, a policeman or prison officer killed on duty, or when the killer had previously been convicted of murder. For the first and only time the government of the day applied a whip to what was effectively a death penalty bill. The Labour Party decided not to oppose it and so put a stop to Silverman's alternative Bill.

The Archbishop of Canterbury was its most enthusiastic supporter, giving it his wholehearted blessing. He called it a 'definite improvement on our present system' and thought it would satisfy public opinion 'better than any other course would'. He objected to it being called a compromise bill, for 'one cannot compromise between hanging a man and not hanging him, it does not admit a compromise, you do the one or the other'. He devoutly hoped that if this Act passed this 'long distressing controversy [would be] allowed to pass for a good time into oblivion'. It had damaged the dignity of the country, and, he went on to joke, was 'very unfair to anyone meditating murder'. He also maintained, rather startlingly, that the entire matter was 'not one of deep principle but one of expediency, as one takes into view the general state of the country and public opinion'.[53]

This was too much even for some of the retentionists. Lord Conesford in his speech on the second reading of the bill said that a moral issue was most definitely involved, and that the proposed distinction between capital and non-capital murders would be found to affront morality. It made this an immoral statute.[54] Both Bell and Ramsey agreed, and, in words the import of which was highly censorious of Fisher, described the Homicide Bill as 'morally shocking'.[55] Gowers, later congratulating Bell on his stand, said that he thought Fisher's position 'utterly unimaginative' and 'untenable by any Christian'.[56] Despite this intervention abolitionists felt abandoned by the Church of England. 'By its failure to assist in the crusade against capital punishment the Church of England lost an opportunity for real ecclesiastical leadership' was the judgment of one of their historians.[57]

The repeated failure of governments to include capital punishment within the parameters of public policy decisively enhanced the influence of the House of Lords over the criminal law of murder. In a matter of conscience, as hanging was allowed to remain, where MPs voted free of party allegiance, it was possible, without causing constitutional disruption, for the Lords to assert their will over their usually dominant junior colleagues. Led by the interventionist Goddard himself, they put an end to abolitionist hopes for the total suspension of the death penalty in 1948 and 1956, forced the withdrawal of one compromise measure and consented to another similar proposal only when it came to be sponsored by a Tory Government.[58] Without Government backing the bills were doomed in the Lords. With the bishops divided and unsure, and Fisher so confidently proposing reforms, there were no moral misgivings about retaining capital punishment in some form.

Public opinion still supported the Lords, but to a lesser extent than before. Between 1948 and 1956 approval for trial suspension had risen in the population as a whole from 13% to 34%, and disapproval had fallen from 69% to 45%. Opinion in the Church of England had mirrored those moves, approval increasing from 10% to 32%, disapproval falling from 72% to 48%. So too had opinion in the Kirk (approval rising from 12% to 30%, disapproval falling from 70% to 44%) and among non conformists in England (approval rising from 17% to 35%, disapproval falling from 66% to 42%). Catholic opinion, on the other hand, had moved much further, approval rising from 15% to 45%, disapproval falling from 66% to 35%. Jewish opinion stayed static, approval declining one point from 40% to 39% and disapproval also declining from 42% to 37%. Approval amongst other religious groups rose from 30% to 40%, disapproval declining from 50% to 37%. Opinion amongst those of no religious belief closely shadowed that of the mainstream churches other than the Catholic, approval rising from 16% to 36%, disapproval falling from 65% to 42%.[59]

Of those who had recently made up their mind against capital punishment almost all said that a major factor was the unease which recent hanging cases had generated, a quarter of the respondents mentioning the Ellis case in particular. Twelve per cent were worried about miscarriages of justice. Those who became opposed to capital punishment did so as a result of specific cases while those who approved of it did so because of murder in general and the danger to children and the old.

From the surveys it is clear that political allegiance was the main barometer of attitude. There was no majority among supporters of any party for suspension, but the strongest showing for it was among Labour and Liberals. As for the churches, the two by law established, the Church of England and the Church of Scotland, were the least likely to support suspension. Most noticeable was the change in Catholic opinion, there being a three-fold increase in Roman Catholics supporting suspension despite the silence of the church hierarchy on the subject.[60] There was little sign of the mainstream churches leading the way; rather they followed in the wake of public opinion, or even lagged behind. It was entirely understandable that the abolitionists should almost despair of them. They were the heirs of their fathers, and their fathers had slain the prophets. Without them, despite them, a few crusading spirits, many Quaker, some Jewish, others isolated individuals within the churches and without, had struggled tirelessly, and seemingly endlessly against the noose. At last they could see the light. One gloried over his foes:

> The principal defenders of hanging have always been the most tradition-bound bodies of the nation: the House of Lords, the Bishops' Bench, the upper ranks of the gowned and wigged profession. Yet in spite of their power and influence over the public mind, chunk after chunk of sacred tradition has been wrenched from their hands: the pillory and the ducking chair, the stake and the gibbet, the cat-o-nine-tails; and within the next few years the strangling cord will be wrested from them too.[61]

16 In the Valley of the Shadow

The Ministry of Chaplains in the Modern Prison Service: 1946–1969

According to our view of Christianity, it ought to be as difficult in a Christian State to find a Christian clergyman to assist at the deprivation of human life, as, thanks to the humane instincts of the common mass, it seems difficult to obtain a wretched mercenary to do the killing. Is it too much to expect to hope that some day the chaplains of the gaols will vindicate their Christianity; and, as one man, petition Parliament against death-punishment . . . We say again, let the gaol chaplains, with one accord, lift their voices in solemn condemnation of the barbarous, the ignorant practice of judicial man-killing; nor will their appeal to the wisdom of Parliament be less benevolent, less Christianlike, if assisted by the dulcet accents of, here and there, a bishop.

Punch[1]

It is curious, but until that moment I had never realized what it means to destroy a healthy, conscious man. When I saw the prisoner step aside to avoid the puddle I saw a mystery, the unspeakable wrongness of cutting a life short when it is in full tide. This man was not dying, he was alive just as we are alive. All the organs of the body were working – bowels digesting food, skin renewing itself, nails growing, tissue forming – all toiling away in solemn foolery. His nails would still be growing when he stood on the drop, when he was falling through the air with a tenth of a second to live. His eyes saw the yellow gravel and grey wall, and his brain still remembered, foresaw, reasoned, even about puddles. He and we were a party of men walking together, seeing, hearing, feeling, understanding the same world; and in two minutes, with a sudden snap, one of us would be gone, one mind less, one world less.

George Orwell[2]

Experience affects different people in different ways, and never more so than for those most intimately involved in the mechanics of judicial death. Two prominent hangmen, John Berry and Albert Pierrepoint, after lifetimes in the job, announced that they were total abolitionists, though their motives for such statements may be questioned. Governors, veterans of executions, could severally testify to the humanity or the horror of it. One would witness that the detrimental effects on those participating were terrible, another that, as professionals, they were unscathed. Some prison officers would volunteer to take part in dozens of hangings, others would view participation as an unpleasant duty, while always it was the policy for those on the death watch to retire and leave it to others who did not know the felon to deliver him to the scaffold. It was considered too traumatic for those who had lived with him to have to watch him die.

More intimately involved than anyone, more personally committed, more engaged in their full humanity were the chaplains, who in the case of prisoners under sentence of death had a unique and vital role from his first day on remand to his last moment on earth. If the role of the late eighteenth and early nineteenth-century chaplains could be typified as inducing confession, and that of the later Victorian chaplains as seeking conversion, that of the twentieth-century chaplains was giving consolation. That is, of course, a gross generalization, and all three purposes overlapped throughout the whole period, but nonetheless it accurately describes the main emphasis of each era.

In the immediate aftermath of the Second World War many men joined the prison service, as governors, or chaplains, or frequently as officers, to be part of an agency for reform. In the war they had often served with the sort of men and boys whom they would find within the prison and Borstal system. Change was in the air and many wanted to be part of it. The evidence of retired governors and chaplains suggest that none had given very much thought to the question of capital punishment before he joined up. A person who wished to be a Borstal housemaster would not be over-exercised by what he would consider to be the distant possibility of being governor of a local prison. Some chaplains did their best to stay away from the gaols where hangings took place; some governors refused promotion so that they would not be posted to such prisons; some would delay joining the service until hanging had been abolished.[3]

One experienced former chaplain records how before he joined the prison service he did not have any particular views on capital punishment. Nor was he specifically asked about it at his interview, but nonetheless he was aware that if he had said he would not take part he would not have been appointed. Active dissent on such an issue would not have been tolerated. However, 'it did not loom large in the consideration to join up'.

> One knew it would be part of the job, accepted it as part of the regime. It was so much part of the system that one on the whole accepted it although unhappily. It was always there and had always been there, you accepted it. It was very easy being at Dartmoor on a limb and out in the wild. Preoccupied with local concerns it was very easy not to keep abreast of what was happening in London.

Another who joined in 1951 had a ruder awakening. At the age of thirty-one he left a remote rural parish, and was sent to Strangeways where executions were common. He had not given much thought to capital punishment before joining and now he was to work in a hanging gaol straight from the parish. He began by taking the conventional position that capital punishment was the just desert for murder, but soon, his experience of the bizarre nature of the whole process and what it did to people changed his attitude completely. Not that all chaplains were to become abolitionists. Some, especially Evangelicals, persisted in defending capital punishment as a just penalty, citing the usual verses from the Old Testament.

If, in the immediate post-war period, hanging were not in the forefront for chaplains when they joined up, by the early 1960s it was impossible for new recruits to evade the issue. One who joined full-time in 1963 acknowledged that 'this question took a vital place in my mind':

> To minister to and accompany the condemned was seen as a possible obligation and responsibility for anyone who became a chaplain. Deep in one's heart one realized it would be a traumatic task and extremely demanding and one sincerely hoped that it would never become a reality to be fulfilled. But should it do so, one committed oneself to God to enable and to provide all the essential qualities to fulfill the role.

Every chaplain knew when he was appointed that he might have to serve in the condemned cell.[4] Training was rudimentary. Often it consisted of a fortnight's general experience in a major prison, but with nothing specific about capital punishment. There were no guidelines and the style of ministry was up to each chaplain.[5]

In local prisons the care of capital cases was the most important part of the job. The same chaplain would deal with the prisoner from remand to trial, to appeal, and to execution. While on remand, a period which could last for up to four months, those accused of murder would be visited every day by the chaplain. Often the chaplain and governor would attend the trial, both to share the experience with the accused, and to gain greater insight into the offence. The execution was set for three weeks after sentence unless there was an appeal. That stopped everything until the appeal could be heard, leading to a delay of six to ten weeks. Following the rejection of an appeal a period of not less than fourteen and not more than eighteen days – three clear Sundays – was allowed before the execution took place. If there were doubt as to the mental state of the prisoner after he had been condemned there was a statutory inquiry when three Home Office officials took evidence from everyone connected with him, and the chaplain was always consulted. Such was the desire of many chaplains to get a reprieve that they might be tempted to exaggerate any mental disorder. Evidence given to the Royal Commission suggested that some chaplains saw that their role in such a process should be crucial, and seemed to view with equanimity the giving of an objective judgment.[6] Other chaplains would consider such a burden insupportable and all would be faced with the dilemma of breaching confidentiality. Some successfully intervened. One told of how a condemned prisoner gave him information about himself shortly before the day of his execution. The chaplain contacted the Bishop of Ripon (who had been to confirm the man) who then sent the information to the Home Secretary and secured a reprieve.[7]

Other than the governor, whose involvement was considerable but remained very formal, the chaplain was the one person who saw the condemned prisoner through the whole process. The guarding officers were spared the end, except on the occasion when the murderer they had watched asked them to be present. The chaplain got to know the condemned person very well, visiting every day, once, twice or even three times, often for along periods. He would see him on his own and it was the only time the two officers with him would leave. Evening visits were especially good. A chaplain might make a morning social visit to play draughts or chess, and an evening one when he would ask the officers to stand outside while he talked of serious spiritual things. While the officers would 'tactfully' steer away from any discussion of the crime and its impending punishment, the chaplain would often encourage talk about such things. One reprieved murderer recalls such a conversation. 'You are going to die in just under three weeks,' the chaplain said. 'I know that you will feel better if you talk to me about your sin, my son. Make your peace and ask to be forgiven and you will go and stand equally with other men.' The murderer, a devout Catholic, was, however, indifferent to his ministrations, although pleased to see him: 'He could not get near to me and I could not reach out to him.'[8]

Ministry had to be very gentle and very sensitive. Every word had to be weighed. It was ministry to an individual in crisis and every case was different. One man might be confirmed in his last days, another talk about boxing; one might want communion in his last minutes, another a cigarette.[9] No one rejected the chaplain though some held him at a distance, initially regarding him with suspicion as someone who was trying to put a seal of respectability on the whole proceedings. Usually, however, they were willing to talk and see him as a friend. He was the one person among staff in a non-disciplinary relationship, and was assumed to be well-disposed. They would sometimes stop him short at a particular point, but often they would become increasingly dependent on 'their' chaplain,[10] and invariably they would ask 'you'll be there, won't you?'

Many responded very gratefully to specifically religious ministrations, especially in their last days when the appeal had been rejected and the hope of reprieve had gone.[11] As soon as the Home Secretary's decision was known to the governor he would immediately communicate the fact to the chaplain who would 'get down there fairly soon afterwards'. 'It was in the last few days', acknowledged one chaplain, 'that one got a wonderful chance to help a man.'[12]

Henry Graham, a soldier hanged in 1925 for the murder of his wife, walked to the gallows chanting 'O, Lamb of God, I come!'.[13] Henry Jacoby was one among many who were confirmed before their execution. Such condemned cell confirmations were as moving for the officiants as for the confirmands. When twenty-three year old Russell Pascoe was baptized and confirmed in the condemned cell in December 1963, the Bishop of Bristol found in the occasion a dramatic 'reminder that no one is beyond God's reach.'[14]

Catholicism had an equally powerful appeal. Roger Casement, the Irish patriot executed for treason in 1916, embraced the Catholic faith in his last days, and while he enjoyed discussing the more arcane points of theology with Fr Casey, the Roman Catholic chaplain at Pentonville, he 'sobbed like a child' when making his first confession.[15] William Joyce, better known to the British public as Lord Haw Haw, who was condemned to death for treason after the Second World War, found in Captain Mervyn-Davies, the Anglican chaplain at Wormwood Scrubs, and his colleague at Wandsworth, men of rare sympathy, with whom he could discuss metaphysics, philology, and religion. Joyce's letters to his wife are full of mention of the conversations he had with and the consolation he received from these chaplains.[16] Before death he professed a firm belief in God as 'the supreme reality', but despite the urging of one of his Catholic friends he saw no need to be reconciled to the faith of his fathers. He thankfully accepted, however, the blessing offered him by Fr Marshall-Keene, an old acquaintance who visited him in the condemned cell. Yet in the hour before his death, on the morning of 3 January 1946, he received communion from the hands of the Anglican chaplain while, as the execution took place, some of his family and friends attended one of the several Requiem Masses being said for him by Catholic priests in London and Ireland.[17] Another non-practising Catholic, Timothy Evans, was visited three times a week by Fr Joseph Francis. Fr Francis found him 'an easy man to contact and attentive to spiritual advice'. As a result Evans began attending Mass and Benediction on Sundays, and asked to receive the sacrament before the end. This he did after making his last confession – a confession of innocence not of guilt – and receiving absolution.[18] Some remained unresponsive. One Roman Catholic chaplain was terribly upset because his prisoner would not make confession and refused the sacrament. The priest took the reserved sacrament with him to the scaffold in case the man changed his mind at the last moment. He did not.

Each chaplain followed his own line of ministry but each knew there was 'a final point, a *terminus ad quem* towards which both he and the prisoner were working'.[19] It was a race against time. For everyone's sake, not least those carrying out the execution, the role of the chaplain was vital. He could prepare the prisoner to meet his end 'manfully':

If they are given the proper preparation they can go to the gallows with their chins right up and face death manfully. It is the preparation that one is able to give them that makes the chaplain's contact so valuable.[20]

Testimony to the value of the work of the chaplain is almost unanimous. One prominent former governor had no doubt that 'chaplains who were able to establish a good rapport with prisoners in these circumstances, helped and supported them enormously and in the final resort helped many of them to go to their death bravely, and with dignity and resignation'.[21] Writing of his prison years a former uniformed officer expressed the belief that the calm with which most murderers met their end was largely the result of the ministrations of the chaplain.[22] On the eve of his execution James Hanratty wrote a long letter to his parents, the last paragraph of which was full of praise for the Catholic priests who had visited him, Fr Keogh from Brixton, a 'fine gentleman' who came 'to give me that extra little bit of courage', and Fr Hulme from Bedford who would also help him to keep his 'courage and spirits up'.[23] It mattered not what faith the condemned person espoused. Another governor had 'watched with admiration' how Anglican chaplains, Roman Catholic priests, and Jewish rabbis had prepared the condemned to die, 'continuing to walk beside them even on that last walk to the scaffold, so that the continuity of spiritual comfort would not be broken'.[24] Sometimes, however, denominational divisions or a reluctance to let in outsiders could militate against the pastoral care of those in their charge. Both the Roman Catholic and Anglican chaplains objected to the visits which Canon Palmer, a Roman Catholic parish priest, made to Edith Thompson at her own request. Thereupon the Prison Commissioners refused to allow him to attend on her.[25]

Rarely did the condemned ask about the actual execution. Often a chaplain would consider it important to tell him it would be very quick, death would be instantaneous, and not to be frightened. Sometimes he would tell him that he had placed a crucifix opposite where he would stand, through the noose, so that he would see the act of salvation on the cross, and look on another executed man as he died. The chaplain would invariably spend the hour before the end with the prisoner, and if he were confirmed, he would celebrate holy communion. It was more difficult when this was not appropriate, leaving a whole hour for the most sensitive conversation. Time would be taken in prayer or the reading of scripture. Sometimes the time would not be enough, and an individual on the edge of doom, interrupted before he had finished reading a psalm, might struggle with his executioners. With unfailing precision, they would enter the condemned cell, pinion the man, walk him briskly through a hidden partition in the cell wall to the gallows, place the noose over his head and pull the lever. From start to finish the whole process took from nine to twenty-five seconds.[26] He was literally dead on time.

In those last seconds there was no written form stipulating what the chaplains should say since the use of the burial service or even sentences from it had been banned in 1927. Perhaps he would murmur, 'unto God's protection we commit you', or 'the Lord bless you and keep you'. Some Roman Catholic priests would give the absolution. After the execution the chaplain signed the public notice, and after the coroner's inquest, buried the corpse in the prison grounds attended by the governor, the foreman of works, and two officers. Then at last, the final duty done, the chaplain would walk in a garden, go away for a few days, or return to visit another prisoner in the condemned cell.

Chaplains responded in various ways to what was for most a traumatic experience. Arguing the rights and wrongs of the punishment does not seem to have been one of them. As participants they remained reticent as to the merits of the thing. It was not for them to say.[27] One governor could not recall ever discussing the ethics of capital punishment with any of the chaplains. Nor did the condemned tax them as to their views on the death penalty. It was not important. The penalty existed, and staff could either resign the service or work with it to attain the best end they could. Public expression of their views was also uncommon. Despite a general feeling of relief among chaplains when hanging was abolished not many had been prepared to speak out against it. They were few in number, isolated, and widely scattered, and, unlike governors, with little sense of cohesion, or opportunity to present a considered chaplaincy view. They were also hampered by what they perceived to be their obligations under the Official Secrets Act, although in this they seem to have acquiesced somewhat more than others working within the Prison Department. Two abolitionist 'Memorials' organized by the NCACP were presented to the Prime Minister of the day in 1956 and 1962.[28] To the former one Jewish and five Anglican chaplains, all of whom had previously retired from the service, appended their names. Five serving governors added theirs. Six years later seven current Anglican chaplains signed. At last at their conference in 1969 the question of presenting a chaplaincy view on the issue was raised, caution was urged and options pointed out, but before any decision could be made on how to proceed, were this desirable, Parliament took the matter out of their hands. The chaplains never realized the hope which *Punch* had expressed in them over a century before.

Yet none was untouched, although some remained reluctant to admit to the full the depth of distress their involvement caused them. The seemingly phlegmatic Baden Ball, in his description of his work at Wandsworth, refers in passing to the toll taken of his 'health and well-being'.[29] Doubts as to the legitimacy of the death penalty were not an element in this. It was not for him to question the Home Secretary's decision about the luckless Derek Bentley, rather it was his task to prepare him to face his death with 'sublime faith' in God's will.[30] In its spare record of duties done the 1952–1953 Chaplain's Journal at Wandsworth nonetheless reveals far more fully than Ball the crushing burden a chaplain in a major hanging jail had to carry. Ball was daily visiting two prisoners under sentence of death (Livesey and Alcott) from 19

November 1952. A third (Curtis) was added on 4 December, and on the day of the passing of the death sentence upon him (11 December), Bentley became the fourth. For one week Ball had to visit four men who were about to die; for two further weeks three. Two executions and one respite reduced the number to one by 19 January 1953. Bentley alone remained. But the strain of such ministry, lasting over two months, was proving too much. The last recorded visit to Bentley was on 23 January. The following day the chaplain, hardly surprisingly, fell ill, returning from sick leave a week later, after Bentley's hanging on the 28th.[31] In his autobiography Baden Ball made no mention of this, and indeed strongly implied that he attended the execution himself. He resigned later that year.[32]

Chaplains who alleged that hanging had a minimal effect on those involved might therefore be so insensitive themselves as not to feel it, as some of their predecessors undoubtedly were, or, more likely, might be so much a part of the prison culture as to conceal it, as Baden Ball seems to have done. In evidence to the Royal Commission, one former prisoner (a conscientious objector in the First World War) said that he could recall one execution at Winchester and was amazed to read the evidence of the chaplains. According to his testimony there was throughout 'an atmosphere of tension on prison officers and prisoners alike, a tendency to gossip about the morbid details'.[33] A former General Secretary of the Prison Officers' Association openly acknowledged the terrible strain of the death watch, and admitted to having nightmares of being hanged himself.[34]

Those most distressed by the experience, or who could not cope with it, left the service. So traumatized was one Roman Catholic priest by his first hanging that he walked out of prison work. A former Anglican chaplain testified that it was 'some years after leaving the prison service' before he was free from 'the haunting picture of an execution'.[35] Another, who admittedly had served for less than two years between 1948 and 1949, and had witnessed only one execution, cast doubt on the evidence of prison officials in general and chaplains in particular on the grounds that all, 'except perhaps a few rebellious spirits', would have assented to 'the body of prison conditioned belief'.[36] It was neither manly to be distressed by, nor dutiful to question, what went on. A more experienced chaplain, the Revd Joseph Walker, agreed with him that the outward appearance of prison officials did not mean that they were not deeply affected. He knew of two such who became very ill as a result of their execution work.[37] Another witness before the Royal Commission had been a chaplain for about four years, during which time he had attended the execution of one prisoner. He would not state categorically that his experiences were directly responsible for his poor state of health, but he had 'little doubt that the emotional strain of that time was a contributory factor', and he fully supported what Walker had told the Commission.[38]

The hanging of women seems to have had the most profoundly unsettling effect on the participants. Such discrimination between the sexes may strike us oddly today but these views were once commonplace. George Bernard Shaw in his play *Saint Joan* graphically portrayed the chaplain who advocated capital punishment in the abstract, but when faced with its reality, in the burning of a woman, recoiled in horror at her fate and at himself.

> For Christ's sake pray for my wretched guilty soul. I am not a bad man . . . I meant no harm. I did not know what it would be like. I did not know what I was doing. You don't know, you haven't seen. It is so easy to talk when you don't know. You madden yourself with words; you damn yourself because it feels grand to throw oil on the flaming hell of your own temper. But when it is brought home to you; when you see the thing you have done, when it is blinding your eyes, tearing your heart, then . . . O God take away this sight from me! O Christ, deliver me from this fire that is consuming me![39]

Glanville Murray had left the service after the execution of Mrs Thompson in 1923. Her death had particularly preyed on his mind. This may in part have been the result of a guilty conscience since she had voiced indignant objections to his ministrations which had frequently consisted in pressing her for a confession she was not going to make. By the end he had much regretted this tack, being entirely convinced of her innocence.[40] Such was her state on the morning of the execution that 'it seemed utterly impossible to believe what we were there to do. My God the impulse to rush in and save her by force was almost too strong for me.'[41]

The Revd Joseph Walker, formerly chaplain of Liverpool and Manchester prisons, who resigned after suffering heart attacks following the death of Margaret Allen in 1949, had 'no doubt that the emotional strain of the events connected with this execution was one of the factors leading to [his] breakdown'.[42] He had gone 'into the prison service without any definite views at all on hanging' but left it 'with the definite view that a woman should not be hanged'. As he watched the hanging of Mrs Allen he 'felt . . . that it was bestial and brutal'.[43]

The ordeal was greatest in the case of those chaplains who became very friendly with the condemned person.

> The chaplain has shared his waiting period, shared his sufferings, he has sympathized with him, and had become joined to him in a very real spiritual and mental sense. When the man is executed the chaplain suffers with him just as he has suffered with him all the time he has been waiting for execution. I think the chaplain is more likely to suffer from something of that sort than anyone else in the whole of the prison. The officers who sit with the prisoner during the waiting period, will not be affected because

they are not expected to attend the execution. The officers who attend at the execution do not know the prisoner very well.[44]

Although the chaplains were involved as priests speaking in God's name, many felt an element of guilty complicity in their participation. One recorded how he reluctantly complied with the governor's request to take a condemned man to the chapel so that the executioner, sitting in the Principal Officer's box in the Centre and disguised in a peaked cap, could observe him. Fr Matthew O'Brien, the Roman Catholic priest at Leeds prison in the 1950s, took his charge to the chapel ostensibly to show him some fine prints in the missal, but in reality to keep him out of the way while the gallows were being tested. The prisoner was not fooled: 'I know why I am here. They're testing that thing down there, aren't they?' The chaplain replied that they were. He could not have told him anything else. If he had, he would not have trusted him again.[45]

Another chaplain felt 'dirtied and sullied and corroded' by being part of the process. He was preaching the gospel of the uniqueness of each creation, and men would die. At 8.40 in the morning he was giving a prisoner communion, at 8.55 shaking his hand, and two hours later burying him. This was a Christian gloss on Orwell's observation. Each execution was totally traumatic, a bereavement every time. As soon as he had been involved in a hanging he began to realize that it was 'a corrosive experience for everyone concerned'. It was corrosive for all the staff involved, even though they would often not admit it. One governor related how he could not get any volunteers to be on the death watch. Another that he could not help asking himself 'why, when one was called upon to superintend an execution, one should have been affected with such a keen sense of personal shame'.[46] For the chaplain it was corrosive spiritually and emotionally in that the existence of a man in the condemned cell overshadowed everything else: 'prison life went on, but before you left each day you had to visit that man'. There was 'an oppressive urgency'. It was corrosive for the institution:

> Chaplains were part of the rehabilitative exercise pointing to the future and yet overshadowing all was that this was a place of death. Non-hanging prisons had a different feel. There was a positive drive and thrust at the time towards rehabilitation. Originally all prisons were locals, and had to do with containment, but immediately after the War the rehabilitative ideal was increasing. Yet this archaic vestige was 'hanging' over you. The public saw prisons as purely punitive places for corporal and capital punishment, but idealistic governors and chaplains wanted to bring about change, introducing new programmes. The chaplain was at the very centre of creative work. Hanging ran counter to all this.[47]

17 Choose Life

The Death Throes of Hanging: 1957–1969

I have set before you life and death, blessing and cursing: therefore
choose life, that both thou and thy seed may live.

Deuteronomy 30.19

Scroop: Let him be punish'd, sovereign, lest example
            Breed, by his sufferance, more of such a kind.
King Henry: O! Let us yet be merciful.
Cambridge: So may your highness, and yet punish, too.

William Shakespeare[1]

Hanging, as it turned out, had been granted a temporary respite, not a reprieve. The Homicide Act attempted to do what the Royal Commission on Capital Punishment had concluded was not practicable, namely, to divide murder into one category for which the penalty would remain hanging, and another for which it would be life imprisonment. As many predicted, the Homicide Act and its distinctions soon proved to be unworkable and immoral. The assumption underlying it was not that some murders were more heinous than others, and therefore deserved hanging, while others did not; it was that some murderers thought before they acted and so could be deterred. No account was taken of degrees of moral culpability, and for this reason its application was soon found to be profoundly unsatisfactory. As in the eighteenth century punishment and justice had been severed with disastrous moral results. A farmer who in a rage shot his wife would hang, whereas had he bludgeoned her to death with the shotgun stock he would not. A bank robber who in making his escape ran over and killed a policeman would die for it; a poisoner who with premeditation and deliberation had slowly killed his victim, but who unaccountably remained outside the capital criteria, would not.

Further, the Act was soon shown to be ineffective. It was not having the desired and expected deterrent effect on those categories of murder which were still capital. The 1961 Government Red Book, *Murder*, showed that the proportion of capital murders had gone up from 12.1% in 1952 to 18.7% in 1960. Nor had the fears of those who predicted an increase in the murder rate as a result of partial abolition been realised. The Red Book showed no increase in murder and manslaughter on the grounds of diminished responsibility since 1957. Indeed the proportion of non-capital murders declined from 87.9% in 1952 to 81.3% in 1960.[2] Ironically, an Act designed to maintain the limited effectiveness of capital punishment against its critics had merely strengthened their case for complete abolition.

Between March 1957 when the Homicide Act came into force and December 1964 when Silverman introduced his Abolition Bill into the Commons forty-eight people were sentenced to death for capital murder, but only twenty-nine were executed, an average of between three and four a year. While 1960 saw seven hangings, and 1961 four, the number fell to two in each of the succeeding three years. Despite the greater gravity of post–1957 capital murders over pre–1957 ordinary murders just under 40% were reprieved, a drop of only 5% from the pre–1957 period. Even the judiciary were coming to believe that abolition was preferable to the perpetuation of these seemingly arbitrary executions. Fisher's hopes for a less clumsy system were being dashed.

The first murderer to suffer under the new Act, the first for nearly two years, John Vickers, was executed on 23 July 1957. Christian Action organized an all night vigil at the Quaker headquarters in Marylebone Road which six members of Parliament attended. Pentonville, after a gap of five years, experienced two executions in as many weeks. Marwood, the second man to die, was a local lad, well-known to many of the occupants of the cells. He had been condemned for the killing of a policeman in a drunken brawl, and many people had anticipated and hoped for a reprieve. On the eve of his hanging there was a riot in the prison which 'disturbed even more the atmosphere surrounding the death cell, its inmate and guards'.[3] During the turmoil pages torn from a Bible floated down from a solitary cell. The following morning mounted police had to be summoned to control the 1,000 strong crowd outside the prison gates. At the time of his death there was an awful silence broken by a little girl saying 'Poor Mr Marwood'. Many considered that his crime was not sufficiently heinous to merit the full rigour of the law. Other cases also gave rise to concern. Grave doubts were expressed about the guilt of James Hanratty, the 'A6 murderer'. The Roman Catholic parish priest who had visited him believed in his innocence and took the extraordinary step of going public on the issue.[4] Demonstrations continued unabated outside hanging prisons to such an extent that the Home Secretary was asked to consider keeping the time and date of executions secret. He declined.[5]

Collins continued to preach abolitionist sermons from his influential pulpit in St Pauls. The NCACP, which had suspended its activities after the passing of the Homicide Act, was revived and revitalized by Gollancz. In December 1960 he announced that he would launch a new campaign which would 'be continued unremittingly' until total abolition was secured. Joint chairman with him in the new enterprise was Gerald Gardiner, and Canon Edward Carpenter, treasurer of Westminster Abbey, added ecclesiastical weight to the executive committee. They were convinced that support for abolition had been increasing enormously among 'the more thoughtful sections of the community' and that one last effort would secure final victory.

The Conservative Government remained unmoved. The Home Secretary, Rab Butler, turned down demands from Chuter Ede for a new inquiry into the Evans' case after the publication in 1961 of Ludovic Kennedy's careful study of it. He further refused to do Silverman's bidding and scrap the Homicide Act, and denied that any promise had been made to review its workings after five years. While the crime wave continued he could not contemplate any dilution in the armoury of justice. The time, as ever, was not ripe.

Yet it was soon to be. The end was now near. And the Church of England, as had so often been the case with capital punishment in the past, was to be in on the kill. But with a difference. In less than a decade it had undergone a complete revolution in its attitude. The church had been converted. The accepted norms of centuries were discarded almost overnight. In the 1950s more and more of the clergy had become concerned about the issue of the death penalty. As their interest in it grew so too had their opposition to it. At the episcopal level Bell had no longer stood alone. Several of his colleagues were abolitionist, and the Archbishop of York, albeit with reservations, was firmly in the abolitionist camp. The momentum for change within the hierarchy of the church grew enormously. This was consolidated first by the replacement of the reactionary Fisher by Ramsey in 1961. They were poles and generations apart. Ramsey had been a pupil at Repton when Fisher had been Headmaster, and their relationship throughout their adult life was largely dominated by this fact. Fisher did not want him as his successor, for in reality Ramsey was the successor to the tradition begun by Temple, carried on by Bell, and interrupted by Fisher. The arguments they deployed on the issue of capital punishment and other matters might often be similar but their attitudes were very different.

The second factor was the completion of a process of a change of opinion among the Anglican bishops which had been gaining slow momentum over the previous decade. This was brought about by the coming to office, at long last, and within a very short space of time, of a whole generation of younger and more critical bishops, replacing men who in many cases had held office for decades. Of the twenty-nine diocesan bishops in the Province of Canterbury twenty-one had been appointed between 1956 and 1962 and sixteen of these twenty-one were new to the episcopacy; of the fourteen in the Northern Province eight had been appointed in the same period and six of them were new bishops. Their predecessors had held sway for many years, and their replacement within so short a period signalled a revolution. The change in atmosphere was extraordinary. No longer were abolitionists the vociferous minority among the episcopate; retentionists, rather, were the moribund dinosaurs.[6]

The Diocese of Southwark under its radical new bishop, Mervyn Stockwood, and his suffragan John Robinson, both ardent campaigners for abolition, led the way in the Southern Province. Stockwood, an avowed socialist, realized that it was vital to secure the victory of the Labour Party in order to bring about the abolition of the death penalty. The Tories had to go. In October 1961, while Robinson declared from the pulpit at Canterbury that 'one last shove' would see the end of capital punishment in England, one of the junior South Bank clergy, the Revd F. P. Coleman, introduced a motion into the Lower House of Convocation urging Parliament to suspend the death penalty for five years. Despite the intervention of the Archdeacon of Dudley, a former prison chaplain, who urged again the deterrent case for the 'sparing use of execution', the motion was carried by a large majority.

Buoyed up by this decision, the following month Bishop Mortimer of Exeter, an erstwhile retentionist, pressed in the Lords for a change in the Homicide Act to bring about abolition. Again his lucid and concise speech made a considerable impact.[7] The church press, Anglican and Roman Catholic, was deluged with letters which, as printed, were evenly balanced for and against hanging.[8] The Archbishops of Canterbury and Westminster appeared on a television documentary as the leading representatives of their respective confession's views. Ramsey appeared thoughtfully noncommittal, urging individual Christians to give the subject the appropriate measure of serious thought. Cardinal Godfrey reiterated the traditional position of the Roman Church: the state had the right and even the duty to kill if, in its own judgment, the life of the community was threatened by a particular sort of crime.[9]

Early in the New Year Mervyn Stockwood decided to take the issue to the Upper House of the Convocation of Canterbury. Aware that some of the older bishops might oppose abolition or procrastinate on the issue, and fearing that the episcopal bench might be divided, in January 1962 he brought before Convocation a compromise motion that hanging be abolished for an experimental period and then reviewed.[10] He 'reminded' a rather surprised gathering of the often ignoble role of their predecessors in the hundred and fifty year campaign to abolish hanging. It was time now for them to lead the way. He believed that hanging was a denial of the gospel, and that the state by practising it was taking to itself the prerogative of God.[11]

Stockwood found everybody in agreement with his aims if not always with his arguments, for not all were as absolutist as he. Yet although some of the bishops reiterated the old Thomist arguments of the state being justified, and even compelled to take life in its own preservation, they conceded that developments in the modern perception of crime, and the ending of a specifically Christian society, had rendered them largely irrelevant. Mortimer, the seconder of Stockwood's motion, made two very important new points.

The first was that the sort of offender whom Aquinas typified as 'pernicious', or as 'a source of corruption to the whole society', would now be categorized as a sexual psychopath and incarcerated in a mental asylum. Most murderers were domestic and hardly corresponded to Thomist categories. The second was that in modern society murder often posed less of a threat to the welfare of society than prostitution, drug-peddling, and the exploitation of human need and poverty,[12] all offences for which capital punishment was not exacted.

Oliver Tomkins, Bishop of Bristol, another of Stockwood's generation, and a close friend of George Bell, said that the real moral question was 'did a murderer *deserve* to die?' On lines similar to Camus, he argued that the death penalty could not be justified in a secular society. There was a very solid and continuous Christian tradition of moral theology that in certain circumstances the state was justified in taking life, not on the basis of 'the sub-Christian *lex talionis*', but only if it could be shown that such an act of retribution itself included the possibility of redemptive and remedial action. He was sure that it was only in a society which believed unshakeably in the reality of eternal life and the reality of judgment by a living God that capital punishment could ever be a moral possibility. Changes in society, however, now made this morally untenable. Society was no longer Christian. If death were extinction then any possibility of redemption after death was impossible. Only in a Christian society was it conceivable that the retribution exacted by the death penalty was compatible with the notion of remedial, redemptive action. Precisely because this assumption could not be made with wide and deep assurance by the society in which they lived, Tomkins concluded that the death penalty ought to be abolished: 'A society which could not with confidence assert that a man *deserved* to die had no right to kill him.'[13] Stockwood's motion was passed unanimously.

A last dramatic, and rather pathetic encounter between the old order and the new occurred when the Archdiocese of York debated in full synod a similar motion proposed by Charles Claxton, Bishop of Blackburn. A Labour supporter and a member of the Transport and General Workers Union, he and Stockwood had been friends and political allies since before the Second World War. Together, simultaneously, they launched their campaigns. Archbishop Donald Coggan, like his brother Canterbury, was a firm abolitionist, in part because of the Evans case. Others, such as Gerald Ellison at Chester, a recent convert, considered that the Homicide Act had made a mockery of any notion of retribution. Only one bishop, Maurice Harland, now translated from Lincoln to Durham, opposed Claxton's motion. For the last time, a bishop with considerable personal experience of ministering to the condemned defended the means by which such ministry was made possible. For clergy of the old school, such as Harland was, so unhappy with modern society, so largely starved of genuine response to their ministrations, so largely ignored in their work, so often not needed by the citizens of a secular society, the susceptibility to religious influence of men under the shadow of the gallows was a rich vein of encouragement. In the condemned cell if nowhere else the priest was indispensable: he would be the friend, share the sorrow, hear the confession, save the soul.

When at Lincoln, Bishop Harland had ministered to six condemned men. He had confirmed two, and had communicated three of them just prior to their executions, executions which he had attended. He recounted the story of one of them, a thirty-five-year-old man who had gloried in his infamous murder of a hospital matron in the chapel. The part-time chaplain could not cope, and with a week to go asked the bishop to intervene. He saw him on his own, and as his predecessor King had done so many years before, read him the story of the Prodigal Son. The man burst into tears. Soon he was confirmed, and after receiving the sacrament on his last night, he refused to take any sedative, saying he wanted to pay for what he had done. It was a unique experience for Harland who had never seen a man more fit for his Maker. Had he been given a life sentence, the bishop feared, 'it would have been a continuance of prison life to which he was already accustomed and no conversion might well have occurred'. The whole inexorable procedure of the death penalty rendered a man more susceptible to the gospel day by day. Clinically, Harland detailed the breakdown of the condemned man's resistance to the gospel: first he cannot believe that this will happen to him, then he pins all his hopes on a reprieve, but by the end of the second week 'he feels pretty certain that he is "going through that door" '. Then 'if you are there, in the providence of God, life-and-death and the rest become a reality to him; and the sheer horror of sin, so conspicuously lacking from our day and generation, bursts upon him and upon those who minister to him'. In mercy to the murderer we must not deprive him of his last chance. Harland was convinced that 'with the brutal type' it was doubtful if anything but the certainty of imminent death could bring them to repentance and need for God. Consequently he feared that 'the absolute abolition of the death penalty [would] rob them of their only hope of salvation'. In view of this experience he would find it very difficult to vote for abolition. He considered that the arguments for abolition were unreal 'compared with the reality of dealing with these people in their particular circumstances'. He put an odd twist into the story of the crucifixion:

> I have been reminded so much of the truth expressed by the penitent thief on the cross when he saw Christ and saw himself and was thankful to be crucified. 'We indeed justly, for we receive the due reward of our deeds' – and that is exactly what has been happening in my experience in those who have been glad to pay. The hardest task I have had in this connection has been breaking the news to two men that they have been reprieved, and to help them face up to the fact that they had got to learn to live with

themselves . . . It is in view of my dealings with the murderer, that I find it difficult to vote for this resolution.

Again he complained of the inadequacy of modern society, and clearly thought that the abolition of the death penalty would see the destruction of all moral sense and the passing of the old ways entirely: 'In these days of insensitivity to the sheer fact and horror of sin – and the crowning sin of all is murder – I cannot feel that we should lightly abolish something which is admittedly no deterrent to particular crimes . . . but which [gives] us a consciousness of right and wrong, and the truth of the sanctity of life.'

And that despite the horrors attendant on an execution: it took the bishop 'a good fortnight', when he had been present at 'one of these beastly things, to get it out of [his] system'. Was it such a bad thing, he asked, that the feel of a prison, on the morning of an execution was tense? He thought that 'we need to have brought to us the horror of the fact that these things can be'. The sacredness of human life could easily be forgotten and overlooked.[14]

Canon Hussey, thanking Durham for his words, cited a governor as saying that 'it is in the condemned cell that the gospel comes into its own'.[15] Despite such support, the argument of Bishop Harland, once so influential when Fisher ruled the church,[16] had become increasingly untenable, even ridiculous. Bishop Greer of Manchester damned his account as 'moving but irrelevant', pointing out that 'the logical conclusion of what he has suggested is that it would be very helpful indeed if many people in our parishes, and indeed we ourselves, were under sentence of death'. He referred to the extraordinary accounts of human bravery, endurance and goodness in the Nazi concentration camps and under torture, 'but none of us would on that account say that torture is a thing which might be retained in any judicial system'.[17]

An equally antediluvian action was fought on the biblical basis of capital punishment. Llewelyn Hughes, the Dean of Ripon, and a former Chaplain-General to the Forces, opposed the motion because he feared that they were 'substituting another voice for the voice of Providence and of the Bible'. His Bible made no protest against the death penalty. The law in Genesis fixed the point at which life was forfeit very firmly, and in Old Testament times large numbers of people were judicially done to death. The gospel story centred on the death penalty. There was 'every insistence that the condemned person was innocent, the trial "rigged", authority was cowardly . . . but nowhere [was] there the slightest suggestion that the penalty itself was wrong'. If Christ had been reprieved or condemned to imprisonment for life, the Dean did not 'know where the New Testament story would have gone'. Christ upon the gibbet was an incentive to worship, not a symbol of protest against the death penalty. As for the parables they contained 'examples of the death penalty, obviously approved: wicked husbandmen miserably destroyed; wicked people bound in bundles and burnt'. The Book of Revelation clearly believed that

God would 'exact the death penalty on a simply colossal scale in the end'. The only way to escape this conclusion, asserted Hughes, was to rewrite the Bible or 'agree with modern writers that the God [depicted there] is wicked'.

His church too – 'itself a burner of heretics' – had taken an equally robust attitude to capital punishment until recently when the abolitionist cause had been 'picked up . . . through a social conscience of those who have gone soft'.

Most bizarre of all was the one novel argument he urged for retention: the ritual of the coronation. The motion, thought Hughes, made nonsense of what was 'the magnificent, the truly Christian preaching of the ceremony of the five swords in the coronation service'. 'There', he said, 'you get the matter, in those five swords, put as admirably as the Church of Christ has ever put it'. This was Establishment gone mad.[18] We are not finished yet. The Dean had a very odd view of murder: people should think of the consequences before 'going in for' it. If the gallows were 'the certain consequence' of murder and if 'the idea that they would be avoided was not bolstered up by such motions as this, then I think that fewer assassins would go in for their crimes'.[19]

This extraordinary and lengthy contribution clearly indicates that many of the arguments for and against the death penalty remained virtually unchanged throughout a century and a half, and also that by the 1960s such arguments, taken seriously only half a decade before, had a wondrously dated feel. More, they were absurd. The synod was left speechless. Blackburn, in response, was 'not quite sure what to say'.[20] But one thing he must. Both could cite scripture for their purpose. He reminded him that Sunday by Sunday he stood up and said that 'God desireth not the death of a sinner but rather that he shall turn from his wickedness and live.'[21] It was the last gasp. As the Bishop of Durham and the Dean of Ripon sat down they must have felt their time had gone for ever. The motion passed overwhelmingly with only sixteen members of the Lower House voting with Harland and Hughes.[22]

When the same year the NCACP drew up another Memorial to the Prime Minister signed by prominent people in the arts, sciences, politics, education, law and the church, its signatories included the Archbishop of York, thirty-one diocesan, six suffragan, and two assistant bishops. A similar Memorial in 1956 had attracted the signatures of neither archbishop, and only five diocesans, eight suffragans and two assistant bishops had signed. No Welsh bishop signed either. Nor did any Roman Catholic.

Abolitionist resolutions had already been passed without dissent by the British Council of Churches, the Quaker Meeting of Sufferings, and the Free Church Federal Council, and many other prominent persons including the Lord Chief Justice had declared themselves in a similar way, but a near unanimous vote of the bishops, a volte-face from their recent position, gave a great fillip to the campaigners and increased the chances of getting a bill through the Lords. For the first time the religious undergirding of capital punishment for so long supplied by the Established Church had been withdrawn. A Leader in *The Times* commented that the church had decisively changed its attitude. With the exception of Temple, the bishops had taken no part in the movement for abolition up until the mid-twentieth century, but now, under the leadership of Ramsey, they had aligned themselves as a body with the position of his great predecessor.[23] In this the church was flaunting public opinion, since all opinion polls in 1962 and 1964 registered an 80% majority in favour of hanging.[24] The *Daily Record*, which did not favour abolition, hinted that some of the bishops might have slept during the debate, but it recorded Ramsey as expressing his pleasure 'in a soft voice, as if trying to placate the ghosts of the nineteenth-century bishops who would have burst their gaiters in horror at the suggestions of ending the death penalty'. *The Economist* recognized the significance of this shift: 'The effect of the opinion of the Anglican Church on the views of Conservative backbenchers, can be surprisingly decisive.'[25] Even greater shocks were to come for those episcopal spirits. Where one Archbishop of Canterbury had led his bishops in total opposition to the curtailment of hanging, another was to lead his into unanimous opposition to hanging.

The leader of the Labour Party, Harold Wilson, who had been one of the Committee of Honour of the NCACP in 1956, appointed its chairman, Gerald Gardiner QC, to the House of Lords in 1962 as the prospective Lord Chancellor. So committed an abolitionist was Gardiner that he had previously refused promotion to the Bench, even though he would have been in the Chancery Division, because he was not prepared to share the responsibility with his fellow judges for hanging people.

On Thursday 13 August 1964 the last executions in Britain took place almost unnoticed: Peter Anthony Allen in Liverpool, and Gwynne Owen Evans in Manchester were hanged for the murder of John West, a laundry van driver. Being northern executions they aroused little interest. The *Mirror* recorded the event in nine lines, most of which dealt with the 'silent meditation protest' led by a Preston curate. In Leeds sixteen people held a half-hour vigil, while in Bristol protestors stood silent and bare-headed outside the cathedral.[26]

In October Labour won the general election, and this time abolition would not be sacrificed to other considerations. Accorded a unique mention in the Queen's Speech, the veteran Sydney Silverman introduced a Private Member's Bill for abolition in December, and the Cabinet allowed time for debate. Opinion polls consistently showed a three to one majority in favour of retention, predominantly on retributive rather than deterrent grounds. It was important, in order to ease the passage of so unpopular a measure, to gain the moral high ground. Lord Longford, Leader of the House, and Gardiner, by then Lord Chancellor, asked Ramsey if he would take charge of the Bill in the Lords and pilot it through. Silverman, that arch-enemy of archbishops, wrote with a formal invitation pointing out that 'it is quite certain that with the bill in your hands the chances of ultimate success would be so much greater'.[27]

Ramsey felt he was only an 'amateur parliamentarian', but he was prepared to stand up to the abuse of the other side, and to cancel other important engagements in so significant a cause. As Temple had done before him, so Ramsey, with the passing of time, had become ever more convinced that hanging had to end. Morally, the injustices of the Homicide Act had shocked him; intellectually, he had found the evidence for the alleged unique deterrent effect of capital punishment to be completely lacking; psychologically, he had become increasingly freed from the old incubus, Fisher, and he knew that in taking the stand he did he represented an almost unanimous episcopate. Counting on the considerable support from the Lord Chancellor and others, he accepted what he considered to be both a duty and a privilege.[28]

While Longford greeted this letter as wonderful news Lord Dilhorne was horrified to hear of it. He thought it monstrous if the impression were given that the enemies of the Bill were less moral than its advocates. *The Economist* had been right in its assessment of the influence the Church of England had on the Tories, but it was in the Lords, so long and so obdurately opposed to abolition, that the effect was most to be felt. In desperation Dilhorne wrote to Ramsey begging him not to pilot the Bill, even threatening him. He and many others felt it would be 'unwise and inappropriate' for the head of the church to move the second reading of a Bill which was so controversial and about which feelings ran so high. He had mentioned this rumour to an old and distinguished member of the House who had commented that if it were true it was 'both shocking and unwise'. Dilhorne had no doubt that if Ramsey sponsored the Bill it would 'give rise to very strong criticism both in the House and outside' which would be 'bound to impair [his] position and that of our church'.[29] Ramsey held out for a long time, but in June, when two civil servants whom he had consulted concurred with Dilhorne, and warned that in the embittered atmosphere his prominence could produce the Bill might not pass, he finally withdrew. He would, however, do all he could to secure its passage.

In the Commons Silverman moved the second reading of his Bill with a powerful, unscripted address. Henry Brooke, a former Conservative Home Secretary, said that because of the anomalies of the Homicide Act he now favoured a trial abolition. His conversion meant that five of the former holders of this office had decided that the death penalty should be abolished.[30] The Bill passed in July 1965.

It then went to the Lords. The Bishop of Chester spoke in the debate, telling the House of his recent change of view. He was now persuaded that the death penalty was a bad punishment, confounding religion, and making nonsense of retribution. The actual procedure, the use of mental and spiritual suffering as a means of punishment, smacked too much of torture.[31] The highpoint was Ramsey's speech.[32] Just like all his predecessors he believed that retribution was a necessary and valid aspect of punishment: 'the wrongdoer suffers punishment because he deserves to; and the recognition on his part that he is getting something that he deserves is a necessary step towards his reformation'. But beyond that there ought to be 'the possibility of reclamation . . . the possibility of a person being alive, repentant, and different'. If this could happen in this world, and not only for the world to come, we should strive for that to be so.

Secondly, the death penalty devalued human life. Proof of its unique deterrent effect might have swayed him but there was no such proof. The Homicide Act had led, as he had predicted, to intolerable moral dilemmas for Home Secretaries. With this pragmatic division between capital and non-capital murders it seemed that law and morality had diverged on the very point where it was imperative for them to coincide.

Life should replace death. Again he used the traditional argument about the violation of society's norms, but this time he argued that that violation could be satisfied by imprisonment:

> The sentence for the crime of murder ought to have a retributive moral seriousness about it: therefore, I believe that the life sentence is right, even though it again and again, and perhaps almost always, be mitigated in practice. The life sentence says to a convicted murderer, 'You have outraged society by killing one of your fellows. You must expect no claim to your old place in society for a very long time, not, indeed, until society can be told that you are on the way to being a different sort of person from what you are now.' I believe that, thus understood, a life sentence carries with it a moral meaning.[33]

In a significant omission he never said, as all his predecessors including Temple had done, and as he himself had done before, that there was a right for society to take the life of its citizens.

All this was delivered with gravitas, without attempt to elicit an emotional response to an emotive issue, and without a touch of self-righteousness.

One of Ramsey's most vociferous opponents was Viscount Kilmuir. In an earlier incarnation as David Maxwell Fyfe he had been the Home Secretary who had let the law take its course in the case of Derek Bentley. Although the Catholic hierarchy had appealed for a reprieve, no intercession had come from Lambeth. Later as Lord Chancellor, along with Lord Dilhorne, he had devised the Homicide Act as the minimum necessary to protect society and deter violence. Then he had received the full and fulsome backing of Archbishop Fisher. The turn around in the Anglican church bewildered and disturbed him. In over forty years in politics he never thought that he 'should see the day when public opinion would be sneered at from the Bench of Bishops and every other part of this House'.[34]

It was enough. For the first time the bishops of the Church of England had wholeheartedly championed an abolition bill, and for the first time an abolition bill was to be approved in the Lords. The Bill passed its Second reading by

204 votes to 104. Ramsey and nine other bishops voted in favour, none against. The Archbishop had ensured that Harland, who would have proved an exception, was engaged elsewhere. Before the Bill became law in November 1965 two amendments were moved. The first required both Houses to declare by affirmative resolution before 31 July 1970 that the Act be extended, otherwise the law would revert to that contained in the Homicide Act 1957. The second, moved in the Lords by the Lord Chief Justice, Lord Parker, gave judges the power to recommend the minimum period to be served before a person sentenced to life for murder could be released. In view of these safeguards the Archbishop of York, who was 'unashamedly for abolition', urged an overwhelming vote in favour of the Bill. At 5.30 pm on 28 October 1965 the Commons accepted the latter amendment. The Murder (Abolition of the Death Penalty) Bill was sent up for Royal Assent on 8 November, and passed into law.[35]

Public opinion was unconvinced and in the years after temporary abolition the majority in favour of hanging reached 85% of the population.[36] The murder of five police officers, including three in one shooting at Notting Hill, in the first two years after the suspension of hanging predictably led to calls for its reimposition. Edward Leadbitter, a Labour MP, told the Home Secretary that if the alternative did not work hanging would have to be reintroduced. Humphrey Berkeley on the other hand, a former Tory MP and then treasurer of the Howard League, warned against emotional responses, and pointed out that in the period 1958–1961 eight policemen had been murdered. *The Times* too warned the Tories not to make hanging a party political matter which it had never been before.[37] Now in opposition, the retentionists found that they too could be skilled propagandists. The Tory MP Duncan Sandys recruited 4–5,000 volunteers to collect signatures for a petition to Parliament which finally ended up with over 40,000. For his pains he was denounced by name from the pulpit of St Pauls by Canon Collins, who accused him of 'trying to frighten people into taking immoral decisions'.[38] Another local petition containing 4,000 names was handed into the House of Commons by the parents of a five-year-old girl who had recently been murdered. One hundred thousand forms were distributed in Glasgow by a pro-hanging committee set up by Walter Wober, a Conservative local councillor.[39]

The experiment, however, survived this early crisis. Physically the reintroduction of hanging was made more difficult by the conversion of the condemned cells for other uses and the destruction of all the apparatus in every prison other than Wandsworth.[40] Nor would the United Kingdom Government provide such apparatus for other countries. Although public opinion remained consistently and increasingly pro-hanging, it was clear that the weight of informed opinion was abolitionist: all the Labour and 30% of the Conservative

MPs, and the majority of civil servants, university dons, journalists, criminologists, and lawyers.[41]

The requisite affirmative motions were carried in December 1969. It was an occasion of remarkable harmony. In the Commons the leaders of all three major parties (Harold Wilson, Edward Heath and Jeremy Thorpe) voted for abolition. The arguments on both sides left the troubled waters of morality and concentrated almost entirely on the equally contentious but less emotive issue of deterrence. The statistical evidence was inconclusive, and members voted according to other criteria, including, of course, ethical. Very few had changed their minds since 1965. Within this miasma of statistical uncertainty many found it impossible to balance the sure evil of the organized and institutionalized killing of known murderers against the predicted saving of unknown and unknowable potential victims. The resolution was carried by 343 votes to 185 on 16 December.

In the Upper Chamber, Lord Gardiner, the Lord Chancellor, made what was described by one onlooker as the greatest speech he had ever heard. Michael Ramsey again spoke, as had another leading left-wing figure in the church, Ian Ramsey, the new Bishop of Durham, the previous day. The latter, a short, stocky Lancastrian, with a strong and unprelatical Northern brogue, forthrightly denounced the death penalty but raised again the question of what substitute should be put in its place, given the terrible effects of lengthy imprisonment.[42] It is a question still with us. Both the archbishops and seventeen other bishops voted in favour. Only Mortimer of Exeter, on the pragmatic grounds of wanting to carry public opinion which he thought would be more likely after a further delay,[43] effectively voted otherwise by serving as a teller against the Government's motion. Most of the judges voted with the bishops. On 18 December the Lords joined the Commons in passing the motion, in their case by a narrower margin of 220 votes to 174. Capital punishment had been relegated to Punch and Judy and Madame Tussauds.[44]

Conclusion

In the centuries following the Renaissance and Reformation the
Churches became narrower and narrower in their interests, until
almost everything that was not ostensibly spiritual or ecclesiastical was
left free from criticism in the name of God and of his commandments.
The social teaching of the church had ceased to count because the
church had ceased to think . . . An institution which possesses no
philosophy of its own accepts that which happens to be fashionable.

R. H. Tawney[1]

When I saw how the head was separated from the body and as it dropped
noisily into the basket, I understood not with my reason but with my whole
being that no theories of the rationality of modern civilization and its
institutions could justify this act; that if all the people in the world, by
whatever theory, had found it necessary, I knew that it was useless, that
it was evil. I knew also that the standard of good and evil was not what
people said or did, not progress, but myself and my own heart.

Leo Tolstoy[2]

'Let him that is without sin' be the executioner. A nation really Christian,
of course, would require a sinless hangman.

Margaret Wilson[3]

Archdeacon Paley justified hanging for theft; the bishops retained it for
shoplifting; Bishop Wilberforce, by his advocacy of discreet, veiled executions,
provided the means to neutralize the demands for abolition; Archbishop
Fisher, by his championing of degrees of murder, attempted to restore the
dignity of capital punishment and so retain it, leaner but fitter than before.
Only at the eleventh hour, and when a Labour Government was openly
advocating it, did the church wholeheartedly take abolition to its heart, and
play a prominent part in winning over the House of Lords.

The Church of England did not stand alone. The other established church, the Scottish Kirk, took a similar stance, and that church which would like to have been accepted on equal terms with its sisters, the Roman Catholic, took an even firmer line in buttressing the civil sword. Status within the state, or at least acceptance, was important. But so too was theology. Two of the churches were in the Catholic tradition of Aquinas, one was Calvinist. The rigid authority of traditional doctrine, or of a legalistic interpretation of proof texts from holy scripture, certainly provided the rationale for their position, and may have propelled them to it. So too at the level of individual conscience. Those who boasted a simple biblical faith, quoted the Old Testament law, and believed in the necessity of conversion to escape the fires of hell, Evangelicals by and large, tended to be in favour of hanging. Those who talked of the spirit of Christ, cited the Sermon on the Mount, and thought that conversion was to do with the whole tenor of life rather than a once-off decision for God or against him, Quakers most obviously, were abolitionist. In their anthropology they also differed. Abolitionists viewed man as made in God's image, moral, rational, and salvageable, straying yet educable; retentionists tended to see man as totally depraved, utterly sinful, and terribly corrupt, straining at the leash to do all manner of evil, restrained only by the hard hand of sacred and secular laws.

The relationship between the Anglican church and the state is a long and intimate one, and the hanging question revealed not merely how consonant with the ethos of a conservative Establishment the church was but also how much that Establishment needed the support of the church. In a Christian country, such as England was, a death penalty devoid of religious sanction could not have survived. It was an issue over which the church could have exercised a moral hegemony and failed to do so. It shadowed public opinion rather than led it. It left the moral highground to Quakers, lapsed Jews, maverick Christians of all denominations, and men and women of none. It could not see with the clarity of a Tolstoy, or a Koestler, or an Orwell, and so compelled people like them to seek a standard of good and evil which came not from the churches but from elsewhere, from the gospels, or from the voice within themselves saying 'this is evil'. Its voice, when heard, uttered the platitudes of Catholic social doctrine and quoted the proof texts of the Pentateuch, all in defence of the right of the state to take the lives of its citizens. It gave law not gospel, and only at the last minute, and again in conformity with government policy, partially redeemed itself. Its failure to do so earlier, its moral lethargy, has contributed to the steady decline of its influence over the ethical and political issues of the day. It had never given a lead to the nation, only a benediction to the state.

Hanging was abolished in this country not as a result of pressure by the churches but because of the crusading efforts of tireless individuals inside Parliament and without, individuals such as Romilly, Ewart, Bright, Neate, Lushington, Tallack, Oldfield, Calvert, Barr, Mrs Van der Elst, Silverman,

Koestler, Gollancz and Gardiner. With few resources and minimal public support they kept up the pressure, mustered the arguments, collected the data, wrote the tracts, held the meetings, and appealed unremittingly to the conscience and the reason of the legislators. With them, latterly, stood only a handful of bishops, but at least they were men of real calibre, and included the three most distinguished in the twentieth century: Temple, Bell, and Ramsey. With these eminent exceptions, most of the time and in large measure the mainstream churches were not interested in the abolitionist cause or actively opposed it. One Christian group alone stands out: at every turn, running every society, campaigning everywhere, were the Quakers. They alone, as a Christian body, were completely and absolutely opposed to the death penalty, even were its abolition to cause an increase in murders.

This whole story does not portray the Church of England in a very favourable light. Perhaps it was no worse than the rest of society, but it should have been better. As so often in the past, a church tied too closely to the state failed to give the necessary moral lead to the nation. Once again it was the radicals, the nonconformists, who went against popular opinion, and persisted, throughout a century and half of largely Pyrrhic victories and outright defeats, in opposing the death penalty which, although it directly affected very few lives, they believed scarred and tainted everyone who lived in a country which maintained it.

It was a cause not important enough for the consideration of the national church most of the time, and when it did consider it, it was to buttress and sustain a system in which it had a major role to play. Its bishops saw judicial hanging as the awesome act of a Christian community fulfilling the will of God; its chaplains lent a religious aura to the whole solemnity, and showed by their solicitous care the concern which the nation church had, not for the preservation of an individual murderer's life, but for the salvation of his sinful soul. Had the church condemned the practice and refused to take part in its execution, hanging would long ago have ended. Who would want to participate in something decreed to be immoral and unChristian? Who would have killed in cold blood knowing that the church condemned the killing?

When the bishops in the Lords did vote *en masse* against the death penalty they carried the day. Latterly a whole generation of younger and more radical bishops had come to the bench. The trends within society were more secular, and within the church more liberal. Increasingly christology took centre stage in theological inquiry, and all knowledge of God was refracted through Christ. There was a greater stress on the social gospel, a rediscovery of the vital ethic of Jesus' teaching, which although it did not condemn the death penalty as such rendered it impossible in practice for anyone to execute it, as the story of the woman taken in adultery (John 8.2–11) made clear. These factors, coupled with the growing unease at the practice of the death penalty, both in that the innocent died, and the guilty were not deterred, and in that the whole process gave a fake religiosity to what was after all the killing of a human being, all created a change in opinion within the church which ultimately bore fruit in the 1960s. It began to repent of what it had done. More than a century and a half after Romilly's shoplifting bill had been defeated by the bishops in the Lords, the bishops in the Lords were to the fore in supporting the complete abolition of the death penalty.

Ironically, now that the churches are largely united in their opposition to capital punishment, it is almost inconceivable that so long as British society remains broadly Christian the death penalty could be reintroduced. To participate in so final a punishment from which the religious sanction has been withdrawn would pose insurmountable difficulties for many people. A secular society on the other hand, or perhaps one in which fundamentalist religion was predominant, could witness the reimposition of the noose or, more likely, execution by lethal injection, or some other sanitized method. It would no longer be a sacred act of human sacrifice, the due recompense for sin, but humane extinction, the putting to sleep of a dangerous animal, the eradication of a pest. Basil Montagu drew this distinction two hundred and fifty years ago. Then it was hardly accurate since it was Christians who maintained the bloody punishments he condemned. Now it may be more true:

> Atheism is a school of ferocity . . . and having taught its disciples to consider mankind as little better than a nest of insects, they will be prepared, in the fierce conflicts of a party, to trample upon them without pity and extinguish them without remorse.[4]

Chronology

	Acts of Parliament: 25 Geo. II, c.37 refers to the 37th statute passed in the 25th year of the reign of King George II.
1706	Abolition of literacy test for benefit of clergy.
1723	Waltham Black Act (9 Geo. I, c. 22).
1752	Murder Act (26 Geo. II, c. 37). Gibbetting given legal sanction.
1760	First use of 'the drop' at execution of Earl Ferrers.
1783	Newgate replaced Tyburn as the place of execution.
1785	Paley's *Principles of Moral and Political Philosophy*. Madan's *Thoughts on Executive Justice*.
1789	Last burning of a woman.
1790	Burning of women abolished.
1808	Society for the Diffusion of Knowledge Upon the Punishment of Death and the Improvement of Prison Discipline [SDKPD]. First attempt in Parliament to get repeal of a capital statute.
1810	Romilly introduced his Shoplifting Bill. Archbishop Sutton and six other bishops voted against.
1812	Lord Byron spoke in the Lords against capital statutes.
1817	Shelley witnessed execution in Derby.
1818	Romilly commited suicide.
1819	Select Committee on Criminal Law as Relates to Capital Punishment for Felonies.
1820	Capital punishment abolished for shoplifting, theft, sending threatening letters, and destroying silk or cloth in a loom or frame.
1823	Waltham Black Act virtually repealed.
1825	Capital punishment abolished for assaulting or obstructing a revenue officer.
1827	Peel began revision of the criminal code.
1828	Society for the Diffusion of Information on the Subject of Capital Punishments [SDISCP] organized under Allen to succeed SDKPD.

1829	Last execution for horse stealing.
1831	Last execution for sheep and cattle stealing and maiming.
1832	Last Gibbetings (Jobling and Cook).
	Whatley's *Thoughts on Secondary Punishments*.
	Wix's *Reflections*.
	Capital punishment abolished for cattle, horse, sheep stealing.
1833	Last juvenile hanged.
	Capital punishment abolished for housebreaking.
1833–6	Royal Commission on Criminal Law.
1834	Gibbetting abolished.
1834–5	Capital punishment abolished for returning from transportation, sacrilege, and letter-stealing.
1836	Capital punishment abolished for coining and forgery.
1837	Capital punishment abolished for burglary from dwelling-houses.
	Hanging reduced to sixteen offences.
1839–40	Wordsworth's *Sonnets Upon the Punishment of Death*.
1840	Execution of Courvoisier.
	Thackeray wrote 'Going to see a man hanged'.
1841	Dickens published *Barnaby Rudge*.
	Hanging for rape abolished.
	Hanging reduced to seven offences.
1846	Dickens wrote letters to *Daily News*.
	Society for the Abolition of Capital Punishment [SACP] replaced SDISCP.
1847	Lords Select Committee on Criminal Law.
1848	Ewart introduced a total abolition bill.
1849	Ewart introduced a total abolition bill.
	Dickens wrote to *The Times*.
	Last woman to be executed for murder of her baby.
1850	Ewart introduced a total abolition bill.
1854	Execution of Moses Hatto at Aylesbury.
1854–7	Alfred Dymond Secretary of the SACP.
1856	Lords Select Committee on Capital Punishment (Wilberforce Committee).

Phillips' *Vacation Thoughts*.
Hardy witnessed execution of Elizabeth Brown.

1861   Number of capital offences reduced to four.

1864–6   Royal Commission on Capital Punishment (Richmond Commission).

1866   Howard Association effectively replaced SACP.
            Last public hanging in Scotland (Joe Bell for murder, at Perth).

1868   Mill's speech in Commons.
            Capital Punishment Act Amendment (31 Vict., c. 24).
            25 May: Last public hanging in England (Michael Barrett executed at Newgate for Fenian bomb outrage on 13 December 1867 when twelve were killed at Clerkenwell).
            13 August: First private hanging (Thomas Wells for murder).

1888   Aberdare Committee.

1900   Oldfield's Survey of episcopal and judicial opinion.

1901   Bell required to be rung only after the execution.

1902   Rule requiring a black flag to be hoisted revoked.

1908   The Childrens Act (8 Edw. VII, c. 67) prohibited capital punishment for those under sixteen.

1920   Penal Reform Committee of the Friends formed.

1921   Howard League for Penal Reform formed out of an amalgamation of the Howard Association and the Penal Reform League.

1922   The Infanticide Act (12 and 13 Geo. V, c. 18) abolished hanging for mothers who killed new-born children.

1923   Execution of Edith Thompson.
            William Temple's letter on capital punishment.

1924   Labour Government.

1924   Home Office instructed governors to keep comments stereotyped.
            November: National Council for the Abolition of the Death Penalty [NCAP] founded as a coordinating body embracing many varieties of abolitionist.

1927   Chaplains instructed not to use the burial service at executions.
            Publications of Roy Calvert's *Capital Punishment in the Twentieth Century*.

1928   Private Members Bill on Capital Punishment passes by one vote in the Commons. For the first time the Commons had voted for abolition.

1929   First full debate on capital punishment this century.

1930   January: William Temple preached John Howard Sermon on 'the Ethics of Punishment'.
July: House of Commons Select Committee on Capital Punishment (Barr Committee).

1931   Fall of the Labour Government.
Sentence of Death (Expectant Mothers) Act abolished hanging for pregnant women.

1933   Death of Roy Calvert.
The Children and Young Persons Act (23 Geo. V, c. 12) abolished hanging for those under eighteen when the offence was committed.
4 May: the last time a reporter was present at an execution (of Parker and Probert at Wandsworth).

1934   Launch of abolitionist journal, *The Penal Reformer*.

1935   William Temple's article in *The Spectator*.

1937   Mrs Van der Elst's survey of episcopal opinion.

1938   First full debate in Commons for nearly a decade.

1944   October: Death of Temple.

1947   November: Labour Government introduced Criminal Justice Bill without abolition clause.

1948   15 April: Commons passed abolition amendment to Criminal Justice Bill.
2 June: Lords deleted abolition clause.
15 July: Commons passed Government's compromise death penalty clause.
20 July: Lords rejected it.
22 July: Commons agreed to omit it.
18 November: Announcement of a Royal Commission.

1949–53 Royal Commission on Capital Punishment (Gowers Commission).

1949   8 March: Timothy Evans hanged.

1953   27 January: Derek Bentley hanged.
15 July: John Christie hanged.

1955   13 July: Ruth Ellis hanged. The last woman to be hanged in UK.
              August: National Campaign for the Abolition of Capital Punish-
              ment [NCACP] initiated.
              10 November: Government rejected all major recommendations
              of the Royal Commission.

1956   February: Government attempted to reform law of murder. Com-
              mons reject this and pass an abolitionist motion.
              10 July: Lords rejected this bill.
              8 November: Announcement of Homicide Bill.

1957   21 March: The Homicide Act (5 and 6 Eliz. II. c. 11) became law.

1962   Canterbury Convocation voted for abolition.
              York Synod voted for abolition.

1964   13 August: last hangings in UK (Peter Allen at Liverpool, Gwynne
              Evans at Manchester for murder).
              21 December: Commons approved Murder (Abolition of Death
              Penalty) Bill.

1965   9 November: The Murder (Abolition of Death Penalty) Act (13
              and 14 Eliz. II, c. 71).

1969   16, 18 December: affirmative motions passed in Commons and
              Lords.

Notes

Fuller publication details for the works cited will be found in the Bibliography

1 The Universal Medicine

1. Said by the late-eighteenth-century judge, Sir Francis Buller, when sentencing at Maidstone. He was 'more learned than humane', his learning being shown in this unattributed quotation from a seventeenth-century essay 'On Punishment' from the *Political Thoughts and Reflections* of George Savile, Marquis of Halifax (1633–1695).
2. *The Merchant of Venice*, Act IV, scene 1.
3. An editorial in *The Times*, 25 July 1872.
4. Extract from Mr Clarkson's *Portraiture of Quakerism*, 1806, cited in Basil Montagu, *Opinions Upon the Punishment of Death*, vol. 1, 1809, pp. 45–46.
5. Cicero, *Caius Rabirius* IV, v.
6. See Francesco Compagnoni, 'Capital Punishment and Torture in the Tradition of the Roman Catholic Church', *Concilium* (120) 1978, pp. 39–53. Tertullian (*De Idololatria* ch. 17), Origen (*Contra Celsum* iii.7), Cyprian, Lactanticus (*Divinae Institutiones* VI xx 15–17), and Augustine (*Epistles* 133, 152–4) all expressed their opposition to the execution of criminals.
7. Pieter Spierenburg, *The Spectacle of Suffering*, 1984, p. 33. For a full appraisal of Luther's attitude to capital punishment see C. E. Maxcey, 'Justice and Order: Martin Luther and Thomas More on the Death Penalty and Retribution', *Moreana* XX, 79–80 (Nov. 1983), pp. 17–33.
8. Fenton Bresler, *Reprieve*, 1965, p. 18.
9. *Parliamentary Debates* (Commons), New Series, vol. v (23 May 1821), cols. 923f.
10. Philippa Maddern, *Violence and Social Order: East Anglia 1422–1442*, 1992, pp. 72f., 116f., 129.
11. Thomas Fowell Buxton, *Parliamentary Debates*, op. cit., col. 917. J. A. Froude, the Victorian historian, described the statement as 'abominable nonsense'. For a critical appraisal of the data see Leon Radzinovicz, *A History of the English Criminal Law and its Administrations from 1750*, vol. I, 1948, pp. 139–142.
12. *Parliamentary Debates*, op. cit., col. 918.
13. 'Have mercy upon me, O God, according to thy lovingkindness: according unto the multitude of thy tender mercies blot out my transgressions.'
14. Bresler, *Reprieve*, p. 25. The recitation of the 'neck verse' was abolished in 1706 when both literate and illiterate became eligible for benefit of clergy. The principle was finally abolished altogether in 1827.
15. Evidence before the Select Committee in 1819. During the reigns of the four Georges, 1714–1830, 156 new offences were made punishable by death.
16. For instance in 1811 there were 404 sentences of death in England with a population of 10 million, while in France with a population of 27 million

there had only been 264 (mentioned by MacKintosh in *Parliamentary Debates* (Commons), New Series, vol. ix (21 May, 1823), col. 406.

17. William Paley, *Works with a Life by Alexander Chalmers*, 1819, vol. II, p. 16.

18. Lawrence Stone, 'Homicide and Violence' in *The Past and Present Revisited*, 1987.

19. Prior to the Judicature Acts of 1873–75 few pleadings and no indictment could be amended: any and every error was fatal. In 1841, for instance, Lord Cardigan was charged with the murder of 'Harvey Garnett Phipps'. In fact he had killed 'Harvey Garnett Phipps Tuckett'. The judge had no recourse other than to direct the jury to acquit.

20. Radzinovicz, *History*, vol. I, p. 27. This was an argument which was to buttress the death penalty right up until the 1950s and beyond, when several cases of miscarriages of justice began seriously to undermine it.

21. *Parliamentary Debates* (Commons), vol. xix (29 March 1811), col. 647.

22. Ibid., col. 631.

23. 9 Geo. I, c. 22.

24. Radzinovicz, *History*, vol. I, pp. 49–79. For the definition of the genesis and use of the Black Act see E. P. Thompson, *Whigs and Hunters*, 1975.

25. Lord Ellenborough, Chief Justice, *Parliamentary Debates* (Lords), vol. xvi (30 May 1810), p. 324.

26. Sir James MacKintosh, *Parliamentary Debates* (Commons), New Series, vol. ix (21 May 1823), col. 405.

27. William Ewart, *Parliamentary Debates* (Commons), 3rd Series, vol. xi (27 March 1832), col. 950.

28. J. Sydney Taylor (anonymously authored), *Anti-Draco, or Reasons for Abolishing the Punishment of Death in the Case of Forgery by a Barrister of the Middle Temple*, 1830, pp. 36–7.

29. In conversation with Sir James MacKintosh, *Parliamentary Debates* (Commons), vol. xxxix (3 March 1819), col. 787.

30. Samuel Romilly, *Observations upon Thoughts on Executive Justice*, 1786, pp. 18–22.

31. See the important and little used article by B. E. F. Knell, 'Capital Punishment: its administration in relation to juvenile offenders in the nineteenth century and its possible administration in the eighteenth', *British Journal of Criminology*, vol. 5, 1965, pp. 198–207. It conclusively refutes the much-repeated assertion that children were regularly executed in both eighteenth- and nineteenth-century England.

32. Radzinowicz, *History*, vol. I, pp. 12–13.

33. Knell, 'Capital Punishment', p. 200.

34. G. Gardiner and N. Curtis-Raleigh, 'The Judicial Attitude to Penal Reform', *LQR*, April 1949, p. 8; Knell, 'Capital Punishment', p. 198 n. 2.

35. Knell, 'Capital Punishment', p. 199. Of the 103 cases he unearthed of children sentenced to death – almost all for theft and none for murder – between 1801 and 1836 not one was actually executed.

36. London 1701. This 'overtly humanitarian' line was followed by George Ollyffe in *An Essay Humbly Offer'd, for an Act of Parliament to Prevent Capital Crimes, and the Loss of many Lives, and to Promote a desirable Improvement and Blessing in the Nation*, London 1731.

37. 26 Geo. II, c. 37.
38. Edward Gibbon Wakefield, *Facts Relating to the Punishment of Death in the Metropolis*, 1832, Appendix pp. 208–9. Between 1800 and 1832 four murderers were hanged at Reading of whom three were publicly dissected (*Reading Mercury*, 17 March 1877, p. 2).
39. Ruth Richardson, *Death, Dissection, and the Destitute*, Penguin edn, pp. 35f, 76, 179.
40. Radzinowicz, *History*, vol. I, pp. 714–722. For a good example see the letter from Paris to the *Morning Herald* where the author wonders that in the land of 'Bibles, Tracts, and Missions' huge crowds gather to watch the public execution of a criminal: 'Oh! if the people of England did but know one thousandth part of what is said and thought throughout civilized Europe ... I cannot but think they would demand the abolition of capital punishments' (21 January 1832).
41. Quoted in Louis Masur, *Rites of Execution*, 1989, p. 29.
42. Charles Dickens, *Barnaby Rudge*, 1841, ch. lxxiv.
43. *Parliamentary Debates* (Commons) New Series, vol. v (23 May 1821), col. 926. Sir Thomas Fowell Buxton, an evangelical with Quaker sympathies, was MP for Weymouth and the successor to Wilberforce in the anti-slavery campaign.
44. So Douglas Hay, 'Property, Authority, and the Criminal Law', in *Albion's Fatal Tree*, 1975, p. 56; Clive Emsley, *Crime and Society in England, 1750–1900*, 1987, pp. 203–214; Frank McLynn, *Crime and Punishment in Eighteenth Century England*, 1991 edn, pp. xii, 260.
45. Robert Peel, *Parliamentary Debates* (Commons), New Series, vol. xxii (1 April 1830), col. 1180.
46. *Parliamentary Debates* (Commons), vol. xxxix (2 March 1819) col. 787.
47. Radzinovicz, *History*, vol. I, pp. 152–3.
48. *Reading Mercury*, 21 March 1803.
49. *Parliamentary Debates* (Commons), vol. xix (29 March 1811), col. 625.
50. McLynn, *Crime and Punishment*, p. 260.
51. Figures published in the *Christian Pocket Magazine* in August 1822 indicate that 5107 persons were sentenced to death in England in the years 1817 to 1820, of whom 427 were executed.
52. William Cobbett, *Parliamentary History of England*, vol. xix (13 May 1777), cols. 237f.
53. George Hardinge, *Miscellaneous Works*, vol. I, 1818, p. 146.
54. Hay, 'Property', pp. 22 and 57. Despite this citation it will be obvious from my explanation of the origin and nature of the Bloody Code that I am in large agreement with Radzinovitz, J. H. Langbein (Albion's Fatal Flaws', *Past and Present*, 98, 1983, pp. 96–120) and Lawrence Stone (*The Past and Present Revisited*, 1987, pp. 241–251) rather than with Hay, Thompson, McLynn and others who see the eighteenth-century criminal justice system as the product of a deliberate conspiracy by a ruling elite against the lower classes. It was never so systematic as their argument would suggest, nor do its attributes easily align themselves with this theory, as their critics point out.
55. *Parliamentary Debates* (Commons), vol. xix (29 March 1811), col. 616.

56. Samuel Johnson, *The Rambler*, 20 April 1751, no. 114; *The Yale Edition* 1969, vol. IV, p. 242.

57. John Locke in *Two Treatises of Government*, the Second Treatise passim, especially sections 3, 85, 87, 88, 94, 139, 171.

58. Ibid., s. 172.

59. J. A. Sharpe, *Crime in Early Modern England 1550–1750*, 1984, p. 150.

60. R. H. Tawney, *Religion and the Rise of Capitalism*, Penguin edn 1938, pp. 192–4. The compliance of the Established Church is still apparent in the area of criminal justice even if Waterman is right in his contention that Christian thinkers played a far more dynamic role in political economy than Tawney allowed (*Revolution, Economics, and Religion*, 1991).

61. Gilbert Burnet, *Exposition of the XXXIX Articles*, 1699, p. 529.

62. Ibid., p. 530.

63. Joseph Butler, *Fifteen Sermons*, Sermon viii, On Resentment, 1726.

64. In introducing his *Principles of Moral and Political Philosophy* Paley excused the lack of references in the following terms: 'I make no pretensions to perfect originality. I claim to be something more than a mere compiler. Much no doubt is borrowed' (Paley, *Works*, vol. I, p. lvii). Indeed it was. All his arguments on the criminal justice system were commonplaces of the early and mid-eighteenth-century assize sermons (see Randall McGowen, ' "He Beareth Not the Sword in Vain": Religion and the Criminal Law in Eighteenth-Century England', *Eighteenth-Century Studies*, (21) 1981, pp. 192–211, esp. pp. 199f.

65. Dugald Stewart in a letter to Sir Samuel Romilly, 28 June 1810, in the latter's *Memoirs*, vol. II, 1840, pp. 304–305. Neither Stewart nor Dr Parr, another regular correspondent of Romilly, shared in this adulation of a national institution. As late as 1836, however, the *Second Report on Criminal Law*, prefaced its recommendations for reform with a lengthy critique on his views.

66. Paley, *Works*, vol. II, p. 6.

67. Ibid., p. 5.

68. Ibid., p. 1.

69. Ibid., p. 4.

70. Ibid., p. 8.

71. Ibid., p. 27. Colonel Frankland believed that it was the aggregate of suffering, not the individual who suffers, which counted: 'It should never be forgotten, that even a multitude of mild punishments might produce a greater sum of human suffering, than a smaller number of severe punishments, without more effectually obtaining the end proposed': *Parliamentary Debates* (Commons), col. xix (29 March 1811), col. 639.

72. Elsie Hughes-Buller, *Tales of a Grandmother*, unpublished ms. 1937, p. 6.

73. Gerald Howson, *The Macaroni Parson*, 1973, p. 219.

74. Colonel Frankland expressed similar sentiments in the 1811 Commons' debate: 'as a moral agent he may be spotless . . . his motive may have been sublime' yet for his deeds die he must that others may be deterred by his suffering from his actions. He has his consolation. 'He may die a martyr. He may go to his reward under another dispensation' (*Parliamentary Debates*, op. cit., col. 633). Oliver Goldsmith had already decried this view: 'when by favour or ignorance justice

pronounces a wrong verdict, it then attacks our lives since in such a case the whole community suffers with the innocent victim' (*The Citizen of the World*, 1762, Letter LXXX in *Collected Works* vol. II, p. 328).

75. William Hazlitt, 'On the Clerical Character', 31 January 1818, *Collected Works*, vol. III, p. 276.

76. M. L. Clarke, *Paley: Evidences for the Man*, 1974, pp. 131f.

77. Martin Madan, *Thoughts on Executive Justice*, 1785, p. 4.

78. Randall McGowen, 'He Beareth Not', pp. 206–7.

79. Samuel Romilly, *Observations on a Late Publication Entitled Thoughts on Executive Justice*, 1786, p. 6.

80. Sir Samuel Romilly, *Memoirs*, vol. I, p. 89.

81. McGowen, 'He Beareth Not', pp. 206–7.

82. John Fletcher, *The Penitent Thief*, 1773, p. 6.

83. Ibid., p. 8.

84. Letter to Jeremy Bentham, 1803, printed in Appendix B to Basil Montagu, *An Inquiry into the Aspersions upon the late Ordinary of Newgate*, 1815, pp. 17–22. Some confusion exists over this letter. Montagu also included it in his *Opinions Upon the Punishment of Death*, vol. II, 1812, pp. 187–191, where the date is incorrectly given as 1783. In addition, the letter quoted above is often confused with another rather sour letter from Forde to Bentham also dated 1803 in the latter's *Works*, vol. xi, edited by John Bowring, Tait, Edinburgh, 1843, p. 143. The text is as follows:

Your own investigation of the subject will furnish you with many documents as well as arguments on the subject of executions; better calculated than anything I have said to do away the disgrace which they are to our country; and from you they will have weight. Pursue them, I beseech you, to the abolishing of executions, and you will deserve ten thousand times more from this country than ever Howard did. My situation in life is too insignificant to have any attention paid to my opinions. Besides, as one of the Alderman said, when I expressed some such thought as I have now given to you – 'Pray, be quiet, Doctor, and keep your mind to yourself! If there were no executions, there would be no occasion for an Ordinary.'

85. Recounted in Alfred Dymond, *The Law on its Trial*, 1865, pp. 287f.

2 The Ripened Fruit

1. George Hardinge, *Miscellaneous Works*, vol. I, 1818, pp. 63f.

2. James Boswell, *Life of Johnson*, 19 September 1777, vol. III, p. 167,

3. Martin Madan, *Thoughts on Executive Justice*, 1785, pp. 26–30.

4. Peter Linebaugh, *The London Hanged*, 1991, p. 89.

5. William Calcraft, executioner for London and Middlesex from 1829 until 1874.

6. *Parliamentary Debates* (Commons), 3rd Series, vol. cxii (11 July 1850), col. 7276.

7. Edward Wakefield, *The Hangman and the Judge*, 1833, p. 2.

8. Edward Wakefield, *Facts Relating to the Punishment of Death in the Metropolis*, 1832, p. 167 . This goes back to the sixteenth and possibly fifteenth centuries,

see J. A. Sharpe, ' "Last Dying Speeches": Religion, Ideology, and Public Execution in Seventeenth-Century England', in *Past and Present*, 107, 1985, pp. 144–67.

9. *The Malefactors' Register or New Newgate and Tyburn Chronicle*, 1810, quoted in Potter, *The Fatal Gallows Tree*, p. 69 and more fully in Brian Lane, *The Murder Club Guide to the Eastern and Home Counties*, p. 78.

10. Wakefield, *Facts*, p. 173.

11. Ibid., pp. 155–6.

12. Ibid., p. 87.

13. Ibid., pp. 153–4.

14. Ibid., p. 152.

15. Royal Commission Evidence, paras. 1248–1255.

16. For a detailed account of this part of the drama see 'The Condemned Sermon' by Edward Gibbon Wakefield, in *Popular Politics*, 1837, pp. 97–103.

17. Michael Ignatieff, *A Just Measure of Pain*, 1978, p.21.

18. City of London Record Office (CLRO) Crooke *Sermons* 1695 p. 2, quoted in Ignatieff, *A Just Measure*, p. 22. See also Michel Foucault's 'The Spectacle of the Scaffold', chapter 2 of *Discipline and Punish*, Penguin 1979.

19. Boswell, *Life*, vol. III, p. 145, letter to Charles Jenkinson, 20 June 1777. Dodd may have been the first but he was not the last. Two years later the Revd James Hackman, who had himself been present at Dodd's departure, was hanged for the murder of his lover (Leon Radzinowicz, *History*, vol. 1, p. 464, n. 45). In 1811 the Revd Peter Vine, vicar of Hartland, was executed for the rape of an eleven-year-old girl and the murder of the man sent to apprehend him (Brian Lane, *The Murder Club Guide to South West England and Wales*, pp. 54–7).

20. That his end gave rise to concern is evidenced in the number of sermons preached on his fate. See, for instance, John Camplin's sermon 'occasioned by the Execution of William Dodd LLD', *The Evidence of Christianity not weakened by the Frailty of its Ministers*, 29 June 1777.

21. John Villette, *A Genuine Account of the Behaviour and Dying Words of William Dodd, LLD*, 1777, pp. 17–21. John Wesley concurred in this view. He had visited Dodd on several occasions and each time came away ever more convinced of his penitence and of the presence of God with him (*Journal*, 1827, vol. 4, p. 99, 25 May 1777). Such conversion narratives played an important role in executions in the American colonies: see Daniel Williams, ' "Behold a Tragic Scene Strangely Changed into a Theater of Mercy": The Structure and Significance of Criminal Conversion Narratives in Early New England', *American Quarterly*, 38, no. 5, 1986, pp. 827–847.

22. Boswell, op.cit., pp. 139–148.

23. Pieter Spierenburg, *The Spectacle of Suffering*, 1987, Cambridge, p. 63.

24. Boswell, *Life*, vol. IV, p. 208, 18 April 1783,

25. Horace Walpole, *Journal of the Reign of King George the Third*, 1859, vol. II, p. 124.

26. J. A. Sharpe, *Crime in Early Modern England 1550–1750*, 1984, pp. 161–163.

27. This was certainly so in the United States in the eighteenth century where manuals for ministers attending executions even included a suggested form of confession. See Louis Masur, *Rites of Execution*, 1989, pp. 33–5, 39–40.

28. William Alberry, *A Millenium of Facts in the History of Horsham and Sussex, 947–1947*, 1947, p. 310.
29. William Tallack, *Howard Letters and Memories*, 1905, p. 140, n. 1.
30. Letter from the Revd W. Cooksey to *The Times*, 27 March 1924.
31. The Revd William Kingsbury, *The Execution of a Malefactor Improved as a Warning especially to Young Persons*, 24 March 1805, p. 6.
32. Ibid.
33. Cyril Pearl, *Victorian Patchwork*, 1972, p. 63.
34. CLRO Crooke, *Sermons*, 1695, p. 2, quoted in Ignatieff, *A Just Measure*, p. 23.
35. Alberry, *A Millenium of Facts*, p. 306.
36. Wakefield, *Facts*, p. 157.
37. Samuel Richardson, *Familiar Letters on Important Occasions*, 1741, Routledge, 1928, No. 160, p. 219.
38. E. P. Thompson, *Whigs and Hunters*, p. 154.
39. John Potter, *The Fatal Gallows Tree*, p. 69.
40. Thomas Wontner, *Old Bailey Experience*, 1833, p. 161.
41. Peter Linebaugh, 'The Ordinary of Newgate and His Acount' in *Crime in England 1550–1800*, 1977, p. 252.
42. Boswell, *Life*, vol. I. pp. 273f., Summer 1754.
43. Linebaugh, *The London Hanged*, p. 33.
44. Bernard Mandeville, *An Enquiry into the Causes of the Frequent Executions at Tyburn*, 1725, p. 19.
45. Cited in Philip Priestley, *Victorian Prison Lives*, 1985, p. 238.
46. Mrs Fry related these and other opinions about the deleterious effects of capital punishment to Sir Samuel Romilly, (*Memoirs*, vol. III, pp. 332–3), to Dr Samuel Favell (*A Speech on the Propriety of Revising the Criminal Law*, 1819, p. 36), and to Sir Thomas Buxton (*Parliamentary Debates* vol. xxix, (2 March 1819), col. 822).
47. Wontner, *Old Bailey Experience*, London 1833, p. 154.
48. Pierce Egan, *Life in London*, 1821, p. 281.
49. Diary entry for 24 February 1817, quoted in F. Cresswell's *The Life of Elizabeth Fry*, 1856, p. 110.
50. Wontner, *Old Bailey Experience*, p. 162.
51. John Wesley, *Journal*, vol. 4, pp. 96, 99.
52. Quoted in C. E. Vulliamy, *John Wesley*, Epworth Press, 3rd edn 1954, p. 158.
53. *Life of Mr Silas Told Written by Himself*, 1786, p. 77. His relationship with another Ordinary, Mr Moore, was much better. In 1767 Moore invited Told to pray extempore with Mrs Brownrigg, to sing hymns, and receive communion (p. 114).
54. This description comes from John Thomas Smith who as young man was admitted to an audience with Dr Forde, and accompanied him to the execution of Governor Wall. See *A Book for a Rainy Day*, 1905 edn, pp. 177–180.
55. Basil Montague, *An Inquiry into the Aspersions upon the late Ordinary of Newgate*, 1815, pp. 63–75.
56. Malcolm Cheney, *Chronicles of the Damned*, 1992, p. 21.
57. Montagu, *An Inquiry*, p. 65.
58. *Old Bailey*, pp. 163–5. A recently published book (Cheney, *Chronicles*) based on

the extant portions of his diary for 1823–4 identifies this person as Mr Baker (p. 69).

59. Cheney, *Chronicles*, pp. 72f.
60. *Old Bailey*, p. 167.
61. Ibid., p. 167–8. For the ministrations of some 'benevolent ladies of Nottingham' to John Jones, a Lincolnshire murderer, in 1841, see Thomas Beggs' 'The Royal Commission and the Punishment of Death', *Social Science Review*, N.S.3, 1865, pp. 154f.
62. *An Account of the Experience and happy death of Mary Voce, who was executed on Nottingham Gallows, on Tuesday, March 16th, 1802, for the Murder of her own Child*, reproduced as appendix 2 of the Penguin edition of George Eliot's *Adam Bede*, 1980, pp. 589ff. This story provided the germ of her novel and of the depiction of the condemned cell contrition of Hetty Sorel.
63. John Fletcher, *The Penitent Thief*, 1773, pp. 9–21.
64. *Mrs Lachlan's Narrative of a Conversion of a Murderer in Letters addressed to a Clergyman*, 1832, p. 117.
65. Ibid., p. 130.
66. Ibid., p. 151.
67. Ibid., p. 181.
68. Ibid., p. 185.
69. Ibid., p. 284.
70. Ibid., pp. 284f. Similarly a Nottinghamshire lady declared John Jones to be 'a child of God if ever there was one', and sent him a white camellia to wear at his execution (Beggs, 'The Royal Commission', p. 155).
71. Ibid. p. 286.
72. C. J. Williams, *Cook, the Murderer*, 1832, pp. 22f.
73. The very similar role of the clergy in the care of the condemned and in the panoply of executions in early modern Germany is documented in Richard van Dülmen, *Theatre of Horror*, 1990, especially pp. 63–65, 74–78, 119–124.

3 Narrowing the Noose

1. *Parliamentary Debates* (Lords), 3rd Series, vol. vi (6 September 1831), cols 1176f..
2. William Wordsworth, *Sonnets upon the Punishment of Death, 1839–1840*, first published in *The Quarterly Review*, December 1841, sonnet IV.
3. Sir Thomas More, *Utopia*, 1516. Jeremy Taylor, 'Ductor Dubitantium, or the Rule of Conscience in all their General Measures', *Works* ed. A. Taylor, vol. x, pp. 70–71. For a good summary see C. E. Maxcey, 'Justice and Order: Martin Luther and Thomas More on the Death Penalty and Retribution', *Moreana XX*, 79–80 (Nov. 1983), pp. 17–33.
4. William Eden, *Principles of Penal Law*, 1771; Sir William Blackstone, *Commentaries on the Laws of England*, 4 vols, 1765; Samuel Johnson, *The Rambler: No. 114*, 1751; Oliver Goldsmith, *The Citizen of the World*, 1762, Letter lxxx, and *The Vicar of Wakefield*, 1766, ch. xxvii; Jeremy Bentham, *Introduction to Principles of Morals and Legislation*, 1780.

5. Frank McLynn, *Crime and Punishment in Eighteenth-Century England*, 1991, p. 308.

6. *Parliamentary Debates* (Commons), vol. xxxix (2 March 1819), cols 781f. See Leon Radzinowicz, *History* vol. I, pp. 422f.

7. 'His case stands out in the history of the administration of criminal law in this period as perhaps the first to stir the public conscience, and to force it to question whether the absolute capital punishment was socially, and morally justifiable for all the offences for which it was appointed (Radzinowicz, *History*, vol. I, pp. 451, 467–472). On the implications of the Dodd affair see also Gerald Howson, *The Macaroni Parson*, 1973, pp. 226–229, and John Burke, 'Crime and Punishment in 1777: the Execution of the Revd Dr William Dodd and Its Impact upon his Contemporaries' in W. B. Thesing (ed.), *Executions and the British Experience from the 17th to the 20th Century*, 1990, pp. 59–75.

8. William Cobbett, *Parliamentary History of England*, vol. xix (1777–8), cols 234–42.

9. Charles Simpson, 'Friends and Capital Punishment', *Friends Quarterly Examiner*, LXVII, 1923, p. 170.

10. Benjamin Rush, *An Inquiry into the Effects of Public Punishments Upon Criminals and Upon Society*, 1787, pp. 15–18; 'An Inquiry into the Consistency of the Punishment of Murder by Death with Reason and Revelation' in *Essays Literary, Moral, and Philosophical*, 1798, pp. 164–182.

11. Louis Masur, *Rites of Execution*, 1989, pp. 64f.

12. The Society for Diffusing Information on the Subject of Capital Punishment and Prison Discipline: *Tract I: Address with an account of a Visit to Warwick Gaol*, 1817.

13. Charles Speare, *Essays on the Punishment of Death*, 13th edn. 1851, p. 214.

14. *Edinburgh Review*, 1821, quoted in Simpson, 'Friends and Capital Punishment', p. 173.

15. Not 1809 as many historians have stated. See Basil Montagu's *An Account of the Origin and Object of the Society for the Diffusion of Knowledge upon the Punishment of Death and Improvement of Prison Discipline*, 1812, p. 7, and *The Third Report of the Society*, 1816, p. 11.

16. In the period 1808 to 1818 Montagu wrote the following: *Opinions Upon the Death Penalty*, 2 vols, 1809 and 1812; *An Examination of Some Observations upon a Passage in Dr Paley's Moral Philosophy on the Punishment of Death*, 1810; *An Account of the Origin and Object of the Society for the Diffusion of Knowledge upon the Punishment of Death and Improvement of Prison Discipline*, 1812; *An Inquiry into the Aspersions upon the late Ordinary of Newgate, with some Observations upon Newgate and upon the Punishment of Death*, 1815; *Some Inquiries respecting the Punishment of Death for Crimes without Violence*, 1818.

17. Joseph John Gurney in a letter to his wife, 28 August 1833, quoted in Augustus Hare's *The Gurneys of Earlham*, 1895, vol. II, p. 77.

18. So eager was the SDKPD to buy books and publish tracts that it ran into debt and had temporarily to suspend proceedings between 1814 and 1815 (Montagu, *The Third Report of the Society*, 1816, p. 11).

19. Sir Samuel Romilly, *Memoirs*, 1840, vol. I, p. 7.

20. Quoted in Patrick Medd, *Romilly*, 1968, p. 102.
21. Ibid., p. 24.
22. 1783 (Romilly, *Memoirs*, vol. I, pp. 277f). In contrast to Romilly, Roget had argued in favour of complete abolition, as did another early reformer, Richard Wright, who appropriately styled himself Beccaria Anglicus (*Letters on Capital Punishment addressed to the English Judges*, 1807).
23. Samuel Romilly, *Observations on a Late Publication, entitled, 'Thoughts on Executive Justice'*, 1786.
24. 48 Geo.III, c.129.
25. *Parliamentary Debates* (Commons), vol. xv (9 February 1810), cols 366–71. An amplified version of the text of the speech was also published by Sir Samuel Romilly as *Observations on the Criminal Law of England as it relates to Capital Punishments and on the mode in which it is administered, 1810*.
26. Romilly, *Observations*, p. 21.
27. Ibid., p. 35.
28. Ibid., p. 40.
29. Ibid., p. 76.
30. As Montagu pointed out in a tract inspired by the speech, Dr Paley's reasoning was 'founded on the supposition that it is better for twenty-seven innocent men to suffer, than for one guilty man to escape; for it will not be said that the terror of death, although not inflicted, is not a severe punishment' (*An Examination of Some Observations*, p. 10).
31. Ibid., p. 53–4.
32. *Parliamentary Debates* (1810) op. cit., cols. 371–3. This reverence for Paley's principles among certain MPs continued down to 1965 when Sir Peter Rawlinson commented that in the conditions of the eighteenth century when there were no police 'there had to be the supreme deterrent for almost every crime' (*Parliamentary Debates* (Commons), 5th Series, vol. 716, (13 July 1965), col. 429.
33. E. S. Turner, *May It Please Your Lordship*, 1971, p. 137.
34. Romilly, *Memoirs*, vol. II, p. 325. They were carefully denominated for the opprobrium of posterity by Romilly as the Bishops of London (Randolph), Salisbury (Fisher), Ely (Dampier), Hereford (Luxmore), Chester (Sparke), and Clogher in Ireland (Porter).
35. A few years later the anonymous author of *On the Punishment of Death in the Case of Forgery* appealed again to the episcopacy urging their support in the forgery campaign. The union of church and state ought to have ensured that the people were governed by laws which conformed to the word and will of God. He was confident that there was not one bishop who could read or hear of 'the periodical executions for forgery without the keenest feelings of regret', and yet these executions were all in virtue of enactments made by a legislature of which they were a part (1818, p. 31). Despite his high opinion of them the bishops gave little help to his cause.
36. Romilly, *Memoirs*, vol. III, pp. 100, 147–149.
37. *Parliamentary Debates* (Commons), vol. xix, (29 March 1811), col. 647. Others argued that it was the law itself and not the criticisms of it that damaged national prestige. It brought the nation into disrepute. Mr Abercromby said that 'it was

mortifying that the people of England should remain so long subject to the animadversion of the people of other countries, either directed against the laws or the execution of them, and that foreigners should have it in their power to make Englishmen blush for those laws which put judges and jurors in such a situation that they could not discharge their duty' (Ibid., col. 652).

38. *Parliamentary Debates* (Lords), vol. xxi, (27 February 1812), cols 971–4. Shelley too entered the abolitionist lists with his essay 'On the Punishment of Death', 1815, found in *The Prose Works of Percy Bysshe Shelley*, vol. II, 1880, pp. 245–254.

39. Romilly, *Memoirs*, vol. III, p. 260.

40. Revd J. Charles Cox, *Three Centuries of Derbyshire Annals*, vol. II, 1890, pp. 40–43. This was also the last instance of such a penalty. Shelley witnessed the execution and in a pamphlet contrasted the death of these men with that of Princess Charlotte the day before ('An Address to the People on the Death of the Princess Charlotte', 1817, *Prose Works*, vol. II, 1880, pp. 101–114).

41. Romilly, Memoirs, vol. III, p. 238.

42. *Parliamentary Debates* (Commons), vol. xxxix (2 March, 1819), col. 793.

43. Simpson, 'Friends and Capital Punishment', pp. 171–2.

44. *Parliamentary Debates* (1819), op. cit., col. 799.

45. Ibid., col. 82.

46. Anon, *On the Punishment of Death in the Case of Forgery*, 1818, pp. 11f.

47. Charles Buxton (ed.), Memoirs of *Thomas Fowell Buxton*, 1872, p. 87.

48. John Joseph Gurney, *Memoirs*, vol. I, 2nd edn 1855, p. 157.

49. *The Punishment of Death. A Selection of Articles from the Morning Herald*, vol. II, 1837, pp. 338–340.

50. Edward Gibbon Wakefield, *The Hangman and the Judge, or a Letter from Jack Ketch to Mr Justice Alderson*, 1833, pp. 6, 8.

51. 4 Geo. iv, c. 54.

52. Brougham, *Parliamentary Debates* (Commons), New Series, vol. xviii (7 February 1828), cols. 129f.

53. Letter to John Wilson Croker, 23 March 1820, *Correspondence and Diaries*, vol. I, p. 170.

54. Norman Gash, *Mr Secretary Peel*, 1961, pp. 326–331, 486.

55. Ibid., p. 329.

56. *Punishment of Death No. 3*. Substance of the Speeches of S. Lushington and J. Sydney Taylor at a Public Meeting in Exeter Hall, London, 30 May 1831, Harvey and Darton.

57. Taylor was one of the most incisive and prolific writers of his day. The *Morning Herald* owed most of its success to his contributions as remarkable for their style as for their content. His spirit 'breathed in the glowing appeals, and cogent reasonings, by which the daily press – the great engines of opinion and improvement – co-operated with the distinguished public men whose efforts in the House of Commons, great as they were, would otherwise have been comparatively powerless' (*Writings*, p. xxxiii).

58. J. Sydney Taylor, *Anti-Draco* 1830, p. 45.

59. *The Punishment of Death. A Selection of Articles from the Morning Herald*, vol. I, 1836, p. 117.

60. *Parliamentary Debates* (Lords), 3rd Series, vol. vi (6 September 1831), col. 1178.
61. The last execution for horse-stealing took place in 1829 and for sheep-stealing in 1831.
62. *Parliamentary Debates* (Commons), 3rd Series, vol. xi (27 March 1832), cols 952–3; vol. xiii (30 May 1832), cols 195–200.
63. Harriet Martineau, *The History of England During the Thirty Years Peace, 1816–1846*, vol. II, *1830–46*, 1850, p. 420.
64. *Sonnets Upon the Punishment of Death*, 1839–40.
65. William Tallack, 'A General View of the Subject of Capital Punishment', *Social Science Review*, N. S. 3, 1865, p. 22. An example of such a Prize Essay was that of the Revd James Peggs which was submitted for a competition advertised in the *Lincoln Standard* on 22 August 1838, and published the following year under the title *Capital Punishment: The Importance of Abolition*.
66. Under the Act of 1823 in the case of the last two the death sentence need not be pronounced but may be recorded, which has the effect of a respite. Since 1838 there have been only four executions for High Treason, Roger Casement in 1916, John Amery on 29 December 1945, William Joyce on 3 January 1946 and, after a court-martial, Private Schurch on 5 January 1946. In each case the treacherous acts were committed in time of war.
67. For examples of those who held firmly to the retention of capital punishment for murder see William Cobbett, *Twelve Sermons*, 1823, no. 7 'God's Vengeance against Murderers', pp. 145ff., and Robert Dees, *The Inexpediency of Capital Punishment*, 1835. T. Wrightson, while strongly persuaded of the inexpediency of the death penalty even for murder was aware that the public mind was not yet ready for total abolition and so would not advocate it himself (*On the Punishment of Death*, 1833, p. 92ff.).
68. See Randall McGowen, 'The Image of Justice and Reform of the Criminal Law in Early Nineteenth-Century England', *Buffalo Law Review*, 32, 1983, pp. 89–125 passim, especially p. 116.
69. In contrast to the clerics, the atheist Jeremy Bentham in 1831 espoused a very radical abolitionist position (*Jeremy Bentham to his Fellow Citizens of France on Death Punishment*, 1831,). By giving it so provocative a title, by writing it first in French, and publishing first in France he did little to enhance its influence or effect in England.
70. It looks as though this may be but one aspect of the much wider achievement of Christian Political Economy in the first three decades of the nineteenth century. See A. M. C. Waterman, *Revolution, Economics and Religion: Christian Political Economy, 1798–1833*, 1991, passim, esp. pp. 203–4, 261.
72. Richard Whately, *Thoughts on Secondary Punishments*, 1832, p. 30.
72. Ibid., p. 34.
73. Revd Samuel Wix, *Reflections Concerning the Inexpedience and Unchristian Character of Capital Punishment*, 1832.
74. Ibid., p. 20.
75. Ibid., p. 23.
76. 6 & 7 Will. IV, c. 30. See also *Parliamentary Debates* (Commons), 3rd Series, vol. xxxiii (28 April, 1836), cols. 466–470.

77. Such reforming zeal was also transmitted through the generations: Hoare was the great-grandfather of Lord Templewood, the twentieth-century Tory abolitionist peer.

78. Anon, 'A Protest against Capital Punishment', *Meliora*, vol. V, 1863, p. 357. So also Tallack, 'A General View', p. 23.

4 Technicians of Guilt

1.   Schopenhauer, *Die Welt als Wille*, vol. I, book iv, p. 465.
2.   W. L. Clay, *The Prison Chaplain: Memoirs of the Reverend John Clay*, 1861.
3.   Joseph Kingsmill, *Chapters on Prison and Prisoners*, 3rd edn 1854, p. 377ff; *On the Present Aspect of Serious Crime in England and the Means used for its Punishment and Repression by Government*, London 1857.
4.   Brian Bailey, *Hangmen of England*, 1989, p. 53.
5.   John Laurence, *A History of Capital Punishment*, c. 1923, pp. 162f.
6.   *A Report Made by the Revd W. Russell, Inspector of Prisons, to Her Majesty's Secretary of State for the Home Department, respecting the Circumstances which occurred on the Occassion of the Condemned Sermon in the Chapel of Newgate Gaol, in the Case of the Convict Hocker, and also respecting the Circumstances which took place on the Morning of the Execution*, 6 May 1845, p. 3.
7.   Ibid., p. 6.
8.   Anon, *Experiences of a Gaol Chaplain*, Bentleys Popular Novels 1850, pp. 80–1.
9.   *Parliamentary Debates* (Lords), 3rd Series, vol. lxxx (2 May 1845), cols 32–39. See also Brian Lane, *The Murder Guide to The Eastern and Home Counties*, 1989, p. 54.
10. *Royal Commission* 1864–6, Evidence, para. 1239.
11. By Douglas Jerrold in 'The Moral Lesson of the Gallows', *Punch*, 17 January 1846, x, p. 33.
12. York Castle Chaplain's Journal, York Public Record Office, 22 March 1833.
13. Lincoln Castle Chaplain's Journal, Lincoln Public Record Office.
14. Lancaster Castle Chaplain's Journal, Newbold Revel Prison Service Museum.
15. Ibid.
16. Albert Borowitz, *The Thurtell-Hunt Murder Case*, 1988, p. 189. The murder took place in 1823.
17. Robert Gittings, *Young Thomas Hardy*, Penguin edn 1978, p. 61.
18. This was related by Sir Eardley Wilmott some thirty years after the event (*Parliamentary Debates* (Commons), 3rd Series, vol. cclxii (22 June, 1881), col. 1062).
19. *Parliamentary Debates*, 3rd Series, vol. civ (1 May, 1849), col. 1076.
20. Owen Chadwick, *Victorian Miniature*, 1960, pp. 111–117.
21. C. B. Tayler, *Facts in a Clergyman's Life*, 1849, pp. 169–203.
22. York Castle Chaplain's Journal, York Public Record Office.
23. *Punch*, vol. 39, 15 September 1860, p. 102.
24. *Second Report from Her Majesty's Commissioners on Criminal Law*, 1836, p. 52.
25. This account was given in a speech by Bishop Bell in the House of Lords in 1948, *Parliamentary Debates*, 5th Series, vol. 156 (2 June 1948), cols 125–6.

26. Alexander Campbell, *Capital Punishment Sanctioned by Divine Authority*, 1846, p. 10.

5 A Sentence of Scripture

1. *On Death Punishment*, 1831.
2. *Twelve Sermons*, 1823, p. 154.
3. *Parliamentary Debates* (Commons), 3rd Series, vol. cxii, 11 July 1850, col. 1258.
4. 1 May 1849, quoted in Edwin Hodder, *Life and Work of the Seventh Earl of Shaftesbury*, vol. I, 1886, p. 281.
5. Mrs Lachlan, *Narrative of Conversation of a Murderer in Letters addressed to a Clergyman*, 1832, p. 286.
6. William Turner in vol. II of the Memoirs of the Literary and Philosophical Society of Manchester; Beccaria Anglicus (Richard Wright), *Letters on Capital Punishment addressed to the English Judges*, 1807, pp. 60–77.
7. Revd Samuel Wix, *Reflections Concerning the Inexpedience and Unchristian Character of Capital Punishment*, 1832.
8. He obviously had not come across the passage in John Bullar's *Memoirs of the Revd W. Kingsbury*, 1819, where he hoped that we were 'approaching a period, in which some effectual method will be found of protecting property, without resorting to the sanguinary and unjustifiable punishment of death'.

   The word *Unjustifiable* is here used without ceremony; because no sincere believer in the divine authority of scriptures, can hesitate to maintain, that it is the proper word. The Almighty himself, the sole Lord of life and death, has said: 'Thou shalt not kill'. He has himself marked the only exceptions to this important rule. It must be at the peril of any legislature to go beyond the limit that infinite wisdom has ordained . . . Successful forgery is robbery. The punishment, under the Jewish law, was restoration fourfold . . . Sanguinary punishments defeat their own end, and they obliterate moral distinctions (p. 141).

9. Wix, *Reflections*, p. iii.
10. Ibid. p. 32. For the same point see Beccaria Anglicus, *Letters*, p. 77.
11. It remained so for a considerable time. As late as 1840 Lord John Russell had to remove this crime from a bill abolishing capital punishment for fear that it would not otherwise pass the House of Lords where 'high feelings' had been provoked (Radzinowicz, *History*, vol. IV, p. 322).
12. That such a confusion could arise was hardly surprising since his arguments from scripture were no more than a reiteration of what the Quakers had been saying for years: see *The Yearly Meeting Epistles: 1770–1857*, London 1858, vol. II for the years 1818, 1830 and 1847.
13. Vaughan Thomas, *The Scriptural Character of Civil Punishment Vindicated*, 1830, pp. 4, 14, 20, 25. So also William Cobbett, *Twelve Sermons*, 1823, p. 154.
14. 1846, New York, quoted in Charles Spear's *Essays on the Punishment of Death*, 13th edn, 1851, p. 135.
15. So styled by a group of women in Mississippi who sent him a bookmark

embroidered with the silhouette of a person suspended from the gallows (Masur, *Rites of Execution*, p. 147).

16. Alexander Campbell, *Capital Punishment Sanctioned by Divine Authority*, 1846, p. 15.
17. Ibid., p. 17.
18. Henry Christmas, *Capital Punishments Unsanctioned by the Gospel and Unnecessary*, 1845. See also his later work, *Christian Politics*, 1855, pp. 233–274.
19. Cf. Spear on the Mosaic Code, *Essays*, p. 156.

The opposers of every moral improvement have gone at once to the types and shadows of the old dispensation. The advocates for slavery, the supporters of war, and the opposers of temperance, have all sought rest amid its shadows and darkness.

20. *Letters Upon Capital Punishment by a Student of St Bees College*, 1847, pp. 8–9.
21. Ibid., pp. 18, 38–9.
22. '*Inquisition for Blood;' or the Eternal Obligation on States and Governments to Inflict the Penalty of Death for Wilful Murder by A Witness for 'Judgment, Mercy, and Faith'*, London 1847, p. 5. In the United States comments were more scurrilous. The opponents of the death penalty were denounced not only as radicals, infidels, anarchists and social levelers, but as 'the haunters of dramshops, the frequenters of brothels', 'men of dissolute habits and violent passions'. (quoted in Masur, *Rites of Execution*, pp. 154f.)
23. Charles Phillips, *Vacation Thoughts on Capital Punishment*, 1856.
24. 'Mr Phillips on Capital Punishment', *The Saturday Review*, vol. II, 15 November 1856, pp. 635–7.
25. Spear, *Essays*, p. 150; Charles Neate MP (Oxford), *Considerations on Punishment*, 1857; Lord Hobbart, *On Capital Punishment*, 1861.
26. For instance see John Pell, *The Punishment of Death Proved to be Unlawful*, 1835.
27. *Three Papers on Capital Punishment*, 1856. I: 'Remarks on Capital Punishment in Cases of Murder'.
28. William Tallack, 'A General View', p. 34.
29. Royal Commission, 1865, Evidence, para 3261.
30. Sheldon Amos, *Capital Punishment in England Viewed as Operating in the Present Day*, 1864, p. 6.
31. Spear, *Essays*. On Spear see Masur, *Rites of Execution*, pp. 124–40.
32. Spear, *Essays*, p. 177.
33. Ibid., p. 180.
34. Jelinger Symonds, 'Capital and Prison Punishments', *The Law Magazine or Quarterly Review of Jurisprudence*, vol. IV, 1846, pp. 223–50, esp. pp. 233–5.
35. Spear, *Essays*, p. 184.
36. The battle waged and won by the Calvinist clergy in New York State over such 'dissenting' abolitionists is related in great detail by P. E. MacKey in his *Hanging in the Balance: The Anti-Capital Punishment Movement in New York State, 1776–1861*, 1982.
37. Charles Phillips, *Vacation Thoughts on Capital Punishment*, 1856. Within a few months an Anglican cleric from Lincolnshire, the Revd J. W. Watkins JP, had issued a 'A Brief Reply' in riposte.

38. Campbell, *Capital Punishment*, pp. 26–7.
39. William Blake, *The Everlasting Gospel*, 1818, lines 1–14.
40. Thomas Wrightson, *On the Punishment of Death*, 1833, p. 7.

6 An Open-Air Entertainment

1. James Boswell, *Life of Johnson*, vol. IV, pp. 188f.
2. 'The Fine Old English Gentleman, to be said or sung at all Conservative dinners', 1841, quoted in P. Collins, *Dickens and Crime*, 1965, p. 220. I am indebted to this work throughout this chapter.
3. *The London Prisons*, 1850, p. 196.
4. Albert Borowitz, *Innocence and Arsenic* 1977, p. 47.
5. W. M. Thackeray, 'Going to See a Man Hanged', *Fraser's Magazine*, August 1840, pp. 150–158.
6. In *The Irish Sketch Book* of 1843 he confessed for his part 'to that common cant and sickly sentimentality which, thank God! is felt by a great number of people nowadays, and which leads them to revolt against murder, whether performed by a ruffian's knife or a hangman's rope, whether accompanied with a curse from the thief as he blows his victim's brains out, or a prayer from my lord on the bench in his wig and black cap'. Among others, Henry Rogers accused those wanting to get rid of capital punishment of having an 'ecessive' or 'morbid sentimentality' ('What is to be done with our Criminals?, *The Edinburgh Review*, July 1847, p. 217).
7. Charles Dickens, *Barnaby Rudge*, ch. LXXVII.
8. 28 February, 9, 13, and 16 March 1846.
9. *Daily News*, 28 February 1846.
10. The *Aylesbury News* reports from 26 April to 11 October 1845.
11. Henry Christmas, *Capital Punishments Unsanctioned by the Gospel*, 1845.
12. *Daily News*, 16 March 1846.
13. Robert Johnson claims that 'gala' is derived from 'gallows' (*Death Work*, 1990, p. 5). There is no evidence for such a derivation.
14. Bernard Manderville, *An Inquiry into the Causes of the Frequent Executions at Tyburn*, 1725, pp. 36f. Over a century later these very words were used – though unattributed by Thomas Wrightson to condemn the same display (*On the Punishment of Death*, 1833, p. 34).
15. Joseph John Gurney, *Memoirs, vol. II*, 2nd edn 1855, p. 107.
16. *Parliamentary Debates* (Commons), vol. xxxix, (8 March 1819), col. 905.
17. *Parliamentary Debates* (Commons), 3rd Series, vol. lii (5 March 1840), col. 920.
18. HO 45/681.
19. Cyril Pearl, *Victorian Patchwork*, 1972, p. 31.
20. Robert Graves, *They Hanged My Saintly Billy*, Cassell 1957, p. 264.
21. *Parliamentary Debates* (Commons), 3rd Series, vol. lvi (16 February 1841), col. 659.
22. Ibid., col. 653.
23. Ibid., vol. lii (5 March 1840), col. 932.
24. 'Hanging, Public or Private?', *The Spectator*, 24 November 1849.

25. Thomas Laqueur, 'Crowds, Carnival, and the State in English Executions, 1604–1868' in *The First Modern Society*, ed. A. L. Beier et al, pp. 305–355.

26. *Parliamentary Debates* (Commons), 3rd Series, vol. xxxviii (19 May, 1837), col. 914.

27. Ibid., vol. lv (23 June 1840), col. 32.

28. Coventry Patmore, 'A London Fete', 1853, *Poems* OUP, 1949.

29. *Parliamentary Debates* (Commons), 3rd series, vol. lvi (16 February 1841), col. 653.

30. Mrs Lachlan, *Narrative*, p. 240.

31. Cited in William Tallack, 'The Dignity of English Law', *Friends Quarterly Examiner*, 1870, p. 505.

32. *Daily News*, 9 March 1846.

33. Robert Dees, *The Inexpediency of Capital Punishment*, 1835, pp. 26f.

34. James Boswell, *London Journal, 1762–3*, Yale edn 1950, pp. 251f.

35. 19 October 1769 (Boswell, *Life of Johnson*, vol. II, p. 93, n. 3).

36. 23 June 1784 (*Life*, vol. IV, p. 328; Boswell, *London Journal*, p. 93).

37. J. H. Jesse, *George Selwyn and His Contemporaries*, vol. I, (p. 5.

38. Ibid. vol. IV, pp. 85 and 96. Once again the ubiquitous Boswell was on the scene, visiting Hackman on the morning of his execution, attending chapel with him, and accompanying him in his mourning coach (p. 83).

39. Shepherd Taylor, *Diary of a Medical Student*, pp. 14 and 116.

40. Harold Orel, *The Unknown Thomas Hardy*, pp. 128–9.

41. Robert Gittings, *Young Thomas Hardy*, p. 60.

42. Written in 1919: Orel, op. cit., pp. 129–130.

43. Thomas Hardy, 'On the Portrait of a Woman about to be Hanged', January 1923.

44. In *Wilhelm Meisters Lehrjahre* (1780) Goethe describes the irresistible fascination which ineluctably drew horrified spectators to the 'terrible spectacle'.

45. Masur, *Rites of Execution*, pp. 95–99.

46. As Douglas Jerrold caustically remarked in *Punch*, 17 January 1846.

47. *Capital Punishment not Opposed to the Doctrine of the Christian Religion, considered in two letters by a Priest of the Catholic Church Established in England*, London 1850, pp. 10–11.

48. The following, for instance, were published in 1846: Edward Hancock, *The Groans of the Gallows; the Living Hangman of Newgate*, London Thomas Pynme, *A Plea for the Abolition of Capital Punishment*; Walter Scott, *The Punishment of Death for the Crime of Murder*; Jelinger Symonds, 'Capital and Prison Punishments'; Αμφω, *War and Punishment opposed to Christianity*; Alexander Campbell, *Capital Punishment Sanctioned by Divine Authority*. And in 1847: Henry Rogers, 'What is to be done with our Criminals?'; A Member of the Church of England, *Capital Punishment under the Gospel Dispensation anti-Scriptural;* A Student of St Bees College, *Letters upon Capital Punishment*; George Combe, *Thoughts on Capital Punishment*; 'God is Love', *A Vindication of the Penalty of Death for the Crime of Murder*; A Witness for 'Judgment, Mercy, and Faith', *"Inquisition for Blood"*, or the Eternal Obligation on States and Governments to Inflict the Penalty of Death for Wilful Murder. And in 1849: George Grove, *Divine Authority for the Capital Punishment of Murderers*. And in 1851: 'Rehum', *Capital Punishment Not*

Grounded on Scripture. For an example of the sort of sermons the Society sponsored see Sydney Smith's sermon on their behalf in *Sermons Preached at St Paul's Cathedral*, 1846, pp. 367ff.

49. *The Eclectic Review*, 1848.
50. 'The Moral Lesson of the Gallows', *Punch*, 17 January 1846, x, 33.
51. Daniel Defoe, *Street Robberies Considered*, 1728, pp. 52–54; Bernard Mandeville, *An Inquiry into the Causes of the Frequent Executions at Tyburn*, 1725, pp. 23–4, 36–7; Henry Fielding, *An Inquiry into the Causes of the Late Increase of Robbers etc*, 2nd edn 1751, p. 189.
52. 25 Geo. II, c. 37.
53. Sir William Blackstone, *Commentaries on the Laws of England, IV*, 15th edn 1809, p. 202.
54. Radzinowicz, *History, vol. I*, p. 217.
55. Blackstone, *Commentaries*, p. 202. Deut. 21.22–3 says that a man worthy of death should be hanged on a tree but 'his body shall not remain all night upon the tree, but thou shalt in any wise bury him that day . . . that thy land be not defiled'.
56. For the fullest account of this practice see A. Hartshorne's *Hanging in Chains*, 1891. The prominent public exposure of the corpses of criminals was practised throughout the continent. In Germany people referred to 'the gallows mountain', in Holland to 'the gallows field' *The Spectacle of Suffering*, Spierenberg, p. 57).
57. 2 & 3 Will. IV, c. 75.
58. See the *Morning Herald*, 11, 14, 17, 21 August 1832.
59. *The Punishment of Death: A Selection of Articles from the Morning Herald*, vol. II, 1837, pp. 4–13.
60. Lachlan, *Narrative*, pp. 250–2. Similar disgust at a contemporary public execution (1831) in Edinburgh was expressed by the anonymous author of 'A Protest against Capital Punishments' in *Meliora*, vol. V, 1863, pp. 363–4.
61. 4 & 5 Will. IV, c. 26. See W. A. Munford, *William Ewart MP*, pp. 68–9. Jack White's Gibbet was still standing near Wincanton as late as 1835 when it was burnt down on Guy Fawkes night (Orel, *The Unknown Thomas Hardy*, p. 131).
62. J. Charles Cox, *Three Centuries of Derbyshire Annals*, vol. II, 1890, p. 45.
63. See the Home Office correspondence (28 September to 7 October 1848) on the propriety of allowing Christian burial to executed felons. Since the Roman Catholic priests would say the obsequies in any case, and dissenters might follow suite, it was inexpedient to prohibit Anglican clergy from so doing – HO45/2468.
64. *Parliamentary Debates* (Lords), 3rd Series, vol. lxxix (28 April 1845), cols 1359–1368.
65. *Punch*, vol. 2, June 1842, p. 240. The article, 'Old Bailey Holidays', was written by Jerrold under his pseudonym 'Q'.
66. *Report of Revd W. Russell, Inspector of Prisons, to Her Majesty's Principal Secretary of State*, 6 May 1845, p. 5.
67. Ibid., pp. 3, 6.
68. 'Hanging, Public or Private?', *The Spectator*, 24 November 1849, pp. 111–2. See also Walter Scott, *The Punishment of Death*, p. 39.

69. *Parliamentary Debates* (Commons) 3rd Series, vol. lvi (16 February 1841) cols 647–664.
70. David Cooper, *The Lesson of the Scaffold*, p. 72.
71. *Punch*, vol. 6, 1844, p. 139.
72. *Punch*, vol. 10. 1846, p. 50.
73. *Punch*, vol. 22, 1852, p. 138.
74. *Parliamentary Debates* (Commons) 3rd Series, vol. xc (9 March 1847) col. 1087.
75. Ibid., vol. cxii (11 July 1850), col. 1259.
76. Albert Borowitz, *The Woman who Murdered Black Satin*, pp. 240–1, 249.
77. Jelinger Symonds, 'Capital and Prison Punishments', pp. 226–7.
78. *The Times*, 13 November 1849.
79. Ibid., 19 November 1849.
80. Ibid., 13 November 1849.
81. So argued in Collins, *Dickens and Crime*, pp. 244–248.
82. 'Hanging, Public or Private?', 24 November 1849.
83. Borowitz, *The Woman*, pp. 269–272.
84. Ibid., p. 273.
85. The only evidence for this is the assertion by his biographer, George Saintsbury, that 'the anti-capital punishment fad was one of the special crotchets of mid-nineteenth century Liberalism, and he kept it up for some time: but in his later and wiser days admitted that he was wrong' (*A Consideration of Thackeray*, 1931, p. 56). This is quoted by Radzinowicz, *History*, vol. IV, p. 337, and again by Collins, *Dickens and Crime*, p. 248. Saintsbury himself gives no further substance for his claim, and nor do those who cite him. From the language he uses it is likely that he is imposing his own preferences on his subject, rather than accurately reflecting Thackeray's later views.

7 The 'Scare-Crow Deity'

1. Beccaria, Cesare, *Dei Delitti e Delle Pene*, 1764, p. 101.
2. 'The Gallows Tree', *The Morning Herald*, 21 November 1864, reproduced in Cooper, *The Lesson of the Scaffold*, p. 96. Throughout this chapter I am indebted to this work.
3. Select Committee, 1856, Evidence para. 60.
4. Buckinghamshire Record Office.
5. Walter Jerrold, *Douglas Jerrold and 'Punch'*, 1910, p. 96.
6. Select Committee, 1856, Evidence para. 60.
7. *Parliamentary Debates* (Lords), 3rd Series, vol. cxxxiii (15 May 1854), cols 306–7. Most of the Australian colonies abolished public executions in 1853.
8. Ibid., col. 311.
9. Ibid., vol. cxlii (9 May 1856) col 1055–6.
10. Ibid., col. 251.
11. Ibid., cols 247–250.
12. Edwin Hodder, *The Life and Work of the Seventh Earl of Shaftesbury*, vol. I, 1886, p. 281.
13. *Parliamentary Debates* (Commons) 3rd Series, vol. cxlii (10 June, 1856), col. 1232.

14. Ibid., col. 1241.
15. Ibid., col. 1244.
16. 7 July 1856.
17. Select Committee, 1856, Evidence, para. 79.
18. Ibid., paras. 6–17. One enterprising cleric did his best to distract attention from the demeaning spectacle. In anticipation of its ill-effects, the Revd Kenrick, curate of Horsham, preached a Good Friday sermon deprecating the public execution of John Lawrence which was to take place the the following day. As a result a good many people left the town and the schoolmasters were persuaded to march their scholars in the opposite direction from where the execution was taking place (Albery, *A Millenium of Facts* p. 318).
19. Select Committee, 1856, Evidence, para. 85.
20. Ibid., paras. 85–88.
21. Ibid., paras. 107–109, Report pp. iv–v.
22. Ibid., paras. 26–34. On the issue of whether murderers should receive Christian obsequies see the 1848 Home Office correspondence (HO 45/2468).
23. Ibid., para. 331.
24. Ibid., para. 337.
25. Ibid., para. 334.
26. *Punch*, vol. 31, 26 July 1856, p. 39.
27. George Jacob Holyoake, 'Public Lessons of the Hangman', from *The Morning Star*, 16 November 1864, reissued as a penny pamphlet, pp. 2–3.
28. Joseph Kingsmill, *Chapters on Prison and Prisoners*, 1852.
29. *All the Year Round*, vol. XX, 15 August 1868, pp. 223–5.
30. Horace Creeley, 19 June 1836, New York, cited in P. E. MacKey, *Voices against Death*, 1976, p. xxi. See also MacKey's *Hanging in the Balance*, 1982, pp. 232–319, and Masur, *Rites of Execution*, pp. 113ff.
31. Lord Hobbart, *On Capital Punishment for Murder*, 1861.
32. Thomas Beggs, 'The Royal Commission and the Punishment of Death', *Social Science Review*, N. S. 3., 1865, p. 160.
33. Anon article in *The Westminster and Foreign Quarterly Review* 1 April 1864, 81, Article IV.
34. For instance, Michel Foucault, *Discipline and Punish*, 1979, p. 65; David Garland, *Punishment in Modern Society*, 1990, p. 141; Michael Jasper, ' "Hats Off!"; the Roots of Victorian Public Hangings', *Executions and the British Experience* ed. W. B. Thesing, 1990, pp. 139–148, esp. p. 140.
35. Cited in B. M. Jones, *Henry Fielding, Novelist and Magistrate*, George Allen and Unwin 1933, p. 205.
36. Henry Rogers, 'Essays Theological and Philosophical II: On Public Executions', *Good Words*, April 1865, pp. 104–112.
37. Garland, *Punishment in Modern Society* p. 140; Barry Faulk, 'The Public Execution: Urban Rhetoric and Victorian Crowds, in Thesing, *Executions*, pp. 77–91, pp. 78f.
38. Rogers, 'On Public Executions', p. 112.
39. 'Mr Phillips on Capital Punishment', *The Saturday Review*, vol. II, 15 November 1856, pp. 635–7.

40. James Stephen, 'Capital Punishments', *Fraser's Magazine* LXIX, June 1864, p. 70. As late as 1888 the same author could advocate the reintroduction of capital punishment for fraud (*History of the Criminal Law*, vol. I, 1888, p. 479).

41. *Parliamentary Debates* (Commons), 3rd Series, vol. clxxiii (23 February, 1864), cols 941–946.

42. Ibid., vol. clxxiv (3 May 1864), cols 2055–2064.

43. Ibid., cols 2097f.

44. For a contemporary account see Rogers, 'On Public Executions', pp. 104–5.

45. Royal Commission Evidence, paras, 1148–1263.

46. Ibid., para. 2252–2338.

47. Ibid., para. 3485–3513.

48. Ibid., para. 3259–3484.

49. Report of the Committee of the Society for the Abolition of Capital Punishment, January 1867, p. 3. Copy in the Howard League archives.

50. Letter to William Tallack, 12 June 1865, printed in William Tallack's *Howard Letters and Memories*, 1905, pp. 163f.

51. Radzinovicz, *History*, vol. V, p. 674.

52. *Parliamentary Debates* (Commons), 3rd Series, vol. cxci (21 April 1868), cols 1047–1055.

53. Ibid., col. 1053.

54. Ibid., col. 1051.

55. Thomas Beggs, *The Deterrent Influence of Capital Punishment*, 1868. The importance of Mill's speech can be seen from the number of abolitionists who rushed into print with refutations of his argument, for instance 'Mr Mill's Speech on Capital Punishment' (Anon), *The Westminster Review*, 1869, vol. 35, pp. 429–436, and William Tallack, 'The Dignity and Efficacy of English law as Diminished by the Capital Punishment', *Friends Quarterly Examiner*, 1870 pp. 493–507.

56. *The Times*, 22 April, 1868.

57. Quinlivan, P., and Rose, P., *The Fenians in England, 1865–1872*, pp. 133–138.

58. 31 Vict., c. 24.

59. *Maidstone and Kentish Journal*, 17 August 1868.

60. Section 4 of the Act allowed for the family of the prisoner to be admitted at the discretion of the Sheriff or Visiting Justices to witness the execution. I have no evidence that this extraordinary discretion was ever exercised.

61. Select Committee, 1856, Evidence paras. 63–67.

62. *The Times*, 22 April 1868. This development in the conduct of English executions was mirrored on the continent: the abolition of public executions was enacted in most German states in the 1850s, in the Netherlands in 1860 (with final abolition of the death penalty in 1870), and in Vienna in 1868. In a few other countries, such as Spain, it took place somewhat after 1870, but only in France did it continue for much longer, in fact until 1939. Although the process towards intramural executions is less well documented on the continent than in England, the conclusion of the most recent studies is that there as here it was primarily a consequence of fundamental changes in public sensibility. The 'mockery' which executions had become, and the threat of the rabble were increasing concerns. The last execution in Vienna was like a fair, with hundreds of booths set up

around the corpses which remained hanging on the gibbet until sunset. Drunk on 'Gallows Beer' and replete with 'Poor Sinner Sausages' the crowds at times sang and cheered, at times quarrelled and fought among themselves (Richard van Dülmen, *Theatre of Horror*, p. 108). Thus the abolition of public executions on the continent came about to prevent the dilution of the deterrent effect of capital punishment and the degeneration of the masses, and to mitigate the suffering of the more refined members of the public, rather than out of any concern for the degradation of the felon (Spierenberg, *The Spectacle of Suffering*, pp. 183–206; van Dülmen, Theatre of Horror, pp. 126f.)

63. Cooper, *The Lesson of the Scaffold*, p. 176.
64. William Tallack, *Howard Letters*, pp. 143f.

8 Hanging in Limbo

1. *A Shropshire Lad*, ix.
2. Time and again the Howard Association's Annual Reports refer to their circulation of many pamphlets and papers to anyone who inquired after them. The requests of 'ministers, essayists and members of discussion classes' were all satisfied (1875 Report, p. 11). Papers which the Association published or republished included such titles as 'The Modern Jews on Capital Punishment' (1877) and 'The Sacredness of Human Life' (1879). The Secretary, William Tallack, proved an excellent example of devotion to the cause, turning down an offer to become Secretary of the Peace Society on twice the salary that the Howard Association provided (*Howard Letters*, p. 143).
3. 'Law and Society Frustrated Through the Capital Penalty', The Howard Association, 1872, p. 1.
4. Christopher Wordsworth, 'A Sermon Preached in Westminster Abbey, on Sunday 24 November, 1867'. See the critique of it by William Ball, 'Capital Punishment', *Friends Quarterly Examiner*, 1868, pp. 232–236.
5. William Tallack, 'The Dignity of English Law', *Friends Quarterly Examiner*, 1870, p. 506.
6. P. E. MacKey, *Voices against Death*, p. xxiii, and the same author's *Hanging in the Balance*, pp. 124–217. See also Walt Whitman's scathing denunciation of the clergy in 'A Dialogue', *The United States Magazine and Democratic Review*, 17 November 1845, pp. 360–364.
7. Tallack, 'The Dignity of English Law', p. 507.
8. Ibid.
9. Robert Gibbs, *A History of Aylesbury*, 1885, p. 545.
10. Buckinghamshire Public Record Office, letter from the Revd Martin Smith, curate of Newport Pagnell, to Robert Gibbs, 28 March 1870.
11. Ibid., letter from the Revd John Spencer, Rector, to Robert Gibbs, 22 March 1870.
12. London, 1876.
13. Charles Kingsley, *All Saints day and Other Sermons*, 1878, pp. 57ff.
14. Letter from Bright to William Tallack, 20 November 1876, published in *Howard Letters*, pp. 154–5.

15. Letter from Bright to Tallack, 6 January 1884, *Howard Letters*, p. 157.
16. Editorial in *The Times*, 25 July 1872.
17. J. W. Pease, House of Commons 12 June 1877, reprinted by the Howard Association as 'The Immediate Abolition of Capital Punishment'.
18. 14 March 1878.
19. *Parliamentary Debates* (Commons), 3rd Series, vol. cclxii (22 June 1881), cols 1051–2.
20. Ibid., col. 1052.
21. Ibid., col. 1059. He was wrong. When the Revised Version was published in 1885 the words remained unchanged.
22. Ibid., cols 1067–9.
23. Ibid., col. 1070.
24. Ibid., col. 1080.
25. For instance in 1876 the English gallows were redesigned to provide a scaffold-top lever for releasing the drop, thus eliminating the delay between adjusting the noose, descending the steps and going under the scaffold to draw the bolt (Justin Atholl, *The Shadow of the Gallows*, p. 103).
26. See, for example, Arthur Griffiths, 'Why have a Hangman?', *Fortnightly Review*, vol. 40, 1883, pp. 581–6. He was an advocate of 'reasonable improvements' in the English way of death and deprecated the fashion for looking abroad for fanciful alternatives. He feared that the vain quest for perfection would lead to abolition. It looks as though the Aberdare Committee agreed with him.
27. NCADP, 'Executions' (for private circulation only), nd. pp. 5–6. See also the undated (1889) Home Office memorandum on the employment of hangmen the appendix to which contains an authorative list of miscarriages (HO 144/212/A48697).
28. *The Report of the Committee appointed to Inquire into the Existing Practice as to carrying out of Sentences of Death* . . . (Aberdare Committee), 1888, HO 144/212/A48697/2, p. vii.
29. Ibid., para. 87. That these improvements met with some success is evidence by a 'stictly confidential' Home Office publication, 'Execution of Sentence of Death: Notes as to Practice', 1920, p. 21 which states that Conway's execution in 1891 was the last major bungle (HO 45/25843).
30. Ibid., paras 853–5.
31. Ibid., p. ix, paras 225, and 923.
32. Ibid., p. xiii.
33. For the material on Berry see HO 144/212/A48697A-F.
34. File on Berry, 1902 (PCOM 8/191). Billington too gave cause for concern towards the end of his career. By 1899 he had become 'less temperate than before', and was described as 'nervous and confused' at two executions. The problem was resolved by his death in 1901 (PCOM 8/192).
35. HO 144/212/A48697-F.
36. Home Office Memorandum (nd) HO 144/212/A48697.
37. Ibid.
38. Gordon Honeycombe, *The Murders of the Black Museum, 1870–1970*, p. 94.
39. *The Liverpool Daily Post*, 21 August 1891.

40. Ibid.
41. 4 May 1934, at the execution of Parker and Probert in Wandsworth Prison.
42. Howard Association Annual Report, 1891, p. 5, and Tallack, *Howard Letters*, p. 149.
43. Howard Association Annual Report, 1893, p. 7.
44. For an excellent summary of the victory of the new learning in late Victorian England see Owen Chadwick, *The Victorian Church*, Part II, pp. 1–111. Some radical clerics welcomed the new learning. In 1879 Stewart Headlam, the Christian Socialist leader, preached: 'Thank God that the scientific men have shattered the idol of an infallible book, broken the fetters of a supposed divine code of rules; for so have they helped to reveal Jesus Christ in his majesty . . . He is the Word of God; he is inspiring you, encouraging you, strengthening you in your scientific studies; he is the wisdom in Lyell or in Darwin'. (Alec Vidler, *The Church in an Age of Revolution*, p. 119.)
45. In 1885 Bishop Ellicott of Gloucester condemned the view that man was part of the evolutionary process, while to the end of his life in 1900 the evangelical Bishop Ryle of Liverpool believed in the literal accuracy of Genesis. (Chadwick, *Victorian Church* I, pp. 23f.) Yet as late as 1892 the abolitionist John MacMaster could produce a vast pre-critical tome on the biblical basis of capital punishment – *The Divine Purpose of Capital Punishment*. It was to be the last of its kind.
46. Daniel Rutenberg, 'From Praise of Hanging to the Femme Fatale: Capital Punishment in Nineties Periodicals', *Victorian Periodicals Review* 11 (1978) pp. 95–104. In the early 1900s articles advocating abolition again began to appear, see Tighe Hopkins, 'Capital Punishment: Ineffectual and Mischievous', *Westminster Review*, vol. 155, 1901, pp. 144–9; and Chester Warren, 'Is Capital Punishment Defensible?', *Westminster Review*, vol. 165, 1906, pp. 512–6.
47. Harry Jones, 'Capital Punishment', *The Sunday Magazine*, 21 (1892) pp. 341–343, 417–420.
48. Edward Hancock, 'William Habron's Doom of the Gallows', 1879, printed in Brian Lane (ed.), *The Murder Club Guide to North-West England*, pp. 47f.
49. Josiah Oldfield (Barr), *The Penalty of Death*, 1901. Oldfield was to remain an active campaigner until ripe old age. As late as 12 December 1947 he was writing to the *Church Times* on the issue of capital punishment.
50. John Clifford DD, Arthur Auchmutty, J. Mathieson Forson, T. Gasquoine, John Glasse DD, A. M. Mitchell, and Walter Walsh.
51. Lambeth Palace Archives, Letter from Oldfield to Davidson, 19 April 1907.
52. The remark about the opposition of the bishops to Romilly, long ago as it was, obviously bothered him quite a lot since almost five years later, after he had been handed an abolitionist tract naming them, he wrote to the House of Lords inquiring where the information derived from on this 'most worrying matter'. He was told that it was from Romilly's memoirs where they had been signalled out for posterity (12 December 1911). He was reassured by the rather desperate excuse that 'The obvious explanation of the attitude not only of the bishops but of the other Lords with regard to the capital punishment question, seems to me to be the fact that although you could be hanged for stealing 5/- you never were.' That simply was not true, but even if it had been he should have asked himself

why if the statute were such a dead duck his predecessors had not voted to rescind it.

53. Lambeth Palace Archives, Letter to Oldfield, 22 April 1907.
54. Ibid., Letter to Oldfield, 27 April 1907.
55. H. Montgomery Hyde, *Famous Trials 9: Roger Casement*, p. 137. Cardinal Bourne was not prepared to admit him into the Roman Catholic church unless he expressed 'sorrow for any scandal he might have caused by his acts, public or private'. Casement rebelled: 'They are trying to make me betray my soul.' When it was discovered that he had already been baptized into that confession as an infant the problem was resolved (Brian Inglis, *Roger Casement*, p. 373).
56. David Edwards, *Leaders of the Church of England, 1828–1944*, p. 240.
57. E. D. Girdlestone, *Capital Punishment reviewed in the light of the expedient and the right*, 1904, pp. 15–21.
58. Hypatia Bradlaugh Bonnar, 'The Death Penalty', *The Humane Review*, 1903, vol. 4, p. 138.

9 Sentiment and Salvation

1. 'The Ballad of Reading Gaol', stanza 5
2. *Quod*, London 1928, p. 320.
3. Two American divines had taken issue on this matter, for instance. The Revd Mr Cheever of New York, had argued that 'abolition would be an act of impiety; for the substitution of imprisonment for life would probably make most murderers die in their sins, while it would send many innocent persons unprepared into eternity'. The abolitionist author, Spear, however, had feared that capital punishment might send a fellow-being into the presence of God unprepared and 'reeking of blood'.

   Some divines have even urged that the law was humane; that the perpetrator has been induced to think seriously of divine things, and led to repentance; and in his last hours has confessed the justice of his sentence, and given glory to God. Granting even that such cases have occurred – and they are like angels visits, few and far between – still the law itself appears in no better light. Indeed it appears cruel, even giving it this favourable view. Monstrous law!. To cut off a human being, whose heart has just begun to feel the emotions of returning virtue . . . This is hanging a criminal for very love and kindness (Spear, *Essays*, pp. 126ff).

4. Henry Romilly, *The Punishment of Death*, 1886. (posthumously published).
5. G. W. E. Russell, *Edward King*, 1912, pp. 123–127.
6. Lincoln Public Record Office, letter from Prison Chaplain to the Dean of Lincoln, 12 May 1911.
7. Ibid., letter from Revd Kettlethorpe, rector of Newark, to the Rt Hon G. Russell, 3 April 1911.
8. This view was echoed by many others. In an article entitled 'In Praise of Hanging', W. S. Lilly wrote that a sentence of life imprisonment was merely 'a more cruel and more cowardly mode of inflicting the death penalty . . . it is also in the vast majority of cases a sentence of moral and spiritual death'.

There can be no question whatever that the most hopeful means of working the reformation of a murderer – and by reformation I mean the conversion of his will from bad to good – is supplied by the certainty of his impending execution. However seared his conscience, however atrophied his moral sense, however blurred his vision of judgment to come, this certainty often quickens him into new spiritual life and works, as Schopenauer expresses it 'a great and rapid change in his inmost being' (*The New Review*, 1894, vol. 11, p. 200).

9. John Pitkin, *The Prison Cell in its Lights and Shadows*, 1918. pp. 127ff.

10. John Laurence, *A History of Capital Punishment*, pp. 159–60. Arthur Griffiths, the Inspector for Prisons, agreed that those who welcomed the ministrations of the chaplain were in danger of 'falling into the exaggeration of cant' – *Fifty Years of Public Service*, 1898, p. 337.

11. S. Wood, *Shades of the Prison House*, 1932, pp. 272–275. It should be borne in mind that the author's obvious dislike of and disdain for a mass murderer may have coloured his account. Other accounts of wonderful conversions abound. In his account of his work, the hangman James Berry records many such transformations: *My Experiences as an Executioner*, 1902, pp. 70ff.

12. Letter from H. B. Vaisey to the *Church Times*, 20 January 1956.

13. Laurence, *History* p. 190.

14. John Lee, *The Man They Could Not Hang*. On another occasion, in 1877, the chaplain with great aplomb said prayers by the prone body of a half-hanged man while a new rope was found to finish the job (James Bland, *The Common Hangman*, 1984, p. 150).

15. Blake, *Quod*, p. 329.

16. Justin Atholl, *The Reluctant Hangman*, p. 69. This work was written before the Home Office documents relating to Berry were released under the hundred year rule and so is seriously defective in its portrayal.

17. Berry, *Experiences*, p. 12.

18. Executioners were prone to confess in public to their lack of faith in capital punishment. Compare for instance the profession of the American executioner Robert Elliot that he had always been opposed to the death penalty: 'I am against Capital Punishment', *Collier's Magazine*, 22 October 1938.

19. Oscar Wilde, 'The Ballad of Reading Gaol', stanza 4. The fullest account of the genesis of Wilde's hanging ballad is given in H. Montgomery Hyde's *Oscar Wilde: The Aftermath*, pp. 65–69.

20. N. D. Deuchar, *The Case Against Capital Punishment*, p. 12.

21. A. F. Brockway, *Inside the Left* p. 103.

22. Pitkin, *The Prison Cell*, p. 164.

23. Clifford Richards, *A Prison Chaplain on Dartmoor*, p. 200.

24. Stephen Hobhouse and A. F. Brockway (eds), *English Prisons Today*, 1922, p. 247.

25. Blake, *Quod*, p. 62.

26. J. W. Horsley, *I Remember*, 1912 pp. 101–105.

27. Hobhouse and Brockway, *English Prisons Today*, p. 247.

28. Constance Lytton, *Prison and Prisoners*, 1914, p. 266.

29. Gordon Honeycombe, *The Murders of the Black Museum, 1870–1970*, pp. 48–50.

30. Ibid., p. 150.

31. Justin Atholl, *The Shadow of the Gallows*, p. 63. See also the Home Office papers on this incident: HO 45/10024/A56698.
32. Lambeth Palace Archives, Davidson *Papers*, Letter from Heath to Davidson, 21 March 1908.
33. Ibid., letter from Wenham, 29 October 1926.
34. File on 'Form of Words to be used at an Execution', 1927 (HO 45/25843).
35. File on 'Attendance etc of Chaplains at Executions', 1927 (HO 45 406104/12).

10 Great Expectations

1. 'The Hooded Shape'.
2. Published as *English Prisons Today* ed. Stephen Hobhouse and A. F. Brockway, 1922.
3. Filson Young, *Trial of Frederick Bywaters and Edith Thompson*, 1923. The emotionalism attendant on such executions is shown by a letter which, several years later, W.J. Wenham wrote to Archbishop Davidson referring to this hanging (21 September 1926): 'I have often wondered what a prison chaplain's reflection may be over the body of a hanged woman when he ponders on that beautiful passage of the burial service: "Man that is born of a woman". Man that is born of a woman, how long will you be content to hang her?'
4. For the most recent and fullest account of her life and death see René Weis, *Criminal Justice*, 1988. That the stories may be exaggerated or invented is suggested by the fact that the then Deputy Governor of Holloway later told her nephew that Mrs Thompson was 'calm and dignified' at her execution (Harley Cronin, *The Screw Turns*, p. 33).
5. Howard League Annual Report 1922–23, p. 5. Not all were so shocked. Thomas Hardy wrote a pitiless poem, 'On the Portrait of a Woman about to be hanged', on the eve of the execution.
6. Lord Soper, private communication.
7. Alan Wilkinson, *The Church of England and the First World War*, p. 265.
8. Adam Fox, *Dean Inge*, p. 127.
9. The original article was published in 1922 and republished in *Lay Thoughts of a Dean*, 1926, pp. 148–155.
10. Ibid., p. 152.
11. W.J. Forsythe, *Penal Discipline, Reformatory Projects and the English Prison Commission, 1895–1939*, pp. 10–17.
12. W. R. Inge, 'The Religious Aspect of the Problem' in *The Problem of the Feeble-Minded: An Abstract of the Report of the Royal Commission*, 1909, pp. 89–93, at p. 92.
13. W. R. Inge, *Christian Ethics and Modern Problems*, 1930, p. 271.
14. Forsythe, *Penal Discipline*, p. 154. Such views were not confined to Conservatives or Liberals. In the same year George Bernard Shaw wanted to insert a preface to a Labour Party Research Committee Report in which he would urge euthanasia by 'lethal chambers' for irreformable criminals. The editors refused. (Stephen Hobhouse, *Forty Years On*, pp. 177f.)
15. H. Bodell Smith, *The State Murder of John Griffiths*, 1923, p. 35. Not all were as

responsive or as responsible as Temple. The other bishop whom Dorrity had approached to help in the fight against capital punishment had replied in the words of Alphonse Karr to the French Chamber of Deputies, '*que messieurs les assassins commencent*' ('let the murderers begin').

16. This argument from expediency was supported by one of his canons, Peter Green, in a work on Christian ethics, *The Problem of Right Conduct*, pp. 262f. These views coincided completely with English Roman Catholic teaching at this time which held on the basis of Aquinas that the supreme right of death belongs to God but that that right is for certain purposes, for instance the protection of society, vested in the state. This divine right of the state to kill criminals was expressly laid down in the *Compendium Theologicae Moralis*:

    It is lawful for the state to put to death criminals, and this because the Death Penalty is necessary in the interests of all the members of the State, and is also essential to the existence of the State, which often can only be maintained by the death of criminals. It is admitted that God conferred this power on the State, without which the State would not be able to exist. This power is also recognized in the practice of all governments, by Holy Writ, and by the universal assent of mankind (Quoted in E. Bowen-Rowlands, *The Judgment of Death*, p. 129).

17. Resolution passed by the Meeting of the Society of Friends on 15 January 1923.
18. *The Proceedings of COPEC*, 1924, p. 148.
19. *British Weekly*, 18 January 1894, Quoted in Henry Pelling, *The Origins of the Labour Party*, p. 140.
20. F. A. Iremonger, *William Temple*, p. 332. The Labour churches more or less petered out by the First World War, in part at least because the other churches had taken up their challenge of 'the social gospel', in part because the majority of their members became more exclusively political and gave up on their attempts to clothe socialism in Christianity.
21. Howard League Annual Report 1923–24. Also at their instigation a Parliamentary Penal Reform Group was established which included both Frank Woods, Bishop of Winchester, and Rupert Cecil, Bishop of Exeter.
22. *Parliamentary Debates*, (Commons), 5th Series, vol. 231, (30 October 1929), col. 288.
23. Ibid., col. 290.
24. Ibid., col. 292. While these impassioned pleas were being made by Labour members in the House, a leader of the Established Church was making less impressive comments. The *Daily Mail* (14 March 1929) reported that the Bishop of Norwich, Bertram Pollock, claimed that the period of waiting between sentence and execution was conducive to the reform of the condemned man since one man had told him that 'the lessons of his old Sunday School came back to him in this time of waiting'.

11   *This Son of York*

1. A sermon by the Rural Dean reported in *The Northampton and Country Independent*, 7 February 1931.

2. 'Capital Punishment from the Christian Standpoint', The Roy Calvert Memorial Lecture for 1936.
3. Select Committee on Capital Punishment, 1930, Report, ss. 61–65.
4. As recounted by Canon Hussey to the Synod of York in 1962, Synod Minutes p. 41.
5. Select Committee, 1930, Evidence pp. 374–376.
6. Ibid., paras. 3724–5.
7. Ibid., para. 3736.
8. Ibid., para. 3743.
9. Ibid., para. 3759.
10. Ibid., para. 3760.
11. Ibid., para. 3754.
12. Ibid., paras. 825, 879.
13. Ibid., paras. 883–5.
14. Ibid., para. 893.
15. Ibid., para. 835.
16. Ibid., para. 844.
17. Ibid., para. 852.
18. Ibid., paras. 852–7.
19. Ibid., paras. 904–5, 921.
20. Ibid., para. 3614.
21. Ibid. His sentiments were shared by at least one governor who had gone public. Major Blake, governor of Pentonville since 1919, had written an article in the *Evening News* (9 October 1926) in which he had confessed to feeling 'a bit of a murderer' himself.

    Each of the other prison governors and officials with whom I have discussed the question of capital punishment have admitted to being affected in the same manner . . . If men who, though possibly somewhat hardened, are still eminently humane, feel they have participated in a not altogether creditable proceeding, there must be something fundamentally wrong with a law which has the effect of lessening the self-respect of those whose duty it is to carry it out.

    He was prosecuted and fined for this indiscretion.
22. Select Committee Evidence, paras. 3639–3643.
23. Much later another archbishop would have drawn the same conclusion as they: 'Anyone who says that it is unchristian to hang puts himself out of court' (Letter from Fisher to Bishop Cuthbert of Coventry, 5 July 1956, Lambeth Palace Archives).
24. Select Committee Evidence, paras. 3673–3681.
25. Ibid., para. 4278.
26. Ibid., para. 4358.
27. W.J. Forsythe, *Penal Discipline*, p. 172.
28. Select Committee Report, paras. 284–5.
29. Ibid., paras. 286–294. Specifically
    (i) Genesis ix. 6 was not applied to Cain and this would not be imposed today because it would leave no place for reprieve, nor distinctions between murder, manslaughter, and infanticide.

(ii) If it were binding there are many other binding obligations in the Old Testament: death should be exacted for blasphemy, and sabbath-breaking.

(iii) There is progress in divine revelation and Christ himself repealed the retaliatory law. Jonathan Dymond in his Essay on the Punishment of Death says: 'Our law is Christian Law, and if Christianity by its precepts or spirits prohibits the punishment of death, it cannot be made right to Christians by referring to a commandment which was given to Noah' (Essays, p. 206).

(iv) Lactantius, and Augustine and the early church in general until the fifth century were against Christians taking part in executions. Julian removed Christians from state offices because of this. In later centuries other Christian opposition was heard.

30. See the correspondence in *The Times* 19, 23, and 24 December 1930. One Tory member, Sir Gervais Rentoul QC, later recanted and joined the abolitionist side (*The Penal Reformer*, vol. 6 no. 1, pp. 1–3).

31. *Daily Telegraph*, 17 December 1930.

33. Mrs Louis Donaldson JP, 'Christ and Capital Punishment', nd.

34. This correspondence was published by the NCADP for circulation among its members and MPs. Copy in the Friends Library.

35. The Sentence of Death (Expectant Mothers) Act 1931 prohibited the death sentence being passed on pregnant women, and The Children and Young Persons Act 1933 prohibited the death penalty being imposed on those under 18. The Army and Navy Act of 1930 severely curtailed capital punishment in the armed forces, restricting it to treason and desertion to the enemy. Whereas between 1914 and March 1920 346 servicemen were executed for military offences, between 1939 and 1945 the total was four (Anthony Babington, *For the Sake of Example: Capital Courts-Martial 1914–1920*. pp. 189, 210–212).

36. Lt-Col. C. E. F. Rich, *Recollections of a Prison Governor*.

37. G. F. Clayton, *The Wall is Strong*, pp. 72f.

38. 'Capital Punishment from the Christian Standpoint', The Third Roy Calvert Memorial Lecture, 1936.

39. A Humanist organization closely associated with the Labour churches and the Labour Party.

40. 'Public Opinion and the Death Penalty', the Fourth Roy Calvert Memorial Lecture, 1937.

41. 12th Annual Report, 1936–7, p. 6.

42. William Temple, 'The Death Penalty', NCADP 1935.

43. Chapman Cohen, 'Shall we Go a-Hanging?', *The Penal Reformer* vol. 1. no. 2, October 1934, pp. 10f., and Dr Eric Strauss, 'A Catholic View of Hanging', ibid., vol. 4. no. 1, July 1937, p. 5.

44. Cohen, op.cit. p. 10; Owen Carroll, 'The Shadow of the Gallows', *The Penal Reformer* vol. 1. no. 4, April 1935 pp. 6f; Sir Gervais Rentoul, 'Second Thoughts on Capital Punishment', ibid., vol. 6 no. 1, pp. 1–3. It was not only the abolitionists who could still advocate such a measure. In the April 1935 issue it was reported that Sir Gifford Fox in the House of Commons (referring to recent executions of black Kenyans) had asked if his Rt Hon. Friend was 'aware of the feeling

among white settlers out there who, in large numbers, would very much like to see a public execution'?

45. Home Office File on Mrs Van der Elst, 1935 (HO 45 677344/2a; on Mrs Van der Elst and Brigstock (HO 45 677344/6); on Mrs Van der Elst and Anderson, 1935 (HO 45 677344/10).
46. File on Anderson, 1935 (HO 45 677344/10).
47. File on Abolitionist Meeting (HO 45 677344/16).
48. Charles Gattey, *The Incredible Mrs Van der Elst*, pp. 46–48, 150.
49. She denied that she had commissioned this picture and refused to pay the artist a 200 guinea fee until compelled to do so by a court judgment (*The Times* 30 October 1936).
50. Letter from John Paton to members of the NCADP, entitled 'The Campaign of Mrs Van der Elst', May 1935, copy in the Friends Library.
51. *The Penal Reformer*, vol. 1. no. 4, April 1935, pp. 8f.
52. Henson had taken an active role in the retentionist campaign, defending capital punishment for murder and treason at a meeting in Durham in April 1935.
53. Mrs Van der Elst, *On the Gallows*, pp. 269–279.
54. Gattey, op.cit., p. 46.
55. Hazel Erskine, 'The Polls: Capital Punishment', *Public Opinion Quarterly*, 34, 1970–71, p. 299.

12 Hanging on the Fence

1. *Measure for Measure*, Act III, scene 1.
2. *Pensées*, 704.
3. *Parliamentary Debates* (Lords) 5th Series, vol. 201 (21 February 1957) col. 1194.
4. There were on average 8.2 executions each year from 1930 to 1939, and 13.3 from 1940 to 1946. The figure for the 1930s was the lowest of any decade in the century, while the latter figure corresponds to the norm of 13 executions a year between 1900 and 1949 (*Royal Commission on Capital Punishment*, 1953, Appendix 2, table 6, p. 309).
5. Theodora Calvert, *Capital Punishment: Society takes Revenge*, 1946.
6. Donald MacKinnon, 'Justice', *Theology*, March 1963, p. 102, note.
7. Roald Dahl, 'The Headmaster' in *Boy*, 1984, pp. 144–6. Dahl attributed his loss of faith in Christianity to the brutal administration of justice on the part of Fisher.
8. For the most recent account of the case see Francis Selwyn, *Rotten to the Core? The Life and Death of Neville Heath*.
9. Gallup Poll November 1947, cited in J. B. Christoph, *Capital Punishment and British Politics*, p. 44.
10. 14 April 1948.
11. Educated Catholic opinion was changing on this issue. The editor of *The Catholic Herald* (5 December 1947) wrote: 'We do not think that the Catholics need have the smallest difficulty, in principle, in supporting the abolition of the death penalty . . . In a modern age where punishment is supposed to be corrective is not the continued retention of this engine of retribution an acknowledgment that society has failed.'

12. *The Times*, 25 May 1948.
13. Christoph, *Capital Punishment*, p. 52.
14. These and the results of the other two polls are all given in Christoph *Capital Punishment*, pp. 53ff.
15. *The Methodist Recorder*, 11 December 1947.
16. *The Cardiff Western Mail*, 23 January 1948; Christoph, *Capital Punishment*, p. 53.
17. Viscount Templewood, *Parliamentary Debates* (Lords), 5th Series, vol. clxxxv (16 December 1953), col. 155.
18. F. R. Barry, *Mervyn Haigh*, pp. 18, 165.
19. *Parliamentary Debates* (Lords), 5th Series, vol. 155, (27 April 1948) cols 422–425. Commenting on this passage, a contemporary Christian ethicist wrote: 'The epithets emphasised are unfortunate, but they are characteristic of a widely shared attitude. They show how use and wont can blind even the most humane and Christian mind to a plain truth . . . it is surely unarguable that [hanging even were it necessary] is profoundly shocking. The Death Penalty is so repulsive in itself that it can never be "untimely" to enquire whether it is still necessary' (Sir Walter Moberly, *The Ethics of Punishment*, p. 300).
20. Ibid., cols 426–7.
21. Ibid., cols 481–2.
22. Ibid., col. 483.
23. Ibid., col. 497.
24. By Stanley Jackson in *The Old Bailey*.
25. *Parliamentary Debates* (Lords), 5th Series, vol. 155, (28 April 1948) col. 485. At Common Law the mental element in murder is defined as an intention to kill or cause grievous bodily harm, while an intention to kill is necessary for attempted murder. Thus he who attempts murder is usually more culpable and often more dangerous than an actual murderer. Yet the latter had to be sentenced to death (now to life imprisonment) while the former was usually given a determinate, or occasionally a life, sentence.
26. Ibid., col. 519.
27. Lambeth Palace Archives, Letter to Fisher, 6 May 1948.
28. Ibid., Letter to Adams, 29 May 1948.
29. *Parliamentary Debates* (Lords), 5th Series, vol. 156, (1 June 1948) cols 42–44.
30. Ibid., col. 43.
31. Ibid., col. 48.
32. Emrys Hughes, *Syndey Silverman*, p. 110.
33. Lambeth Palace Archives, letter to the Lord Chancellor, 21 May 1948.
34. *Parliamentary Debates* (Lords), 5th Series, vol. 156, (2 June 1948) cols 124–5.
35. Ibid., col. 126.
36. Ibid., col. 153. The Archbishop's papers reveal him on the defensive over this issue. Stung by the charges levelled at him in the Lords, he wrote to Lord Rochester complaining that he had misrepresented him. Fisher had said that there were certain Christian principles of which he indicated two. The first was the punishment must not be out of proportion to the crime. As an illustration 'and to correct misuse of the text' he had quoted 'an eye for an eye'. It had surprised him that *The Times* should describe his interpretation of that text as

striking when it was merely 'a commonplace of biblical study'. He then went on to quote part of his speech dealing with 'the law of love', and added that he had not thought it necessary to say that this principle was derived from the New Testament as the earlier one was from the Old Testament, for it must have been obvious. It was not 'a quotation from our Lord but it was directly derived, of course, from him' (3 June 1948). In this and other letters to critics he makes his position clearer, but their criticism still stands. Why was he not so clear in Parliament? The first thing he should have done was to draw attention to Christ's repudiation of retaliation (Letter from Revd John Roberts, 8 June 1948).

37. *Parliamentary Debates* (Lords), 5th Series, vol. 185, (16 December 1953) col. 155.

13 Death on the Drawing Board

1. Lambeth Palace Archives, letter to the Archbishop of Canterbury, 22 October 1926.
2. Cabinet Minutes of 8 November 1948 (HO 45/25084/83737).
3. On 18 March 1949 Sir Hartley Shawcross, the Attorney General, wrote to Chuter Ede recommending Geoffrey Warde, Bishop of Lewis, for membership of the Commission. An annotation in pencil beside this merely says 'no Bishops' (HO 45/25084/83737).
4. *Parliamentary Debates* (Commons), 5th Series, vol. 460 (20 January 1949), col. 330.
5. Lord Templewood, for instance, addressing the Howard League, criticized the Government for the interminable delay in setting up the Commission (*The Times*, 25 April 1949).
6. 'Capital Punishment', *New Statesman and Nation*, N.S. xxxix (28 January 1950).
7. H. T. Smith, the Senior Chaplain, with fifteen years of service and the experience of several capital charge cases; J. I. Lane, the Catholic chaplain of Liverpool, with 24 years of service and eight executions; and H. D. Hare, the Anglican chaplain of Liverpool with six years service and two executions.
8. They were later supported not only in their view of the validity of capital punishment for murder, but also in their proposal for greater consultation with chaplains by the evidence of two chaplains from the Scottish Prison Service, J. McC. Campbell, JP, formerly of Barlinnie, and Revd D. McA. Chalmers, chaplain of Saughton for eleven years, with the experience of one execution.
9. Royal Commission Evidence, Memorandum by Prison Chaplains (c).
10. Royal Commission Evidence, para. 1517.
11. Ibid., para. 1462.
12. Ibid., paras. 1465–8.
13. Ibid., Chaplains' Memorandum III.
14. Ibid., col. 1493.
15. Frances Partridge, *Everything to Lose: 1945–60*, Gollancz 1985, p. 111.
16. The *Howard Journal*, (1949–50) vol. 8, pp. 1f..
17. Royal Commission Evidence, Memorandum by the Howard League Appendix B; Memorandum by the Revd Joseph Walker and evidence paras. 7218–7282.

Ludovic Kennedy was researching for his play *Murder Story* at this time, and recalled later how surprised he had been by the revulsion felt by all prison staff at executions: 'Many of those who had to attend executions – doctors, chaplains, and especially prison officers who had sat with the condemned man during his last days and had come to know and like him – said how uneasy they always felt afterwards, as though they had done something discreditable and unclean.' He recorded that a prison chaplain of twenty-eight years service spoke of 'horror, humiliation, and shame' (*On My Way to the Club*, p. 233).

18. Royal Commission Evidence, Memorandum by Fisher 3. Of the 1210 people sentenced to death between 1900 and 1949 553 (45.7%) had had their sentences commuted or respited. 90.8% of the 130 women were spared, and 40.3% of the 1080 men (Royal Commission Report para. 20, p. 6).

19. Charles Gattey, *The Incredible Mrs Van der Elst*, pp. 206f.

20. Royal Commission Evidence, para. 4128.

21. The Scottish chaplain, Chalmers, had never in all his long experience heard a fellow prisoner expresss condemnation of the condemned man, nor ever heard someone say that they would change their ways as the result of an execution. The deterrent effect, he concluded, might exist, but it was secondary. Certain types of murder deserved to be punished by death irrespective of whether this would deter others (Royal Commission Evidence, paras. 5097–5091).

22. A good example is the Revd Baden Ball of Wandsworth who through his knowledge of 'the criminal mind', as he liked to call it, was 'compelled to say that murder has many a time been nipped in the bud because the potential perpetrator feared that if he were caught he might be hanged' (*Prison Was My Parish*, p. 237).

23. Letter from the Revd J. de Blanc to the *Church Times*, 10 February 1950.

24. Lord Asquith, *Parliamentary Debates* (Lords), 5th Series, vol. 185, (16 December 1953), col. 174.

25. Lambeth Palace Archives, letter to Bishop Bell, 25 January 1953. Another change of heart was that of Earl Jowitt who admitted to be much less sure of the retentionist case (*Parliamentary Debates*, op. cit., col. 150).

26. Ernest Gowers, *A Life for a Life?*

14 Godly Butchery

1. John Greenleaf Whittier, *The Human Sacrifice*, 1843, in *Anti-Slavery Poems*, 1888.

2. Karl Mittermaier, *Capital Punishment*, 1865, p. 141.

3. *The Knight and Death and Other Stories*, ET 1991, p. 43.

4. William Robertson Smith, *Lectures on the Religion of the Semites*, A. & C. Black, 3rd edn 1927, p. 370, note 4.

5. Pieter Spierenburg, *The Spectacle of Suffering*, p. 21.

6. René Girard, *Violence and the Sacred*, ET Patrick Gregory, Baltimore 1977, pp. 18–20.

7. Or the Republic as God's Kingdom on earth (Masur, *Rites of Execution*, pp. 26f, 66). In this I strongly disagree with the analysis of Foucault (*Discipline and Punish*) and Garland (*Punishment and Modern Society*, pp. 140f.) who see executions as primarily demonstrations of the power of the State per se.

8. Masur, *Rites of Execution*, p. 26.

9. Radzinowitz, *History*, vol. 1, p. 221.

10. George Horne, *The Providence of God Manifested in the Rise and Fall of Empires*, 1775, Oxford, quoted in Randall McGowan, ' "He Beareth Not the Sword in Vain": Religion and the Criminal Law in Eighteenth-Century England', *Eighteenth-Century Studies* (21), 1981, p. 193.

11. *The Grand Assize; or General Gaol Delivery*, 1795, Cheap Repository.

12. William Pugh, *He is the Minister of God to Thee for Good*, 1765, quoted in McGowan, 'He Beareth Not', p. 198.

13. Richard Coleire, *Kings and Judges the Viceregents of God*, 1729, p. 17.

14. Report of Revd W. Russell, Inspector of Prisons, to Her Majesty's Principal Secretary of State, 1845. The fullest description of the 'religious observances attendant on the punishment of death' is Edward Wakefield's *Facts Relating to the Punishment of Death in the Metropolis*, 1831, pp. 144–171.

15. Nor was it just Tyburn that received this treatment. The 'Hanging in Chains of Francis Fearn' transformed a Loxley Common near Sheffield into Golgotha (Thomas Laqueur, 'Crowds, carnival and the state in English Executions, 1604–1868' in *The First Modern Society*, ed. A. L. Beier et al, p. 341).

16. 'The Moral Lesson of the Gallows', *Punch*, 17 January 1846, p. 33.

17. Laqueur, in *The First Modern Society*, p. 341.

18. John Potter, *The Fatal Gallows Tree*, p. 70. For a fictional account see Thomas Hardy's short story *The Withered Hand*.

19. Michael Jasper, ' "Hats Off!": The Roots of Victorian Public Hangings', in W. B. Thesing, (ed.), *Executions and the British Experience*, p. 143.

20. Potter, *The Fatal Gallows Tree*, p. 71. The blood of the decapitated Louis XVI was similarly venerated. There is some evidence that he saw his own execution in sacrificial terms (Daniel Arasse, *The Guillotine and the Terror*, pp. 61–64).

21. Geoffrey Abbott, *Lords of the Scaffold*, p. 133.

22. On this inversion and its significance see John Lofland, *The Dramaturgy of State Executions*, Patterson Smith, New Jersey, 1977.

23. A. E. Housman, *A Shropshire Lad*, IX.

24. Oscar Wilde, 'The Ballad of Reading Gaol', stanza 3.

25. Owen Carroll, 'The Shadow of the Gallows', *The Penal Reformer*, Vol. 1. No. 4, pp. 6f.

26. Baden Ball, *Prison Was My Parish*, p. 239.

27. Rich, *Recollections of a Prison Governor*, p. 189.

28. René Weis, *Criminal Justice*, Penguin edn p. 282.

29. Barbara Wooton, 'Morality and Mistakes' in *The Hanging Question* ed. Louis Blom-Cooper, pp. 13f. Procedure in the present day United States is on a par with this. What is left of the human being erodes over the final three hours. For electrocution the victim's head is shaved, an action which will 'take just about all the strength a man has out of him . . . like when Delilah cut Sampson's hair' (Robert Johnson, *Death Work*, pp. 92–3). Before the execution the prisoner had to remove all his clothing and put on new denims and 'a white shirt so that he will present a neat appearance to the witnesses now gathering in the Witness Room' – it is like the preparations for a baptism or confirmation, or an operation.

Shaven, showered, and donned in garments the buttons of which have been replaced by Velcro to stop the body being burned during the electrocution, the condemned man is a walking corpse. The death cell becomes like a funeral parlour, where officers and officials talk in hushed tones, and retain a quiet, reserved, and even reverent demeanour. If the condemned man wants coffee he gets it in a paper cup which is 'a precautionary part of the ritual'. As last minute preparations are made the 'two death watch guards take the traditional green carpet from the adjoining cell and roll it out and around the corner so that Richard won't have to walk his last steps on cold concrete'. Perhaps some hint of a recognition that the rite is pagan rather than Christian was shown in the prohibition of religious services on Death Row. Billy Graham, like Christ harrowing Hell, was the only exception. An American chaplain acknowledged that only this ritual made it possible to endure an execution: 'without it, the condemned could not give the expected measure of co-operation to the etiquette of dying' (Byron Eshelman, *Death Row Chaplain*, pp. 15–26).

30. *Royal Commission on Capital Punishment, 1949–1953, Howard League Memorandum Appendix A* by Margery Fry: The Mrs Thompson Execution: Rev Murray.

31. *The Daily Mirror*, 4 July 1955.

32. Eric Strauss, 'A Catholic View of Hanging', *The Penal Reformer*, vol. 4. no. 1, July 1937, p. 5.

33. Select Committee, 1930, Evidence, para., 3723.

34. Spierenberg, *The Spectacle of Suffering*, pp. 32f.

35. Albert Camus, *On Capital Punishment*, 1957, no pagination.

36. Alexander Campbell, *Capital Punishment Sanctioned by Divine Authority*, p. 25.

37. *Les Soirees de Saint-Petersbourg*, Paris 1821, quoted in Arasse, *The Guillotine and the Terror*, p. 54.

38. Lambeth Palace Archives, W. H. Waddams, Prison Commissioner from 1943–6 in a confidential memorandum to Fisher.

39. Arasse, *The Guillotine and the Terror*, pp. 73f.

40. Camus, *On Capital Punishment*.

41. Albert Pierrepoint, *Executioner Pierrepoint*, 1974, p. 200. Although a 'vocation', being a hangman was nonetheless a part-time job. Pierrepoint when not on His Majesty's employ was a publican, running a hostelry, named 'Help the Poor Struggler', near Manchester. More prosaically, a recent writer has attributed his resignation to a dispute over the payment of his fees (Gordon Honeycombe, *The Murders of the Black Museum, 1870–1970*, p. 491).

42. *Executioner Pierrepoint*, p. 99.

43. *Executioner Pierrepoint*, p. 133. Not that all hangmen shared his sentiments. The most recent 'autobiography', *The Hangman's Tale* of Syd Dernley, a miner and assistant executioner, reveals a very different personality, irreligious, ribald and with sense neither of religion, vocation, nor decency. Unlike Pierrepoint, he has remained a staunch defender of hanging and regrets its passing. For many years after his retirement Dernley had the only privately owned gallows in the country erected in his cellar. It had been auctioned off when Cambridge prison closed. There he would 'show friends the ropes'.

44. Act IV, scene 2. Shakespeare satarizes the 'vocational' view of hanging:

– Provost: 'Sirrah, here's a fellow will help you tomorrow in your execution . . . He hath been a bawd.
– Abhorson, an executioner: 'A bawd, sir? Fie upon him! he will discredit our mystery.
– Pompey: . . . Do you call, sir, your occupation a mystery?
– Abhorson: 'Ay, sir, a mystery.
– Pompey: Painting, sir, I have heard say, is a mystery; and your whores, sir, being members of my occupation, using painting, do prove my occupation a mystery: but what mystery there should be in hanging, if I should be hanged, I cannot imagine.

15 Murder by Degrees

1. Thomas Carlyle, *Latter-Day Pamphlets* on 'Modern Prisons', *Works*, vol. 20, p. 71.
2. *The Knight and Death, and Other Stories*, p. 106.
3. Ludovic Kennedy, *On My Way to the Club*, p. 231.
4. See Ludovic Kennedy, *Ten Rillington Place*. Evans received a posthumous pardon in 1966 after hanging had been abolished.
5. The fears of the authorities that the possibility of miscarriages taking place would undermine public confidence in the criminal justice system was justified. One long-serving governor's attitude to hanging was changed totally by this case and by Bentley's, once the full facts had finally emerged. His confidence in the complete reliability of the criminal justice system and in the exercise of the prerogative of mercy was shaken, and from then on he became firmly opposed to any suggestion that the death penalty should be restored (private communication). Bernard Levin has recently written in an article entitled 'Not just a few rotten apples, enough to taint the system' that the Evan's case 'significantly helped to shape [his] life and work' in that it transformed his image of the judicial bench (*The Times*, 30 August 1990).
6. R. T. Paget, et al., *Hanged – and Innocent?*, p. 110. Not all concurred. Canon Dudley Simon of St Michael's Covent, Ham Common, wrote to the press calling for the restoration of the stocks and pillory, and of transportation, and for the introduction of 'pleasant euthanasia' for the criminally insane, and 'dishonourable' execution for murderers (quoted in M. J. Trow, *Let Him Have It Chris*, pp. 107f.).
7. One such convert was Ludovic Kennedy who wrote a play, *Murder Story*, based on this case. To this day Bentley's sister, Iris, places a wreath outside the gates of Wandsworth Prison on the anniversary of his execution. Four decades after his death, debate about the case is still going on. See Paget et al., *Hanged*; David Yallop, *To Encourage the Others*; Francis Selwyn, *Nothing But Revenge*; C. B. Dee and R. Odell, *Dad Help Me Please*; M. J. Trow, *Let Him Have It Chris*. In 1991 a film was released, the Home Secretary reopened the case and a *Times*' Leader called for Bentley's pardon (3 October). A year later the Home Secretary refused the pardon but said that in his opinion Bentley should not have been hanged.
8. *The Times*, 23 February 1953.
9. Lambeth Palace Archives, letter from Fisher, 2 December 1953. As late as 1969 Canon Edward Carpenter was to bewail the same shortcoming: 'little attention had been given by moral theologians in recent years to the legitimacy of capital

punishment within the context of the full Christian faith'. He would have welcomed the setting up of a Commission to explore this question, since he believed that 'every execution suggested to people that the Christian faith is not true' ('The Christian Context' in *The Hanging Question* ed. Blom-Cooper). It is significant that from its inception in 1920 until 1970 no article on the issue of capital punishment had appeared in the leading Anglican journal *Theology*.

10. *Parliamentary Debates* (Commons), 5th Series, vol. 536 (10 February 1955), col. 2072. Little support was forthcoming for the recommendation that the jury be invited to decide on a life or death sentence, although one speaker from the Government backbenches (Major Legge-Bourke) went even further and suggested that this decision should be left to the clergy, the experts in discerning repentance (Ibid., cols 2144–6).

11. Ibid., col. 2074.

12. Ibid., col. 2083.

13. For example, in 1955 Sir Henry d'Avigdor-Goldsmid (Walsall) came to the House as an abolitionist as a result of his experiences as High Sheriff of Kent two years before when he had had to witness 'the obscene mumbo jumbo' of a sentence of death being passed on a girl whom he knew would be reprieved. He also had had to witness an execution. Rather incongruously he maintained that he was an abolitionist on pragmatic grounds, not of conscience (*Parliamentary Debates*, 5th Series, vol. 793 (15 December 1969) cols. 986f.).

14. Quoted in full in L. Marks and T. Van Den Bergh, *Ruth Ellis: A Case of Diminished Responsibility?*, pp. 169–171.

15. Lord Soper (private communication).

16. From J. D. Lang, 16 December 1955.

17. *The Observer*, 11 March 1956.

18. Victor Gollancz, *Capital Punishment: The Heart of the Matter*, p. 7.

19. Ibid., p. 13.

20. A. J. Ayer, the Bishop of Birmingham, Maurice Bowra, Benjamin Britten, Canon Carpenter, Cecil Day Lewis, Christopher Fry, Laurence Housman, Montgomery Hyde, Augustus Johns, the vicar of Leeds, Compton McKenzie, Revd George McLeod, the Bishop of Middleton, J. B. Priestly, Cannon C. E. Raven, Donald Soper, Stephen Spender, Michael Tippett, Peter Toynbee, Very Revd C. L. Watt, Rebbecca West, Harold Wilson, Barbara Wooton, and Ken Younger MP.

21. Francis Selwyn, *Nothing But Revenge*, pp. 174, 181–192.

22. Gerald Gardiner, *Capital Punishment as a Deterrent: and the Alternative*.

23. Tony Benn, *Out of the Wilderness*, 1987, p. 36.

24. *Parliamentary Debates* (Commons), 5th Series, vol. 548 (16 February 1956), col. 2557.

25. Ibid., col. 2562.

26. Ibid., col. 2595.

27. Ibid., col. 2623.

28. Ibid., col. 2634.

29. Ruth Dudley Edwards, *Victor Gollancz*, pp. 641ff.

30. L. John Collins, *Faith Under Fire*, p. 246.

31. *Parliamentary Debates*, (Lords), 5th Series, vol. 198 (9 July 1956), col. 596.

32. Collins, *Faith Under Fire*, p. 246.
33. Lambeth Palace Archives, Letter to Bell, 18 June 1956.
34. Ibid., Letter to Templewood, 28 June 1956.
35. Ibid., Letter to Bell, 25 June 1956.
36. *Parliamentary Debates* (Lords), 5th Series, vol. 198 (9 July, 1956), cols. 595–6.
37. Ibid., cols 597–8.
38. Ibid., cols 798–9.
39. Ibid., cols 625–630.
40. Ibid., cols 654–5.
41. Ibid., col. 694.
42. Ibid., col. 717.
43. Ibid., col. 695.
44. Ibid., cols 697–8.
45. Ibid., cols 713–17.
46. Ibid., cols 746–52.
47. This cheapening of the effect of capital punishment by the activity of the media had long concerned the Archbishop. In letter to the Revd R. H. Nottage, rector of Corringham in Essex, on 30 June 1955 he wrote: 'Modern journalism has created such a monstrous business of emotion and sensationalism out of every murder trial and out of the death penalty as to cheapen the whole process and make it disgusting. What should have been a process of awful dignity has become a matter for trivial sensationalism. There is still much to be said for it but this undignified and trivial age has really so robbed it of any value it can have as to make its abolition necessary.'
48. Lambeth Palace Archives, Letter to Fisher 6 July 1956. One of the five men he had counselled protested his innocence to the last. Harland had had 'serious misgivings' as to whether he were really guilty, and acknowledged that 'his is the sort of case which strengthens misgivings whether the death penalty is justified'. All the same this man 'seemed to desire grace and accepted the inevitable without rancour and with great courage'.
49. *Parliamentary Debates* (Lords) 5th Series, vol. 198 (9 July 1956) col. 597.
50. 5 October 1956.
51. Lambeth Palace Archives, Letter to Bell.
52. Memorial to the Prime Minister, copy held in the Howard League Archive.
53. *Parliamentary Debates* (Lords), 5th Series, vol. 201 (21 February 1957), cols 1193–4. Silverman's biographer scathingly put it that Fisher obviously did not agree with George Meredith's aphorism 'Expediency is man's wisdom, doing right is God's', and had no doubts that he was speaking as the official representative of God in the House of Lords (Hughes, *Sydney Silverman*, p. 155).
54. *Parliamentary Debates* (Lords), 5th Series, vol. 201, col. 1220.
55. Ibid., col. 1229.
56. Lambeth Palace Archives, Letter to Bell, 1957.
57. E. O. Tuttle, *The Crusade Against Capital Punishment*, p. 145.
58. For a rather hagiographical account of the role of Lord Chief Justice see Fenton Bresler's *Lord Goddard*.
59. Christoph, *Capital Punishment*, pp. 117–121.

60. The official position of the Roman Catholic Church was beginning to change. In 1960 at the time of the Chessman execution in the United States the editor of the *Osservatore Romano* (the official organ of the Vatican) wrote that 'the execution of criminals is repugnant to the modern conscience'. John XXIII may be supposed to be the inspiration behind this fundamental change in Vatican attitude (Charles Duff, *A New Handbook on Hanging*, 1954 p. 150). A Catholic Truth Society pamphlet of 1963 (*Capital Punishment* by Revd J. F. McDonald SJ) states the official position which is more or less identical to the traditional Anglican one, and allows Catholics to side with whom they will. The civil power had the God-given right to take the life of an atrocious criminal. This is testified to in scripture. It had been heresy to hold otherwise and in the profession of faith drawn up by Innocent III in 1208 the Waldensian heretics were required to profess their belief in the right of the state to inflict capital punishment. Nowadays Catholics must look at the prevailing conditions in the country and ask 'is the existing order likely to be preserved or threatened if capital punishment were to be abolished?' Catholics may not deny that the state has a right to use capital punishment but may argue that under present circumstances the use of the death penalty is not necessary.

61. Arthur Koestler, *Reflections on Hanging*, pp. 284ff.

16 In the Valley of the Shadow

1. 'The Moral Lesson of the Gallows', *Punch*, vol. 10, 17 January 1846, p. 33.
2. George Orwell, 'A Hanging', in *The Collected Essays* vol. 1, pp. 44–48.
3. A good example of the reforming governor forced to participate in hangings which he passionately opposed was David Waddilove. He had been recruited into the prison service by Alex Paterson as an assistant Borstal housemaster. He later governed both Feltham and Gaynes Hall Borstals before being sent to Pentonville. There in 1959 he had to participate in the hanging of Chrimes and Marwood, the horror of which lived with him. A year later he returned to the Borstal system. After his retirement he became an active and influential member of the Howard League (Obituary in *The Times*, 19 December 1991).
4. The following account of the ministry of a prison chaplain is paraphrased from conversations with two eminent chaplains of great experience in this area, supplemented from other sources.
5. In contrast governor grades were given a far more direct exposure to the procedures involved.
6. Royal Commission, 1949–1953, Evidence para. 1493.
7. Ibid., Howard League Memorandum Appendix B (1).
8. John Edward Allen, *Inside Broadmoor*, p. 34.
9. For a factual account of the care of the condemned see J. Arthur Hoyles, *Religion in Prison*; for dramatic representations see the plays by William Douglas Home, *Now Barabbas . . .* and Ludovic Kennedy, *Murder Story*.
10. Royal Commission Evidence: Prison Chaplains' Memorandum III.
11. J. A. Cole, *Lord Haw Haw*, pp. 269–74.
12. Fenton Bresler, *Reprieve* p. 128.

13. Ibid.
14. Ibid.
15. Brian Inglis, *Roger Casement*, p. 373.
16. Ibid., pp. 296–304.
17. Royal Commission Evidence; Prison Chaplains' Memorandum III.
18. Ludovic Kennedy, *Ten Rillington Place*, pp. 202, 208.
19. Private communication.
20. Royal Commission Evidence.
21. Private communication.
22. Smith, L. W. Merrow, *Prison Screw*, p. 67.
23. Paul Foot, *Who Killed Hanratty?* p. 297. Hanratty often referred to the priests who visited him in his letters home. One parish priest, a Fr Hughes of Bedford, was so concerned after hearing his confession of innocence that he went to the press (pp. 295f).
24. Grew, B. D., *Prison Governor*, p. 109.
25. René Weis, *Criminal Justice*, Penguin edn, p. 288.
26. Royal Commission Evidence, Pierrepoint, para. 8452–3.
27. Peter Crookston, *Villain*, p. 105.
28. Howard League Archives.
29. Baden Ball, *Prison Was My Parish*, p. 240.
30. Ibid., p. 250.
31. Chaplain's Journal, Wandsworth Prison.
32. Ball, *Prison Was my Parish*, p. 251.
33. Royal Commission Evidence, Howard League Memorandum Appendix B (2).
34. Harley Cronin, *The Screw Turns*, p. 26.
35. Royal Commission Evidence, Howard League Memorandum Appendix B (1).
36. Ibid., B (8).
37. Ibid., Memorandum of the Revd Joseph Walker 4–6.
38. Ibid., Evidence para. 7250.
39. *Saint Joan*, scene vi.
40. Weis, *Criminal Justice*, pp. 275 and 301.
41. Royal Commission Evidence, Howard League Memorandum Appendix A by Margery Fry: The Mrs Thompson Execution.
42. Ibid. Walker Memorandum 6.
43. Ibid. Walker, evidence para. 7230–1.
44. Ibid. para. 7243.
45. Crookston, *Villain*, p. 103.
46. Wallace Blake, *Quod*, p. 317.
47. Many chaplains would agree with the letter to *The Times* which said that it was 'a mockery to talk of reforming a penal system where the death penalty remains to deny the basic principle on which reform is founded' (22 January 1947). The Howard League contended that it 'was significant that the first reforms were introduced in Wakefield Prison, and one of the first things done in that prison when the re-modelling took place was to pull down the execution shed and to remove the condemned cell altogether, so that there could not be any association with execution in that prison. When Maidstone was opened on the same lines,

the same thing happened'. (Evidence 3663). For the same view see Hoyles, *Religion in Prison*, pp. 131 and 141.

17 Choose Life

1. *Henry V*, Act II, scene 2.
2. Evelyn Gibson & S. Klein, *Murder*, Home Office Research Unit Report, 1961.
3. *The Times*, 20 December 1991 (obiturary of David Waddilove, former Governor of Pentonville Prison).
4. See Paul Foot, *Who Killed Hanratty?*
5. By Cyril Osborne, a Conservative MP (*The Times* 13 November 1959).
6. This change of heart was being seen throughout the Anglican Communion. Abolitionist resolutions were passed in 1957 by the Synod of the Diocese of Calgary, in 1958 by the Council for Social Service and the Executive Council of the General Synod of Canada, and by the Protestant Episcopal Church in the USA and in 1961 by the Anglican Church in New Zealand: *What do the Churches say on Capital Punishment?*, Friends Conference on Crime and the Treatment of Offenders, 1961.
7. *Parliamentary Debates* (Lords), 5th Series, vol. 235 (9 November 1961), cols 446–449, 501–2.
8. See the *Church Times* and the *Catholic Herald* for November and December 1961.
9. *The Daily Telegraph*, 25 October 1961. The BBC programme *The Death Penalty* was shown on the 24th. Ramsey's comments were recorded before the vote in the Lower House of Convocation.
10. Mervyn Stockwood, *Chanctonbury Ring*, pp. 158–9.
11. Canterbury Synod Debate, pp. 105–109.
12. Ibid., pp. 109–113.
13. Ibid., pp. 119–122.
14. York Synod Debate, pp. 36–41.
15. The speech made at the York Synod is almost identical to the letter sent by Harland to Fisher, and used by the latter in the Lords' debate only six years before.
16. York Synod Debate, pp. 41f.
17. Ibid., p. 43.
18. This dotty argument was not quite new. It had been answered, if answer it needed, a century before by William Ball who pointed out that the 'kingly sword' is for 'prevention and reformation, the distinct reverse of vengeance and blood': the 'sword of state' may not 'be taken in some sanguinary sense' ('Capital Punishment', *Friends Quarterly Examiner*, 1868, pp. 232–236).
19. York Synod Debate, p. 47.
20. Ibid, p. 50.
21. Ibid.
22. Durhan was not without supporters outside of Convocation. Evangelicals in particular were reluctant to give up the traditional position of the church. Derek Kidner, for instance, the Senior Tutor of Oakhill Theological College, produced

a tract on *The Death Penalty* justifying the death penalty on biblical grounds and seeing it very much as part of God's armoury.

23. *The Times*, 18 January 1962.

24. Hazel Erskine, 'The Polls: Capital Punishment', *Public Opinion Quarterly*, 34, 1970–71, p. 299. Later polls indicated a slight drop in opposition to abolition: the National Opinion Poll of November 1964 registered 65.5%, and a Gallup Poll of January 1965 registered 70% in favour of retention.

25. *The Economist* 20 January 1962. One young Roman Catholic Conservative MP, Norman St John-Stevas, also argued that prima facie Christians should oppose the death penalty since it was hard to imagine Jesus insisting on its imposition on a penitent criminal. Its only possible justification was necessity, and he was persuaded that the great weight of evidence gave no support for this (*The Right to Life*, pp. 90–113).

26. Elwyn Jones, *The Last Two to Hang*, p. 87; Brian Lane (ed), *The Murder Club Guide to North-West England*, pp. 37f.

27. Lambeth Palace Archives, Letter from Silverman to Ramsey, 17 February 1965. This and the following two letters are unavailable until 1995, but are quoted in Owen Chadwick's authorized biography, *Michael Ramsey*, pp. 157–162.

28. Lambeth Palace Archives, Letter from Ramsey to Silverman, 19 February 1965.

29. Ibid. Letter from Dilhorne to Ramsey, 26 February 1965.

30. Templewood, Samuel, Morrison, Ede, and Brooke.

31. *Parliamentary Debates* (Lords), 5th Series, vol. 268 (20 July 1965) col. 607.

32. Ibid., col. 633–8. The speech is conveniently reproduced in Michael Ramsey, *Canterbury Pilgrim*, pp. 139–143).

33. *Parliamentary Debates* (Lords), 5th Series, vol. 268, col. 634.

34. Ibid., col. 642.

35. On the course that the amendments took see Frank Dawtry, 'The Abolition of the Death Penalty in Britain', *The British Journal of Criminology* (6), April 1966, pp. 183–192.

36. The Marplan Poll for *The Times* on 24 October 1969, and the *Daily Express* Poll on 5 December both indicated that 85% favoured hanging. Collins and Gollancz were quick to dismiss the significance of this (letter to *The Times* 17 December 1969) pointing out in typically lurid language the fickleness of public opinion: 'it seems that when the vision of the gallows appears on the nation's horizon, eyes bulge and reason is strangled. If the last victim of the executioner happens to arouse pity – like Bentley or Ellis – up go the nays like a flight of doves. If he is a repellent character, like Christie, up go the ayes like a swarm of vultures.'

37. *The Times*, 17 August 1966. There was evidence that the hanging issue was being used for political gain. Five Conservative candidates in Manchester jointly signed a declaration almost fighting the election on the issue. In the West of Scotland it was the main party plank. Stan Orme, the Labour MP for Salford, was virtually accused of being a child-murderer (in the wake of the Moors murders) because he had been a teller for the abolitionists. The Labour MP for Eccles, Carter-Jones, was assailed by vicious propaganda when a child in his constituency was killed. (*Parliamentry Debates*, 5th Series, vol. 793 (15 December 1969), cols 693f, 997).

38. *Parliamentary Debates* (Commons), 5th Series, vol. 793 (16 December 1969), col. 1190.
39. *The Times*, 13 February and 4 June 1968, and 24 June 1969.
40. The Government announced that the dismantlement and refurbishment was complete on 13 March 1967.
41. *The Times*, 11 and 15 December 1969.
42. *Parliamentary Debates* (Lords), 5th Series, vol. 306 (17 December 1969), col. 1157.
43. Ibid., col. 1181–3.
44. It is still retained for treason and for military offences during wartime. Since the abolition of capital punishment for murder no one under British jurisdiction has been executed for any cause.

Conclusion

1. R. H. Tawney, *Religion and the Rise of Capitalism*, Penguin edn 1938, pp. 188–195.
2. Leo Tolstoy, *Confessions*, An Account of an Execution in Paris, 1879.
3. Margaret Wilson, *The Crime of Punishment*, 1931, p. 141.
4. Basil Montagu, *Some Inquiries Respecting the Punishment of Death for Crimes without Violence*, 1818, p. 4.

Bibliography

1 Official Reports

Select Committee on Criminal Law as Relates to Capital Punishment, 1819.
Second Report from Her Majesty's Commissioners on Criminal Law, 1836.
Report of Revd W. Russell, Inspector of Prisons, to Her Majesty's Principal Secretary of State, 1845.
Second Report of the Select Committee on Criminal Law, 1847.
Select Committee of the House of Lords on The Present Mode of Carrying into Effect Capital Punishments, 1856: Report and Evidence.
Royal Commission on Capital Punishment, 1864–6: Report and Evidence.
Select Committee on Homicide Law Amendment Bill, 1874.
Select Committee of the House of Commons on Capital Punishment, 1930: Report and Evidence.
Royal Commission on Capital Punishment 1949–53: Report and Evidence.

2 Public Record Office, Kew

Home Office File on the Execution of William Saville, HO 45/681.
Home Office Correspondence on the Propriety of allowing Christian Burial to Executed Felons, September-October 1848, HO 45/2468.
The Report of the Committee appointed to Inquire into the Existing Practice as to carrying out of Sentences of Death, and the Causes which in several recent Cases have led either to failure or to unseemly occurrences; and to consider and report what arrangements may be adopted (without altering the existing Law) to ensure that all Executions may be carried out in a becoming manner without risk of failure or miscarriage in any respect (the Aberdare Committee), 1888, HO 144/212/A48697/2.
Home Office Memorandum on the employment of hangmen the appendix to which contains an authorative list of miscarriages of Justice, 1889, HO 144/212/A48697.
Home Office File on Berry, HO 144/212/A48697A-F.
Home Office Memorandum (nd [1889]), HO 144/212/A48697.
Home Office File on the Execution of Conway, 1891, HO 144/212/A48697.
Prison Commissioners' File on Billington, 1899–1902, PCOM 8/192.
Prison Commissioners' File on Berry, 1902, PCOM 8/191.

Home Office Confidential Publication, 'Execution of Sentence of Death: Notes as to Practice', 1920, HO 45/25843.

Home Office Memorandum: 'Executions: Function of Chaplain', 1924, HO 45/25843.

Home Office Circular to Prisons: Attendance etc of Chaplains at Executions, 1927, HO 45/25843.

Home Office Memorandum 'Accident to Assistant Executioner', 1928, HO 45/25843.

Home Office File on Mrs Van der Elst, 1935, HO 45 677344.

Cabinet Minutes on Capital Punishment Commission, 1948, HO 45/25084/ 837371.

3   Debates

Parliamentary Debates (Hansard).
The Proceedings of COPEC, Longmans 1924.
Canterbury Convocation: Full Synod Debate 17 January 1962.
York Convocation: Full Synod Debate 15 May 1962.

4   Chaplains' Journals

Lancaster Castle Journal, 1853–1862, Newbold Revel Prison Service Museum.
Wandsworth Prison Journals 1935–1961, HMP Wandsworth.
York Castle Journal, York Public Record Office.
Lincoln Castle Journal, Lincoln Public Record Office.

5   Papers

Bell, Bishop, *Papers*, Lambeth Palace Archives.
Davidson, Archbishop, *Papers*, Lambeth Palace Archives.
Fisher, Archbishop Geoffrey, *Papers*, Lambeth Palace Archives.
Gibbs, Robert, *Papers*, Buckinghamshire Public Record Office, Aylesbury.
Joyce, William, Letters from Prison, Michael Forman Archives, London.
King, Bishop Edward, *Papers*, Lincolnshire Public Record Office.
Temple, Archbishop William, *Papers*, Lambeth Palace Archives.

6   Primary and Secondary Works

A Member of the Church of England, *Capital Punishment under the Gospel Dispensation anti-Scriptural*, 1847.
A Priest of the Catholic Church, *Capital Punishment Not Opposed to the Doctrine of the Christian Religion*, London 1850.

A Student of St Bees College, *Letters upon Capital Punishment*, 1847.

A Witness for 'Judgment, Mercy, and Faith', *'Inquisition for Blood'*, *or the Eternal Obligation on States and Governments to Inflict the Penalty of death for Wilful Murder*, London 1847.

Abbott, Geoffrey, *Lords of the Scaffold: A History of the Executioner*, Robert Hale 1991.

Albery, William, *A Millenium of Facts in the History of Horsham and Sussex 947–1947*, Horsham Museum Society 1947.

Allen, John Edward, *Inside Broadmoor*, W. H. Allen 1952.

Amos, Sheldon, *Capital Punishment in England Viewed as Operating in the Present Day*, Ridgway, London 1864.

Αμφω, *War and Punishment opposed to Christianity*, 1846.

Anon, *Hanging Not Punishment Enough*, London 1701.

Anon, *Three Tracts of the Society for Diffusing Information on the Subject of Capital Punishment and Prison Discipline*, Longman 1817.

Anon, 'On the Punishment of Death in the Case of Forgery', 1818.

Anon, 'Capital Punishment of Forgery', *Edinburgh Review*, vol. 52, 1830–1, pp. 398–410.

Anon, *Experiences of a Gaol Chaplain*, Bentley's Standard Novels, London 1850.

Anon, 'A Protest Against Capital Punishments', *Meliora*, vol. V, 1863, pp. 356–366.

Anon, 'The Prerogative of Pardon and the Punishment of Death', *Westminster and Foreign Quarterly Review*, 81, Article 4, 1864, pp. 405–420.

Anon, 'Reason and Authority against Capital Punishment in any Case', *Social Science Review*, NS, vol. 4, 1865, pp. 415–427.

Anon, 'Calcraft's Calling', *Temple Bar*, vol. xv, 1865, pp. 144–53.

Apsland, Alfred, 'On Capital Punishments', *Transactions of the Manchester Statistical Society*, 1866–7, pp. 67–88.

Arasse, Daniel, *The Guillotine and the Terror*, ET Allen Lane 1989.

Atholl, Justin, *The Shadow of the Gallows*, John Long, Tiptree, Essex 1954.

—— *The Reluctant Hangman: The Story of James Berry, Executioner 1884–1892*, John Long, Tiptree Essex 1956.

Babington, Anthony, *For the Sake of Example: Capital Courts-Martial 1914–1920*, Secker and Warburg 1983.

Bailey, Brian, *Hangmen of England: A History of Execution from Jack Ketch to Albert Pierrepoint*, W. H. Allen 1989.

Ball, Baden, *Prison Was My Parish*, Heinemann 1956.

Ball, William, 'Capital Punishment', *Friends Quarterly Examinar*, 1868, pp. 232–236.

Barr, James, *Capital Punishment from the Christian Standpoint*, The Third Roy Calvert Memorial Lecture, NCADP, London 1936.

Barry, F. R., *Mervyn Haigh*, SPCK 1964.

Beattie, J. M., *Crime and the Courts in England 1660–1800*, OUP 1986.

Beccaria, Cesare, *Dei Delitti e Delle Pena*, 1764.

Beedle, Susannah, *An Essay on the Advisability of Total Abolition of Capital Punishment*, Nichols and Son, London 1867.

Beggs, Thomas, 'The Royal Commission and the Punishment of Death,' *Social Science Review*, N.S.3, 1865, pp. 151–167.

—— *The Deterrent Influence of Capital Punishment, being a reply to the Speech of J. S. Mill Esq. MP*, William Tweedie, London 1868.

Beier, A. L., David Cannadine, J. M. Rosenheim (eds), *The First Modern Society: Essays in English History in Honour of Lawrence Stone*, CUP 1989.

Benn, Anthony Wedgwood, *Out of the Wilderness. Diaries 1963–7*, Hutchinson 1987.

Bentham, Jeremy, *Introduction to Principles of Morals and Legislation*, 1780.

—— *To His Fellow Citizens of France on Death Punishment*, Heward, London 1831.

Berry James, *My Experiences as an Executioner*, Percy Lund, London 1902.

Blake, Wallace, *Quod*, London 1928.

Bland, James, *The Common Hangman: English and Scottish Hangmen before the Abolition of Public Executions*, Henrys, Hornchurch, Essex 1984.

Bleakley, H., *The Hangmen of England*, Chapman and Hall 1929.

Blom-Cooper, L. J., 'The Trial of George Riley', *Criminal Law Review* 1961, pp. 292–296.

—— (ed.), *The Hanging Question: Essays on the Death Penalty*, Duckworth 1969.

Blom-Cooper, L. and Drewry, Gavin (eds), *Law and Morality*, Duckworth 1976.

Bonnar, Hypatia Bradlaugh, 'The Death Penalty', *The Humane Review*, 1903, vol. 4, p. 125–30.

Borowitz, Albert, *Innocence and Arsenic: Studies in Crime and Literature*, Harper and Row 1977.

—— *The Woman who Murdered Black Satin: The Bermondsey Horror*, Ohio State University Press 1981.

—— *The Thurtell-Hunt Murder Case*, Robson Books 1988.

Boswell, James, *London Journal*, 1762–3, The Yale Edition, Heinemann 1950.

—— *Life of Johnson*, 1791, ed. George, Birkbeck Hill, revised L. F. Powell, Clarendon Press, 1934.

Bowen-Rowlands, E., *The Judgment of Death*, Collins 1924.

Bradford, William, *An Enquiry how far the Punishment of Death is Necessary in Pennsylvania*, Pennsylvania 1795.

Bray, Thomas, *Report of Newgate*, SPCK, 1702.

Bresler, Fenton, *Reprieve: A Study of a System*, 1965, Harrap, London.

——*Lord Goddard*, Harrap 1977.

Brockway, A. F. *Inside the Left: Thirty Years of Platform, Press, Prison, and Parliament*, Allen & Unwin 1942.

Brougham, Henry, Lord, *Speeches Upon Questions Relating to Public Rights, Duties, and Interests*, vol. II, A. & C. Black 1838.

Bullar J., *Memoirs of the Rev W. Kingsbury*, London 1819.

Burke, Edmund, 'Some Thoughts on the Approaching Executions', *Works*, vol. IX, F. & C. Rivington 1812, pp. 265–277.

Burleigh, Charles, *Thoughts on the Death Penalty*, Philadelphia 1845.

Burnet, Gilbert, *Exposition of the XXXIX Articles*, 1699.

Butler, Joseph, *Fifteen Sermons*, 1726.

Buxton, Charles, (ed), *Memoirs of Thomas Fowell Buxton*, John Murray, new edn 1872.

Cadogan, Edward, *The Roots of Evil*, John Murray 1937.

Calvert, E. R., *Capital Punishment in the Twentieth Century*, Putnam, London, 5th edn 1936.

—— *The Death Penalty Enquiry: being a review of the evidence before the Select Committee on Capital Punishment*, Gollancz 1931.

—— *Notes on the Punishment of Death*, NCADP nd.

Calvert, Theodora, *Capital Punishment: Society takes Revenge*, NCADP Newsletter, London 1946.

Campbell, Alexander, *Capital Punishment Sanctioned by Divine Authority*, Edinburgh 1846.

Camplin, John, *The Evidence of Christianity not weakened by the Frailty of its Ministers. A Sermon Preached in the Cathedral Church of Bristol on Sunday 29 June 1777, occasioned by the Execution of William Dodd, LLD.*, John Rivington, London 1777.

Camus, A., *On Capital Punishment*, Evergreen Review, New York 1960.

Carlyle, Thomas, *Collected Works*, Chapman & Hall, London 1896–99.

Carroll, Owen, 'The Shadow of the Gallows', *The Penal Reformer* vol. I, no. 4, April 1935.

Chadwick, Owen, *Victorian Miniature*, Hodder 1960.

—— *The Victorian Church*, Part I, 3rd edn A. & C. Black 1971; Part II, 2nd edn A. & C. Black 1972. Both volumes reissued SCM Press 1987.

—— *Michael Ramsey*, OUP 1990.

Cheney, Malcolm, *Chronicles of the Damned: The Crimes and Punishments of the Condemned Felons of Newgate Gaol*, Marston House, Yeovil 1992.

Christmas, Henry, *Capital Punishments Unsanctioned by the Gospel and Unnecessary: A letter to the Revd Sir John Page Wood Bart*, 1845.

—— *Christian Politics: Three Essays on Paley*, London 1855.

Christoph, J. B. *Capital Punishment and British Politics: The British Movement to Abolish the Death Penalty 1945–1957*, Allen & Unwin 1962.

Clarke, M. L., *Paley: Evidences for the Man*, SPCK 1974.

Clay, Walter Lowe, *The Prison Chaplain: Memoirs of the Reverend John Clay*, 1861.

Clayton, G. F., *The Wall is Strong: The Life of a Prison Governor*, Longman 1958.

Cobbett, William, *Twelve Sermons*, London 1823.

Coit, Stanton, *Public Opinion and the Death Penalty*, NCADP, London 1937.

Cole, J. A., *Lord Haw Haw*, Faber 1964.

Coleire, Richard, *Kings and Judges the Viceregents of God. A Sermon Preach'd, July 31, 1729 at the assizes holden at Kingston upon Thames in the County of Surrey*, London 1729.

Collins, L. John, *Faith Under Fire*, Leslie Frewin 1966.

Collins, Philip, *Dickens and Crime*, Macmillan, 2nd edn 1965.

Combe, George, *Thoughts on Capital Punishment*, Edinburgh 1847.

Compagnoni, Francesco, 'Capital Punishment and Torture in the Tradition of the Roman Catholic Church', *Concilium*, 120 (1978), pp. 39–53.

Cooper, David, *The Lesson of the Scaffold*, Allen Lane 1974.

Copinger, W. A., *An Essay on the Abolition of Capital Punishment*, Stevens and Haynes, London 1876.

Cox, J. Charles, *Three Centuries of Derbyshire Annals*, Vol. II, 1890.

—— 'Hanging in Chains', *Antiquary*, vol. 22, November 1890.

Craven, C. M., 'The House of Commons and the Death Penalty', *The Howard Journal*, 7, 1948–9, pp. 205–216.

Cresswell, F., *The Life of Elizabeth Fry*, London 1856.

Crew, Albert, *London Prisons of Today and Yesterday*, Butler and Tanner, London 1933.

Croker, John Wilson, *Correspondence and Diaries*, 2nd edn by L. J. Jennings, 1885, vol. I.

Cronin, Harley, *The Screw Turns*, John Long 1967.

Crookston, Peter, *Villain*, Jonathan Cape 1967.

Cunningham, W., *Christianity and Social Questions*, Duckworth 1919.

Dahl, Roald, Boy: *Tales of Childhood*, Jonathan Cape 1984.

Dawtry, Frank, 'The Abolition of the Death Penalty in Britain', *The British Journal of Criminology*, (6), April 1966, pp. 183–192.

Dee, C. B, and Odell, R., *Dad Help Me Please*, W. H. Allen 1990.

Dees, Robert, *The Inexpediency of Capital Punishment*, Newcastle Literary and Philosophical Society, 7 October, 1834, Newcastle upon Tyne 1935.

Defoe, Daniel, *Street Robberies Considered*, 1728.

Dernley, Syd, *The Hangman's Tale*, Robert Hale 1989.

Deuchar, N. D., *The Case Against Capital Punishment*, Letchworth Printers 1925.

Dicey, A. V., *Law and Public Opinion in England during the Nineteenth Century*, Macmillan 2nd edn 1914.

Dickens, Charles, *Barnaby Rudge*, 1841.

Dixon, W. Hepworth, *The London Prisons*, Jackson and Walford, London 1850.

Donaldson, Lewis, *Christ and Capital Punishment*, NCADP, London n.d.

Du Cane, Edward, *The Punishment and Prevention of Crime*, London 1885.

Duff, Charles, *A New Handbook on Hanging*, Andrew Melrose, London 1954.

Dülmen, Richard van, *Theatre of Horror: Crime and Punishment in Early Modern Germany*, Polity Press, Cambridge 1990.

Dymond, Alfred, *The Law on its Trial, or Personal Recollections of the Death Penalty and its Opponents*, London 1865.

Eden, William, *Principles of Penal Law*, 1771.

Edwards, David, *Leaders of the Church of England, 1828–1944*, OUP 1971.

Edwards, Ruth Dudley, *Victor Gollancz: A Biography*, Gollancz 1987.

Egan, Pierce, *Life in London: or the Day Night Scenes of Jerry Hawthorne Esq.*, Sherwood, Neely and Jones, London 1821.

Eliot, George, *Adam Bede*, 1859.

Emsley, Clive, *Crime and Society in England, 1750–1900*, Longman 1987.

Erskine, Hazel, 'The Polls: Capital Punishment', *Public Opinion Quarterly*, 34, 1970–71, Summer 1970, pp. 290–307.

Eshelman, Byron, *Death Row Chaplain*, Prentice-Hall, New Jersey 1962.

Favell, Samuel, *A Speech in the Propriety of Revising the Criminal Law*, London 1819.

Fielding, Henry, *An Inquiry into the Causes of the Late Increase of Robbers etc*, 2nd edn 1751.

Fletcher, John, *The Penitent Thief, or a Narrative of two women fearing God, who visited in prison a highway-man, executed at Stafford, April the 3rd, 1773, with a letter to a condemned malefactor: and a penitential office for either a true churchman or a dying criminal. By a Country Clergyman*, 2nd edn 1773.

Foot, Paul, *Who Killed Hanratty?*, Jonathan Cape 1971.

Forman, H. B., *The Prose Works of Percy Bysshe Shelley*, vol. II, London 1880.

Forsythe, W. J., *Penal Discipline, Reformatory Projects and The English Prison Commission, 1895–1939*, University of Exeter Press 1990.

Foucault, Michel, *Discipline and Punish: The Birth of the Prison*, Allen Lane 1977; Penguin 1979.

Fox, Adam, *Dean Inge*, John Murray 1960.

Frost, T., 'The Last Gibbet', in W. Andrews, *Bygone Leicestershire*, 1892, pp. 193–203.

Gardiner G. and N. Curtis-Raleigh, 'The Judicial Attitude to Penal Reform', *Law Quarterly Review* 65, April 1949.

Gardiner Gerald, 'Thou Shalt Not Kill', NCACP 1953.

—— *Capital Punishment as a Deterrent: and the Alternative*, NCACP 1955.

Garland, David, *Punishment and Modern Society: A Study in Social Theory*, Clarendon Press 1990.

Gash, Norman, *Mr Secretary Peel: The Life of Sir Robert Peel to 1830*, Longmans 1961.

Gattey, Charles, *The Incredible Mrs Van der Elst*, Frewin 1972.

Gibbs, Robert, *A History of Aylesbury*, Aylesbury 1885.

Gibson, Evelyn, and Klein, S., *Murder*, HMSO 1961.

Girdlestone, E. D., *Capital Punishment reviewed in the light of the expedient and the right*, Society for the Abolition of Capital Punishment, London 1904.

Gittings, Robert, *Young Thomas Hardy*, Penguin 1978.

Goldsmith, Oliver, *Collected Works*, ed. Arthur Friedman, Clarendon Press 1966.

Gollancz, Victor, *Capital Punishment: The Heart of the Matter*, Gollancz 1955.

—— *From Darkness to Light*, Gollancz 1956.

Gordon, Charles, *The Old Bailey and Newgate*, London 1903.

Gowers, Sir Ernest, *A Life for a Life?*, Chatto 1956.

Green, Peter, *The Problem of Right Conduct*, Longman 1930.

Grew, B. D., *Prison Governor*, Jenkins 1958.

Griffiths, Arthur, 'Why have a Hangman?', *Fortnightly Review*, vol. 40, 1883, pp. 581–6.

—— *Chronicles of Newgate*, Chapman and Hall, London 1884.

—— *Fifty Years of Public Service*, London 1898.

Grove, George, *Divine Authority for the Capital Punishment of Murderers*, Worcester 1849.

Groves, David, 'De Quincey's "Daughter of Lebanaon" and the Execution of Mary McKinnon', *Wordsworth Circle*, 19, Spring 1988, pp. 105–6.

Gurney, Joseph John, *Memoirs*, 2 vols, 2nd edn Fletcher and Alexander 1855.

Hancock, Edward, *The Groans of the Gallows, or the Past and Present Life of William Calcraft, The Living Hangman of Newgate*, London 1846.

Hardinge, George, *Miscellaneous Works* ed. J. Nicholls, vol. I, London 1818.

Hare, Augustus, *The Gurneys of Earlham*, 2 vols, George Allen, London 1895.

Hargrove, A. L. 'Britain and the Death Penalty', *The Howard Journal*, 3(2) 1931, pp. 27–32.

Harrop, A. J., *The Amazing Career of Edward Gibbon Wakefield*, Allen & Unwin 1926.

Hart, H. L. A. 'Should the Death Penalty Be Abolished?', *The Listener*, 19 January 1956.

Hartshorne, A., *Hanging in Chains*, London, Fisher 1891.

Hay, Douglas, et al., *Albion's Fatal Tree: Crime and Society in Eighteenth-Century England*, Allen Lane 1975.

—— 'Crime and Justice in Eighteenth- and Nineteenth-Century England', *Crime and Justice*, vol. II, Chicago 1980, pp. 45–84.

Hazlitt, William, 'On the Clerical Character', January 31, 1818, *Collected Works*, vol. III, ed. A. R. Waller and Arnold Glover, Dent 1902.

—— 'Historical View of the progress of Opinion on the Criminal law and the Punishment of Death', *The Edinburgh Magazine and Literary Miscellany*, IV, March 1819, pp. 195–202.

—— 'Parliamentary Report on the Criminal Laws', ibid., V, December 1819, pp. 491–495.

—— 'Criminal Law', ibid., V, January 1820, pp. 26–31.

—— 'On the Punishment of Death', *Fraser's Magazine*, 2 (1831), pp. 666–672.

Heath, Carl, *Crime and Humane Ethics*, Allenson and Co., London 1934.

Heaton, George, *The Clergyman in the Gaol*, Houlston and Stoneman, London 1847.

Hibbert, Christopher, *The Roots of Evil*, Weidenfeld and Nicolson, 1963.

Hobbart, Lord, *On Capital Punishment for Murder*, Parker, London 1861.

Hobhouse, Stephen, *Forty Years On*, James Clarke 1951.

Hobhouse, Stephen and A. F. Brockway (eds), *English Prisons Today: The Report of the Prison System Enquiry Committee*, Longmans 1922.

Hodder, Edwin, *Life and Work of the Seventh Earl of Shaftesbury*, 3 vols, Cassell 1886.

Holyoake, George Jacob, *Public Lessons of the Hangman*, Farrah, London 1864.

—— *Sixty Years of an Agitator's Life*, London 1892.

Home, William Douglas, *Now Barabbas . . .*, Longmans 1947.

Honecker, Martin, 'Capital Punishment in German Protestant Theology', *Concilium* (120), 1978, pp. 54–63.

Honeycombe, Gordon, *The Murders of the Black Museum, 1870–1970*, revd edn, Arrow 1984.

Hopkins, Tighe, 'Capital Punishment: Ineffectual and Mischievous', *Westminster Review*, vol. 155, 1901, pp. 144–9.

Horsley, J. W., *Jottings from Jail*, 1887.

—— *Prisons and Prisoners*, 1898.

—— *'I Remember': Memories of a 'Sky Pilot' in the Prison and the Slum*, Well, Gardiner and Darton, London, 1912.

Howard Association, 'Law and Security Frustrated Through The Capital Penalty', 1872.

—— 'The Modern Jews on Capital Punishment', 1877.

—— 'The Sacredness of Human Life', 1879.

Howson, Gerald, *The Macaroni Parson*, Hutchinson 1973.

Hoyles, J. Arthur, *Religion in Prison*, Epworth Press 1955.

Hughes, Emrys, *Sydney Silverman: Rebel in Parliament*, Blackfriars, Leicester 1969.

Hyde, H. Montgomery, *Oscar Wilde: The Aftermath*, Methuen 1963.

—— *Famous Trials 9: Roger Casement*, Penguin 1964.

Inge, William Ralph, 'The Religious Aspect of the Problem' in *The Problem of the Feeble-Minded: An Abstract of the Report of the Royal Commission*, 1909, pp. 89–93.
—— *Lay Thoughts of a Dean*, London 1926.
—— *Christian Ethics and Modern Problems*, London 1930.
Inglis, Brian, *Roger Casement*, Hodder 1973.
Ignatieff, Michael, *A Just Measure of Pain*, Macmillan 1978.
Iremonger, F. A., *William Temple*, OUP 1948.

Jackson, Stanley, *The Old Bailey*, W. H. Allen 1978.
James, Eric, *John Robinson: A Life*, Collins 1987.
Jerrold, Walter, *Douglas Jerrold and 'Punch'*, Macmillan 1910.
Jesse, John Heneage, *George Selwyn and His Contemporaries*, 4 vols, Bentley, London 1843–4.
Johnson, Robert, *Death Work*, Belmont, California 1990.
Johnson Samuel, *The Rambler*, The Yale Edition vol. IV, ed. W. J. Bate and A. B. Strauss, Yale University Press 1969.
Jones, Elwyn, *The Last Two to Hang*, Macmillan 1966.
Jones Harry, 'Capital Punishment', *Sunday Magazine*, 21 (1892), pp. 341–3, 417–420.
Joyce, J. A., *The Right to Life: A World View of Capital Punishment*, Gollancz 1961.
Kennedy, Ludovic, *Murder Story* (play), Gollancz 1956.
—— *Ten Rillington Place*, Gollancz 1961.
—— *On My Way to the Club*, Collins 1989.
Kidner, Derek, *The Death Penalty: An Ethical and Biblical Exposition*, Falcon Booklets 1963.
Kingsbury, William, *The Execution of a Malefactor Improved as a Warning especially to Young Persons: A Sermon preached at Southampton, March 24th 1805, being the day after the untimely fate of Robert Avery at Winchester, for forgery*, Baker & Son, London 1805.
Kingsley, Charles, *All Saints Day and Other Sermons*, Kegan Paul 1878.
Kingsmill, Joseph, *Chapters on Prison and Prisoners and the Prevention of Crime*, 3rd edn Longman 1854.
—— *On the Present Aspects of Serious Crime in England and the Means used for its Punishment and Repression by Government*, London 1857.
Knell, B.E.F., 'Capital Punishment: its administration in relation to juvenile offenders in the nineteenth century and its possible admistration in the eighteenth', *British Journal of Criminolgy*, vol. 5, 1965, pp. 198–207.
Koestler, A, *Hanged by the Neck*, Gollancz 1961.
—— *Reflections on Hanging*, Gollancz 1955.

Lachlan, Mrs, *Narrative of a Conversion of a Murderer in Letters addressed to a Clergyman*, Simpkin and Marshall, London 1832.

Lane, Brian (ed)., *The Murder Club Guide to London*, Harrap 1988.

—— *The Murder Club Guide to South East England*, Harrap 1988.

—— *The Murder Club Guide to North-West England*, Harrap 1988.

—— *The Murder Club Guide to the Midlands*, Harrap 1988.

—— *The Murder Club Guide to the Eastern and Home Counties*, Harrap 1989.

—— *The Murder Club Guide to South-West England and Wales*, Harrap 1989.

Langbein, J.H., 'Albion's Fatal Flaws', *Past and Present*, 98, 1983, pp. 96–120.

Laurence, John, *A History of Capital Punishment*, Sampson, Low and Masters, London *c* 1923.

Lecky, William, *A History of England in the Eighteenth Century*, vol. VI, London 1887.

Lee, John, *The Man they Could Not Hang*, Arthur Pearson, London n.d.

Leyda, Seraphia, 'Wordsworth's Sonnets *Upon the Punishment of Death*', Wordsworth Circle, 14 (Winter 1983), pp. 48–53.

Lilly, William Samuel, 'In Praise of Hanging', *The New Review*, vol. II, 1894.

Linebaugh, Peter, 'The Ordinary of Newgate and His Account', in *Crime in England 1550–1800* ed. J.S. Cockburn, Methuen 1977.

—— *The London Hanged: Crime and Civil Society in the Eighteenth Century*, Allen Lane 1991.

Locke, John, *Two Treatises of Government* ed. Peter Laslett, CUP 2nd edn 1967.

Lytton, Constance, *Prison and Prisoners*, Heinemann 1914.

McDonald, J.F., *Capital Punishment*, Catholic Truth Society 1963.

McGowen, Randall, ' "He Beareth Not the Sword in Vain": Religion and the Criminal Law in Eighteenth-Century England', *Eighteenth-Century Studies* (21) 1981, pp. 192–211.

—— 'The Image of Justice and Reform of the Criminal Law in Early Nineteenth-Century England', *Buffalo Law Review*, 32, 1983, pp. 89–125.

—— 'A Powerful Sympathy: Terror, the Prison, and Humanitarian Reform in Early Nineteenth Century Britain, *Journal of British Studies*, 25, 1968, pp. 312–334.

—— 'The Body and Punishment in Eighteenth-Century England', *Journal of Modern History*, 59, 1987.

MacKey, P.E., *Voices Against Death, : American Opposition to Capital Punishment 1787–1975* New York 1976.

—— *Hanging in the Balance: The anti-Capital Punishment Movement in New York State, 1776–1861*, New York 1982.

McLynn, Frank, *Crime and Punishment in Eighteenth-Century England*, OUP 1991.

McManners, John, *Death and the Enlightenment*, OUP 1981.

MacMaster, J., *The Divine Purpose of Capital Punishment*, Kegan Paul, Trench, and Trubner 1892.

Madan, Martin, *Thoughts on Executive Justice with Respect to our Criminal Laws, particularly on the Circuit*, 1785.

Maddern, Philippa, *Violence and Social Order: East Anglia 1422–1442*, Clarendon Press 1992.

Mandeville, Bernard, *An Inquiry into the Causes of the Frequent Executions at Tyburn*, London 1725.

Marks, Alfred, *Tyburn tree: Its History and Annals*, Brown, Langham 1905.

Marks, Laurence and Tony Van Den Bergh, *Ruth Ellis: A Case of Diminshed Responsibility*, Penguin 1990.

Martineau, Harriet, *The History of England During the Thirty Years Peace, 1816–1846, vol. II, 1830–46*, Knight, London 1850.

Masur, Louis, *Rites of Execution: Capital Punishment and the Transformation of American Culture, 1776–1865*, OUP, New York 1989.

Maxcey, C.E., *Justice and Order: Martin Luther and Thomas More on the Death Penalty and Retribution'*, Moreana XX, 79–80 (Nov. 1983) pp. 17–33.

Mayhew, H., and Binney J. *The Criminal Prisons of London* Griffin, Bohn and Co. 1862.

Medd, Patrick, *Romilly*, Collins 1968.

Melville, Herman, *Billy Budd*, Penguin edn 1985.

Mittermaier, Karl, *Capital Punishment*, ET by John Macrae Moir, London 1865.

Moberley, W., *The Ethics of Punishment*, Faber 1948.

—— 'Capital Punishment', *The Howard Journal*, 9(1) 1954, pp. 12–17.

Montagu, Basil, *The Opinions of Different Authors upon the Punishment of Death*, 2 vols, Longmans 1809 and 1912.

—— *An Examination of Some Observations upon a Passage in Dr Paley's Moral Philosophy on the Punishment of Death*, Mcreery, London 1810.

—— *An Account of the Origin and Object of the Society for the Diffusion of Knowledge upon the Punishment of Death and Improvement of Prison Discipline*, London 1812.

—— *An Inquiry into the Aspersions upon the late Ordinary of Newgate, with some Observations upon Newgate and upon the Punishment of Death*, Richard and Arthur Taylor, London 1815.

—— *Some Inquiries respecting the Punishment of Death for Crimes without Violence*, Richard and Arthur Taylor, London 1818.

Montagu, Lily, *Capital Punishment and the Old Testament*, NCADP n.d.

Morning Herald, The Punishment of Death, A Selection of Articles (mainly by J. Sydney Taylor), 2 vols. London 1836–7.

Morris, T., and Louis Blom-Cooper, *A Calendar of Murder*, Michael Joseph 1964.

Morris, T., *Crime and Criminal Justice since 1945*, Blackwell 1989.

Mortimer, R. C., *Christian Ethics*, Hutchinson 1950.
Mumford, W. A., *William Ewart MP, 1798–1869*, Collins 1960.

Naish, Camille, *Death Comes to the Maiden: Sex and Execution, 1431–1933*, Routledge 1991.
National Council for the Abolition of the Death Penalty, 'Executions', n.d.
Neate, Charles, *Considerations on Punishment*, Ridgeway, London 1857.

Oldfield, Josiah, *The Penalty of Death*, Bell, London 1901.
—— *Hanging for Murder*, Society for the Abolition of Capital Punishment 1908.
Ollyffe, George, *An Essay Humbly Offer'd, for an Act of Parliament to Prevent Capital Crimes, and the Loss of many Lives, and to Promote a desirable Improvement and Blessing in the Nation*, 1731.
Orel, Harold, *The Unknown Thomas Hardy*, Harvester Press 1987.
Orwell, George, 'A Hanging', in *The Collected Essays, Journalism and Letters of George Orwell*, vol. I, Secker and Warburg, 1968.

Paget, R. T., Silverman, S. and Hollis C., *Hanged – and Innocent*, Gollancz 1953.
Paley, William, *Works with a Life by Alexander Chalmers*, 5 vols, London 1819.
Patmore, Coventry, *Poems*, OUP 1949.
Partridge, S. G., *Prisoner's Progress*, Hutchinson, n.d.
Pearl, Cyril, *Victorian Patchwork*, Heinemann 1972.
Pease, J. W., 'The Immediate Abolition of Capital Punishment', 1877.
Peel, Robert, *Correspondence and Diaries*, 2nd edn ed. L. J. Jennings, London 1885.
Peggs, Revd James, *Capital Punishment: The Importance of Abolition*, London 1839.
Pell, John, *The Punishment of Death Proved to be Unlawful in a Letter to the Marquis of Northampton*, Hamilton, Adams, and Co., London 1835.
Pelling, Henry, *The Origins of the Labour Party, 1880–1900*, OUP, 2nd edn 1965.
Philips, David, ' "A New Engine of Power and Authority": The Institutionalization of Law Enforcement in England, 1780–1830' in *Crime and the Law: The Social History of Crime in Western Europe since 1500*, ed. V. A. C. Gatrell, Bruce Lenman, and Geoffrey Parker, Europa 1980.
Phillips, Charles, *Vacation Thoughts on Capital Punishments*, Brighton 1856.
Phillipson, Coleman, *Three Criminal Law Reformers*, Montclair, NJ 1970.
Pierrepoint, Albert, *Executioner Pierrepoint*, Harrap 1974; Coronet 1977.
Pitkin, John, *The Prison Cell in its Light and Shadows*, Sampson Low, London 1918.
Potter, John Deane, *The Fatal Gallows Tree*, Elek 1965.
Priestley, Philip, *Victorian Prison Lives*, Methuen 1985.

Punishment of Death, No. 3: Substance of the Speeches of S. Lushington and J. Sydney Taylor at a Public Meeting in Exeter-Hall, London, May 10th, 1831, Harvey and Darton, London 1831.

Purcell, William, *Portrait of Soper*, Mowbray 1972.

Pynme, Revd Thomas, *A Plea for the Abolition of Capital Punishment*, 1846.

Quinlivan, Patrick, and Rose, Paul, *The Fenians in England, 1865–1872*, John Calder 1982.

Radzinowitz, Leon, *A History of English Criminal Law and its Administration from 1750*, Stevens & Sons, London.
  vol. I *The Movement for Reform*, 1948.
  vol. IV *Grappling for Control*, 1968.
  vol. V (with Roger Hood) *The Emergence of Penal Policy*, 1986.

Ramsey, Michael, *Canterbury Pilgrim*, SPCK 1974.

Rehum, *Capital Punishment Not Grounded on Scripture*, London 1851.

Rich, Lt Col C. E. F., *Recollections of a Prison Governor*, Hurst and Blackett, London 1932.

Richardson, Ruth, *Death, Dissection and the Destitute: The Politics of the Corpse in Pre-Victorian Britain*, Routledge 1988; Penguin 1989.

Richardson, Samuel, *Familiar Letters on Important Occasions*, 1741, Routledge 1928.

Rickards, Clifford, *A Prison Chaplain on Dartmoor*, Arnold, London 1920.

Rogers, Henry, 'What is to be done with our Criminals?', *The Edinburgh Review or Critical Journal*, vol. lxxxvi, July 1847.

—— 'Essays Theological and Philosophical II: On Public Executions', *Good Words*, April 1865, pp. 104–112.

Romilly, Henry, *The Punishment of Death*, John Murray 1886.

Romilly, Samuel, *Observations on a Late Publication Entitled Thoughts on Executive Justice*, T. Cadell, London 1786.

—— *Observations on the Criminal Law of England as it relates to Capital Punishments and on the mode in which it is administered*, London 1810.

—— *Memoirs of the Life of Sir Samuel Romilly written by Himself*, 3 vols, London 1840.

Rose, G. *The Struggle for Penal Reform: the Howard league and its Predecessors*, Stevens & Sons 1961.

Rude, George, *Criminal and Victim: Crime and Society in Early Nineteenth-Century England*, OUP 1985.

Rumbelow, Donald, *The Triple Tree: Newgate, Tyburn, and Old Bailey*, Harrap 1982.

Rush, Benjamin, *An Inquiry into the Effects of Public Punishments Upon Criminals and Upon Society*, Philadelphia 1787.

—— *Essays Literary, Moral, and Philosophical*, Philadelphia 1798.

Russell, G. W. E., *Edward King, 60th Bishop of Lincoln*, 3rd edn Elder & Co 1912.

Rutenberg, Daniel, 'From Praise of Hanging to the Femme Fatale: Capital Punishment in Nineties Periodicals', *Victorian Periodicals Review*, 11 (1978), pp. 95–104.

St John-Stevas, Norman, *The Right to Life*, Hodder 1963.

Schopenhauer, *Die Welt als Wille und Vorstellung*, 1819.

Sciascia, Leonardo, *The Knight and Death and Other Stories*, Carcanet 1991.

Scott, G. Ryley, *The History of Capital Punishment*, Torchstream Books, London 1950.

Scott, Walter, *The Punishment of Death for the Crime of Murder, Rational, Scriptural and Salutary*, London 1846.

Schwed, R. E., *Abolition and Capital Punishment*, New York 1983.

Sellin, Thorsten, *The Penalty of Death*, Beverly Hills 1980.

Selwyn, Francis, *Rotten to the Core? The Life and Death of Neville Heath*, Routledge 1988.

—— *Nothing But Revenge: The Case of Craig and Bentley*, Penguin 1991. (Originally published as *Gangland*, Routledge 1988).

Sharpe, J. A., *Crime in Seventeenth-Century England: a country study*, OUP 1983.

—— *Crime in Early Modern England 1550–1750*, Longman 1984.

—— ' "Last Dying Speeches": Religion, Ideology, and Public Execution in Seventeenth-Century England', *Past and Present*, 107, 1985 pp. 144–167.

—— *Judicial Punishment in England*, Faber 1990.

Shaw, Bernard, *Saint Joan*, 1924.

Shelley, Percy Bysshe, 'On the Punishment of Death', 1815, In *Prose Works* ed. Harry Buxton Forman, vol. II, Reeves & Turner 1880.

—— 'An Address to the People on the Death of Princess Charlotte', 1817, ibid.

Simpson, C. R., 'Friends and Capital Punishment', *Friends Quarterly Examiner* LXVII, 1923, pp. 169–177.

Smith, H. Bodell, *The State Murder of John Griffiths: An Appeal to Humanity and the Churches*, Daniel, London 1923.

Smith, John Thomas, *A Book for a Rainy Day, or Recollections of the Events of the Years 1766–1833* ed. Wilfred Whitten, Methuen 1905.

Smith, L. W. Merrow, *Prison Screw*, Jenkins 1962.

Smith, Sydney, *Sermons Preached at St Paul's Cathedral*, Longmans 1846.

Sorell, Tom, *Moral Theology and Capital Punishment*, OUP 1987.

Spear, Charles, *Essays on the Punishment of Death*, London and Boston, 13th edn 1851.

Spierenburg, Pieter, *The Spectacle of Suffering*, OUP 1984.

Squire, Henry, *On the Behaviour of the Sinful: A Sermon delivered in the Old Meeting, Gaol Street, Great Yarmouth on Sunday April 8th 1849, while the Murderer Rush was under Sentence of Execution*, 1849.

Stephen, James, 'Mr Phillips on Capital Punishment', *Saturday Review*, 15 November 1856, vol. II. pp. 635–7.

—— 'Capital Punishments', *Fraser's Magazine LXIX*, June 1864, pp. 753–69.

—— *History of the Criminal Law*, 3 vols., 1888.

Stephen, Leslie, *Essays on Freethinking and Plainspeaking*, Longmans 1873.

—— *The English Utilitarians*, vol. I, Duckworth 1900.

Stockwood, Mervyn, *Chanctonbury Ring*, Hodder 1982.

Stone, Lawrence, *The Past and Present Revisited*, Routledge & Kegan Paul 1987.

Symonds, Jelinger, 'Capital and Prison Punishments', *The Law Magazine or Quarterly Review of Jurisprudence*, vol. IV, 1846, pp. 223–50.

Tallack, William, 'A General View of the Subject of Capital Punishment', *Social Science Review*, N.S.3, 1865, pp. 20–36.

—— 'Capital Punishment Illustrated by a few very recent Facts', 1867.

—— 'Capital Punishment in England and Wales', Howard Association, n.d.

—— 'The Dignity and Efficacy of English Law as Diminished by the Capital Punishment', *Friends Quarterly Examiner*, 1870, pp. 493–507.

—— *Howard Letters and Memories*, Methuen 1905.

Tawney, R. H., *Religion and the Rise of Capitalism*, John Murray 1926; Penguin 1938.

Tayler, Revd C. B., *Facts in a Clergyman's Life*, London, Seeleys 1849.

Taylor, Jeremy, *Works* ed. A. Taylor, Longmans 1852.

Taylor, J. Sydney, *Anti-Draco or Reasons for Abolishing the Punishment of Death in the case of Forgery, by a Barrister of the Middle Temple*, Ridgeway, London 1830.

—— *Selections from the Writings*, C. Gilpin, London 1843.

Taylor, Shephard, *The Diary of a Medical Student during the Mid-Victorian Period 1860–1864*, Jarrold 1927.

Teeters, N. G., *Hang by the Neck*, Thomas, Illinois 1967.

Temple, William, 'The Ethics of Punishment', *The Howard Journal III (1)*, 1930, pp. 12–18.

—— 'The Death Penalty', NCADP, reprinted in *The Spectator*, 1935.

Templewood, Lord, *The Shadow of the Gallows*, Gollancz 1951.

Thackeray, W. M. 'Going to See a Man Hanged', *Fraser's Magazine XXII*, August 1840, pp. 150–158.

Thesing, William B. (ed.), *Executions and the British Experience from the 17th to the 20th Century: A Collection of Essays*, McFarland, USA 1991.

Thomas, Keith, *Man and the Natural World: Changing Attitudes in England 1500–1800*, Allen Lane 1983; Penguin 1984.

Thomas, Vaughan, *The Scriptural Character of Civil Punishment Vindicated in a Sermon Preached at St Mary's Church on 22nd July, 1830*, Oxford 1830.

Thompson, E. P., *Whigs and Hunters*, Allen Lane 1975.

Tidmarsh, M, Halloran, J. D., Connolly, K. J., *Capital Punishment*, Sheed and Ward 1963.

Told, Silas, *Life of Mr Silas Told Written by Himself with a Note to the Serious and Candid Reader by John Wesley*, 1786, Epworth Press 1954.

Tolstoy, Leo, *Confessions*, 1879.

Trow, M. J., *Let Him Have It Chris*, Constable 1990.

Turner, E. S. *May It Please Your Lordship*, Michael Joseph 1971.

Turner, G. D., *The Alternatives to Capital Punishment*, NCADP 1938.

Turner, William, *Essay on Crimes and Punishments*, Manchester 1785.

Tuttle, E. O., *The Crusade Against Capital Punishment*, Stevens & Sons 1961.

Tyburn Nuns, *They Died at Tyburn*, Tyburn Convent, London 1961.

Van der Elst, Violet, *On the Gallows*, London 1937.

Vicars, Rayleigh, 'Should Capital Punishment be Abolished?', *The Gentleman's Magazine*, vol. 279, 1895, pp. 308–317.

Vidler, Alec, *The Church in an Age of Revolution*, Hodder 1961.

Villette, John, *A Genuine Account of the Behaviour and Dying Words of William Dodd, LLD*, London 1777.

Wakefield, Edward Gibbon, *Facts Relating to the Punishment of Death in the Metropolis*, London 1832.

—— *The Hangman and the Judge, or a Letter from Jack Ketch to Mr Justice Alderson*, Effingham Wilson, London 1833.

—— *Popular Politics*, Charles Knight, London 1837.

Walpole, Horace, *Journal of the Reign of King George the Third* ed. Dr Doran, vol. II., London 1859.

Warren, Charles, 'Is Capital Punishment Defensible?', *Westminster Review*, vol. 165, May 1906, pp. 512–6.

Waterman, A. C., *Revolution, Economics and Religion: Christian Political Economy, 1798–1833*, CUP 1991.

Watkins, J. W., *A Brief Reply to Mr Commissioner Phillip's Thoughts on Capital Punishment*, London 1858.

Webster, Edward, *Remarks on Capital Punishment in Cases of Murder*, London 1856.

Weis, René, *Criminal Justice: The True Story of Edith Thompson*, Hamish Hamilton, 1988: Penguin 1990.

Wells, Gabriel, *On Capital Punishment*, Heinemann 1929.

Wesley, John, *Journal*, vol. IV Kershaw, London 1827.

What do the Churches Say about Capital Punishment?, Friends Conference on Crime and the Treatment of Offenders, 1961.

Whately, E. Jane, *The Life and Correspondence of Richard Whately DD*, 2 vols., Longman 1866.

Whately, Richard, *Thoughts on Secondary Punishments*, London 1832.

Whitman, Walt, 'A Dialogue', *The United States Magazine and Democratic Review*, 17 November 1845, pp. 360–364.

Whittier, John Greenleaf, *Anti-Slavery Poems: Songs of Labor and Reform*, Cambridge, Mass. 1888.

Wilkinson, Alan, *The Church of England and the First World War*, SPCK 1978. London.

Williams, C. J., *Cook, The Murderer or the Leicester Tragedy*, Thomas Richardson, Derby 1832.

Williams, Daniel, ' "Behold a Tragic Scene Strangely Changed into a Theater of Mercy": The Structure and Significance of Criminal Conversion Narratives in Early New England', *American Quarterly*, 38, no. 5, 1986, pp. 827–847.

Wilson, Margaret, *The Crime of Punishment*, Jonathan Cape 1931.

Wix, Samuel, *Reflections Concerning the Inexpedience and Unchristian Character of Capital Punishment*, London 1832.

Wontner, Thomas, *Old Bailey Experience by the Author of The Schoolmaster's Experience in Newgate*, Frazer, London 1833.

Wood, S., *Shades of the Prison House: A Personal Memoir*, Williams and Norgate, London 1932.

Wordsworth, Christopher, 'On the Punishment of Death for Wilful Murder: A Sermon Preached in Westminster Abbey on Sunday 24 November 1867', 2nd edn Rivingtons, London 1867.

Wordsworth, William, *Sonnets Upon the Punishment of Death, Quarterly Review*, December 1842.

Wright, Richard [Beccaria Anglicus], *Letters on Capital Punishment addressed to the English Judges*, Johnson, London 1807.

Wrightson, Thomas, *On the Punishment of Death*, London 1833, 3rd edn 1837.

Yallop, David, *To Encourage the Others*, W. H. Allen 1971; Corgi 1990.

Young, Filson, *Trial of Frederick Bywaters and Edith Thompson*, Notable British Trials Series, William Hodge, Edinburgh and London 1923.

Zelmanowits, J, 'Is there such a thing as Capital Punishment?', *British Journal of Criminology*, II, 1, July 1961.

Index of Names

Index of Subjects